Takane & Hana

11

STORY AND ART BY

Yuki Shiwasu

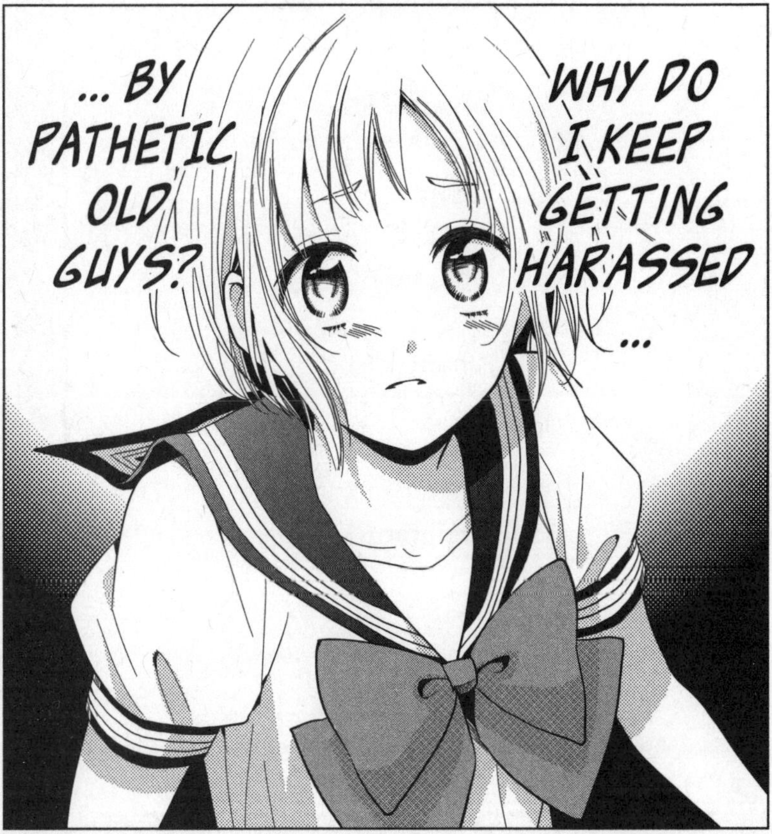
WHY DO I KEEP GETTING HARASSED ...
... BY PATHETIC OLD GUYS?

Takane & Hana

11

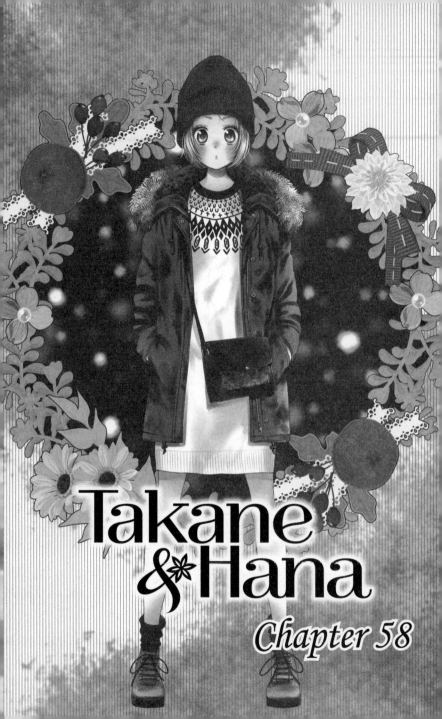

Takane &*Hana

Chapter 58

Valuables

SQUEAK

SQUEAK

TAKANE LIKES TO KEEP THINGS SPOTLESS.

Y'KNOW, YOU CAN PROBABLY JUST GET THE HOUSEKEEPER TO POLISH EVERYTHING, EXCEPT MAYBE THE FISH TANK.

I GUESS, BUT I'D RATHER NOT.

GLEAM

GLEAM

WHEN THINGS ARE TRULY VALUABLE...

...I LIKE TO CARE FOR THEM MYSELF TO BE SURE THEY'RE HANDLED PROPERLY.

I POLISH THEM PERSONALLY.

THAT'S WHAT IT MEANS TO TAKE GOOD CARE OF SOMETHING.

Hmm...

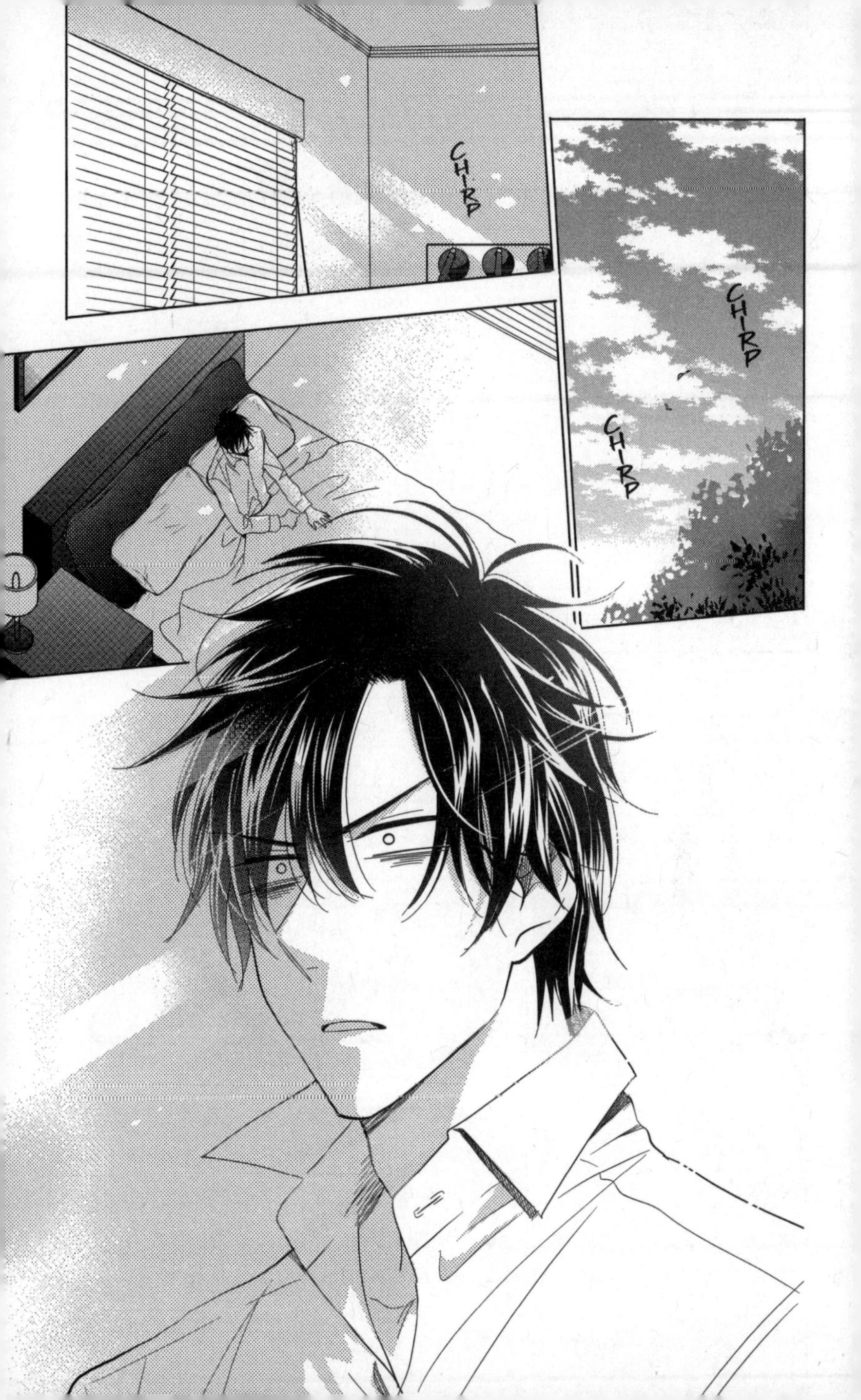
CHIRP
CHIRP
CHIRP

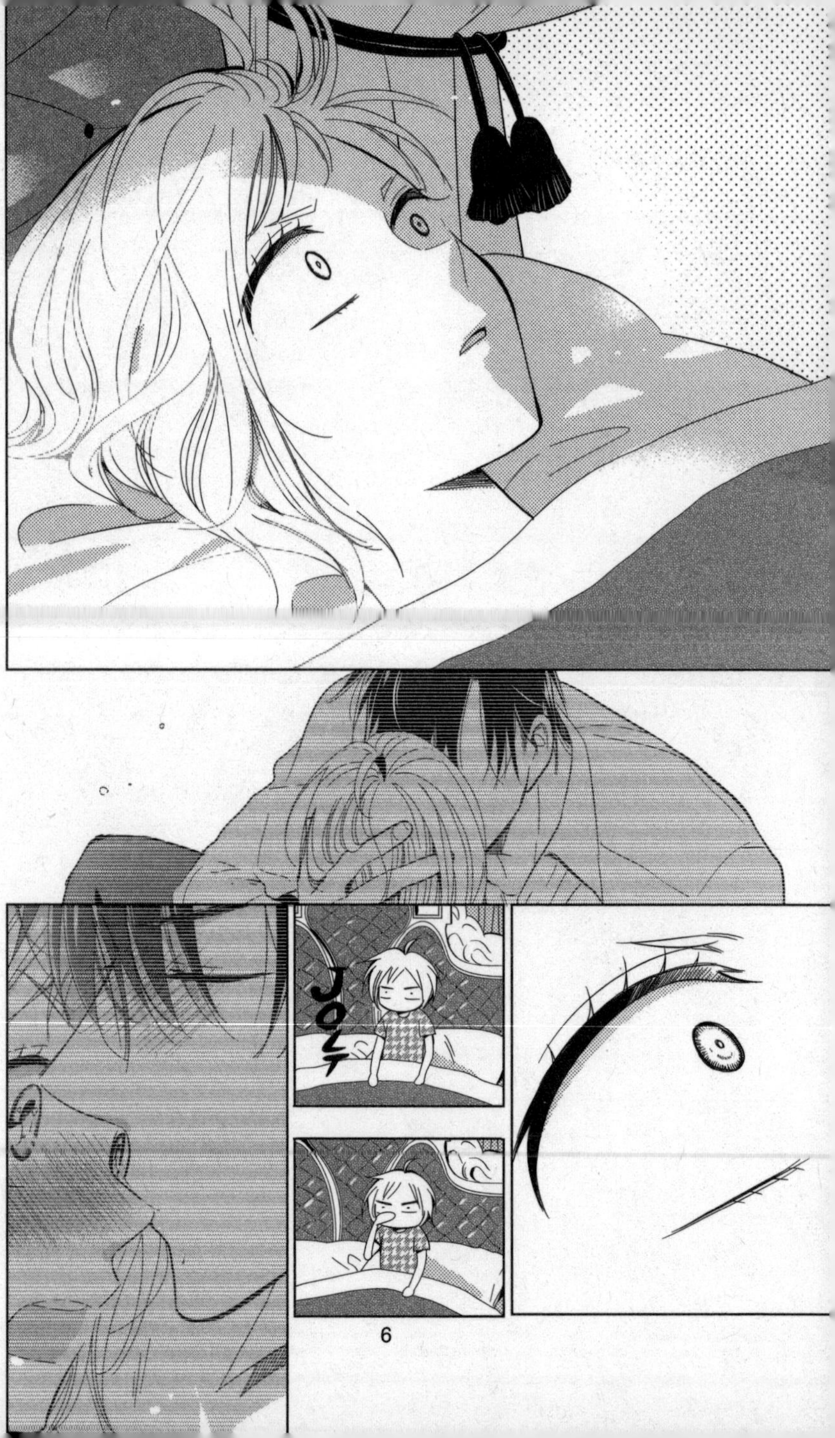
JOLT

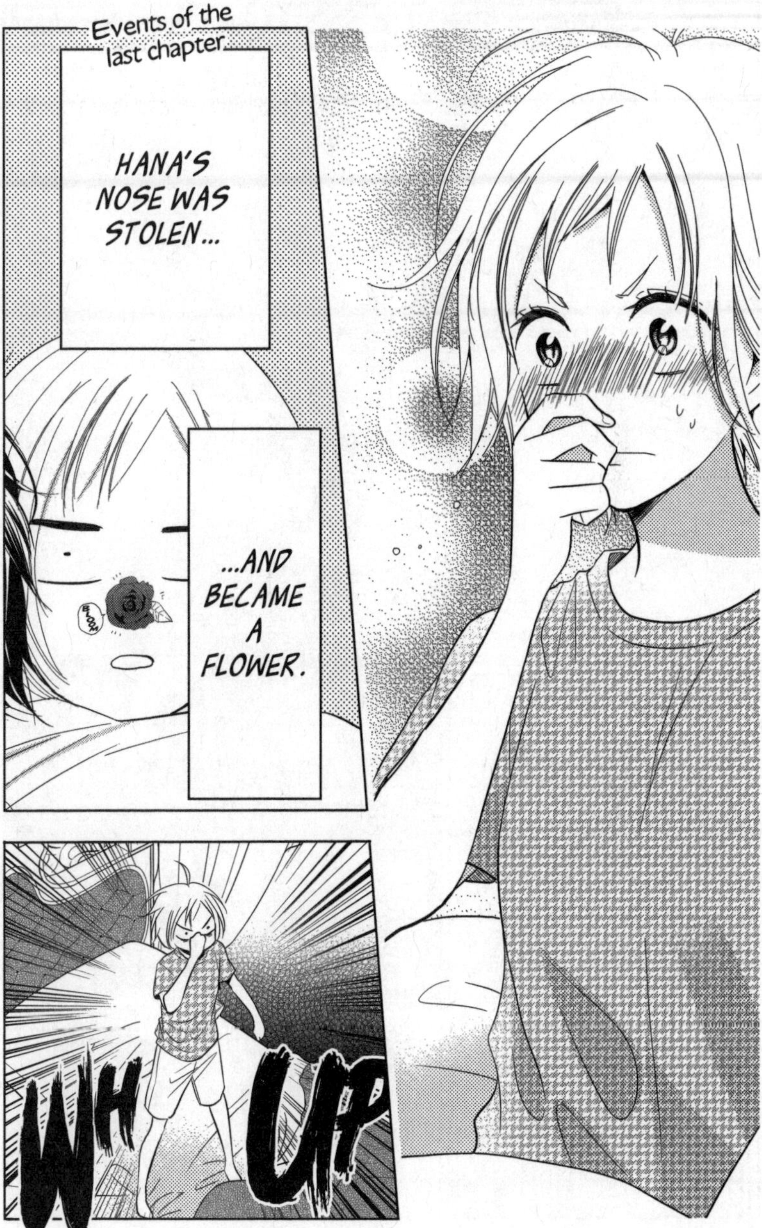
Events of the last chapter
HANA'S NOSE WAS STOLEN...
BLOOM
...AND BECAME A FLOWER.
WH UP

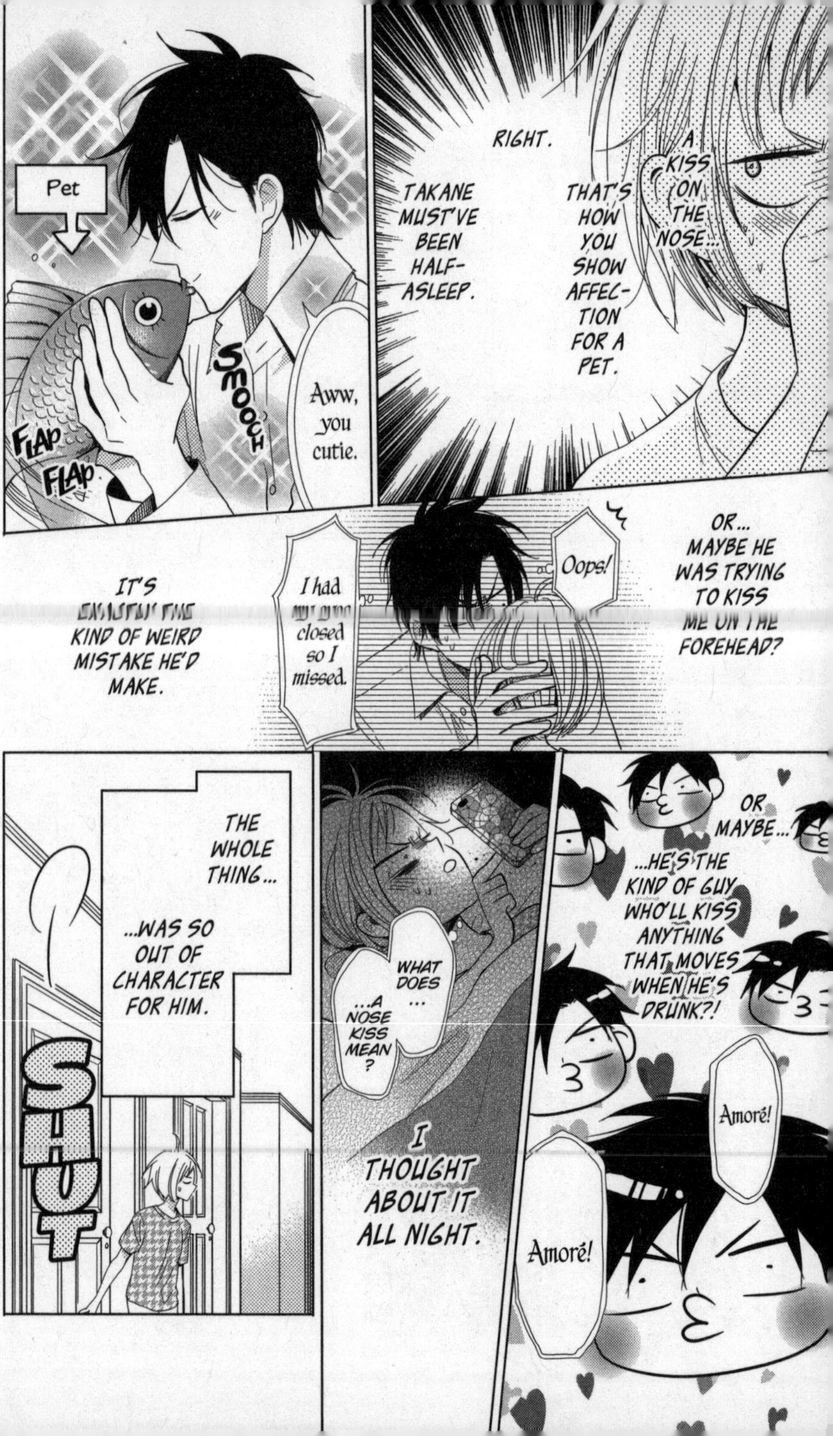
A KISS ON THE NOSE...
RIGHT.
THAT'S HOW YOU SHOW AFFECTION FOR A PET.
TAKANE MUST'VE BEEN HALF-ASLEEP.
Pet
SMOOCH
Aww, you cutie.
FLAP
FLAP
OR... MAYBE HE WAS TRYING TO KISS ME ON THE FOREHEAD?
Oops!
I had
closed so I missed.
IT'S
KIND OF WEIRD MISTAKE HE'D MAKE.
OR MAYBE...
...HE'S THE KIND OF GUY WHO'LL KISS ANYTHING THAT MOVES WHEN HE'S DRUNK?!
Amoré!
Amoré!
WHAT DOES...
...A NOSE KISS MEAN?
I THOUGHT ABOUT IT ALL NIGHT.
THE WHOLE THING...
...WAS SO OUT OF CHARACTER FOR HIM.
SHUT

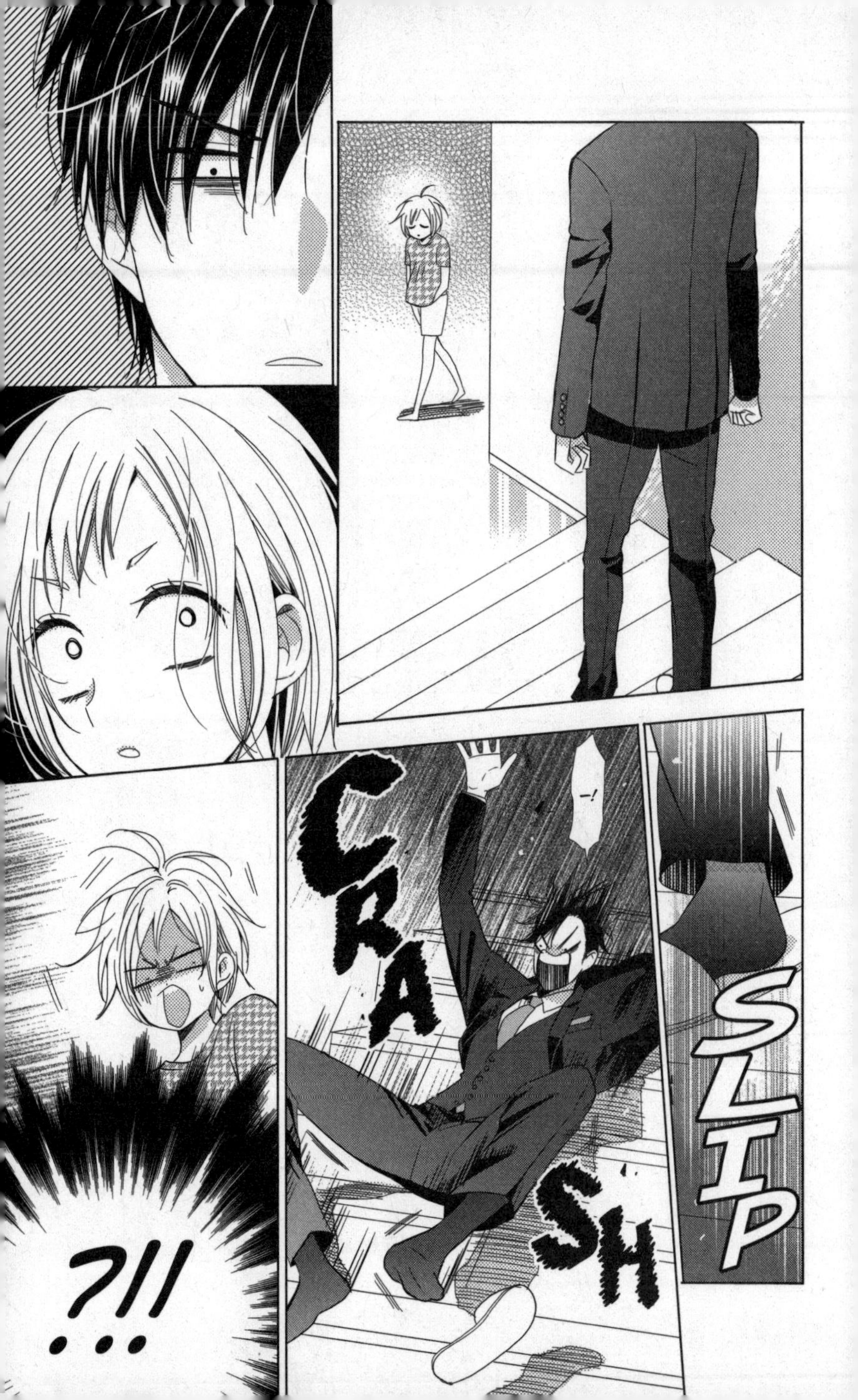
SLIP
—!
CRASH
?!!
...

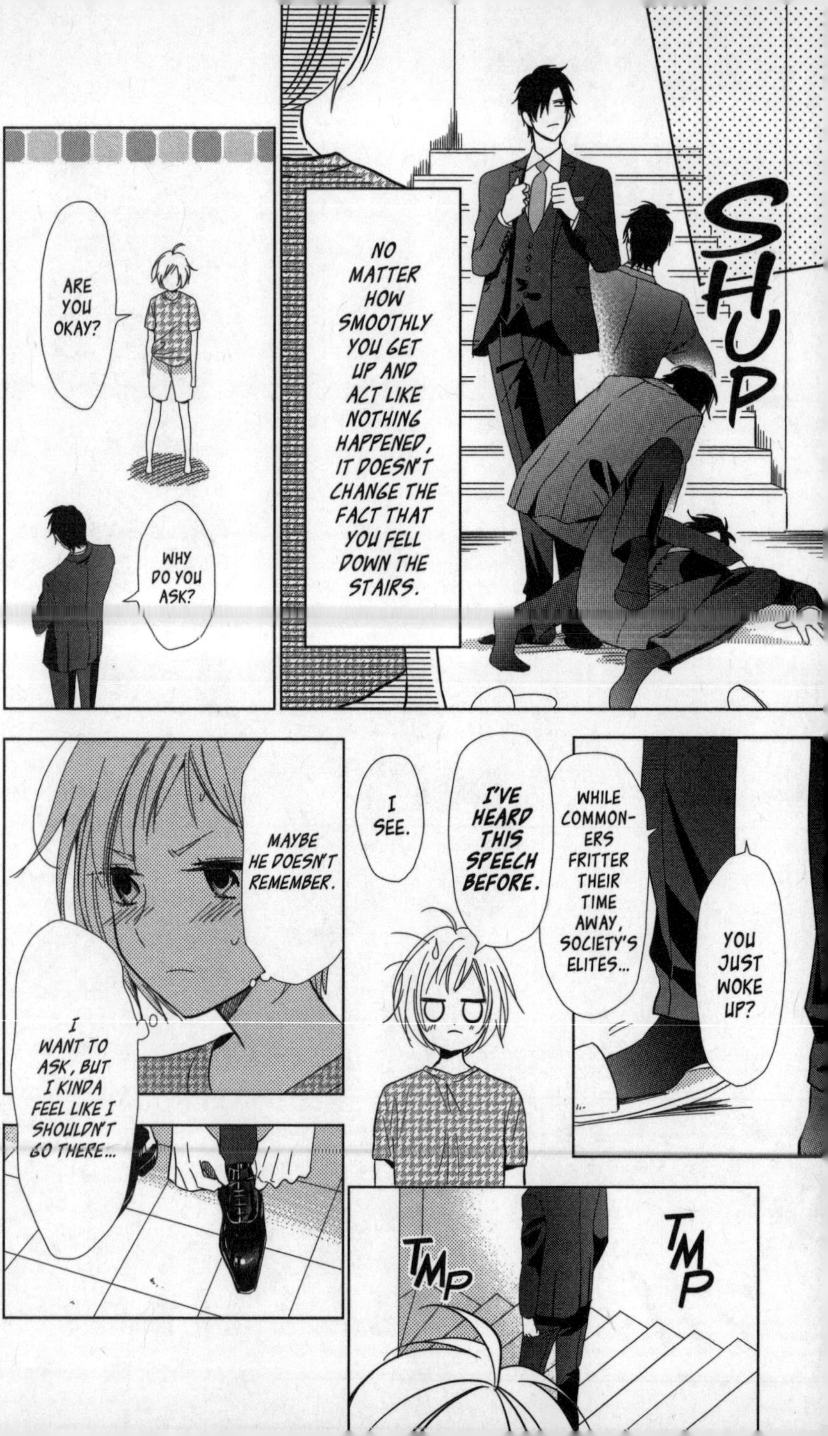
SHUP
NO MATTER HOW SMOOTHLY YOU GET UP AND ACT LIKE NOTHING HAPPENED, IT DOESN'T CHANGE THE FACT THAT YOU FELL DOWN THE STAIRS.
ARE YOU OKAY?
WHY DO YOU ASK?
YOU JUST WOKE UP?
WHILE COMMONERS FRITTER THEIR TIME AWAY, SOCIETY'S ELITES...
I'VE HEARD THIS SPEECH BEFORE.
I SEE.
MAYBE HE DOESN'T REMEMBER.
I WANT TO ASK, BUT I KINDA FEEL LIKE I SHOULDN'T GO THERE...
TMP
TMP

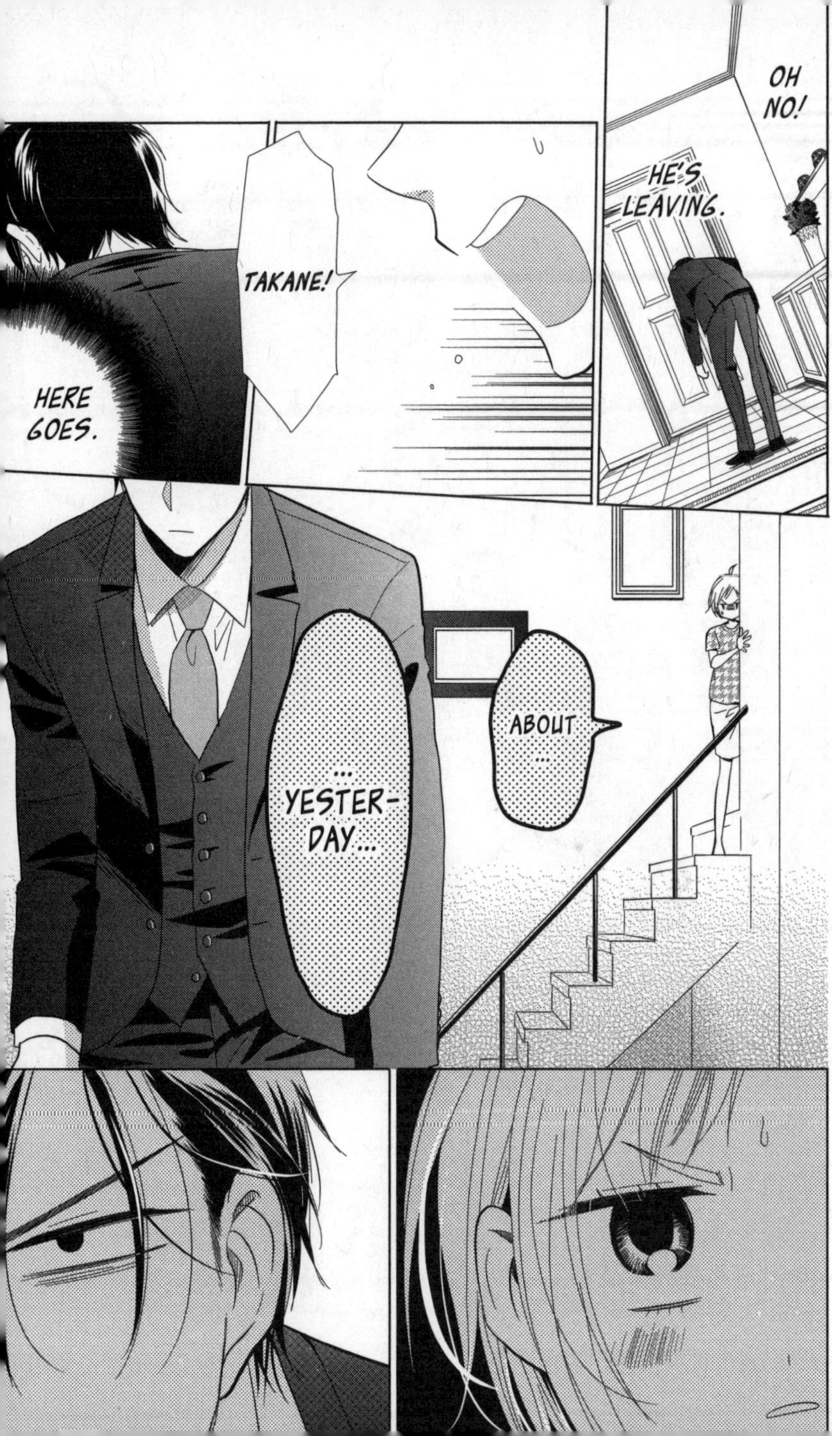
OH NO!
HE'S LEAVING.
TAKANE!
HERE GOES.
ABOUT ...
... YESTER-DAY...

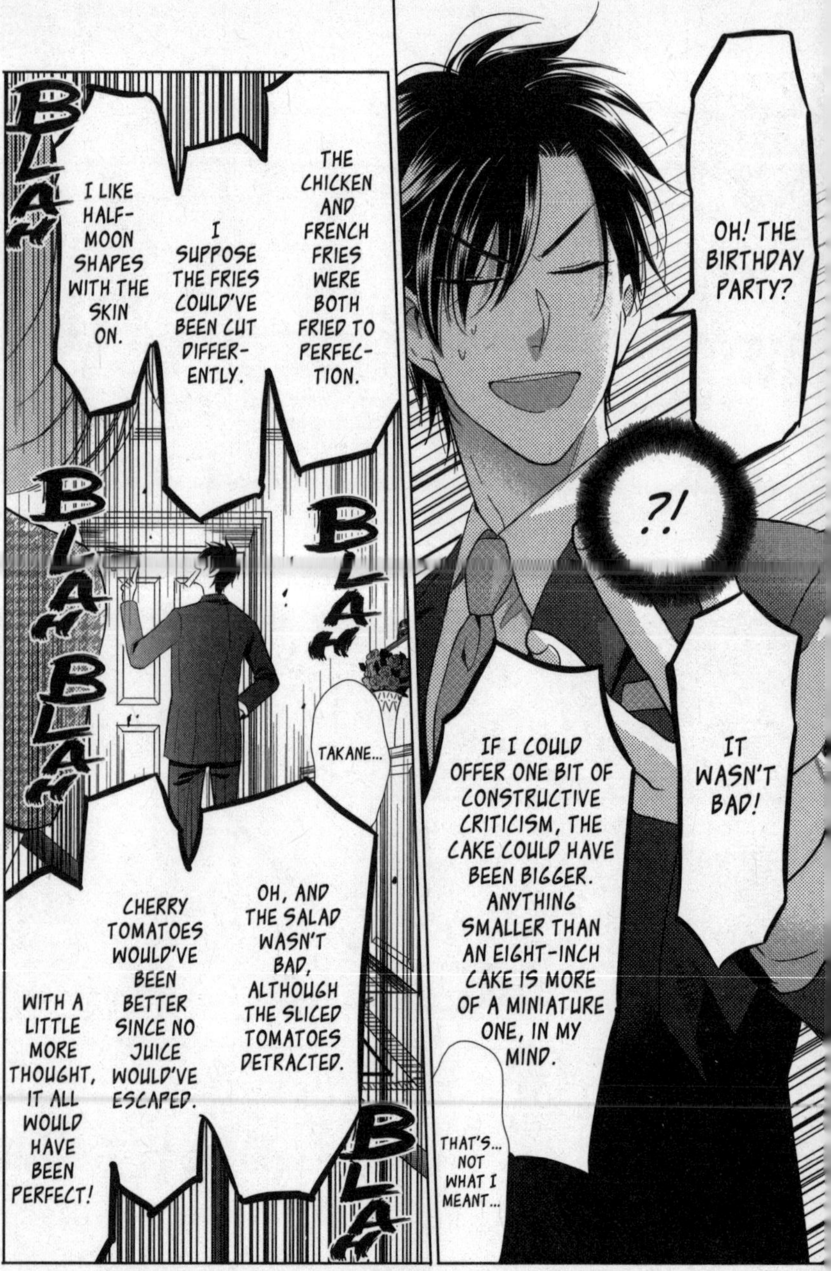
OH! THE BIRTHDAY PARTY?
?!
IT WASN'T BAD!
IF I COULD OFFER ONE BIT OF CONSTRUCTIVE CRITICISM, THE CAKE COULD HAVE BEEN BIGGER. ANYTHING SMALLER THAN AN EIGHT-INCH CAKE IS MORE OF A MINIATURE ONE, IN MY MIND.
THAT'S... NOT WHAT I MEANT...
THE CHICKEN AND FRENCH FRIES WERE BOTH FRIED TO PERFECTION.
I SUPPOSE THE FRIES COULD'VE BEEN CUT DIFFERENTLY.
I LIKE HALF-MOON SHAPES WITH THE SKIN ON.
BLAH
BLAH
BLAH
BLAH
TAKANE...
OH, AND THE SALAD WASN'T BAD, ALTHOUGH THE SLICED TOMATOES DETRACTED.
CHERRY TOMATOES WOULD'VE BEEN BETTER SINCE NO JUICE WOULD'VE ESCAPED.
WITH A LITTLE MORE THOUGHT, IT ALL WOULD HAVE BEEN PERFECT!
BLA

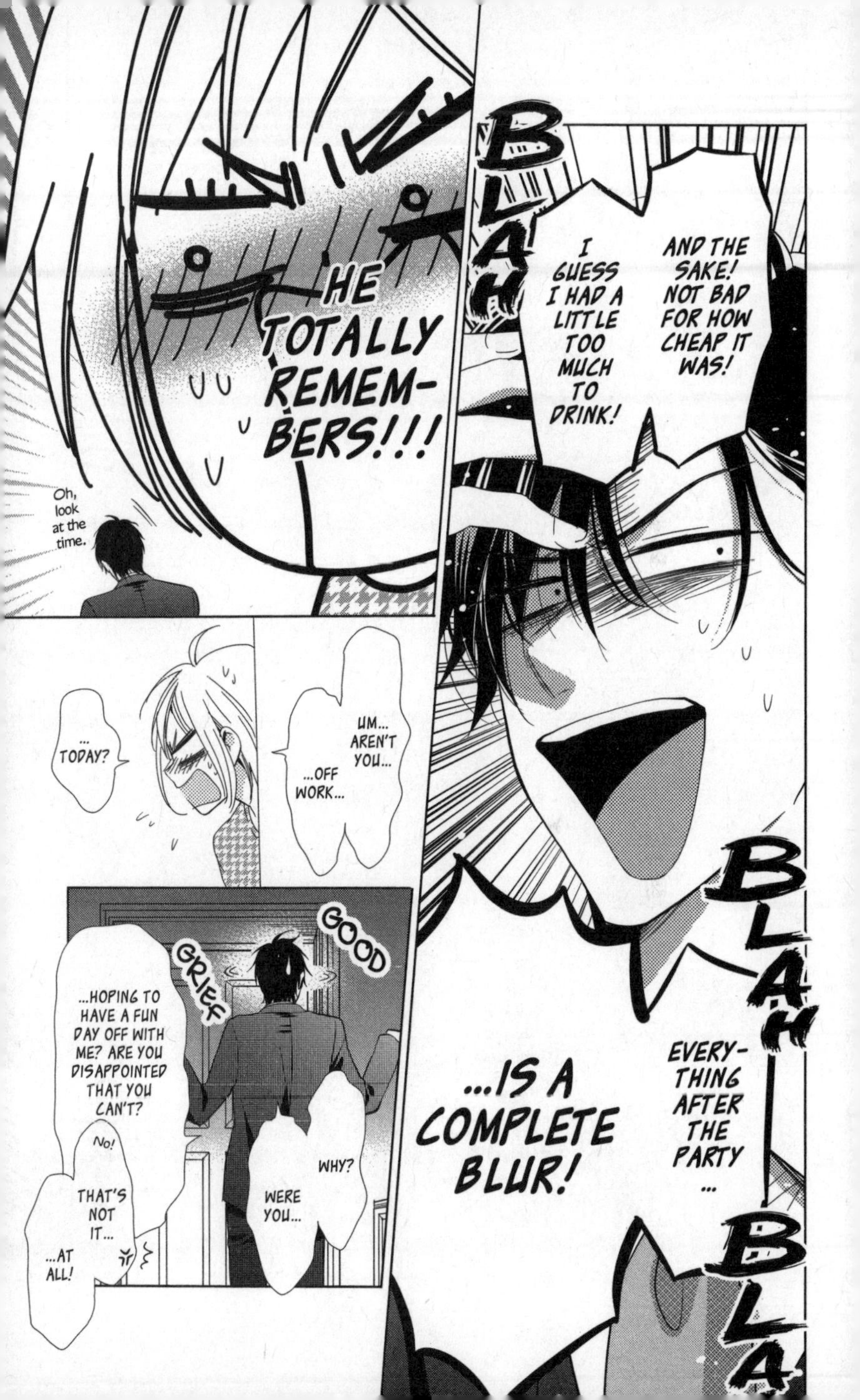
BLAH
AND THE SAKE! NOT BAD FOR HOW CHEAP IT WAS!
I GUESS I HAD A LITTLE TOO MUCH TO DRINK!
BLAH
EVERYTHING AFTER THE PARTY...
...IS A COMPLETE BLUR!
BLA
HE TOTALLY REMEMBERS!!!
Oh, look at the time.
UM... AREN'T YOU...
...OFF WORK...
...TODAY?
GOOD GRIEF
WHY?
WERE YOU...
...HOPING TO HAVE A FUN DAY OFF WITH ME? ARE YOU DISAPPOINTED THAT YOU CAN'T?
No!
THAT'S NOT IT...
...AT ALL!

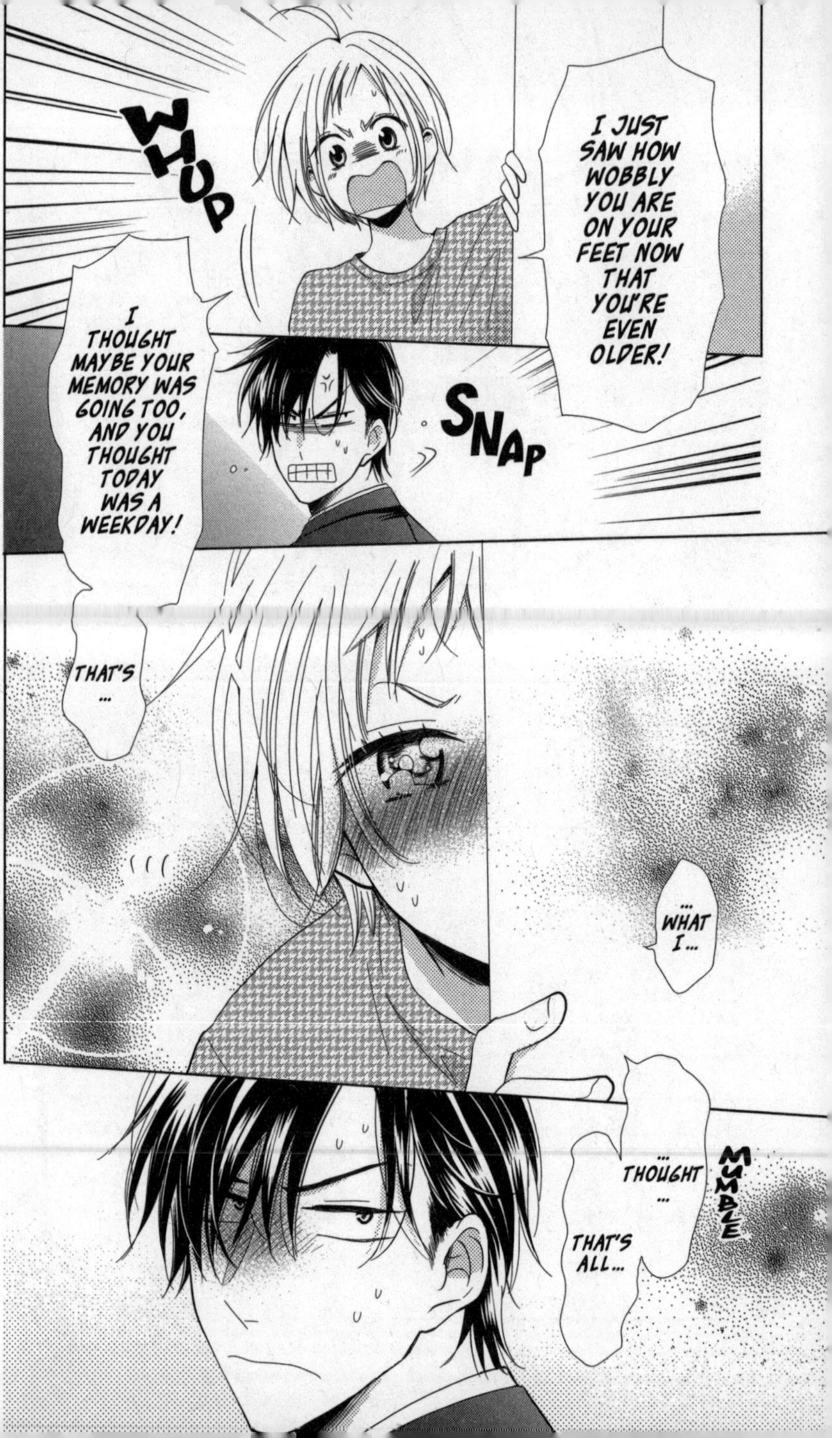
I JUST SAW HOW WOBBLY YOU ARE ON YOUR FEET NOW THAT YOU'RE EVEN OLDER!
WHUP
SNAP
I THOUGHT MAYBE YOUR MEMORY WAS GOING TOO, AND YOU THOUGHT TODAY WAS A WEEKDAY!
THAT'S...
...WHAT I...
...THOUGHT...
THAT'S ALL...
MUMBLE

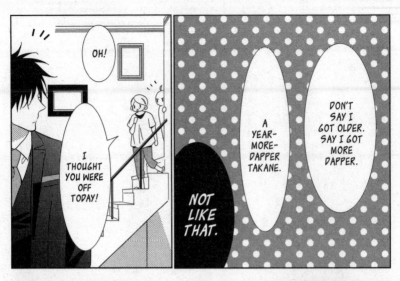

DON'T SAY I GOT OLDER. SAY I GOT MORE DAPPER.
A YEAR-MORE-DAPPER TAKANE.
NOT LIKE THAT.
OH!
I THOUGHT YOU WERE OFF TODAY!
MY GRANDFATHER ASKED ME TO STOP BY.
AH.
OF COURSE. FOR YOUR BIRTHDAY.
HAVE A GOOD TIME.
I'LL SEE YOU LATER.
PLEASE GIVE YOUR GRANDFATHER OUR REGARDS.
SHUT
Hungover
Breakfast is ready.
Okay.

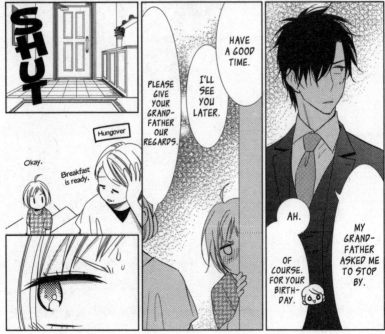

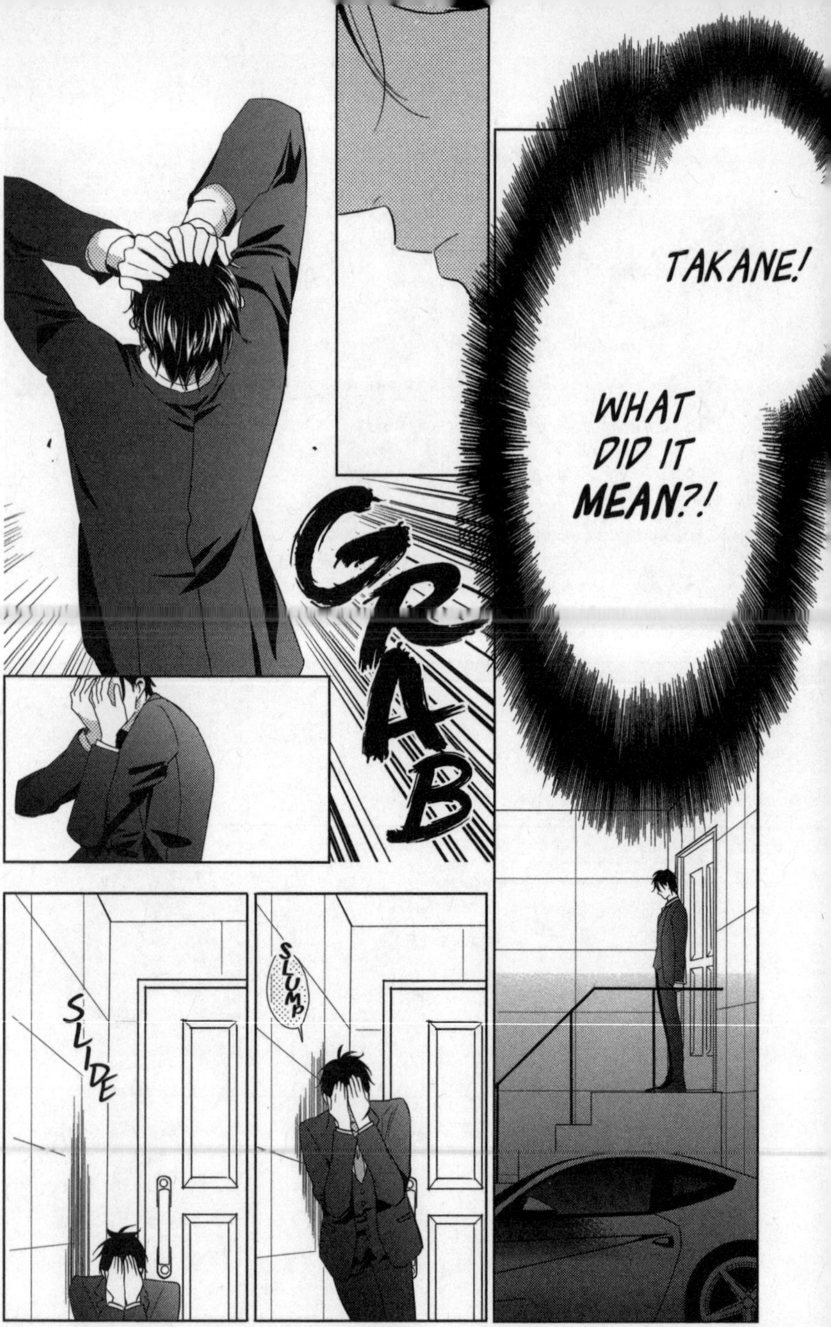
TAKANE!
WHAT DID IT MEAN?!
GRAB
SLUMP
SLIDE

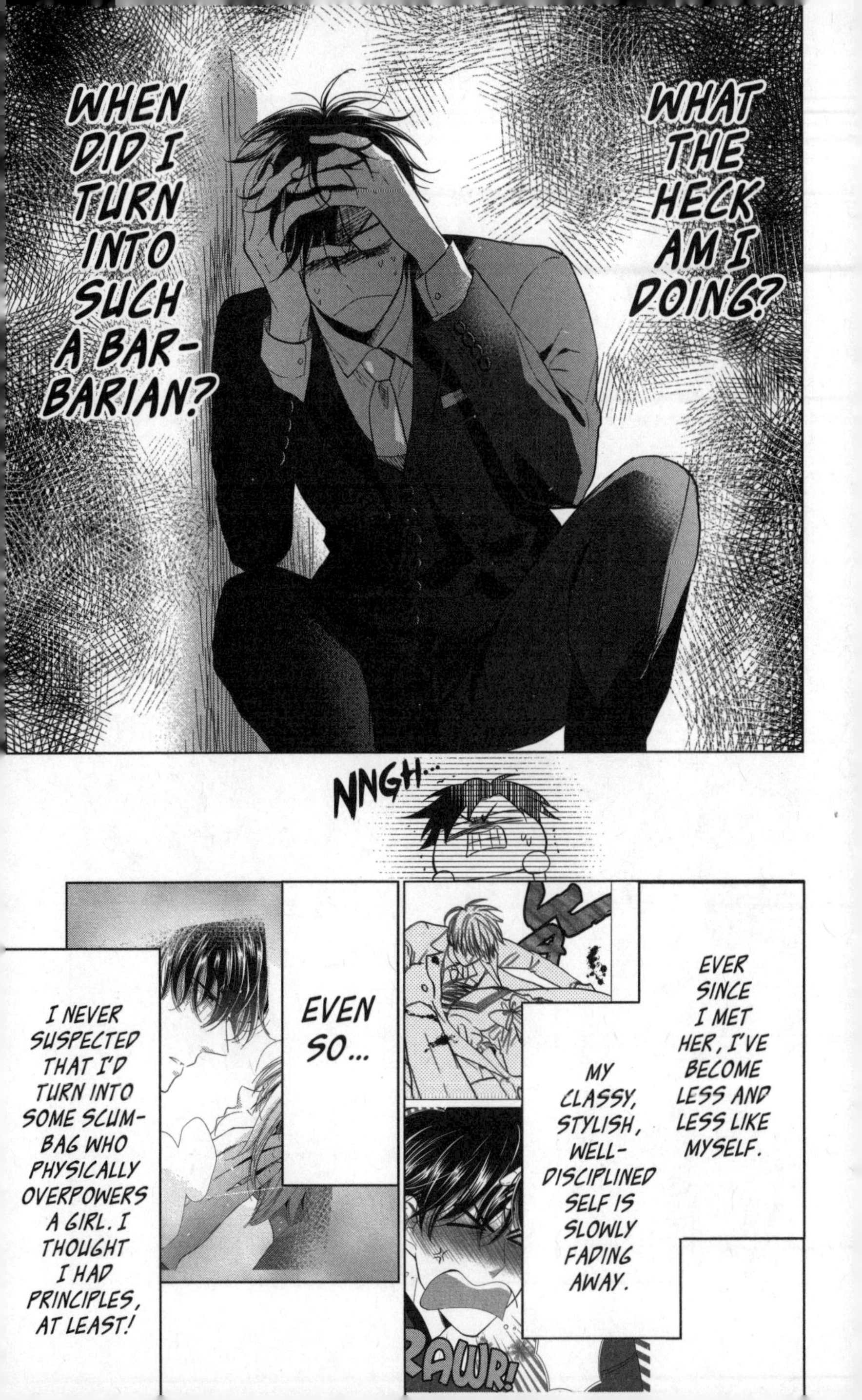
WHAT THE HECK AM I DOING?
WHEN DID I TURN INTO SUCH A BAR-BARIAN?
NNGH...
EVER SINCE I MET HER, I'VE BECOME LESS AND LESS LIKE MYSELF.
MY CLASSY, STYLISH, WELL-DISCIPLINED SELF IS SLOWLY FADING AWAY.
EVEN SO...
I NEVER SUSPECTED THAT I'D TURN INTO SOME SCUM-BAG WHO PHYSICALLY OVERPOWERS A GIRL. I THOUGHT I HAD PRINCIPLES, AT LEAST!

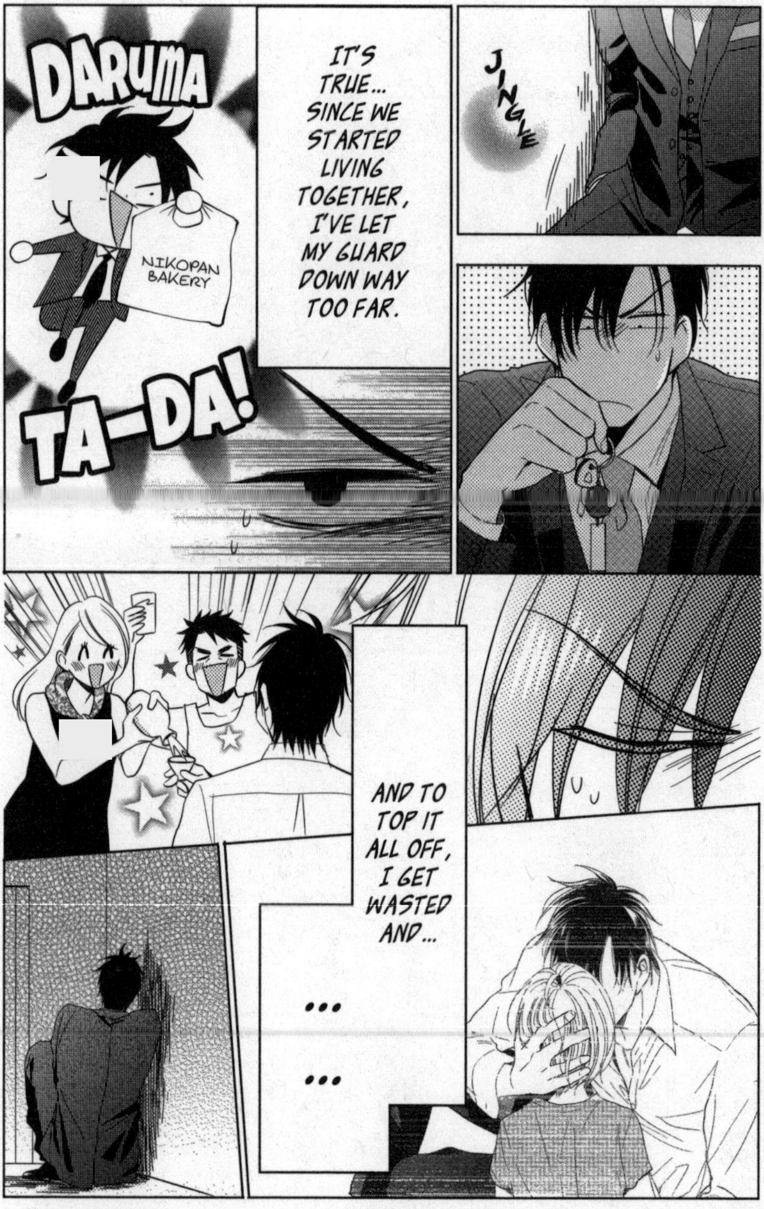
JINGLE
IT'S TRUE... SINCE WE STARTED LIVING TOGETHER, I'VE LET MY GUARD DOWN WAY TOO FAR.
DARUMA
NIKOPAN BAKERY
TA-DA!
AND TO TOP IT ALL OFF, I GET WASTED AND...
...
...

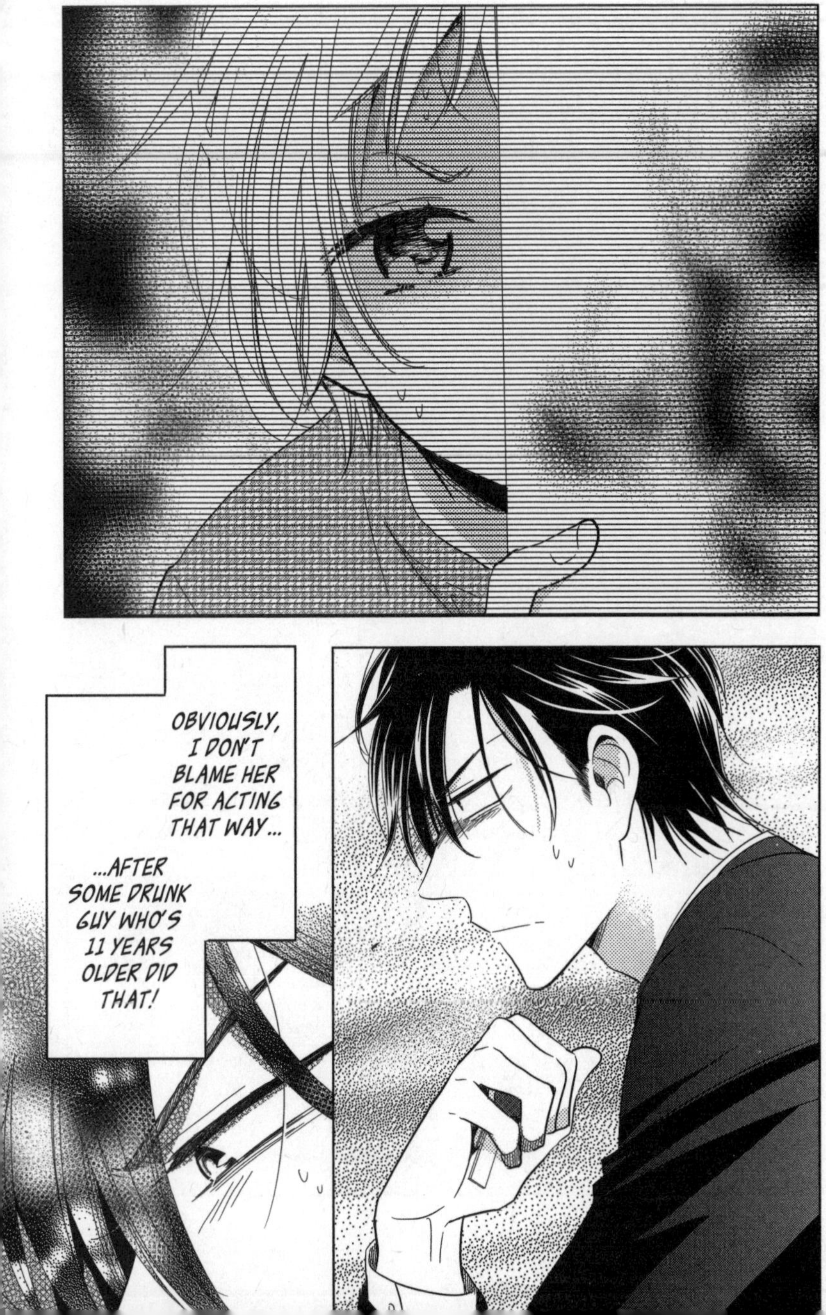
OBVIOUSLY, I DON'T BLAME HER FOR ACTING THAT WAY...
...AFTER SOME DRUNK GUY WHO'S 11 YEARS OLDER DID THAT!

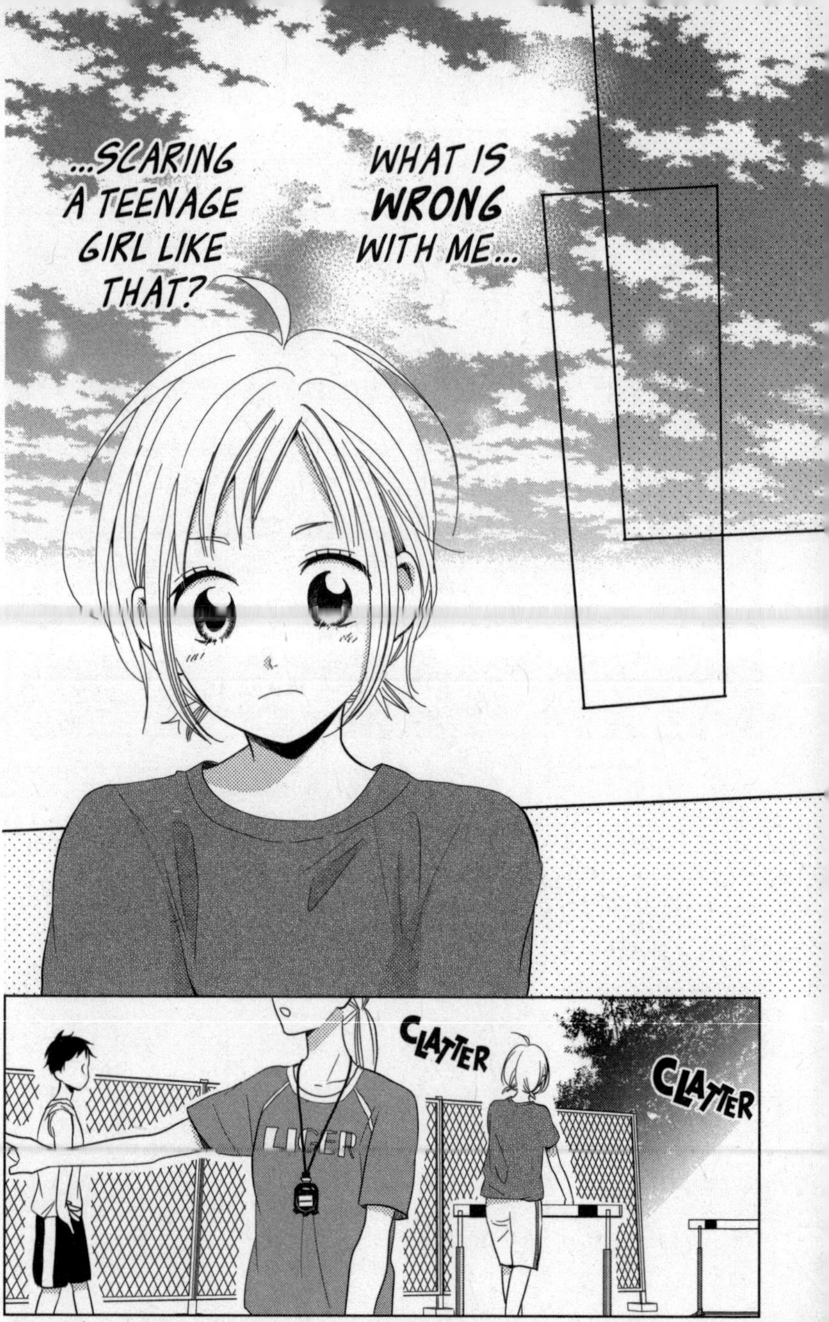
WHAT IS WRONG WITH ME...
...SCARING A TEENAGE GIRL LIKE THAT?
CLATTER
CLATTER
LIGER

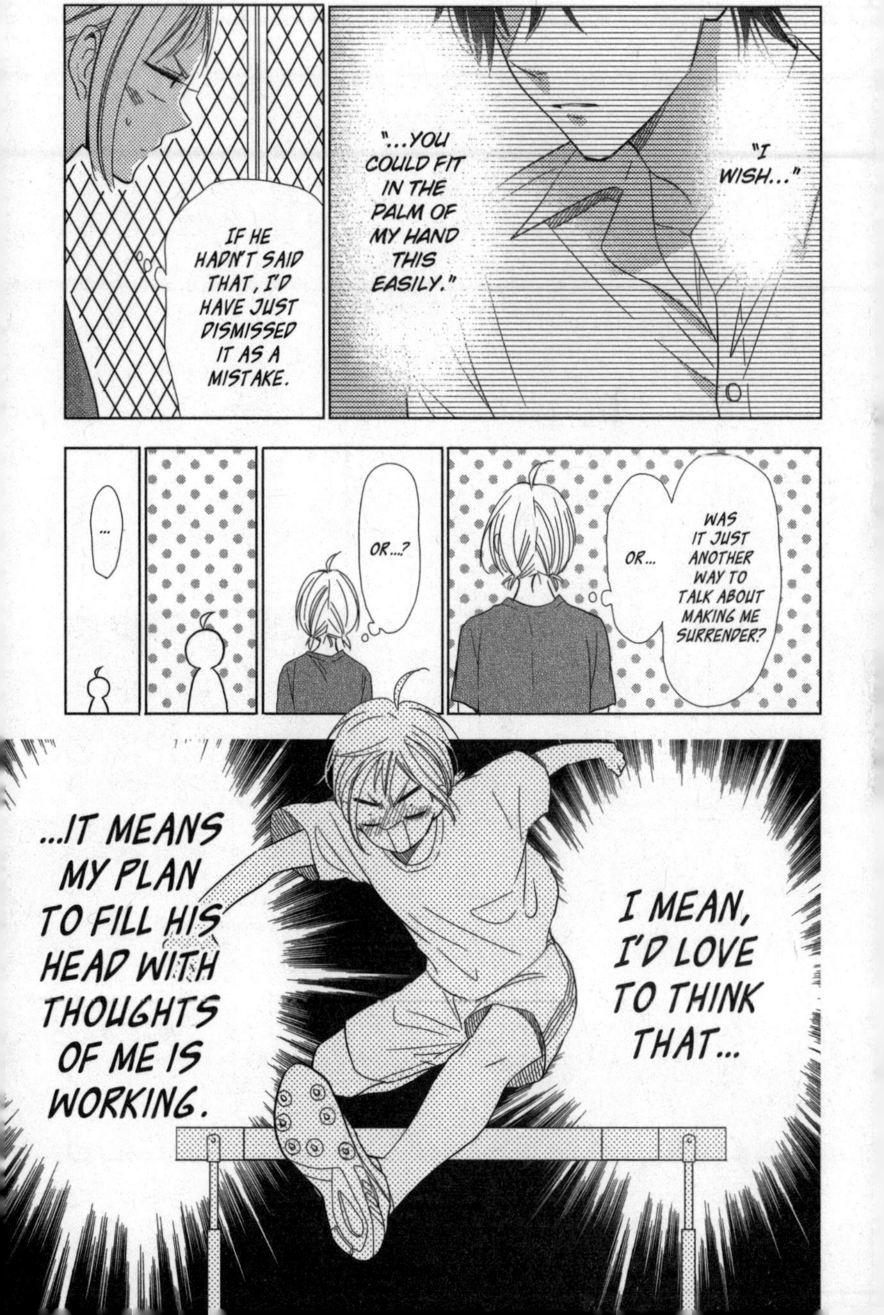
"I WISH..."
"...YOU COULD FIT IN THE PALM OF MY HAND THIS EASILY."
IF HE HADN'T SAID THAT, I'D HAVE JUST DISMISSED IT AS A MISTAKE.
WAS IT JUST ANOTHER WAY TO TALK ABOUT MAKING ME SURRENDER?
OR...
OR...?
...
I MEAN, I'D LOVE TO THINK THAT...
...IT MEANS MY PLAN TO FILL HIS HEAD WITH THOUGHTS OF ME IS WORKING.

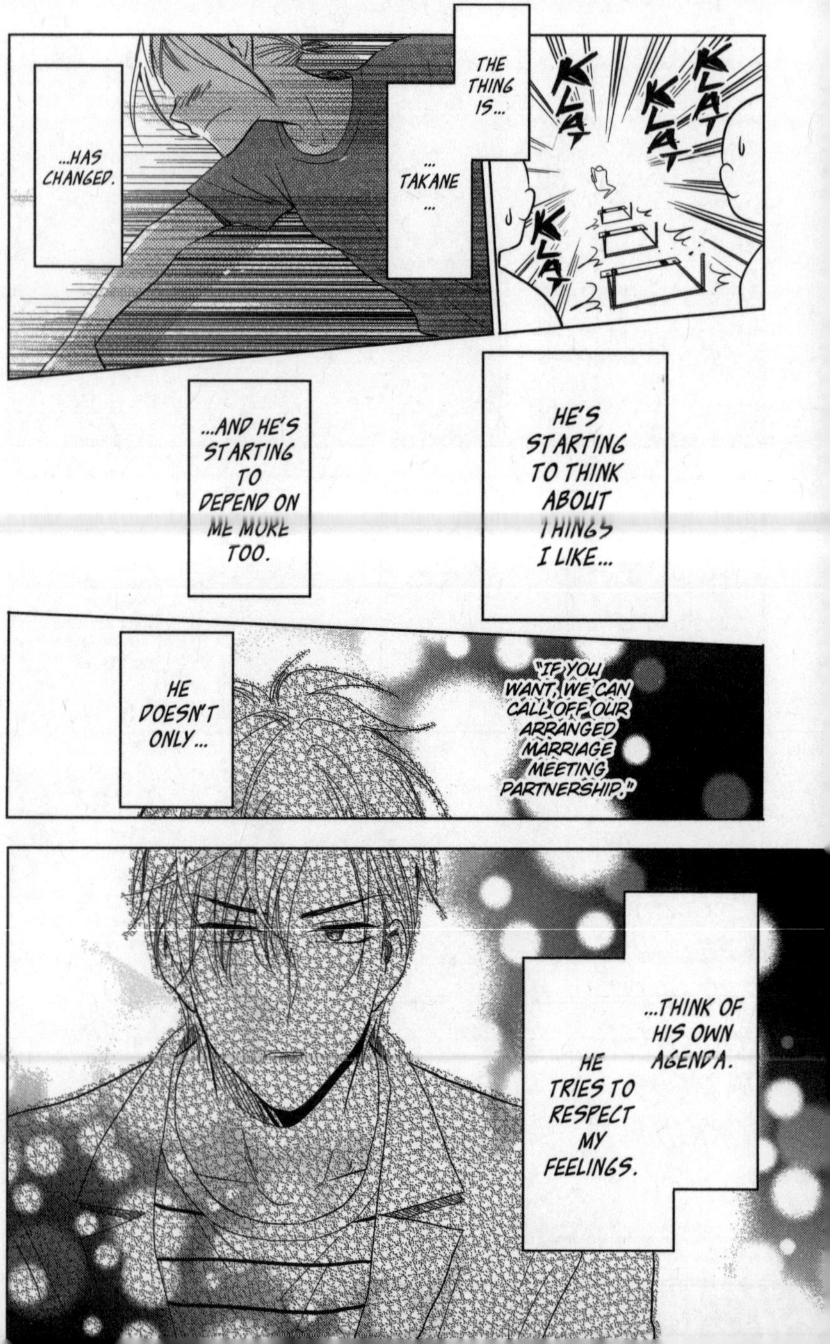
KLAT
KLAT
KLAT
KLAT
THE THING IS...
...TAKANE...
...HAS CHANGED.
HE'S STARTING TO THINK ABOUT THINGS I LIKE...
...AND HE'S STARTING TO DEPEND ON ME MORE TOO.
"IF YOU WANT, WE CAN CALL OFF OUR ARRANGED MARRIAGE MEETING PARTNERSHIP."
HE DOESN'T ONLY...
...THINK OF HIS OWN AGENDA.
HE TRIES TO RESPECT MY FEELINGS.

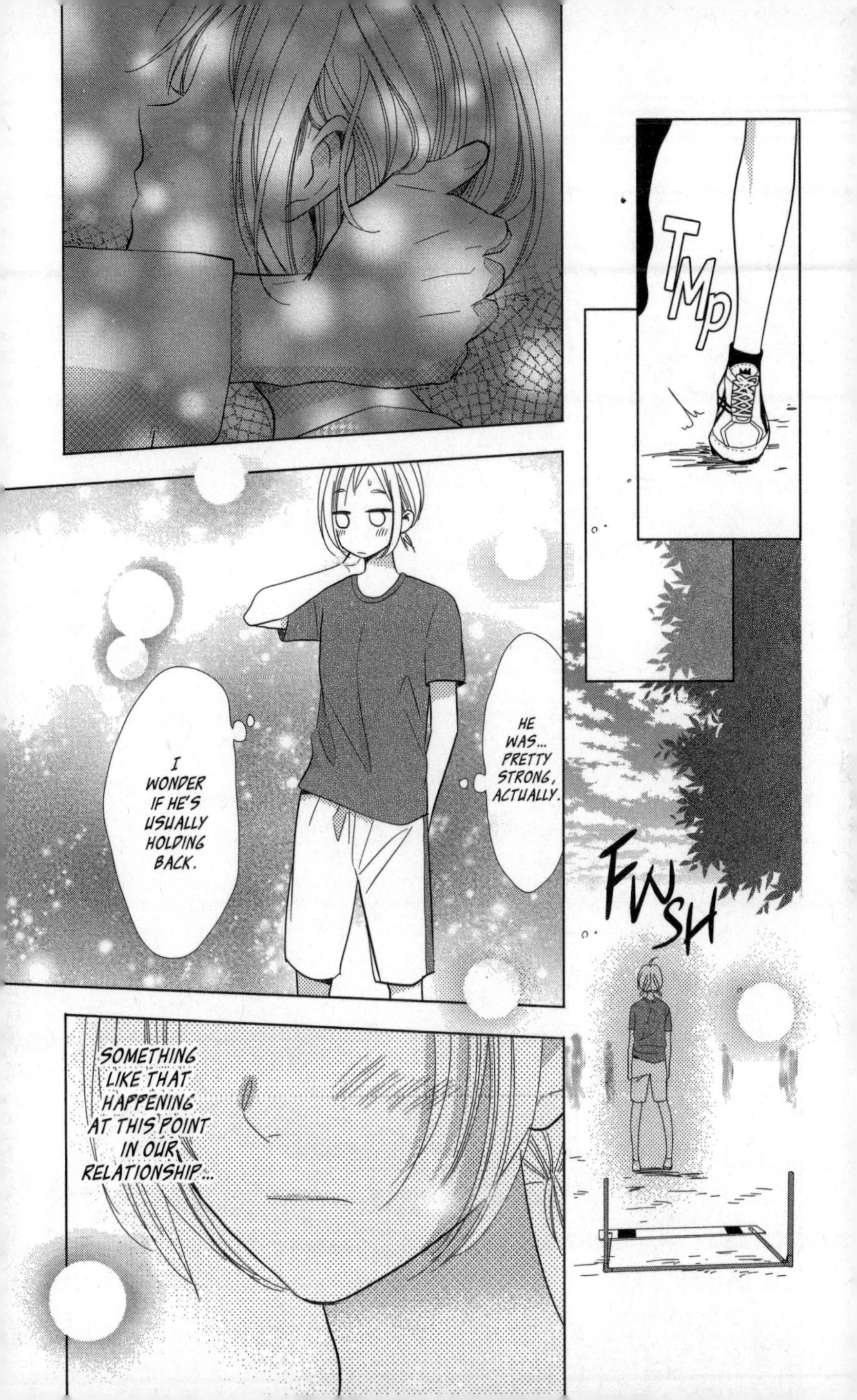
TMP
FWSH
HE WAS... PRETTY STRONG, ACTUALLY.
I WONDER IF HE'S USUALLY HOLDING BACK.
SOMETHING LIKE THAT HAPPENING AT THIS POINT IN OUR RELATIONSHIP...

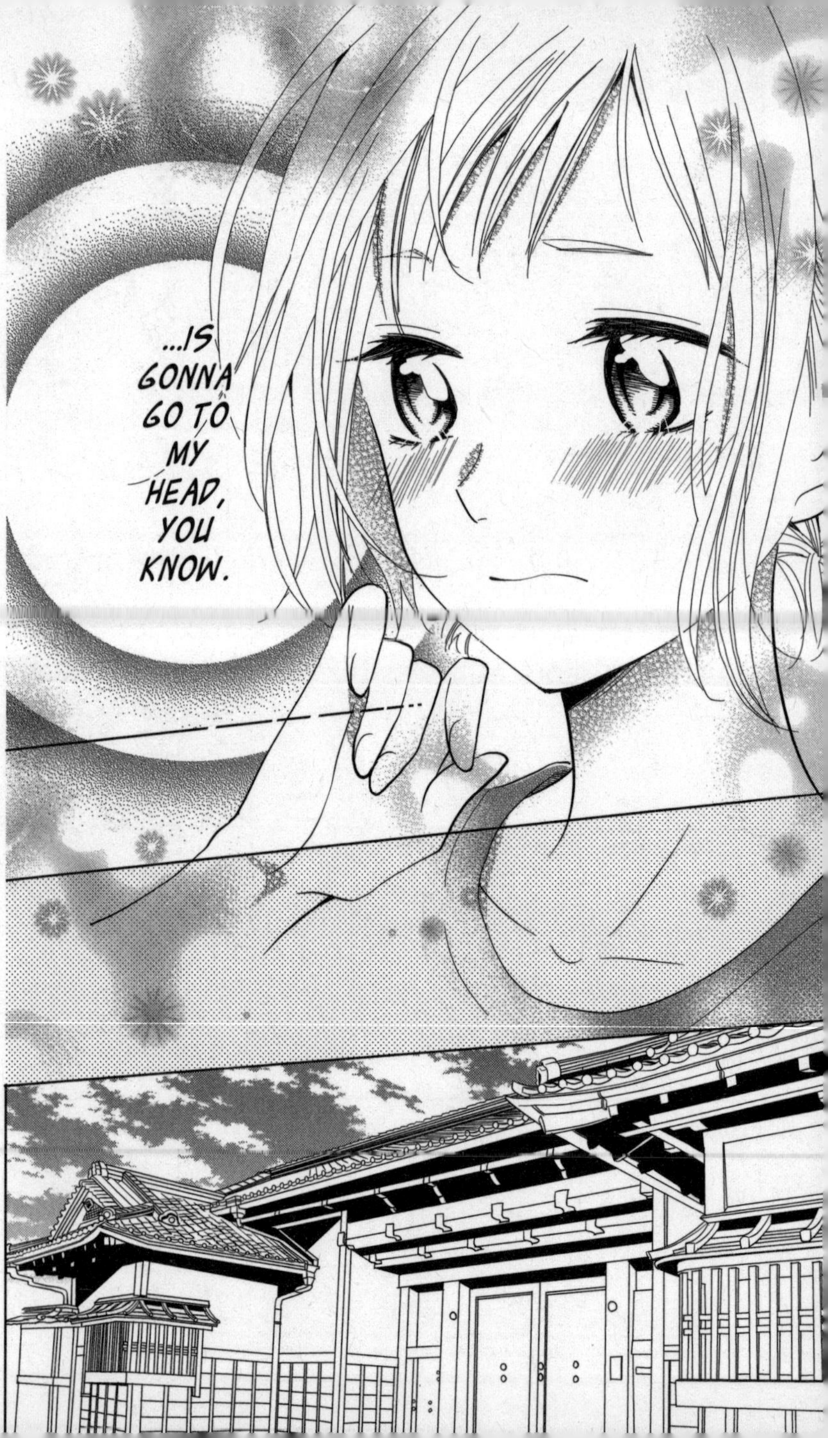
...IS GONNA GO TO MY HEAD, YOU KNOW.

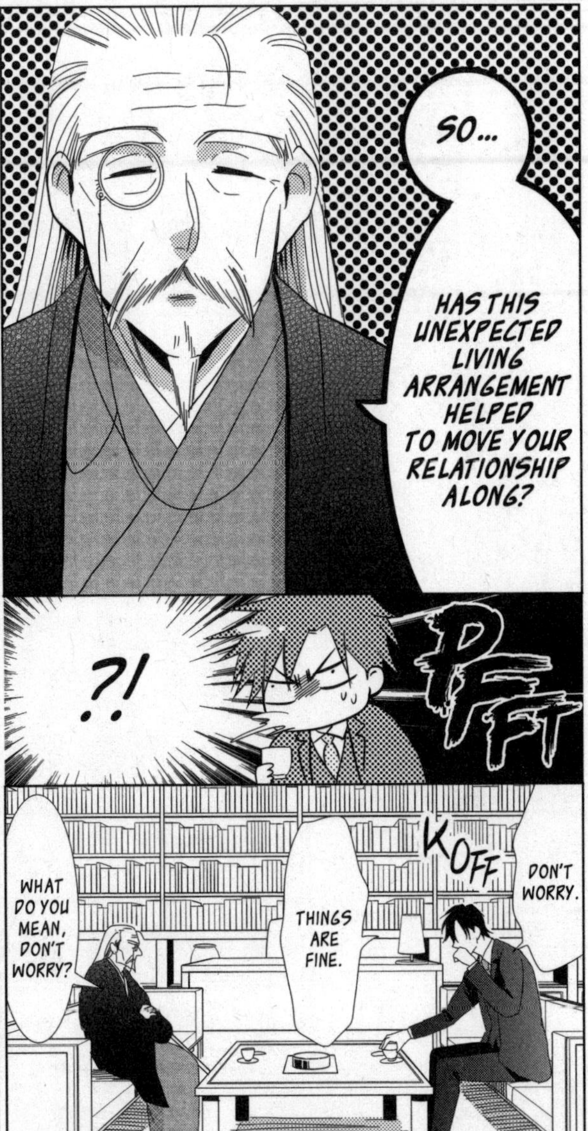
SO...
HAS THIS UNEXPECTED LIVING ARRANGEMENT HELPED TO MOVE YOUR RELATIONSHIP ALONG?
PFFT
?!
DON'T WORRY.
KOFF
THINGS ARE FINE.
WHAT DO YOU MEAN, DON'T WORRY?

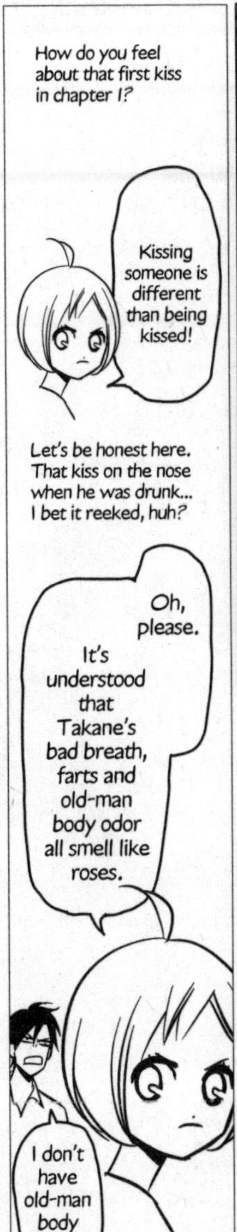
How do you feel about that first kiss in chapter 1?
Kissing someone is different than being kissed!
Let's be honest here. That kiss on the nose when he was drunk... I bet it reeked, huh?
Oh, please. It's understood that Takane's bad breath, farts and old-man body odor all smell like roses.
I don't have old-man body odor!

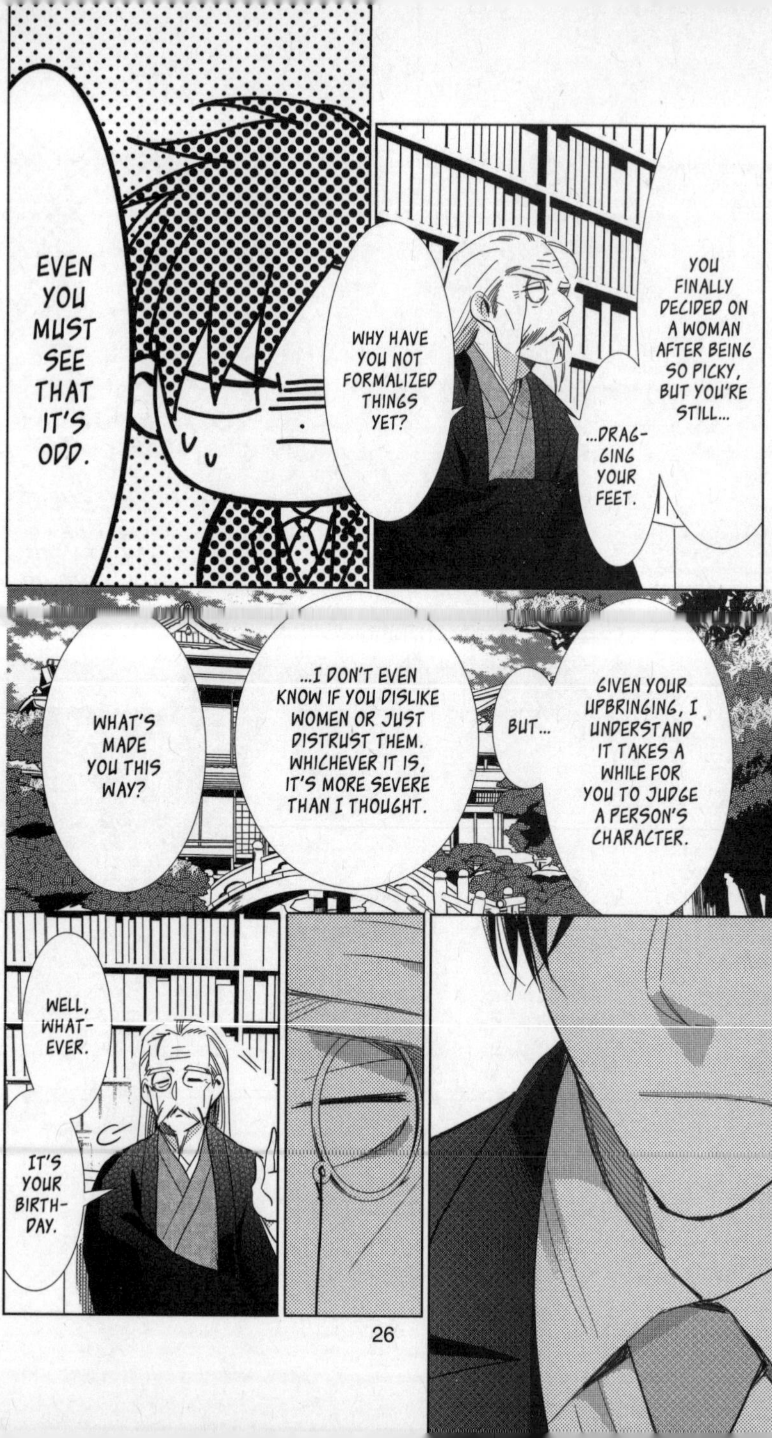
YOU FINALLY DECIDED ON A WOMAN AFTER BEING SO PICKY, BUT YOU'RE STILL...
...DRAG-GING YOUR FEET.
WHY HAVE YOU NOT FORMALIZED THINGS YET?
EVEN YOU MUST SEE THAT IT'S ODD.
GIVEN YOUR UPBRINGING, I UNDERSTAND IT TAKES A WHILE FOR YOU TO JUDGE A PERSON'S CHARACTER.
BUT...
...I DON'T EVEN KNOW IF YOU DISLIKE WOMEN OR JUST DISTRUST THEM. WHICHEVER IT IS, IT'S MORE SEVERE THAN I THOUGHT.
WHAT'S MADE YOU THIS WAY?
WELL, WHAT-EVER.
IT'S YOUR BIRTH-DAY.

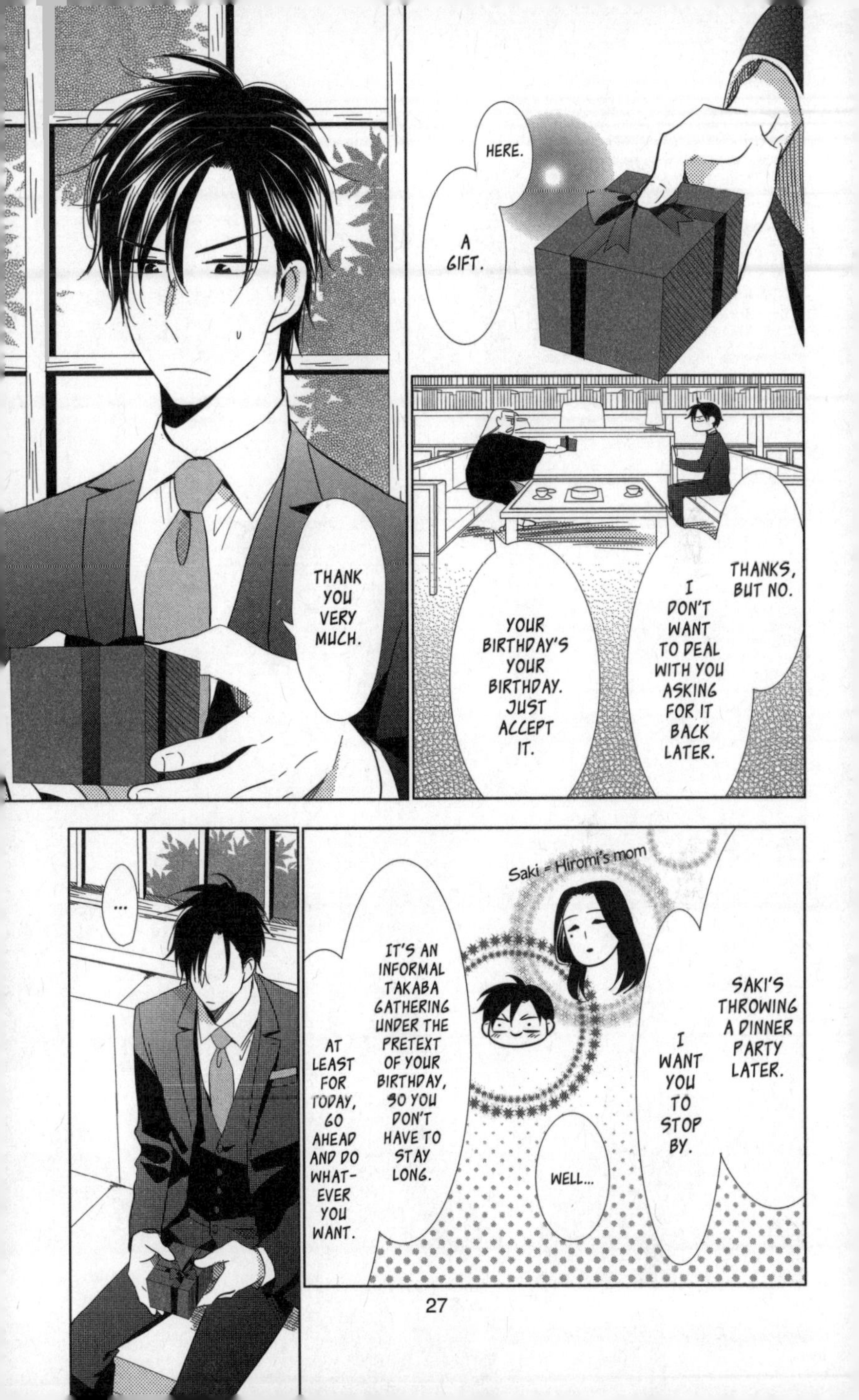
HERE.
A GIFT.
THANKS, BUT NO.
I DON'T WANT TO DEAL WITH YOU ASKING FOR IT BACK LATER.
YOUR BIRTHDAY'S YOUR BIRTHDAY. JUST ACCEPT IT.
THANK YOU VERY MUCH.
SAKI'S THROWING A DINNER PARTY LATER.
I WANT YOU TO STOP BY.
Saki = Hiromi's mom
WELL...
IT'S AN INFORMAL TAKABA GATHERING UNDER THE PRETEXT OF YOUR BIRTHDAY, SO YOU DON'T HAVE TO STAY LONG.
AT LEAST FOR TODAY, GO AHEAD AND DO WHATEVER YOU WANT.
...

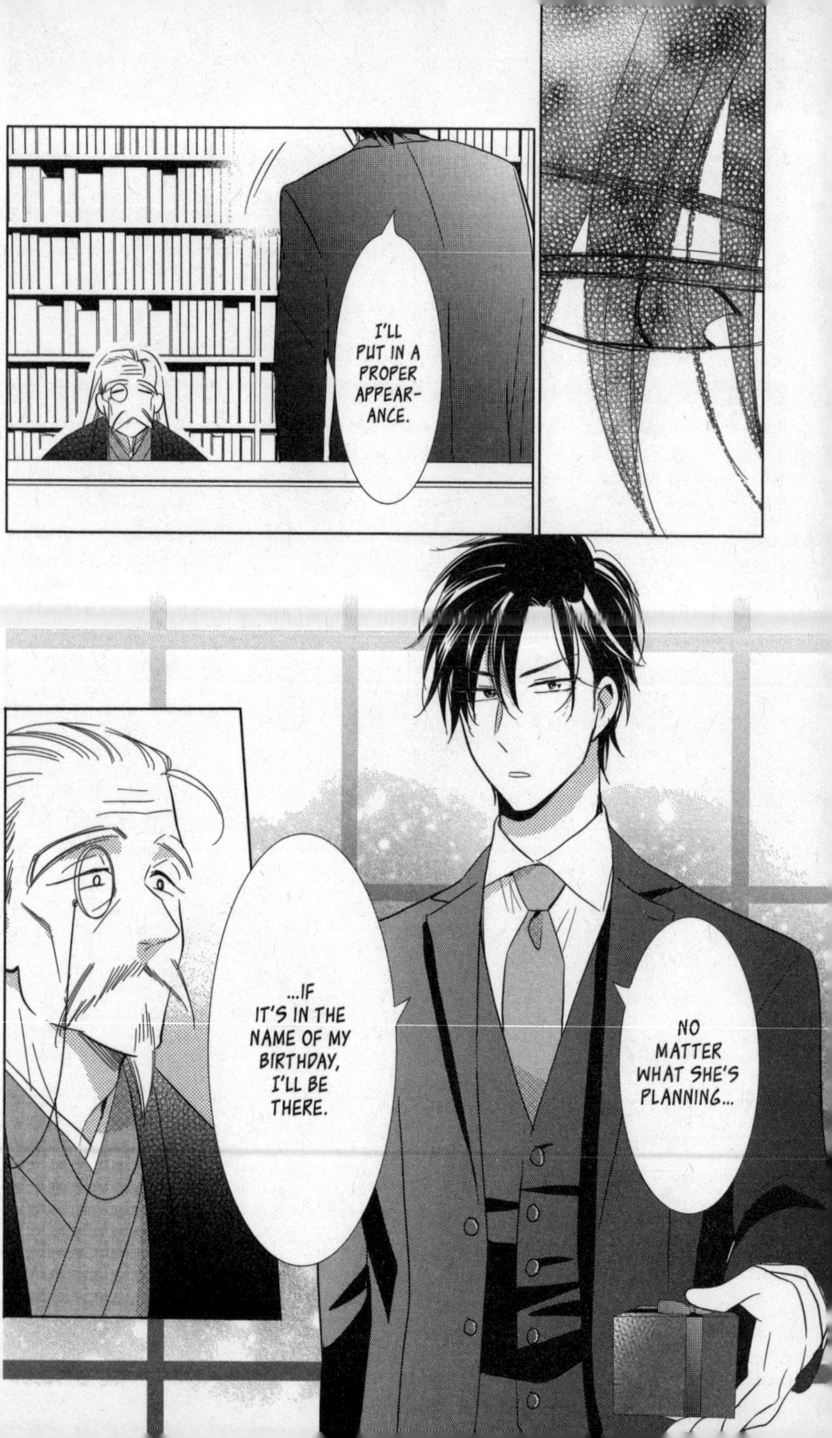
I'LL PUT IN A PROPER APPEAR-ANCE.
NO MATTER WHAT SHE'S PLANNING...
...IF IT'S IN THE NAME OF MY BIRTHDAY, I'LL BE THERE.

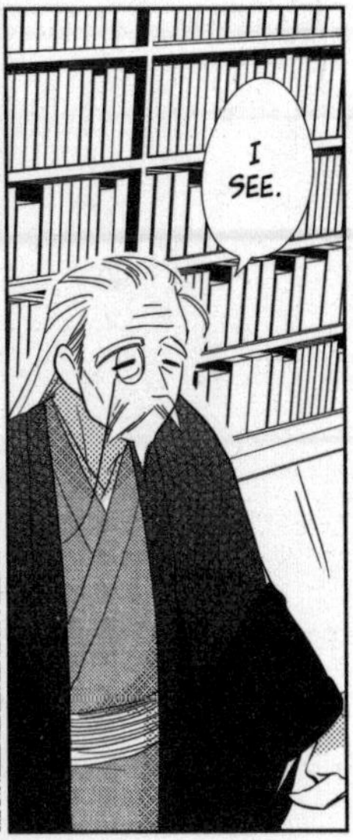
I SEE.

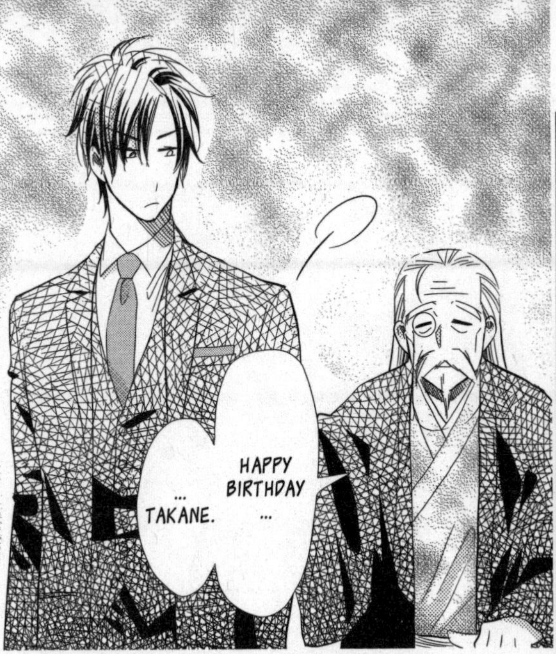
HAPPY BIRTHDAY ...
... TAKANE.

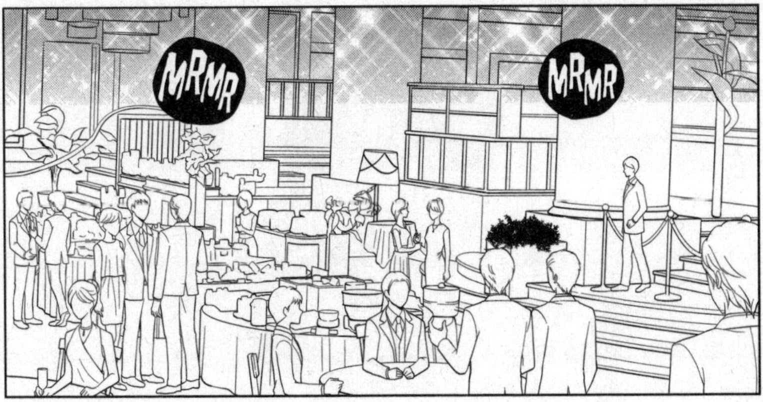
MRMR
MRMR

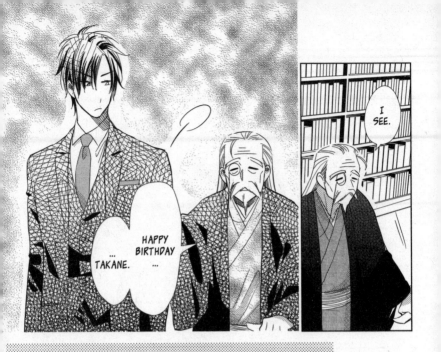

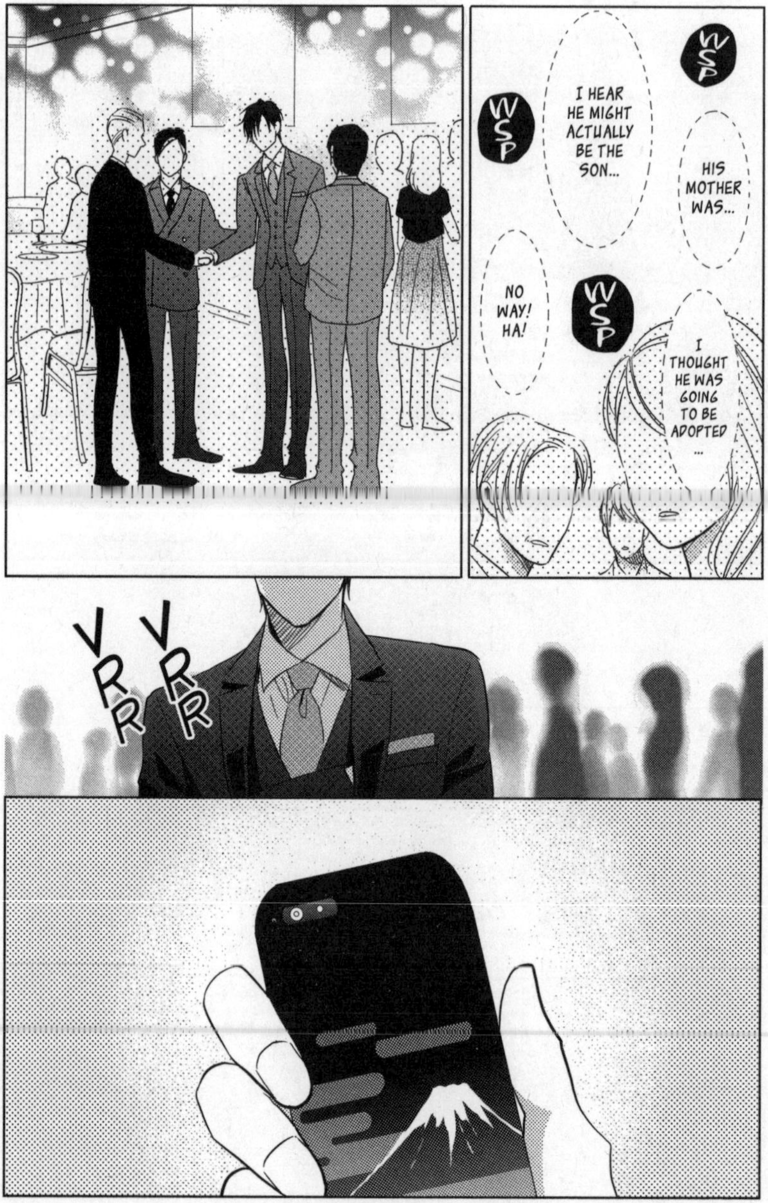
WSP
HIS MOTHER WAS...
I HEAR HE MIGHT ACTUALLY BE THE SON...
WSP
I THOUGHT HE WAS GOING TO BE ADOPTED...
WSP
NO WAY! HA!
VRR
VRR

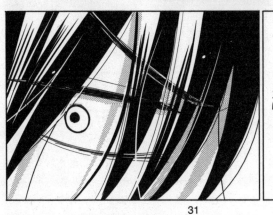

TAKANE?

WHAT'S WRONG? IT'S YOUR BIRTHDAY! WHY THE LONG FACE?

31

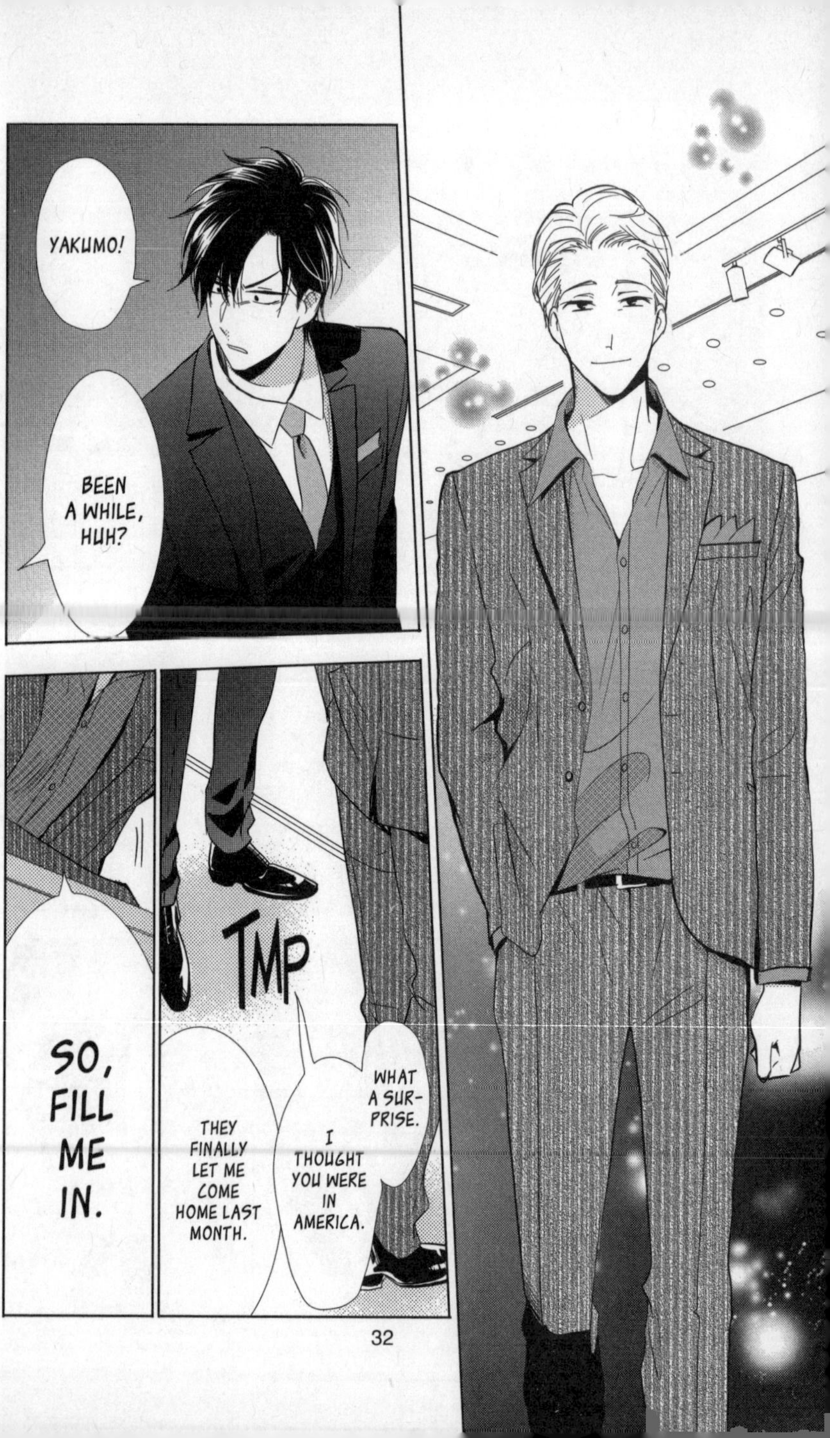
YAKUMO!
BEEN A WHILE, HUH?
TMP
WHAT A SUR-PRISE.
I THOUGHT YOU WERE IN AMERICA.
THEY FINALLY LET ME COME HOME LAST MONTH.
SO, FILL ME IN.

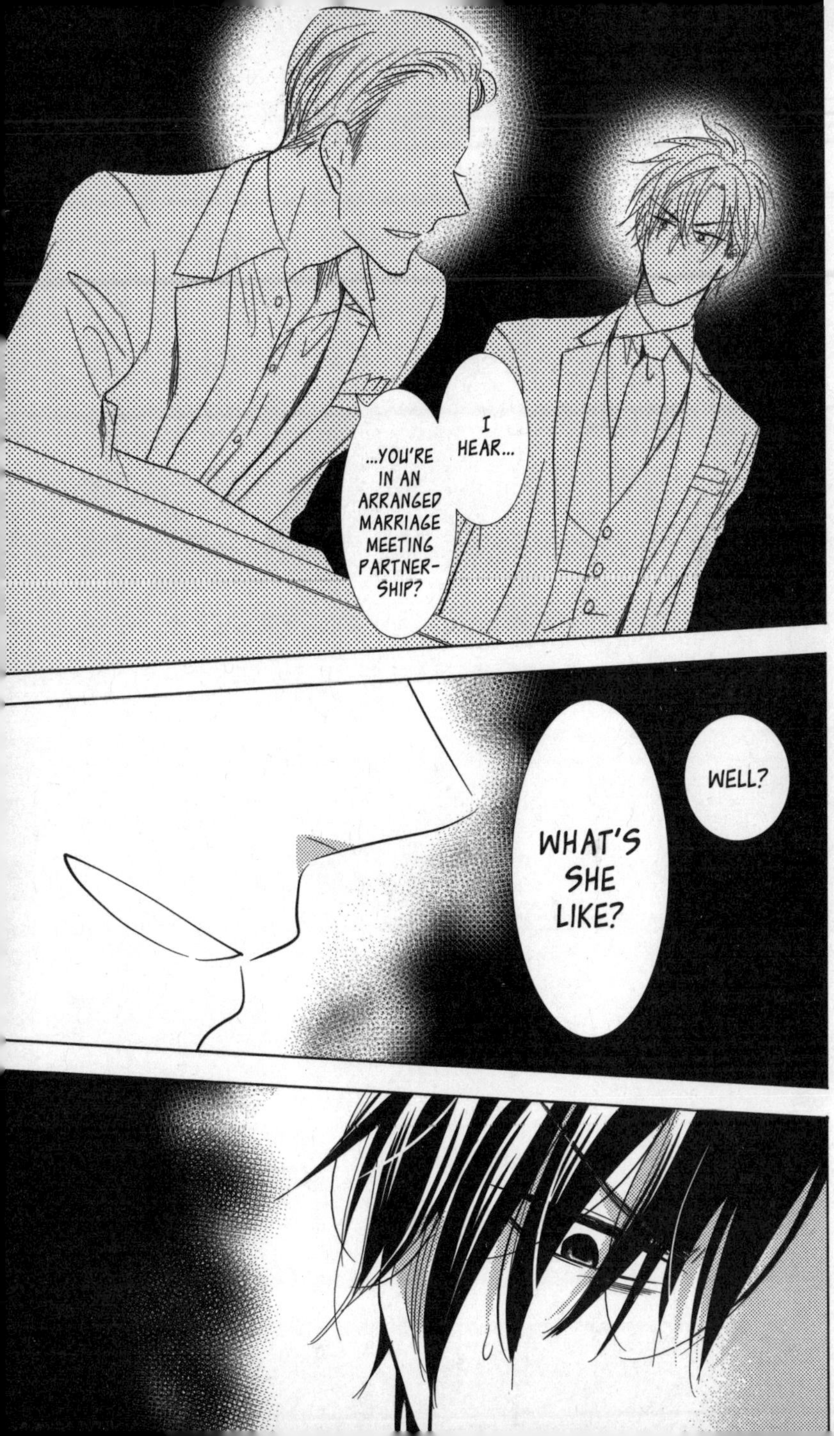
I HEAR...
...YOU'RE IN AN ARRANGED MARRIAGE MEETING PARTNER-SHIP?
WELL?
WHAT'S SHE LIKE?

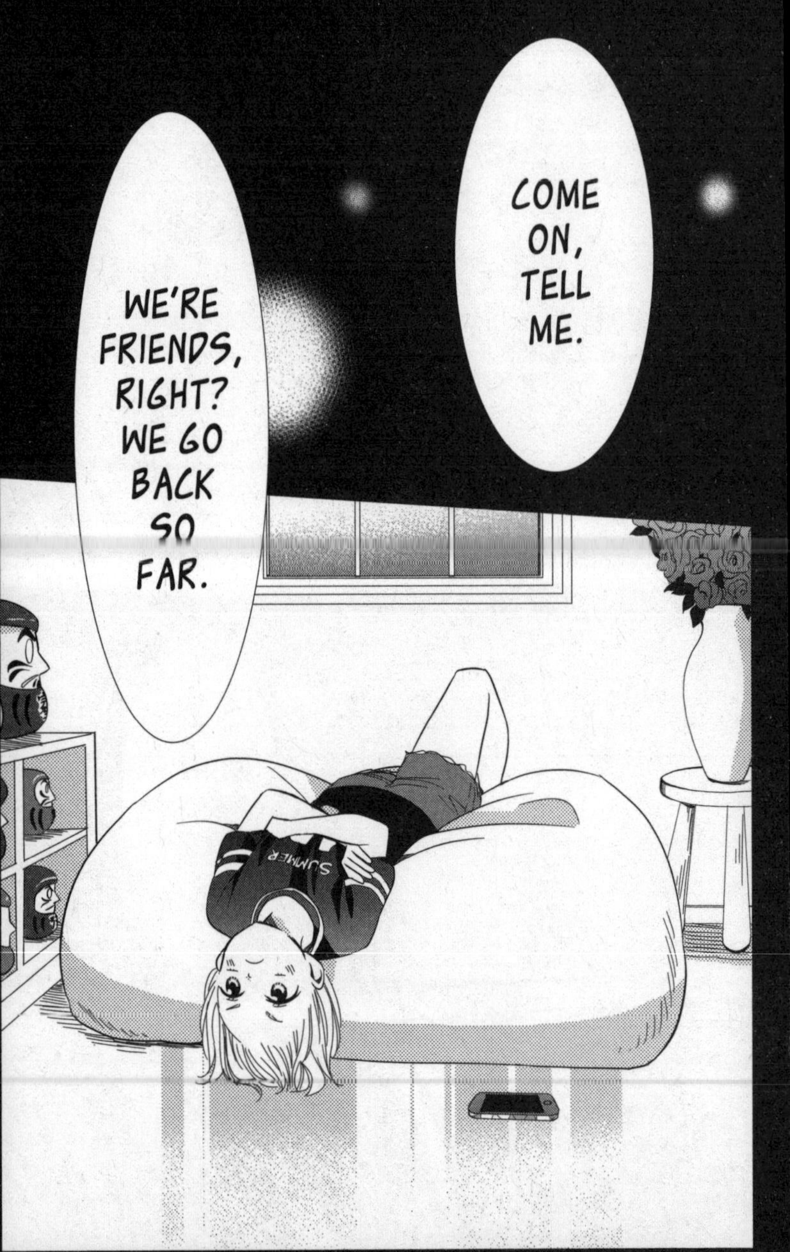
COME ON, TELL ME.
WE'RE FRIENDS, RIGHT? WE GO BACK SO FAR.
SUMMER

Two People Passing Each Other

WHEN WE PASS EACH OTHER IN A NARROW HALLWAY...
STROLL
GOOD MORNING.
MORE LIKE GOOD AFTERNOON.
STROLL
DODGE
...FOR SOME REASON, TAKANE...
...STOPS RIGHT IN THE MIDDLE AND PATIENTLY WAITS FOR ME TO QUICKLY SLIP AROUND HIM.
3-2
NONOMURA
IT'S LIKE A FACE-OFF BETWEEN A CAR AND A PEDESTRIAN.
IS HE BEING SERIOUS OR IS HE JUST MESSING WITH ME? I CAN'T TELL...

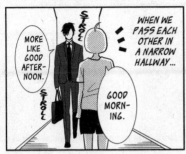

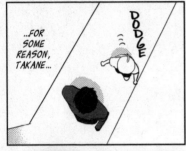

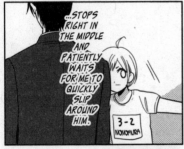

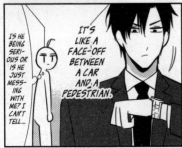

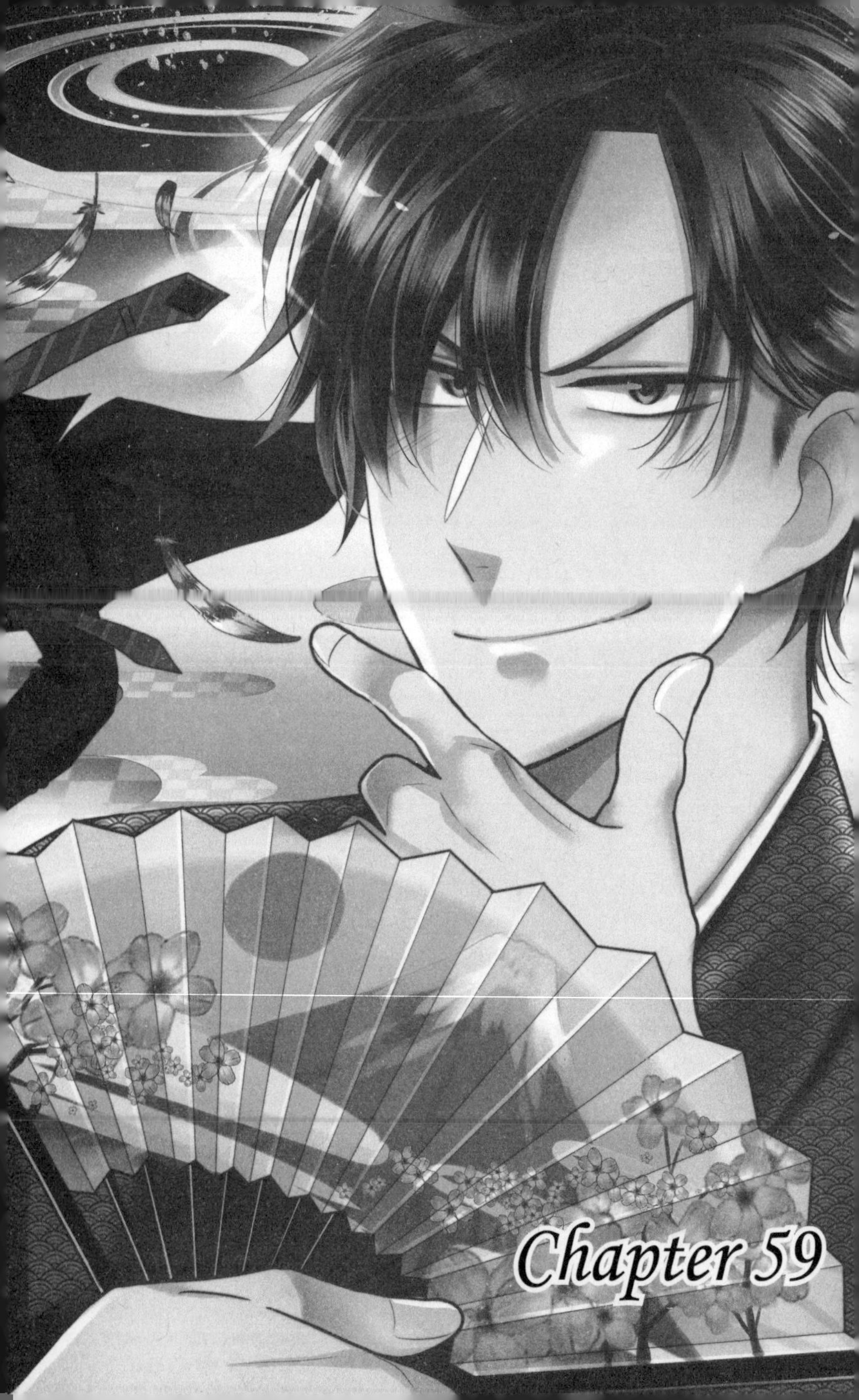
Chapter 59

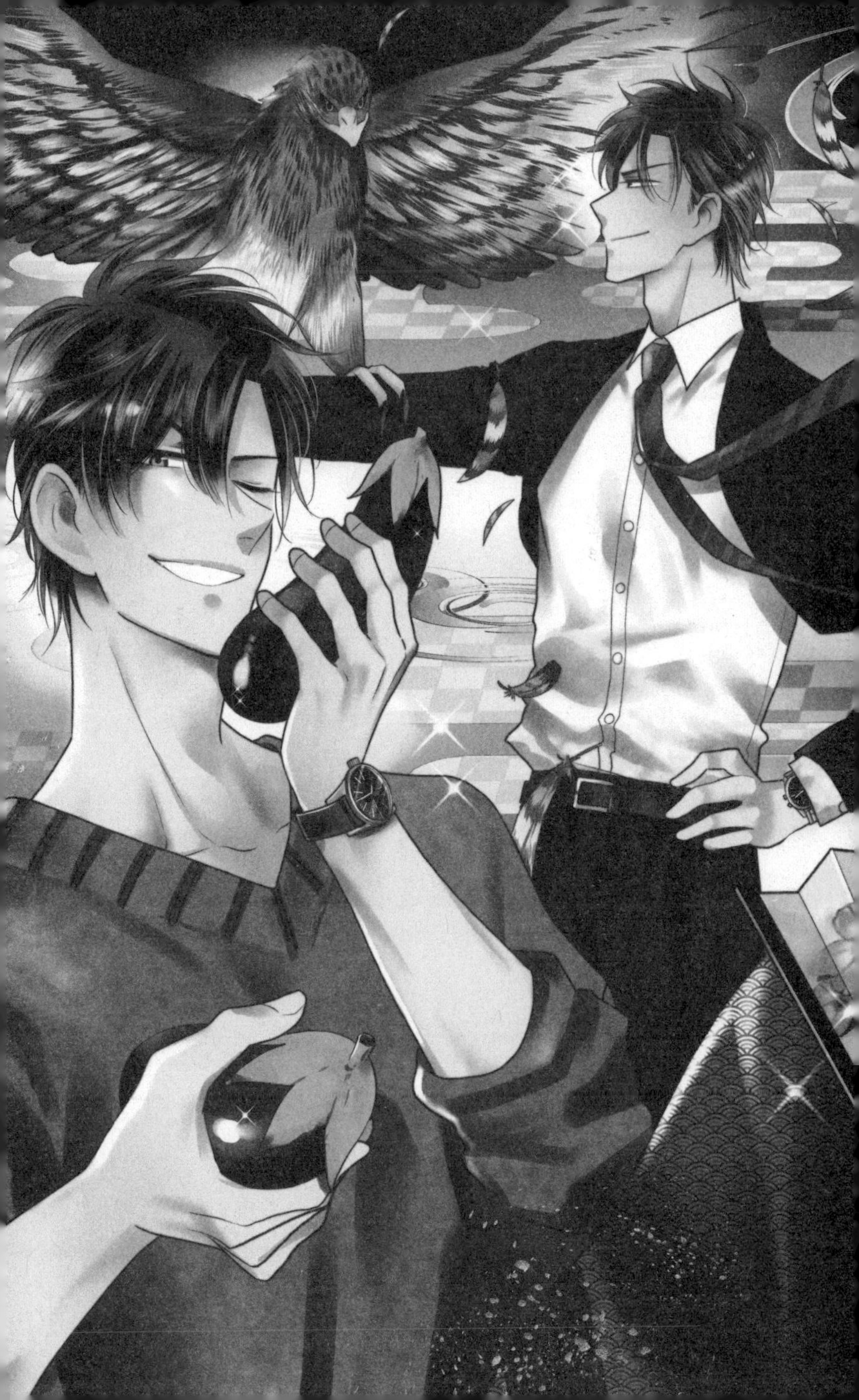

Nickname

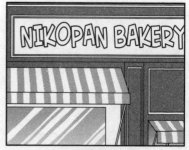

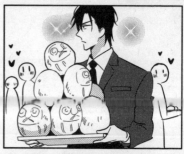

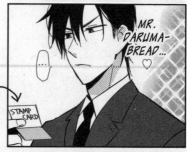

NIKOPAN BAKERY
WSP WSP
HE'S BACK! THAT MYSTERIOUS, GOOD-LOOKING BUSINESSMAN WHO COMES IN SO OFTEN.
GOSH, HE'S SO HANDSOME...
MR. DARUMA-BREAD...
...
STAMP CARD
Hana makes him bring it.

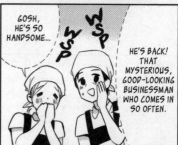

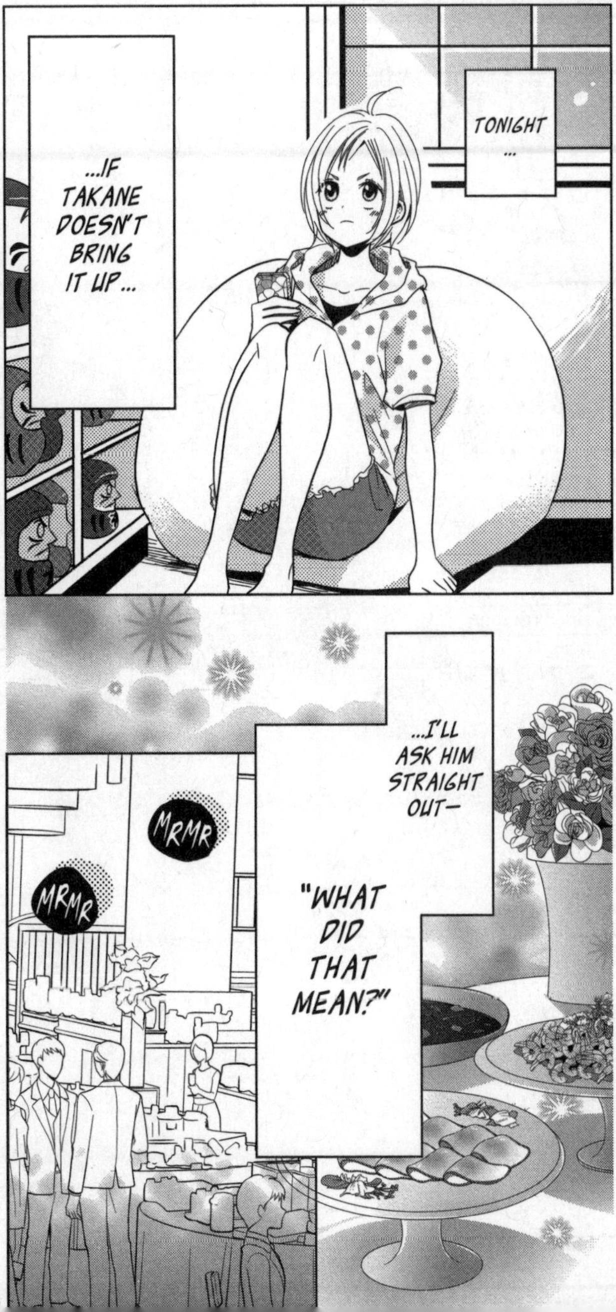
TONIGHT ...
...IF TAKANE DOESN'T BRING IT UP...
...I'LL ASK HIM STRAIGHT OUT—
"WHAT DID THAT MEAN?"
MRMR
MRMR

• The opening color pages of chapter 59 •

I realize it's a bit over-the-top, considering the mood of the chapter. However, when the magazine came out, it came with the following sales copy:

1. Takane

2. Takane

3. Takane

The first dream you have in the New Year will be about me.

Both Mt. Fuji and *taka* (hawk) are associated with Takane, but I'm not sure about the eggplant.* Is it his eyes? His eyes are the color of eggplants. That's gotta be it.

• What is sales copy? •

The sales copy goes on the frontispiece of the magazine where the manga is serialized. People who buy the compiled graphic novels don't often get to see it, though.

I can't introduce all of them, but I'll pick out a few for you to read. (To be continued)

*In Japanese culture, it is considered good luck for one's first dream of the New Year to be of Mt. Fuji, a hawk and an eggplant.

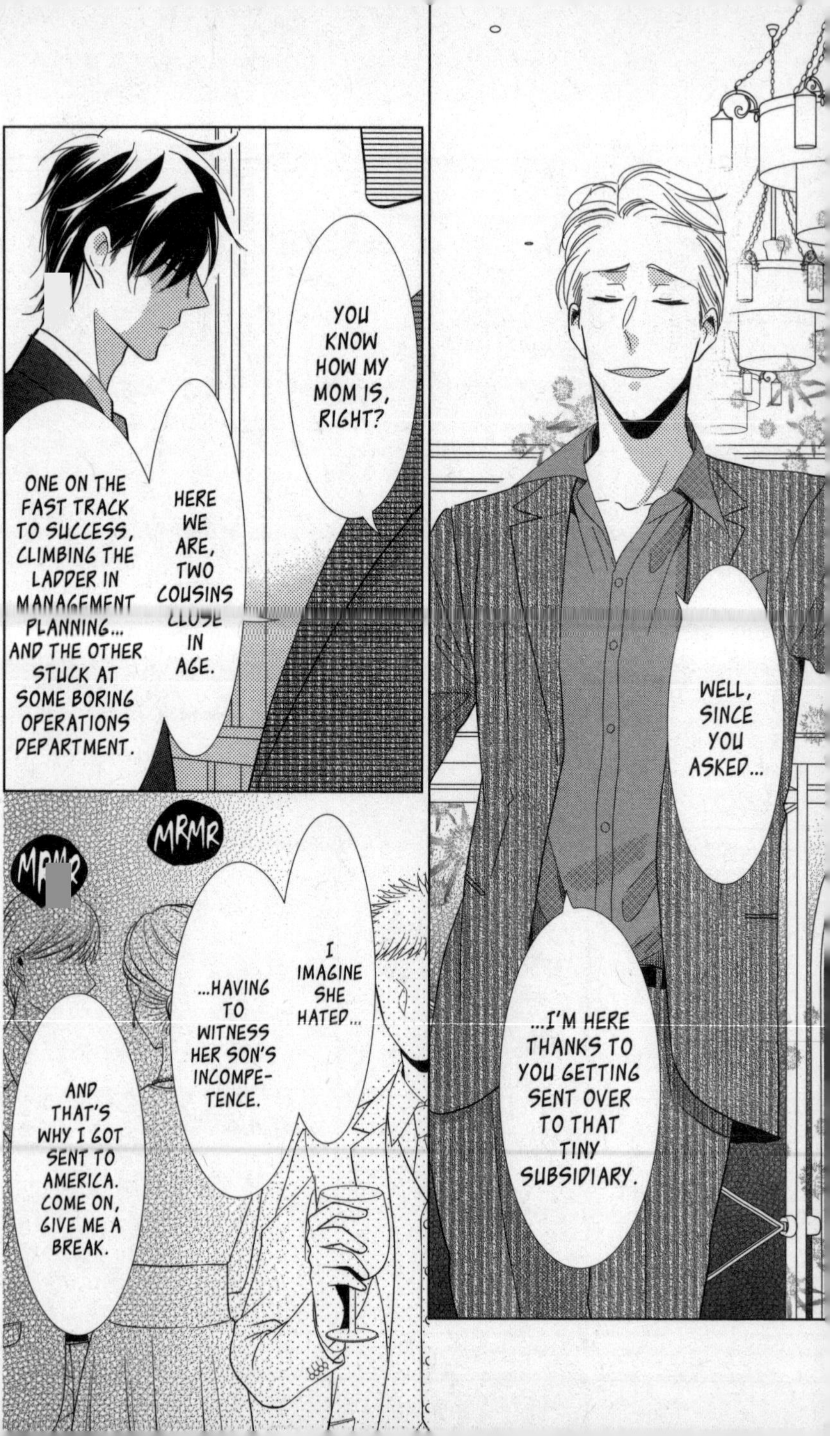
WELL, SINCE YOU ASKED...
...I'M HERE THANKS TO YOU GETTING SENT OVER TO THAT TINY SUBSIDIARY.
YOU KNOW HOW MY MOM IS, RIGHT?
HERE WE ARE, TWO COUSINS CLOSE IN AGE.
ONE ON THE FAST TRACK TO SUCCESS, CLIMBING THE LADDER IN MANAGEMENT PLANNING... AND THE OTHER STUCK AT SOME BORING OPERATIONS DEPARTMENT.
MRMR
I IMAGINE SHE HATED...
...HAVING TO WITNESS HER SON'S INCOMPETENCE.
AND THAT'S WHY I GOT SENT TO AMERICA. COME ON, GIVE ME A BREAK.

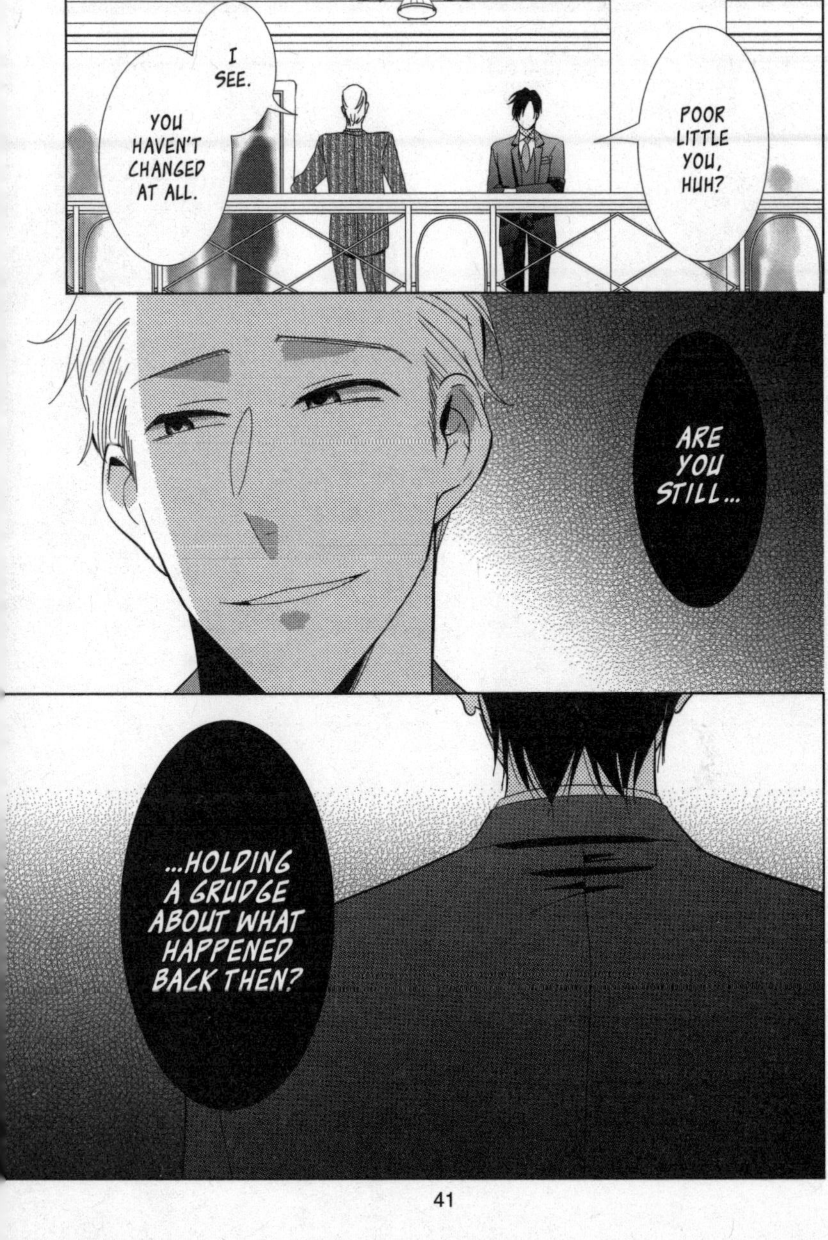
POOR LITTLE YOU, HUH?
I SEE. YOU HAVEN'T CHANGED AT ALL.
ARE YOU STILL...
...HOLDING A GRUDGE ABOUT WHAT HAPPENED BACK THEN?

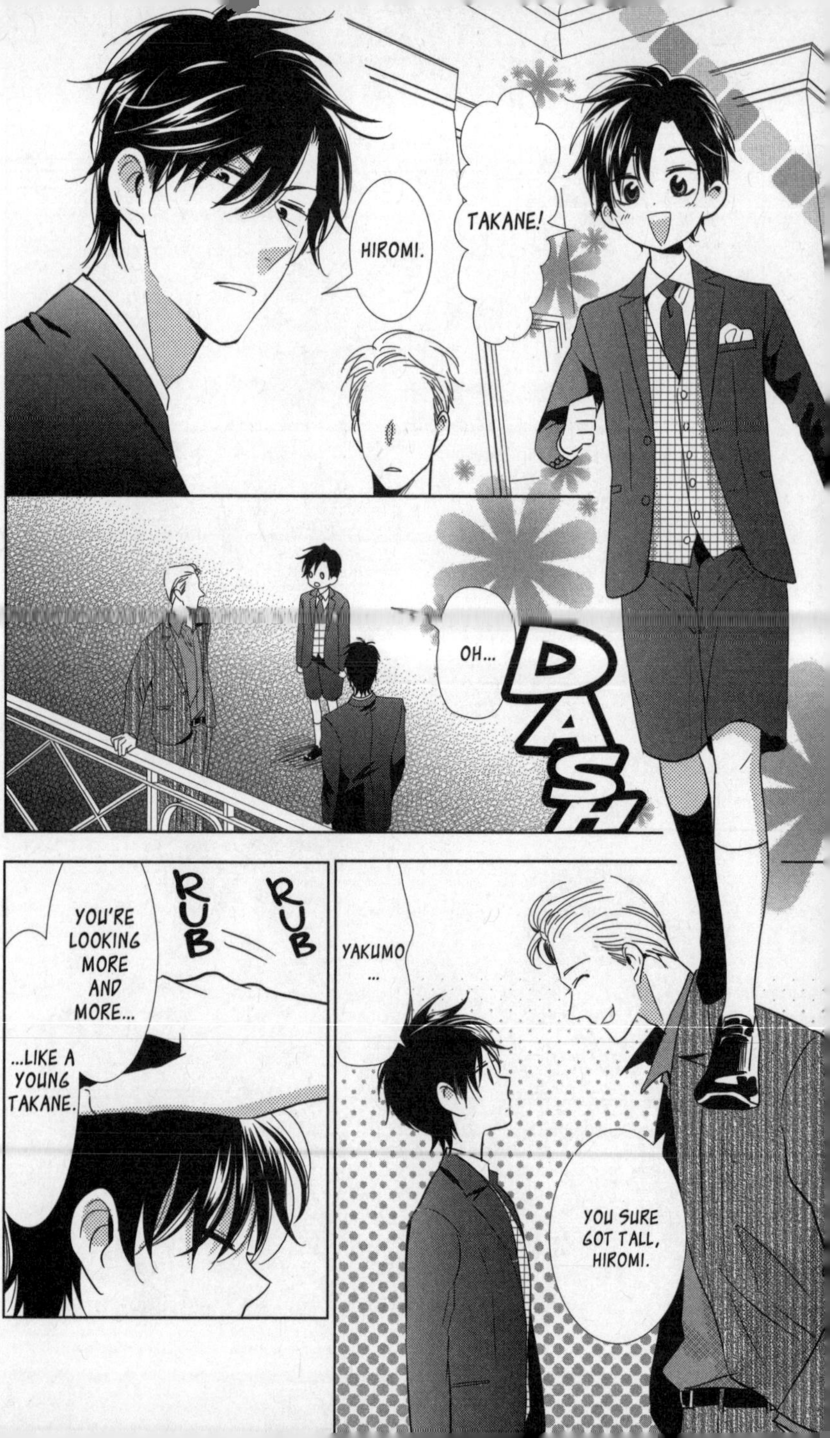
TAKANE!
HIROMI.
OH...
DASH
YAKUMO...
YOU SURE GOT TALL, HIROMI.
RUB RUB
YOU'RE LOOKING MORE AND MORE...
...LIKE A YOUNG TAKANE.

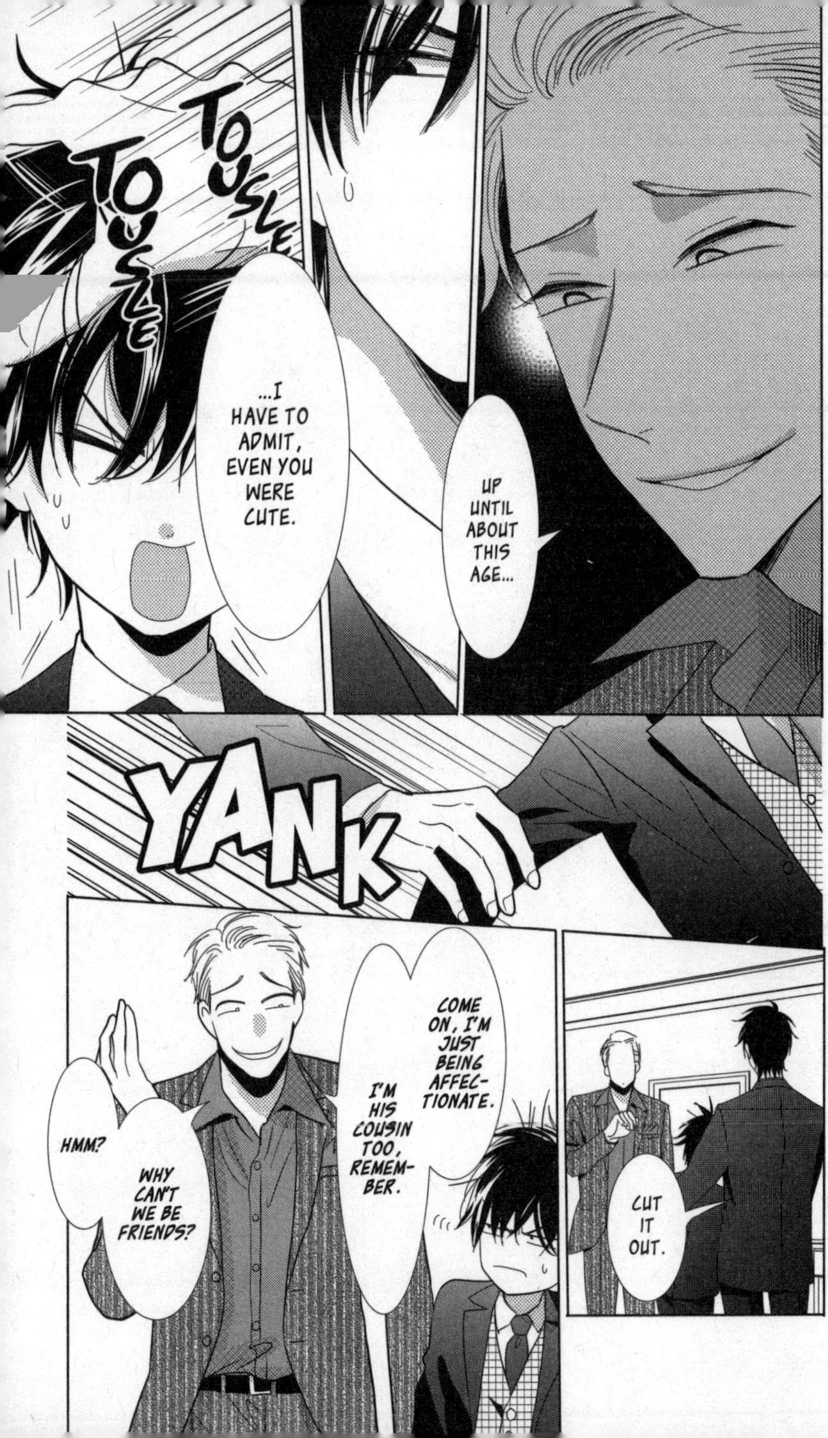
UP UNTIL ABOUT THIS AGE...
TOUSLE
TOUSLE
...I HAVE TO ADMIT, EVEN YOU WERE CUTE.
YANK
CUT IT OUT.
COME ON, I'M JUST BEING AFFECTIONATE.
I'M HIS COUSIN TOO, REMEMBER.
HMM?
WHY CAN'T WE BE FRIENDS?

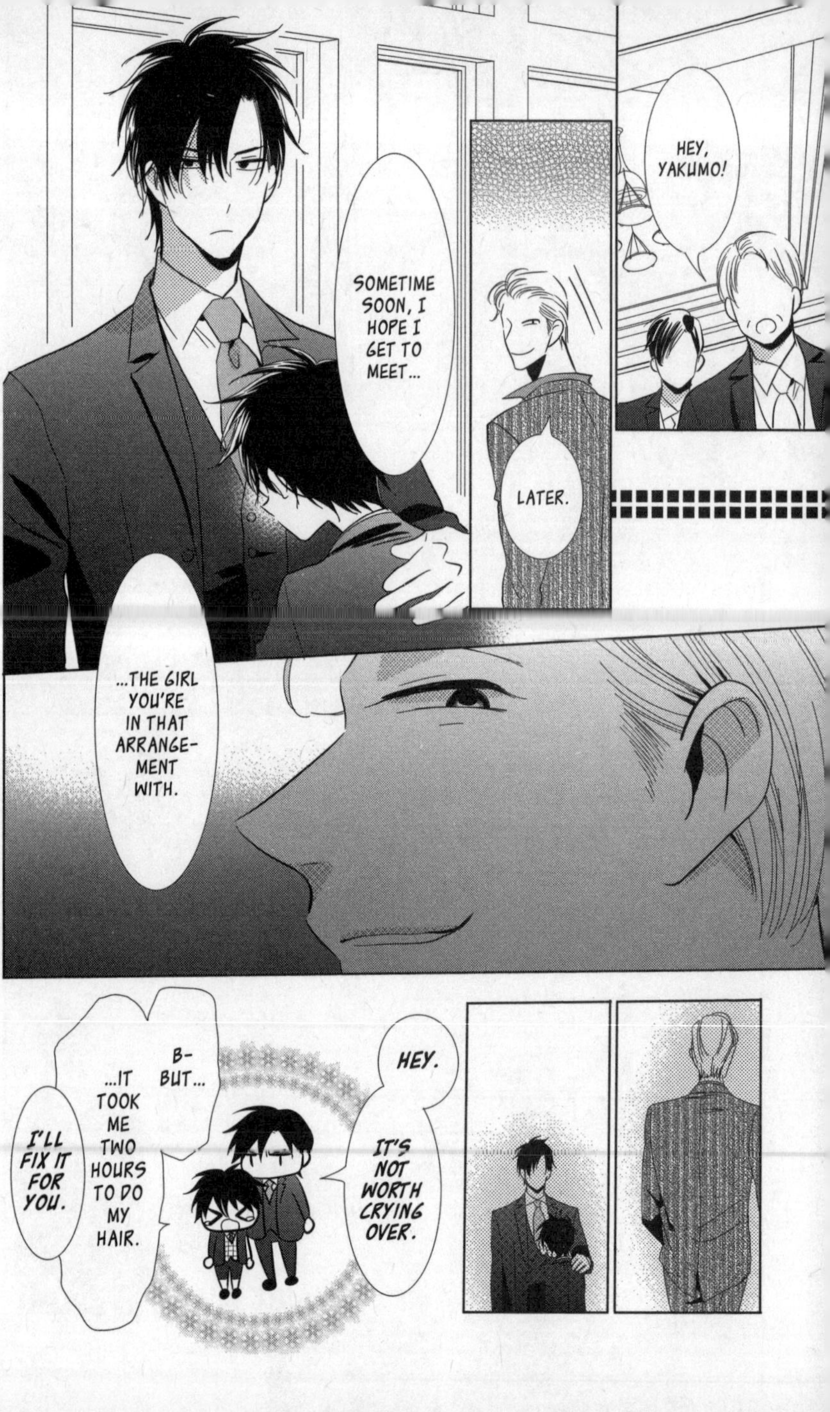
HEY, YAKUMO!
LATER.
SOMETIME SOON, I HOPE I GET TO MEET...
...THE GIRL YOU'RE IN THAT ARRANGE-MENT WITH.
HEY.
IT'S NOT WORTH CRYING OVER.
B-BUT...
...IT TOOK ME TWO HOURS TO DO MY HAIR.
I'LL FIX IT FOR YOU.

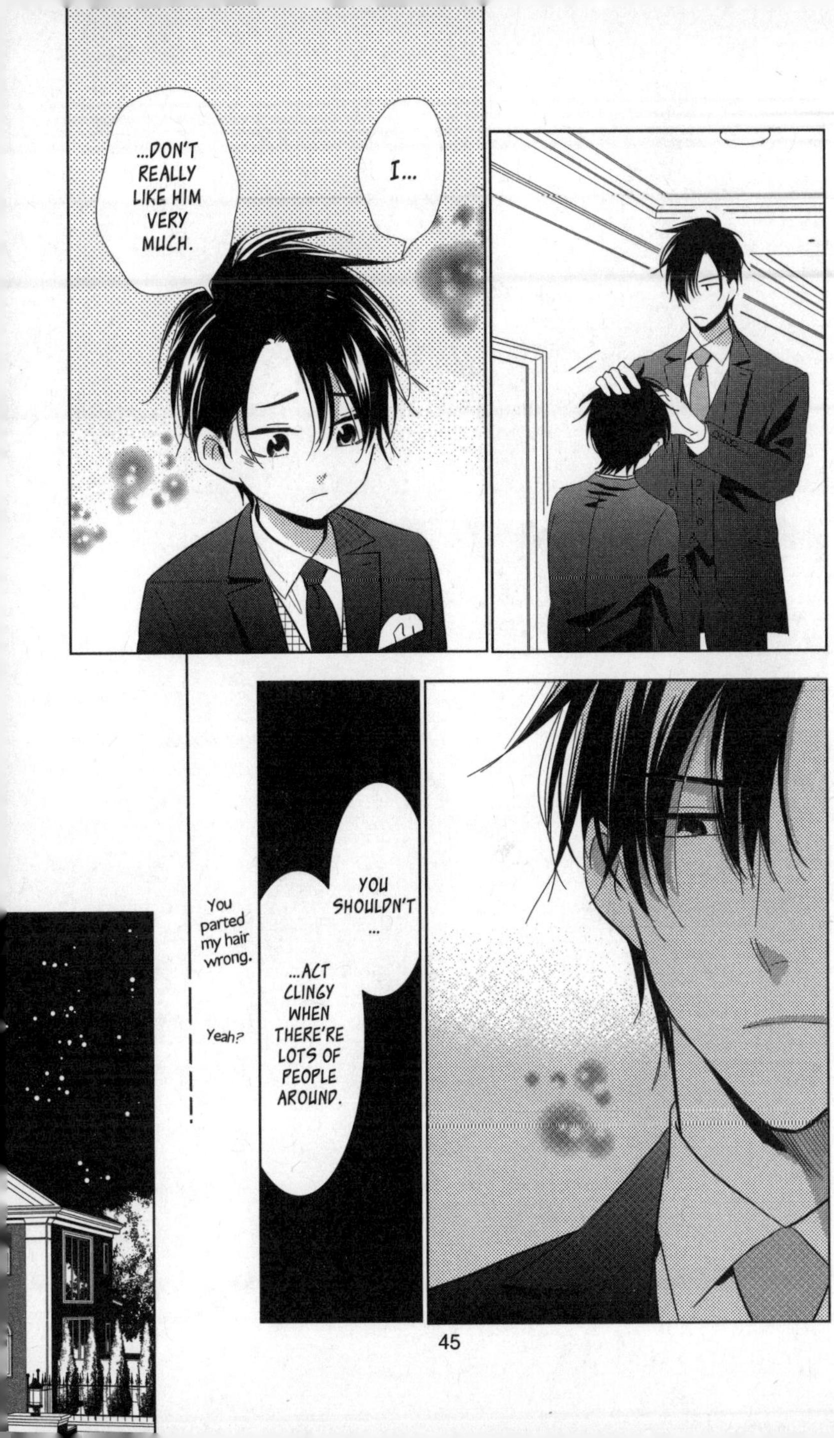
I...
...DON'T REALLY LIKE HIM VERY MUCH.
YOU SHOULDN'T ...
...ACT CLINGY WHEN THERE'RE LOTS OF PEOPLE AROUND.
You parted my hair wrong.
Yeah?

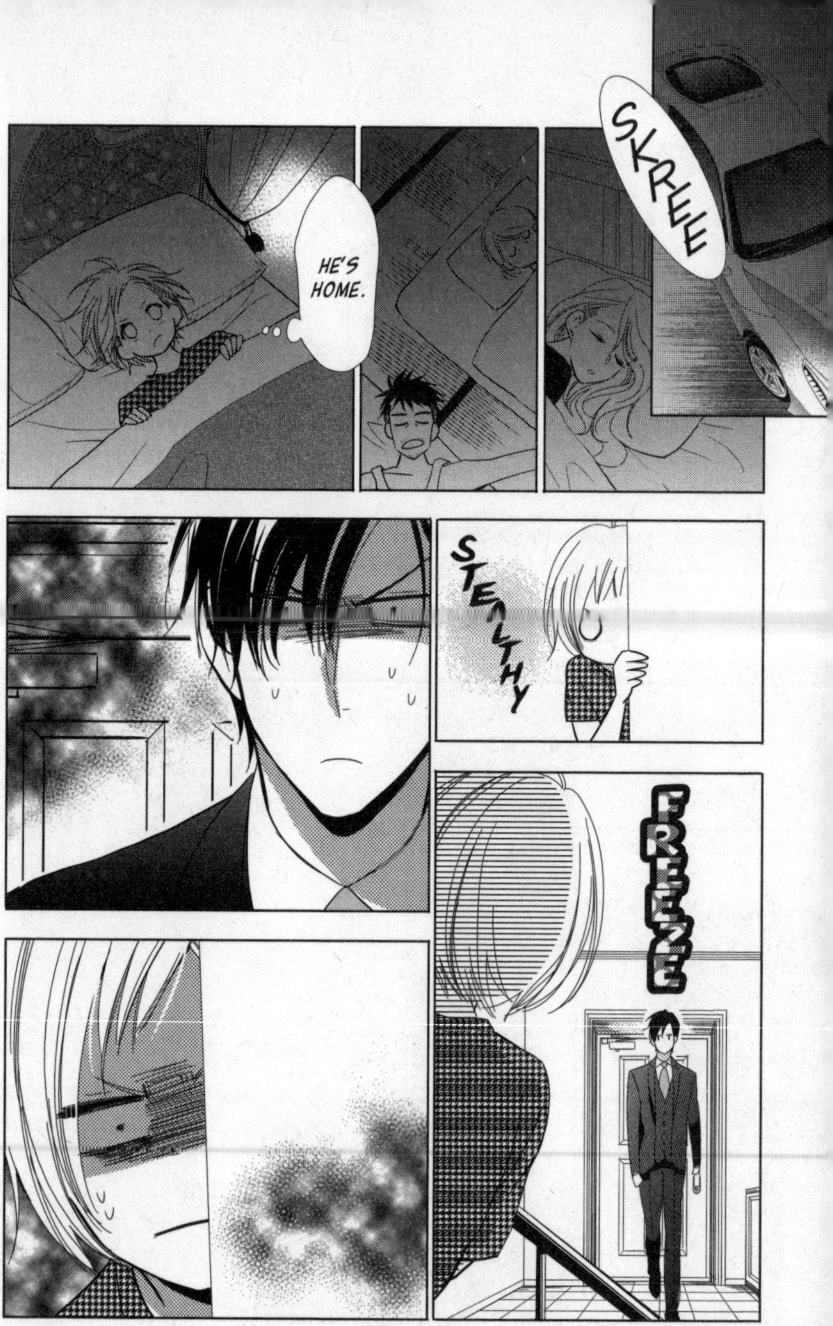
SKREE
HE'S HOME.
STEALTHY
FREEZE

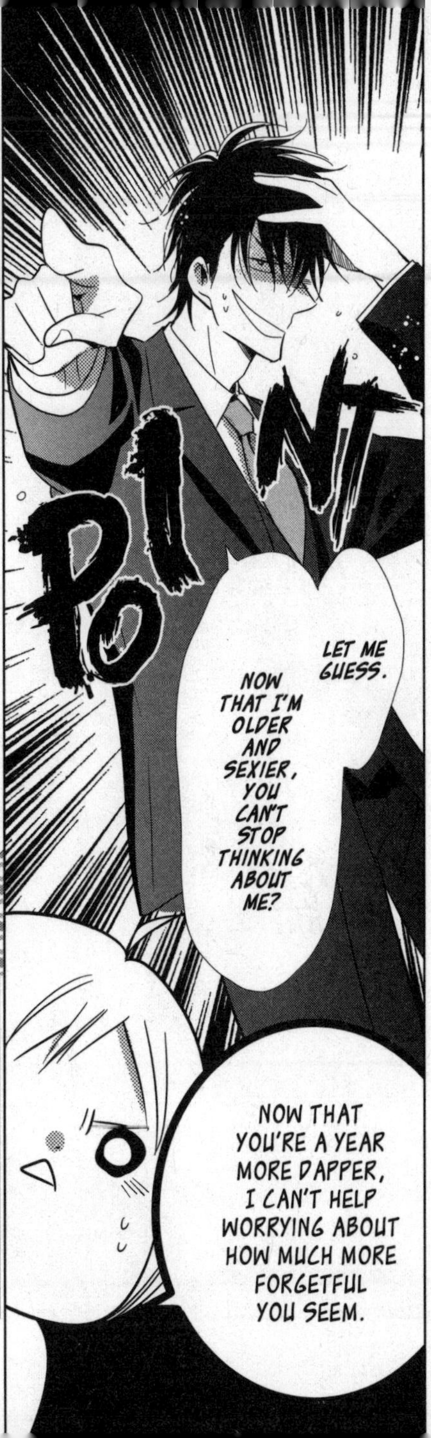
LET ME GUESS.
NOW THAT I'M OLDER AND SEXIER, YOU CAN'T STOP THINKING ABOUT ME?
POINT
NOW THAT YOU'RE A YEAR MORE DAPPER, I CAN'T HELP WORRYING ABOUT HOW MUCH MORE FORGETFUL YOU SEEM.

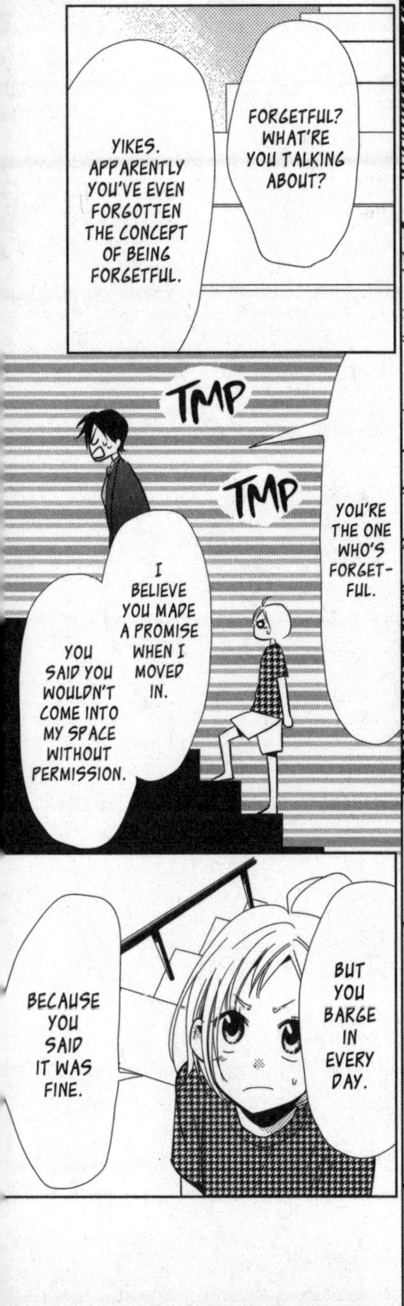
FORGETFUL? WHAT'RE YOU TALKING ABOUT?
YIKES. APPARENTLY YOU'VE EVEN FORGOTTEN THE CONCEPT OF BEING FORGETFUL.
YOU'RE THE ONE WHO'S FORGET-FUL.
TMP
TMP
I BELIEVE YOU MADE A PROMISE WHEN I MOVED IN.
YOU SAID YOU WOULDN'T COME INTO MY SPACE WITHOUT PERMISSION.
BUT YOU BARGE IN EVERY DAY.
BECAUSE YOU SAID IT WAS FINE.

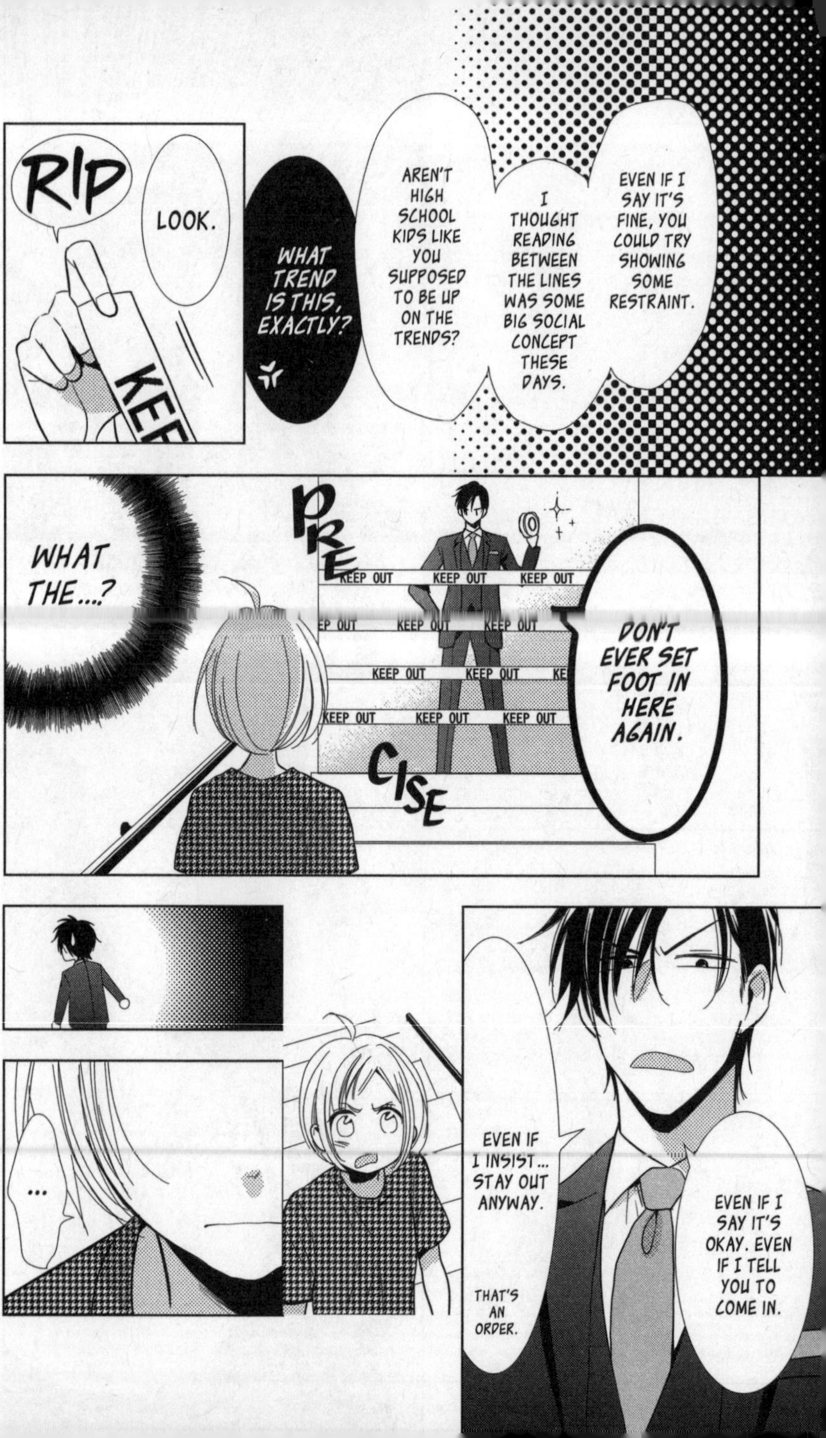
EVEN IF I SAY IT'S FINE, YOU COULD TRY SHOWING SOME RESTRAINT.
I THOUGHT READING BETWEEN THE LINES WAS SOME BIG SOCIAL CONCEPT THESE DAYS.
AREN'T HIGH SCHOOL KIDS LIKE YOU SUPPOSED TO BE UP ON THE TRENDS?
WHAT TREND IS THIS, EXACTLY?
LOOK.
RIP
KEE
DON'T EVER SET FOOT IN HERE AGAIN.
PRE
KEEP OUT KEEP OUT KEEP OUT
CISE
WHAT THE...?
EVEN IF I SAY IT'S OKAY. EVEN IF I TELL YOU TO COME IN.
EVEN IF I INSIST... STAY OUT ANYWAY.
THAT'S AN ORDER.
...

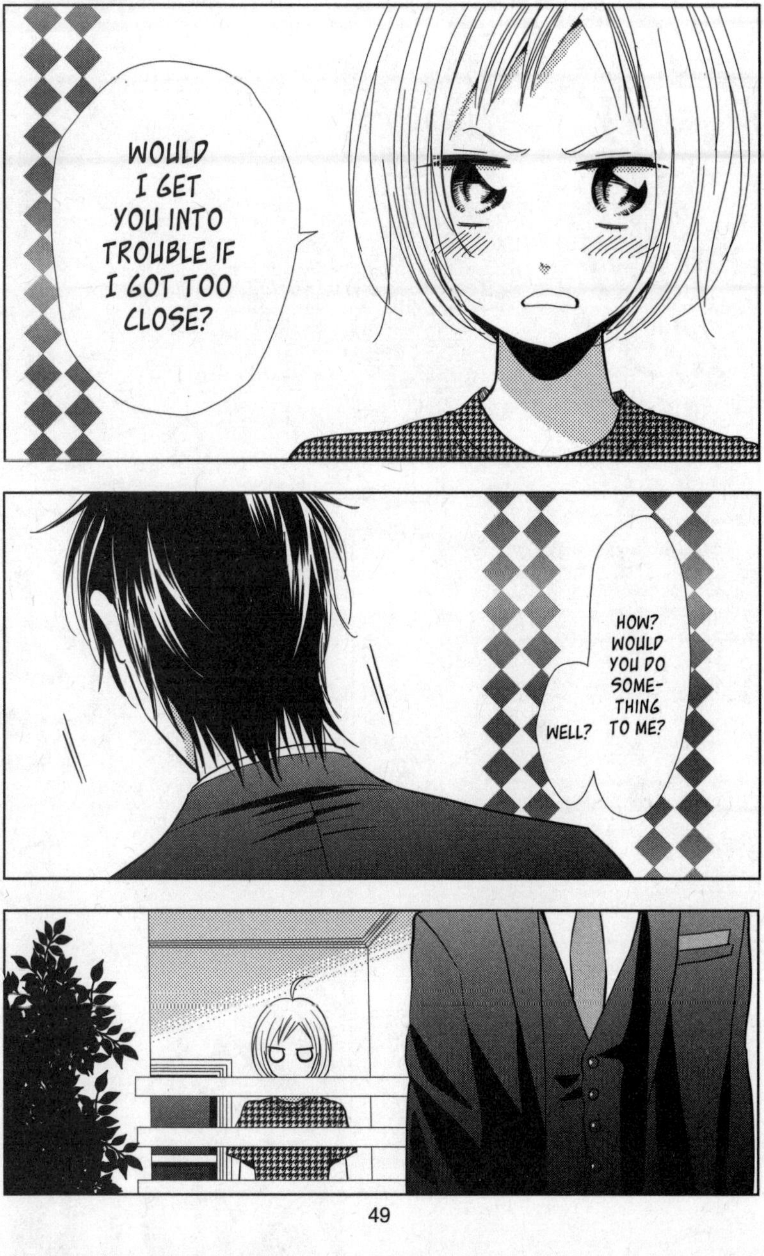
WOULD I GET YOU INTO TROUBLE IF I GOT TOO CLOSE?
HOW? WOULD YOU DO SOME-THING TO ME?
WELL?

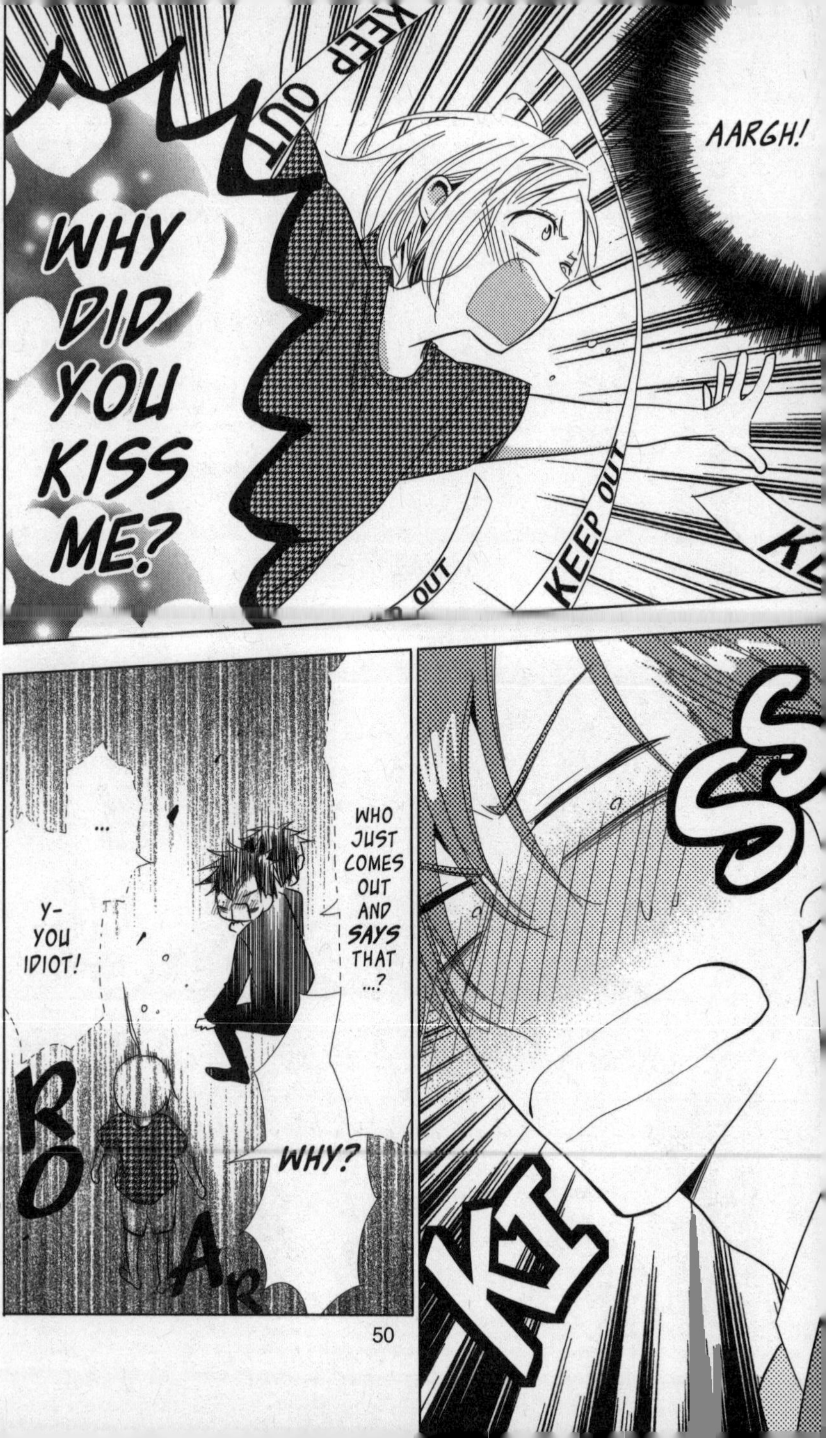
KEEP OUT
AARGH!
WHY DID YOU KISS ME?
KEEP OUT
WHO JUST COMES OUT AND SAYS THAT ...?
WHY?
...
Y-YOU IDIOT!
ROAR

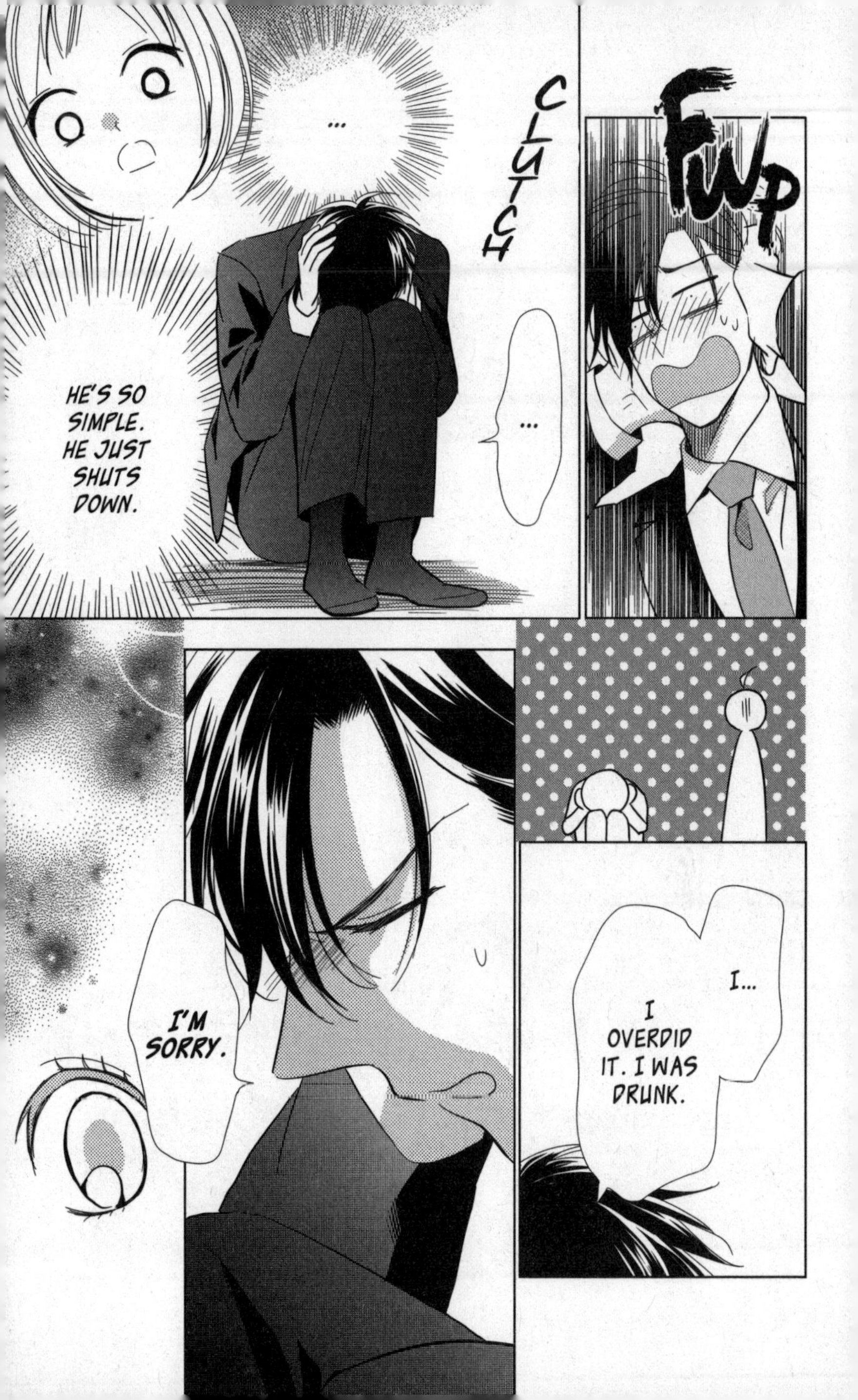
FWP
CLUTCH
...
...
HE'S SO SIMPLE. HE JUST SHUTS DOWN.
I...
I OVERDID IT. I WAS DRUNK.
I'M SORRY.

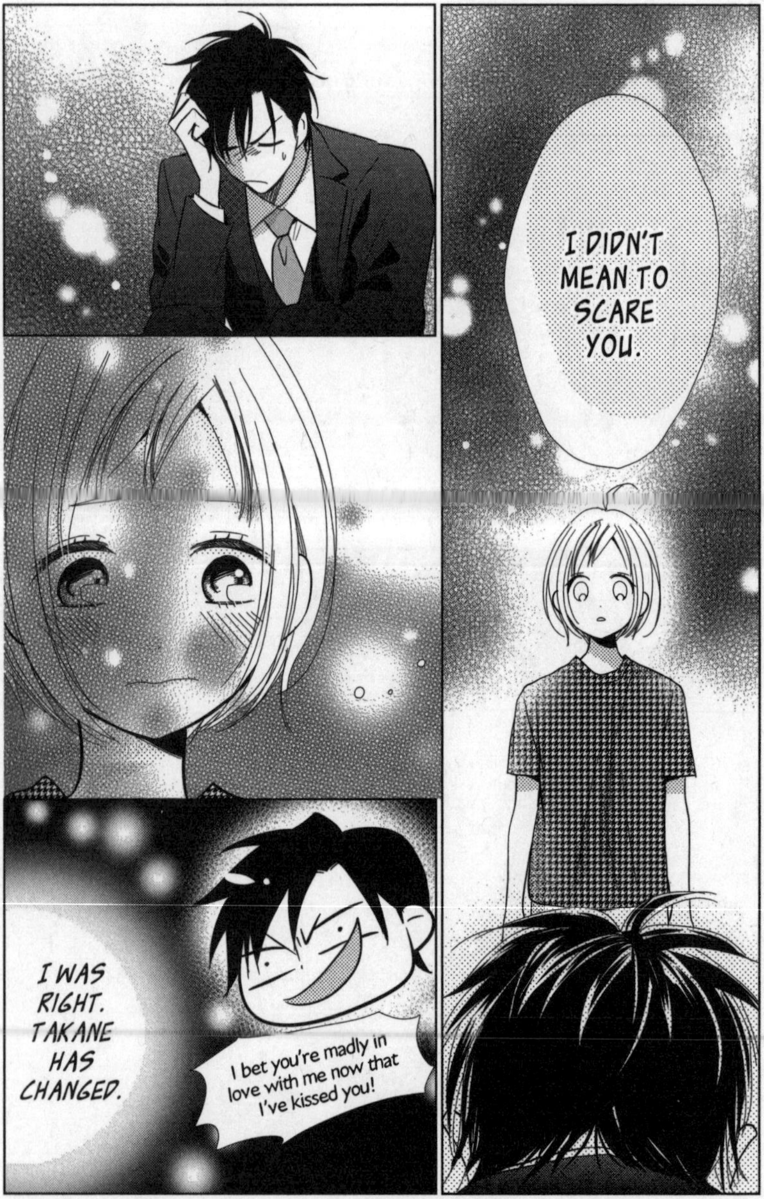
I DIDN'T MEAN TO SCARE YOU.
I bet you're madly in love with me now that I've kissed you!
I WAS RIGHT. TAKANE HAS CHANGED.

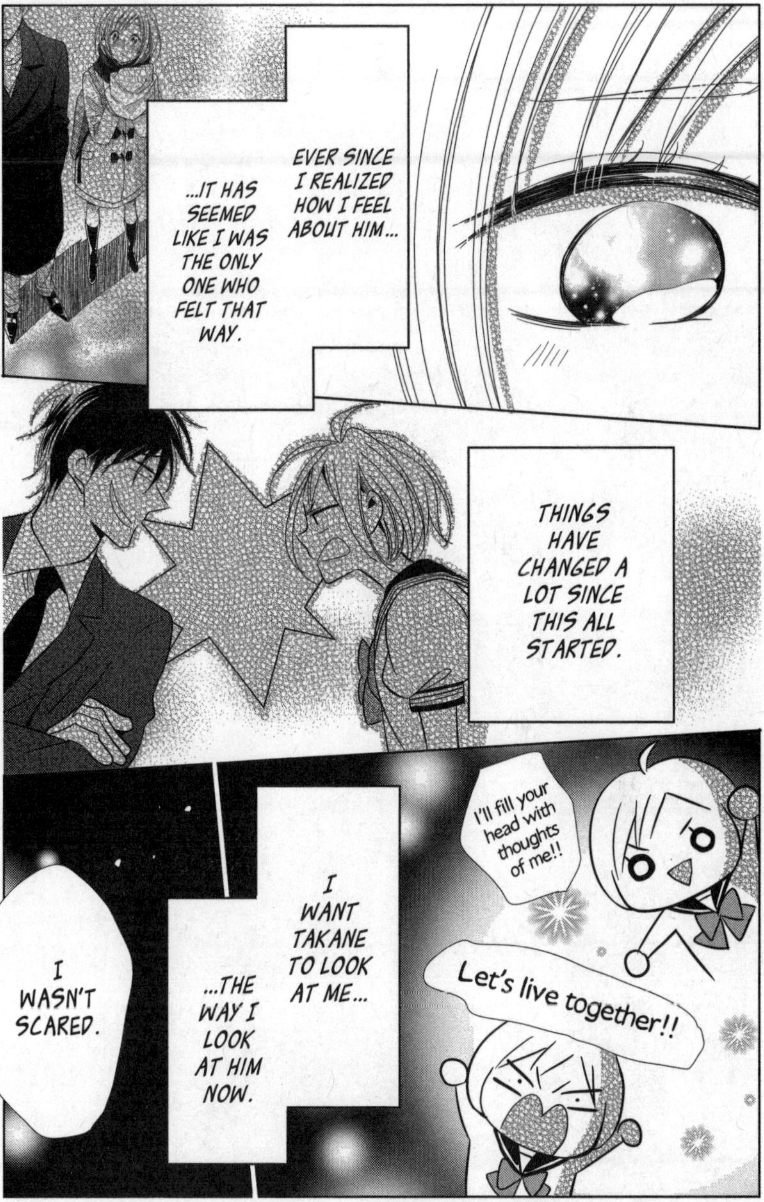
EVER SINCE I REALIZED HOW I FEEL ABOUT HIM...
...IT HAS SEEMED LIKE I WAS THE ONLY ONE WHO FELT THAT WAY.
THINGS HAVE CHANGED A LOT SINCE THIS ALL STARTED.
I'll fill your head with thoughts of me!!
Let's live together!!
I WANT TAKANE TO LOOK AT ME...
...THE WAY I LOOK AT HIM NOW.
I WASN'T SCARED.

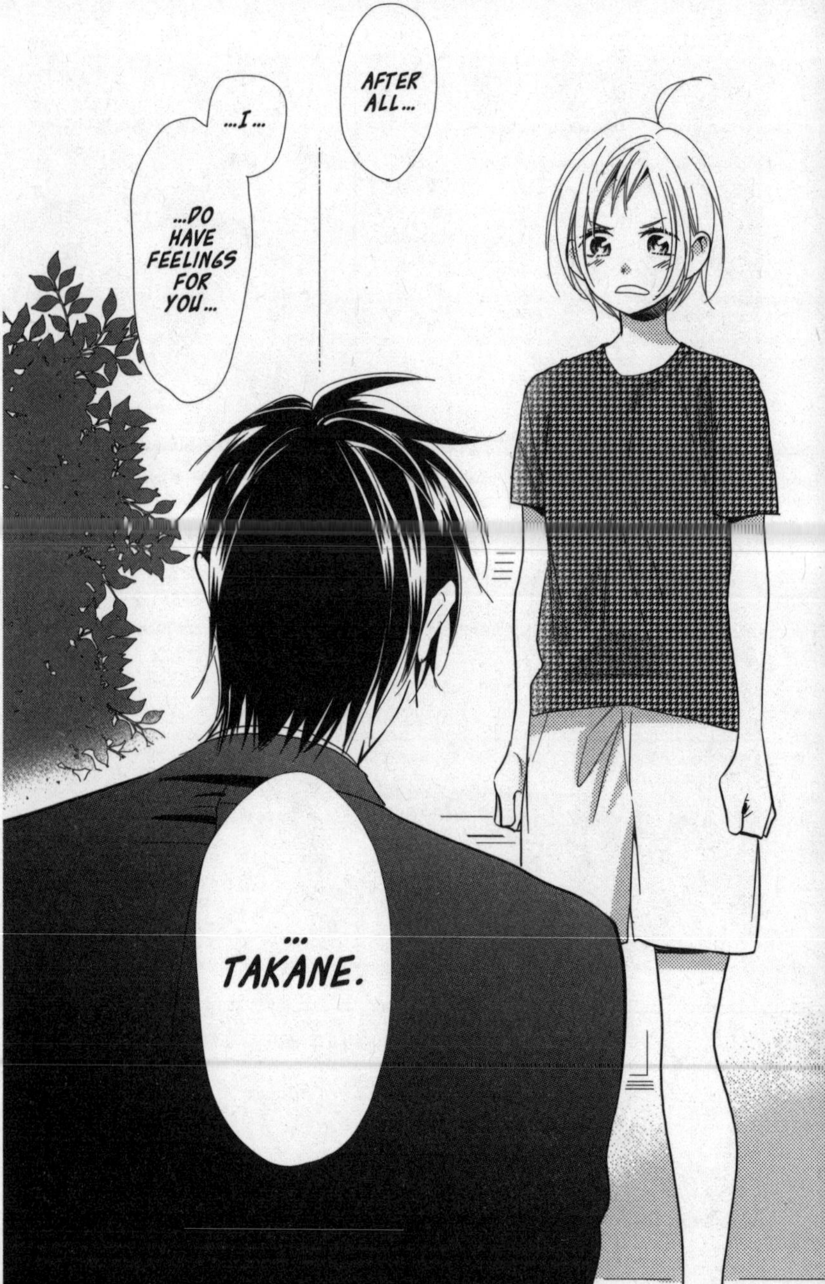
AFTER ALL...
...I...
...DO HAVE FEELINGS FOR YOU...
...TAKANE.

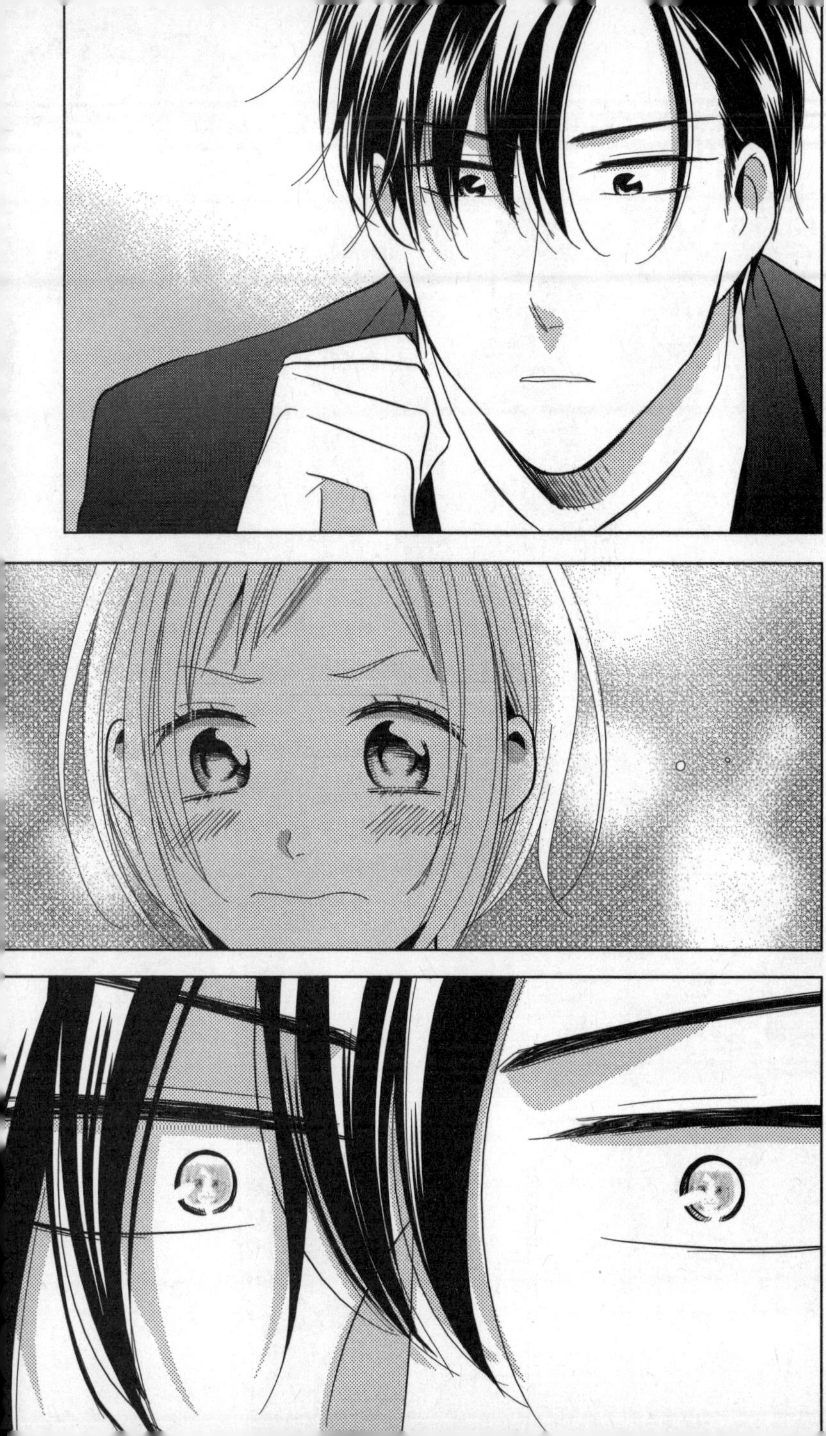

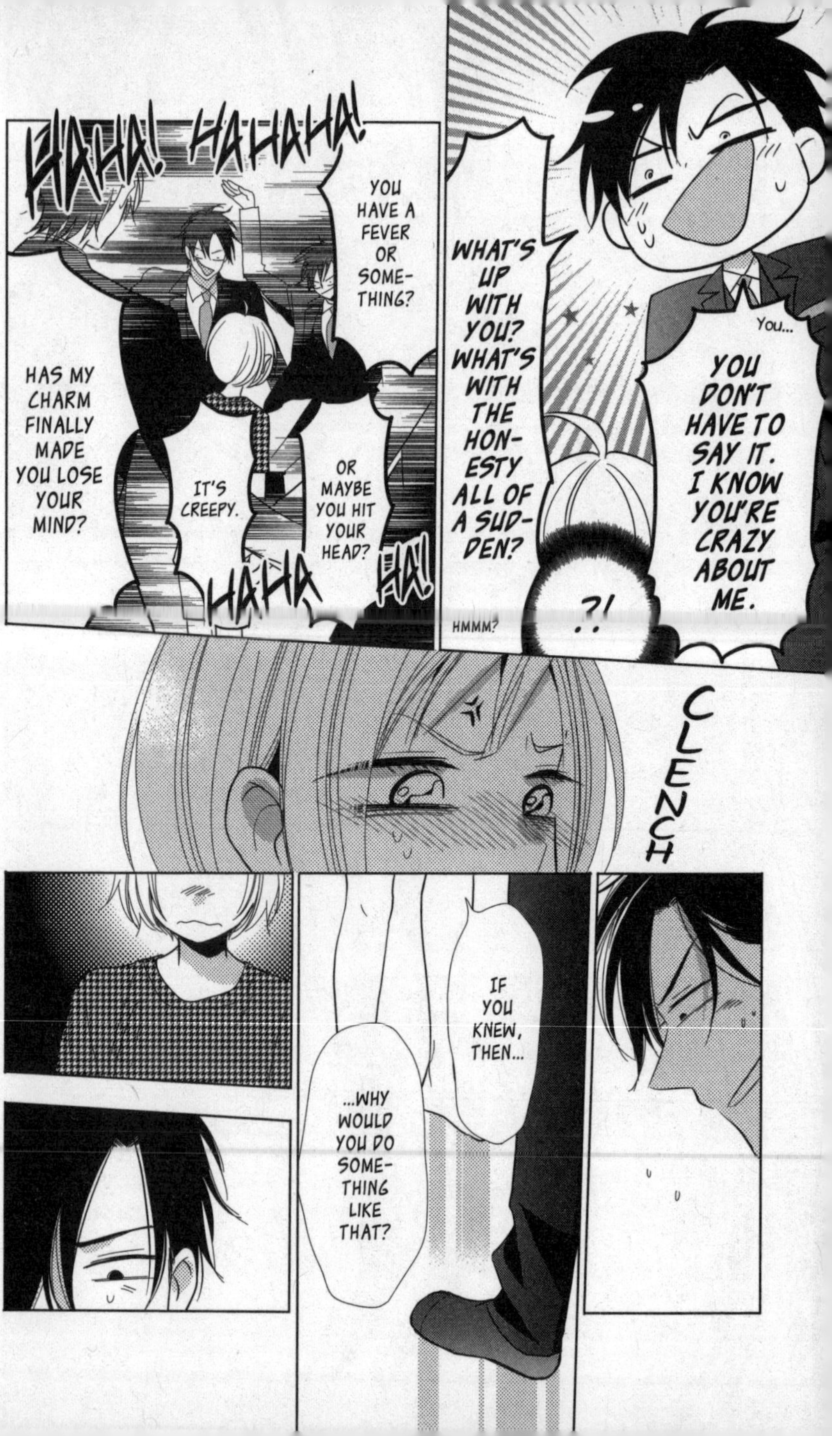
You...
YOU DON'T HAVE TO SAY IT. I KNOW YOU'RE CRAZY ABOUT ME.
WHAT'S UP WITH YOU? WHAT'S WITH THE HON-ESTY ALL OF A SUD-DEN?
?!
HMMM?
HAHA! HAHAHA!
YOU HAVE A FEVER OR SOME-THING?
OR MAYBE YOU HIT YOUR HEAD?
IT'S CREEPY.
HAS MY CHARM FINALLY MADE YOU LOSE YOUR MIND?
HAHA HA!
CLENCH
IF YOU KNEW, THEN...
...WHY WOULD YOU DO SOME-THING LIKE THAT?

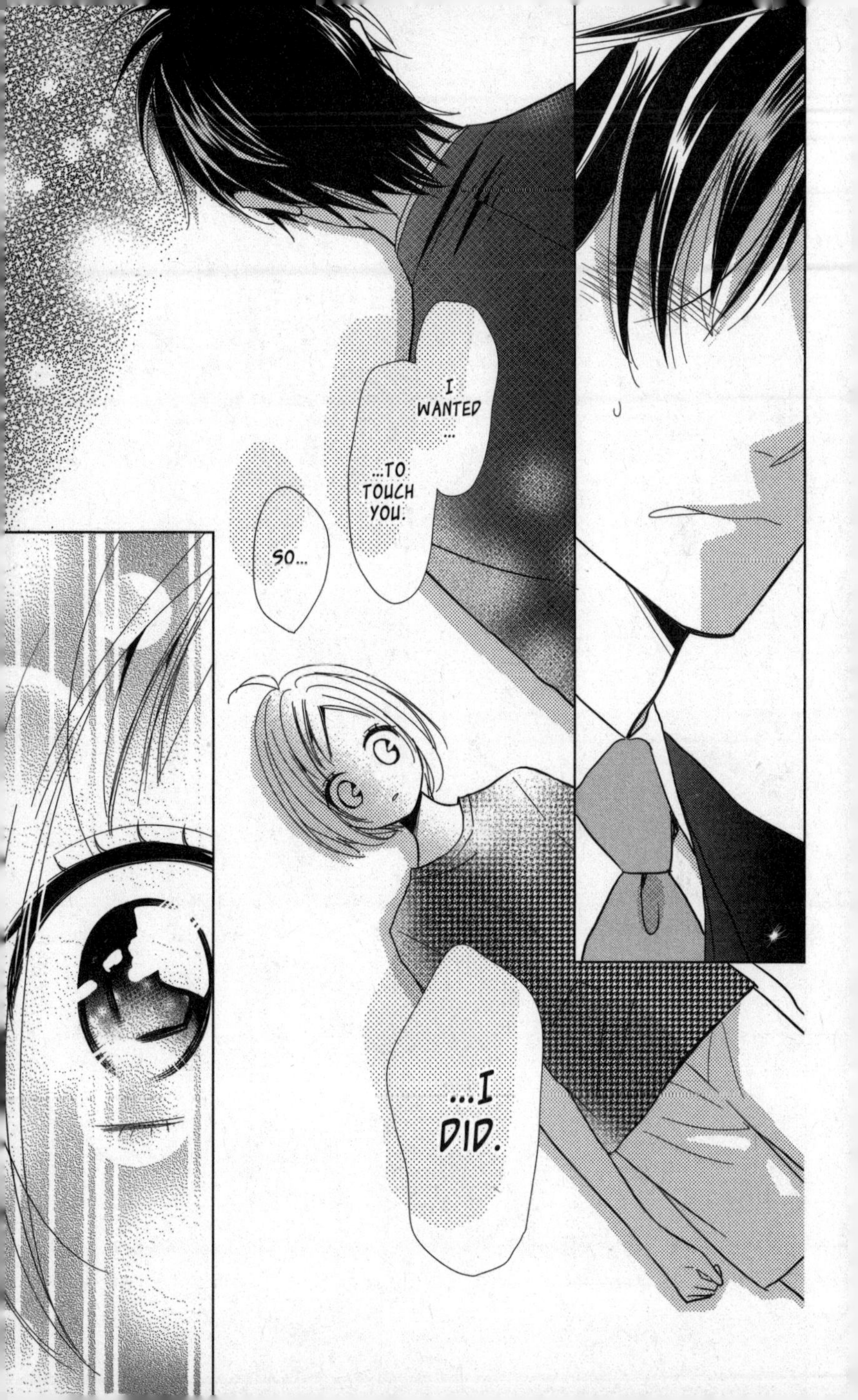
I WANTED ...
...TO TOUCH YOU.
SO...
...I DID.

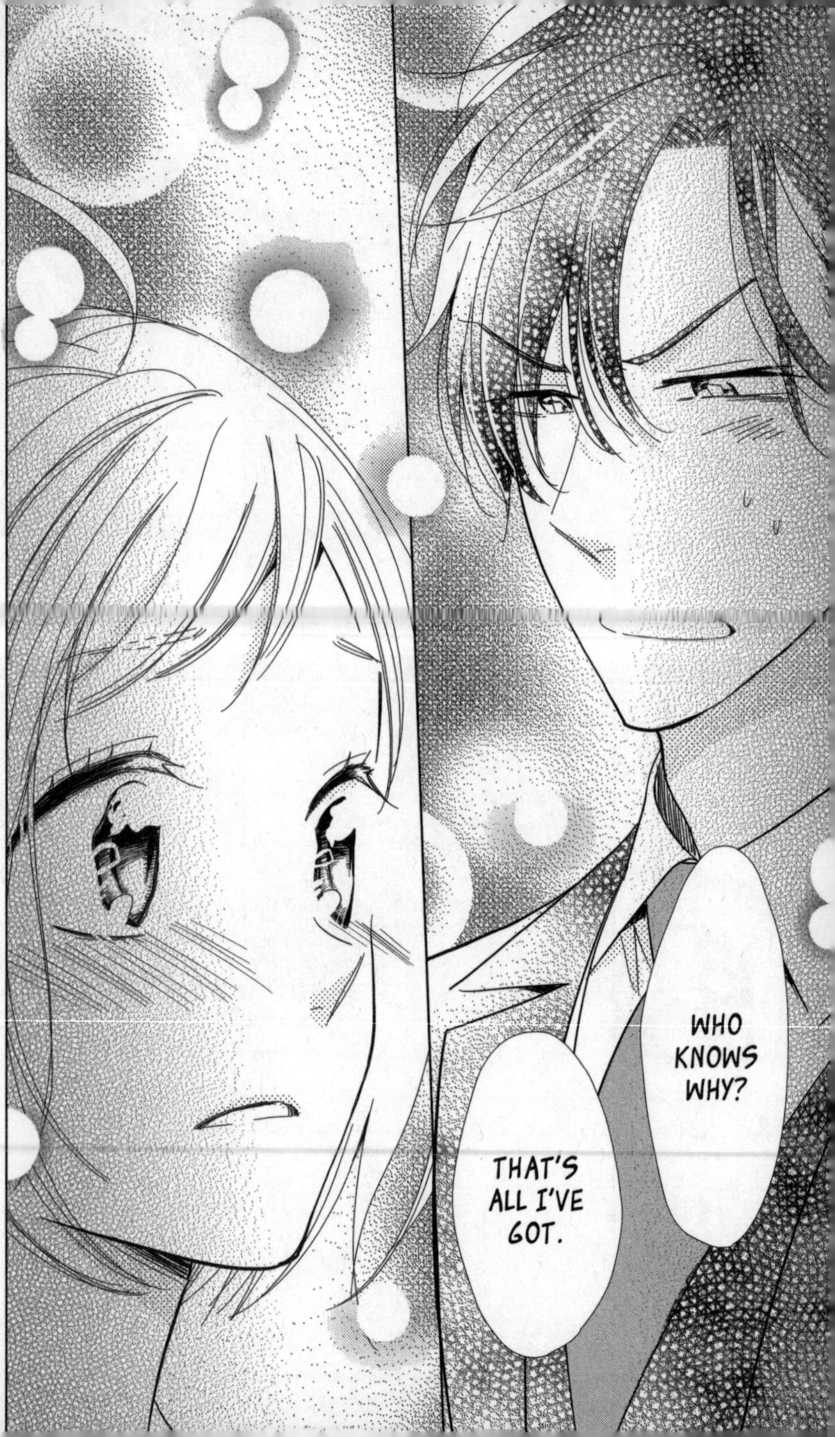
WHO KNOWS WHY?
THAT'S ALL I'VE GOT.

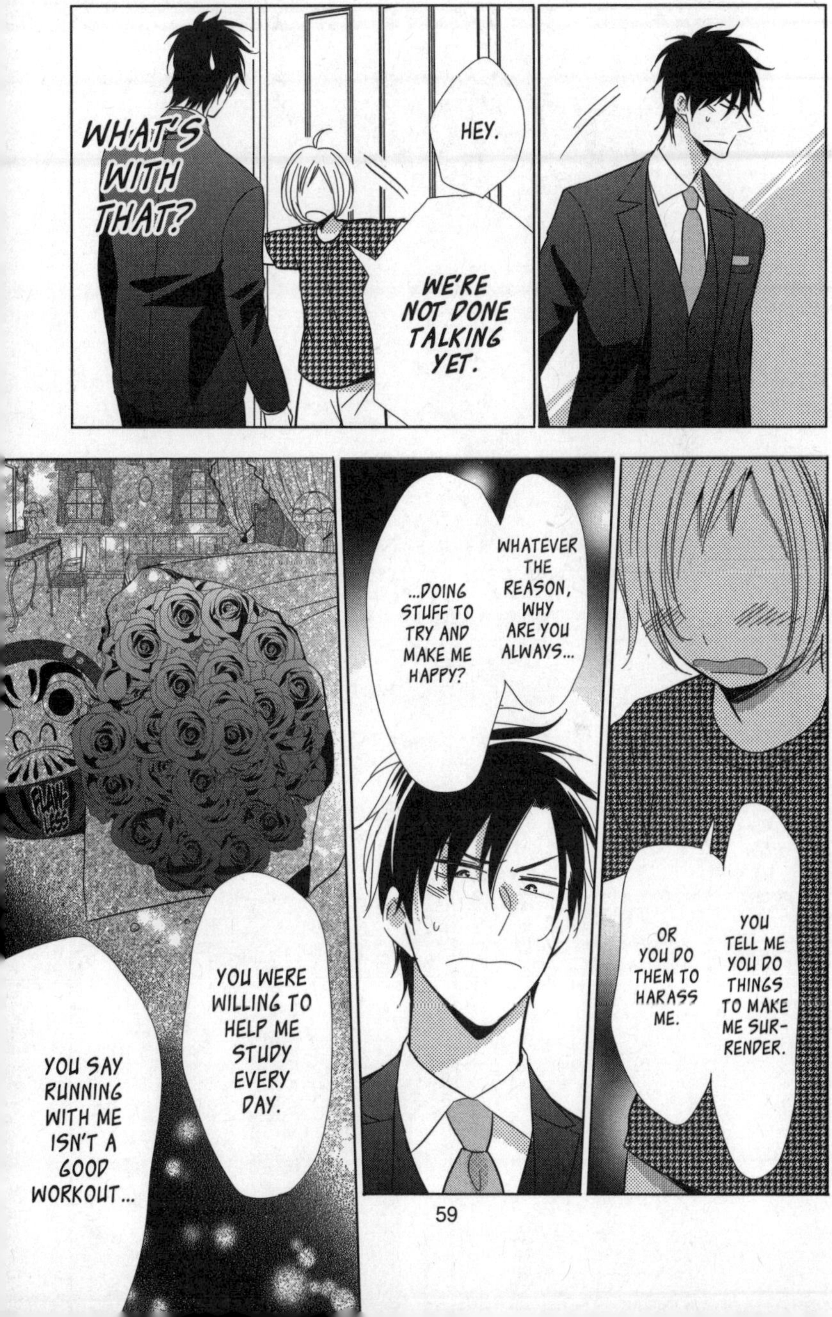
HEY.
WE'RE NOT DONE TALKING YET.
WHAT'S WITH THAT?
YOU TELL ME YOU DO THINGS TO MAKE ME SUR-RENDER.
OR YOU DO THEM TO HARASS ME.
WHATEVER THE REASON, WHY ARE YOU ALWAYS...
...DOING STUFF TO TRY AND MAKE ME HAPPY?
YOU WERE WILLING TO HELP ME STUDY EVERY DAY.
YOU SAY RUNNING WITH ME ISN'T A GOOD WORKOUT...

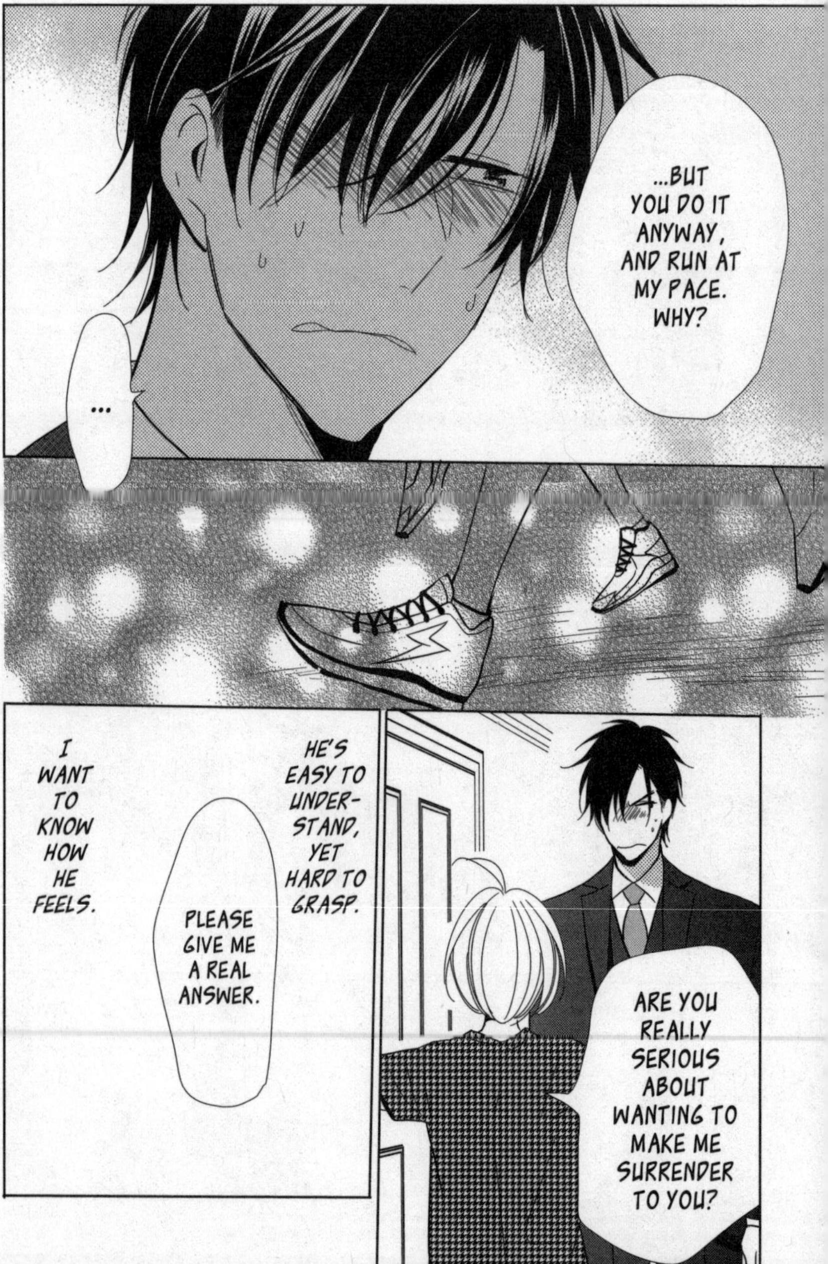
...BUT YOU DO IT ANYWAY, AND RUN AT MY PACE. WHY?
...
ARE YOU REALLY SERIOUS ABOUT WANTING TO MAKE ME SURRENDER TO YOU?
HE'S EASY TO UNDER-STAND, YET HARD TO GRASP.
PLEASE GIVE ME A REAL ANSWER.
I WANT TO KNOW HOW HE FEELS.

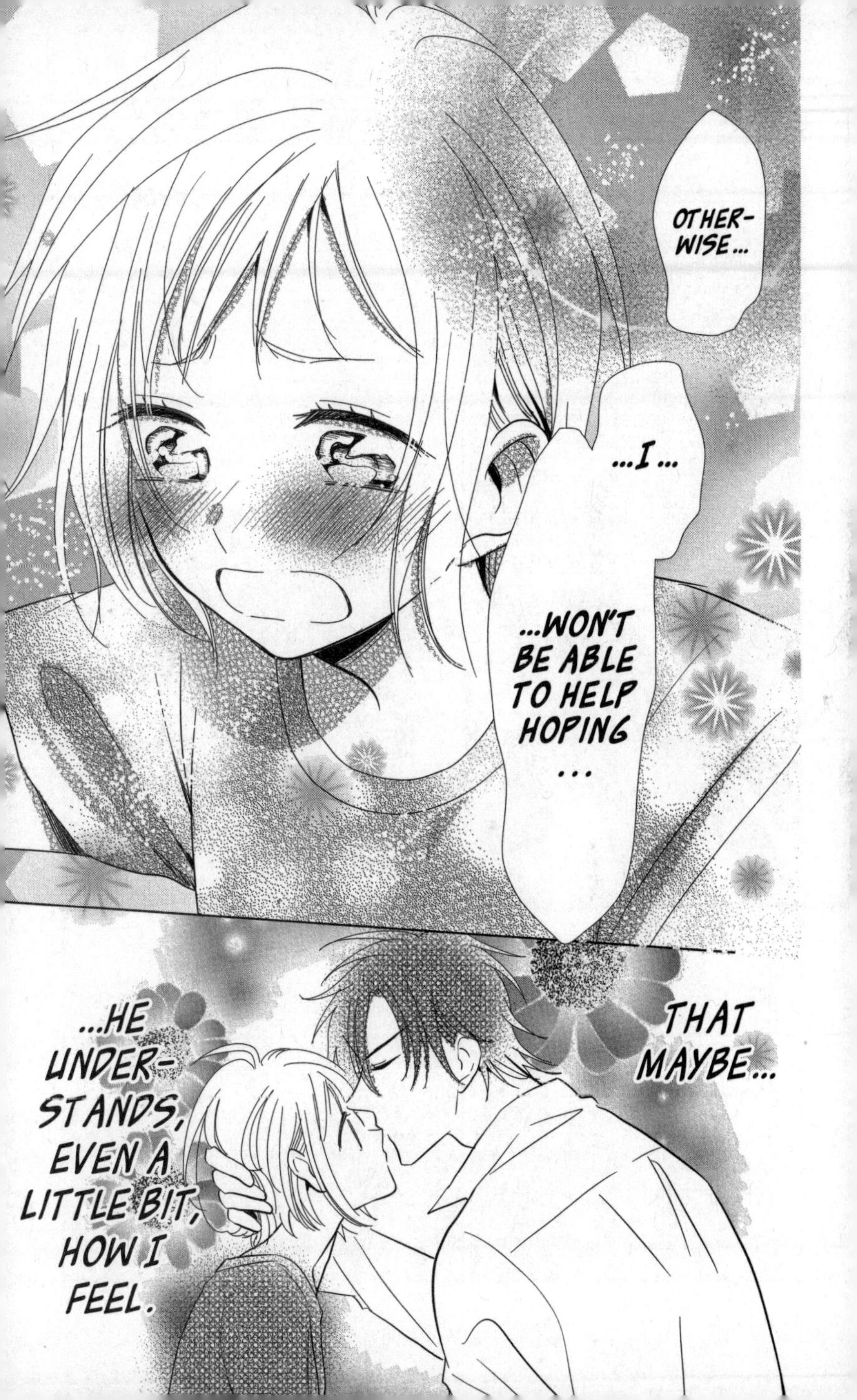
OTHER-WISE...
...I...
...WON'T BE ABLE TO HELP HOPING...
THAT MAYBE...
...HE UNDER-STANDS, EVEN A LITTLE BIT, HOW I FEEL.

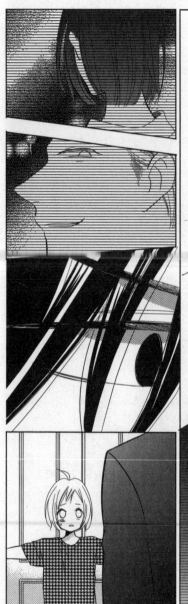

I JUST WANTED TO BELIEVE THAT.

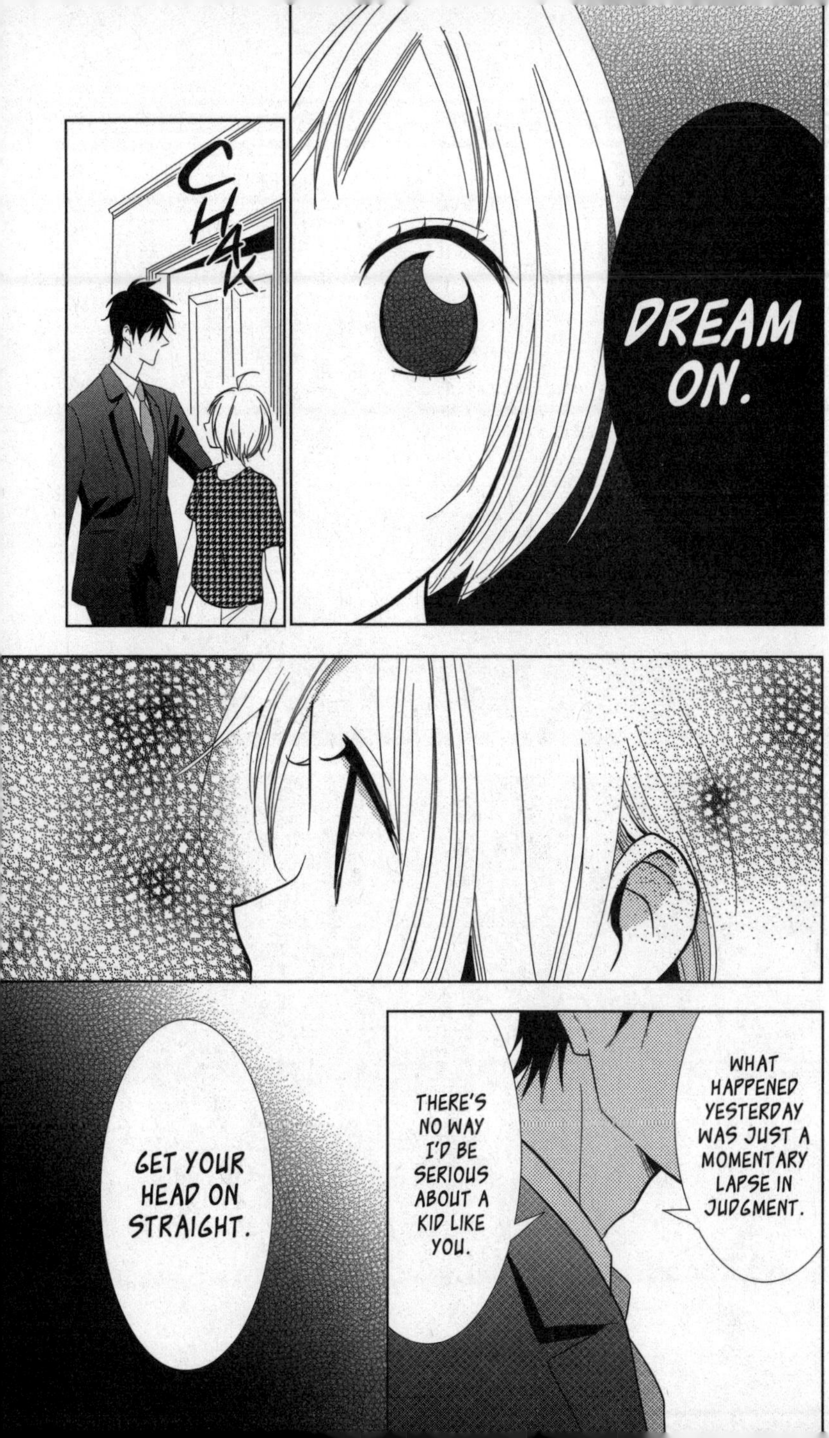
DREAM ON.
CHAK
WHAT HAPPENED YESTERDAY WAS JUST A MOMENTARY LAPSE IN JUDGMENT.
THERE'S NO WAY I'D BE SERIOUS ABOUT A KID LIKE YOU.
GET YOUR HEAD ON STRAIGHT.

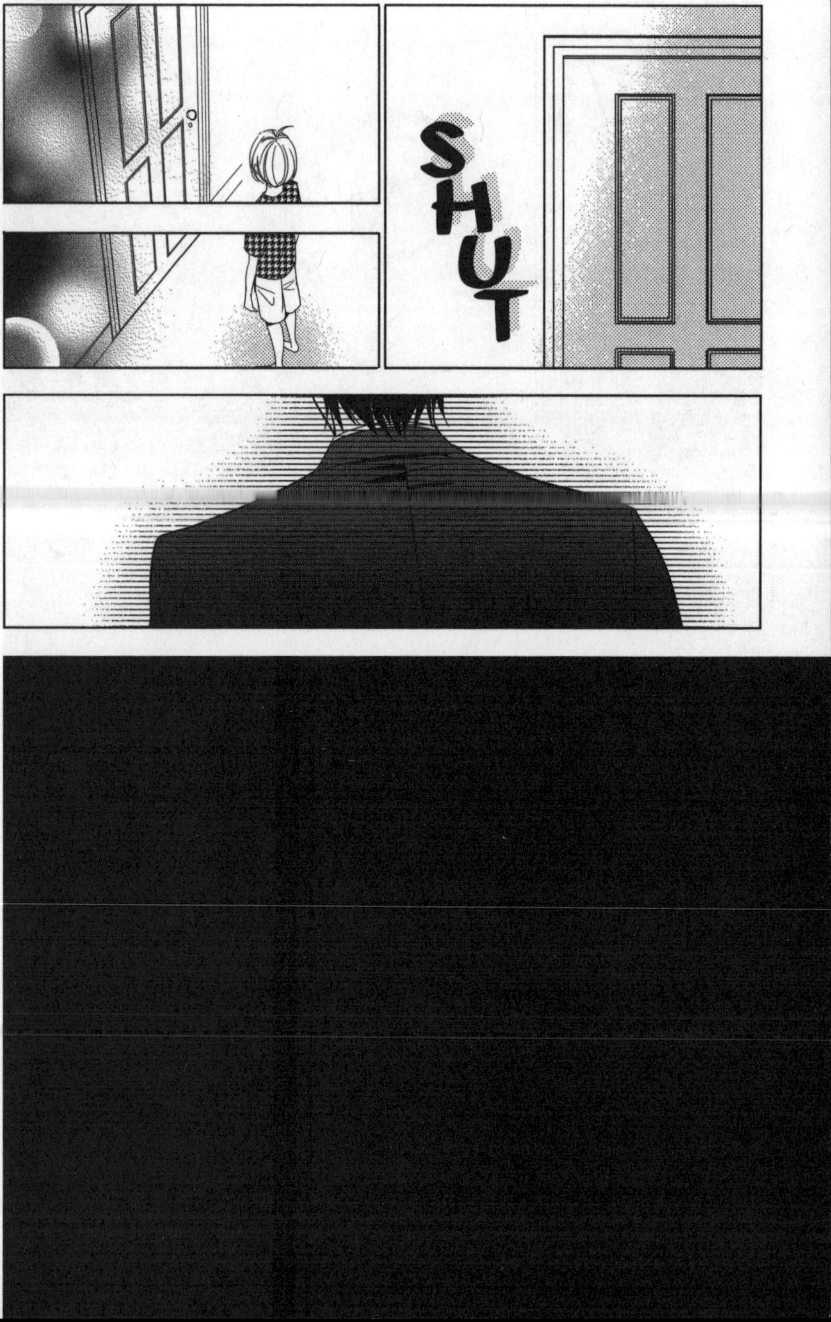
SHUT

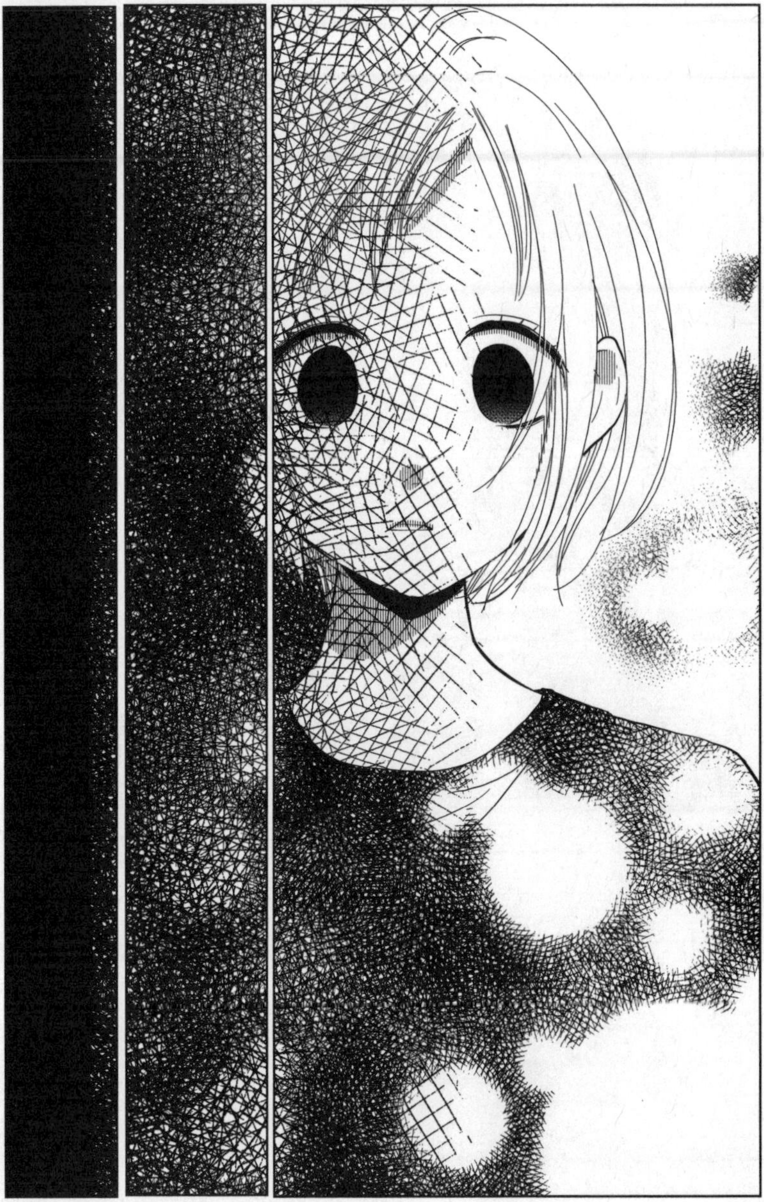

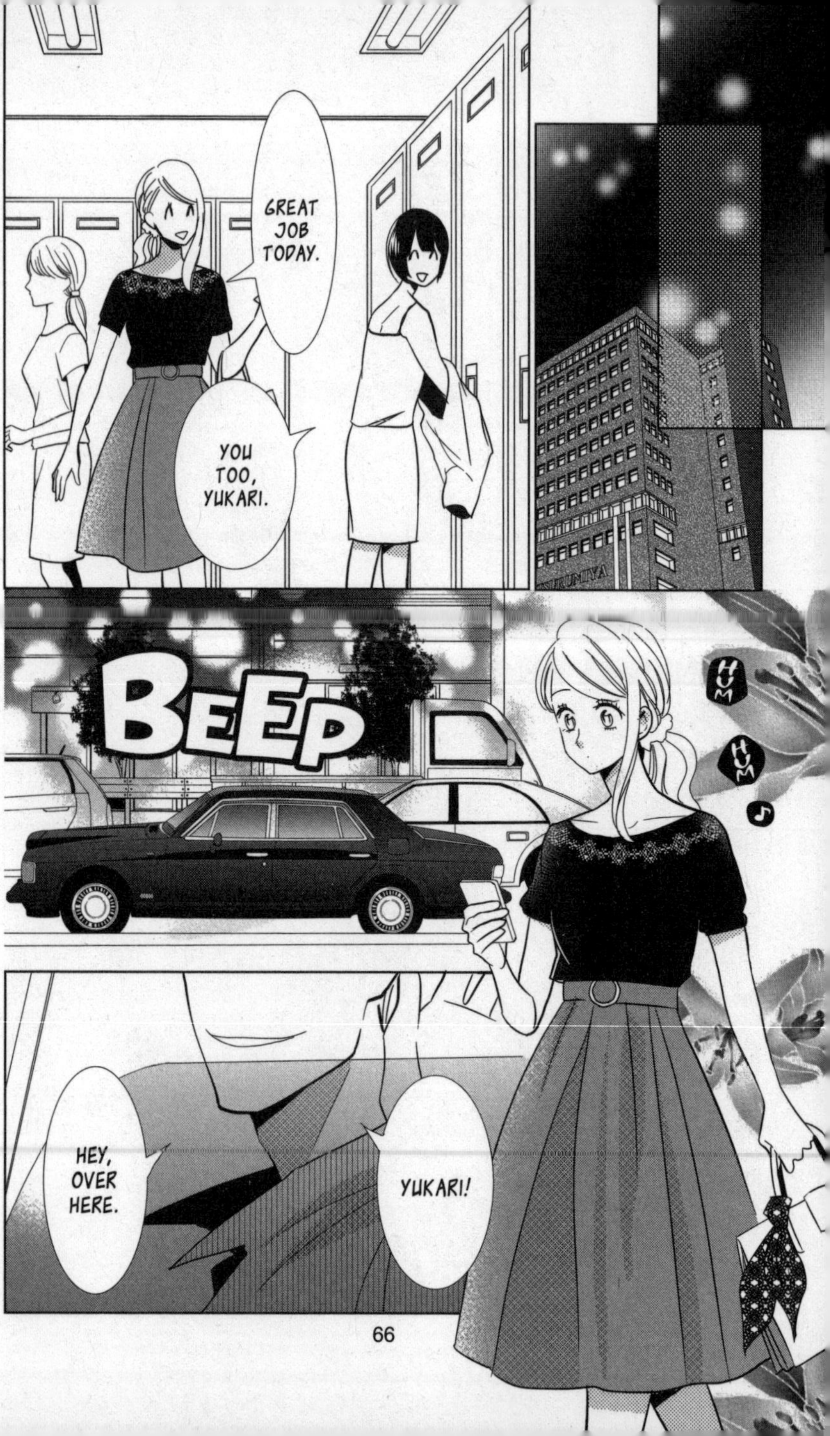
GREAT JOB TODAY.
YOU TOO, YUKARI.
HUM HUM ♪
BEEP
YUKARI!
HEY, OVER HERE.

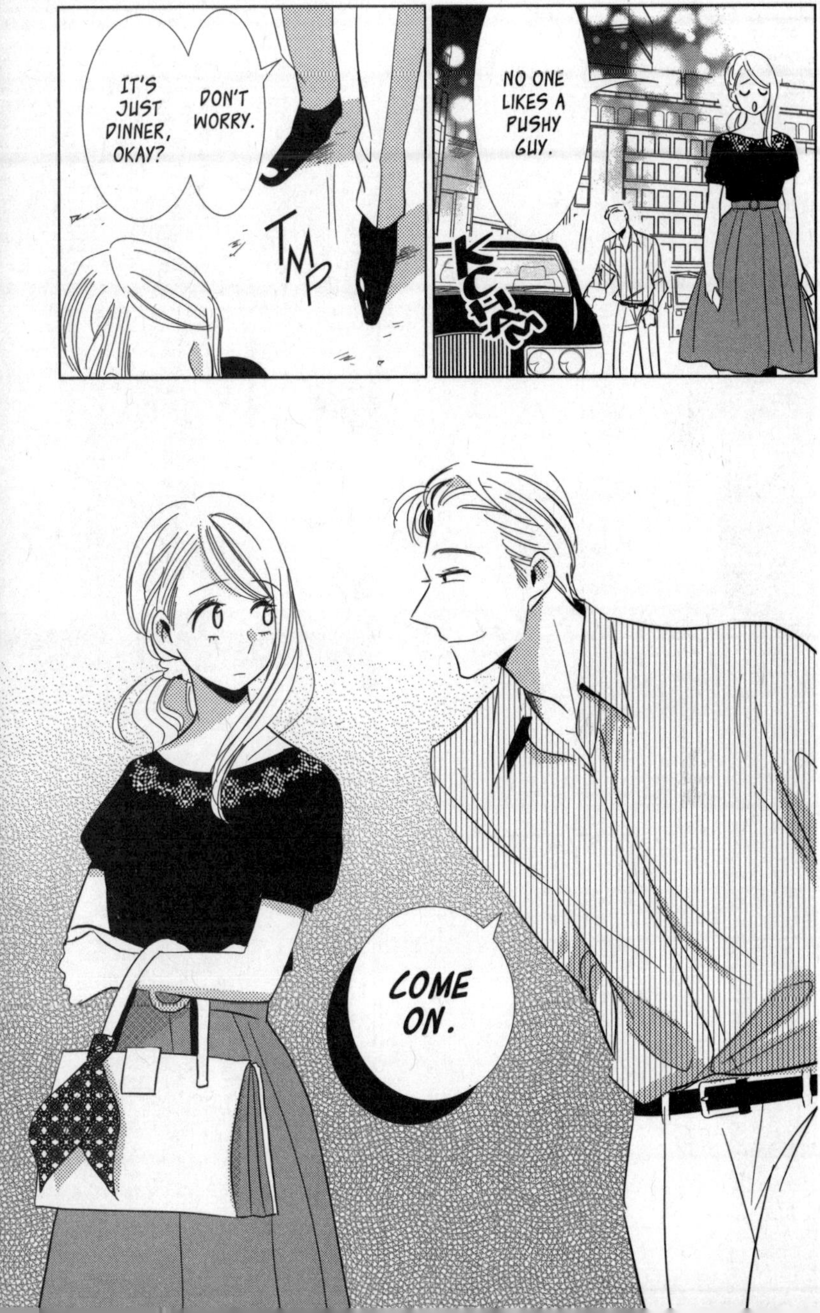
NO ONE LIKES A PUSHY GUY.
KCHAK
DON'T WORRY.
IT'S JUST DINNER, OKAY?
TMP
COME ON.

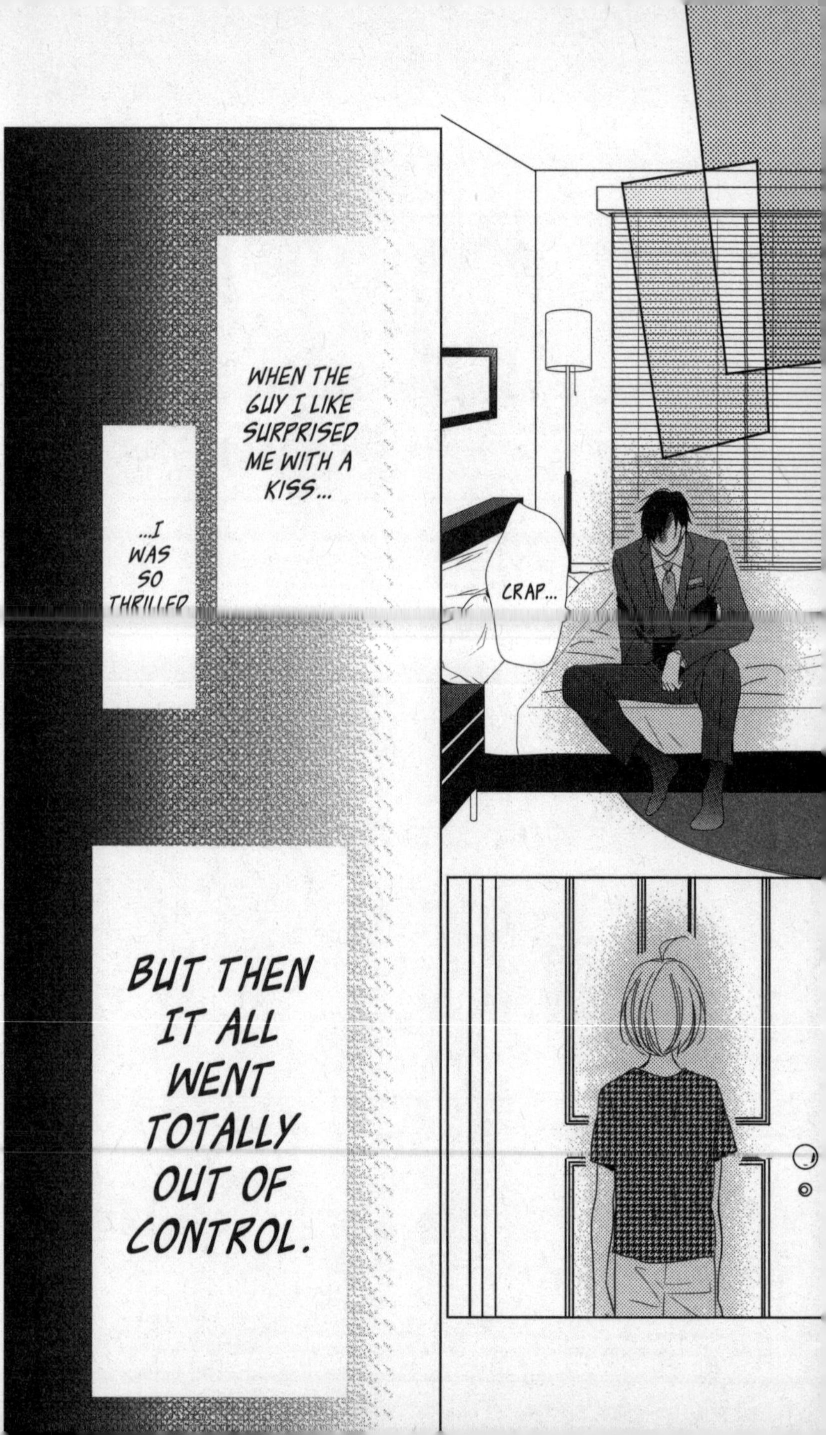
CRAP...
WHEN THE GUY I LIKE SURPRISED ME WITH A KISS...
...I WAS SO THRILLED
BUT THEN IT ALL WENT TOTALLY OUT OF CONTROL.

Chapter 60

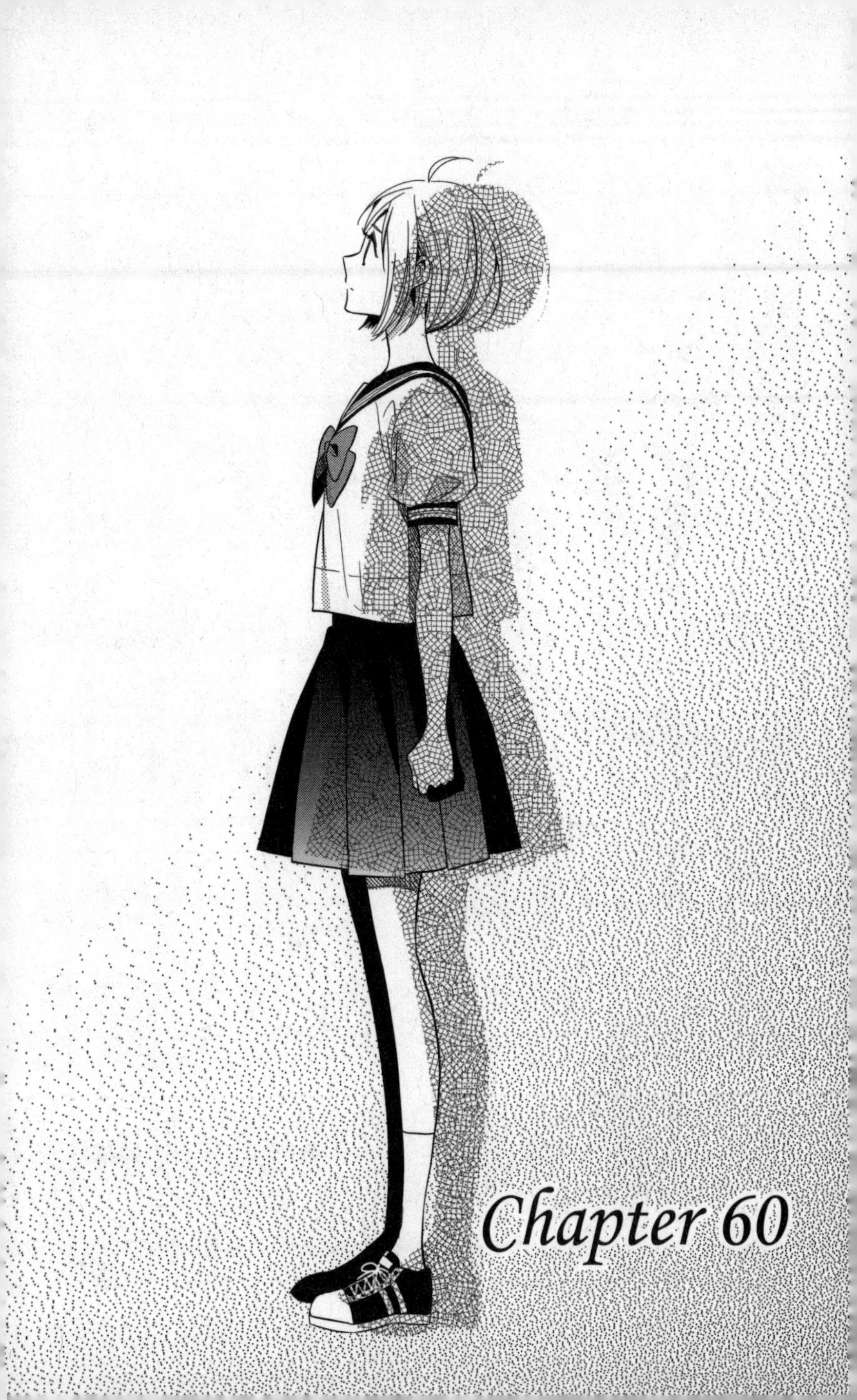

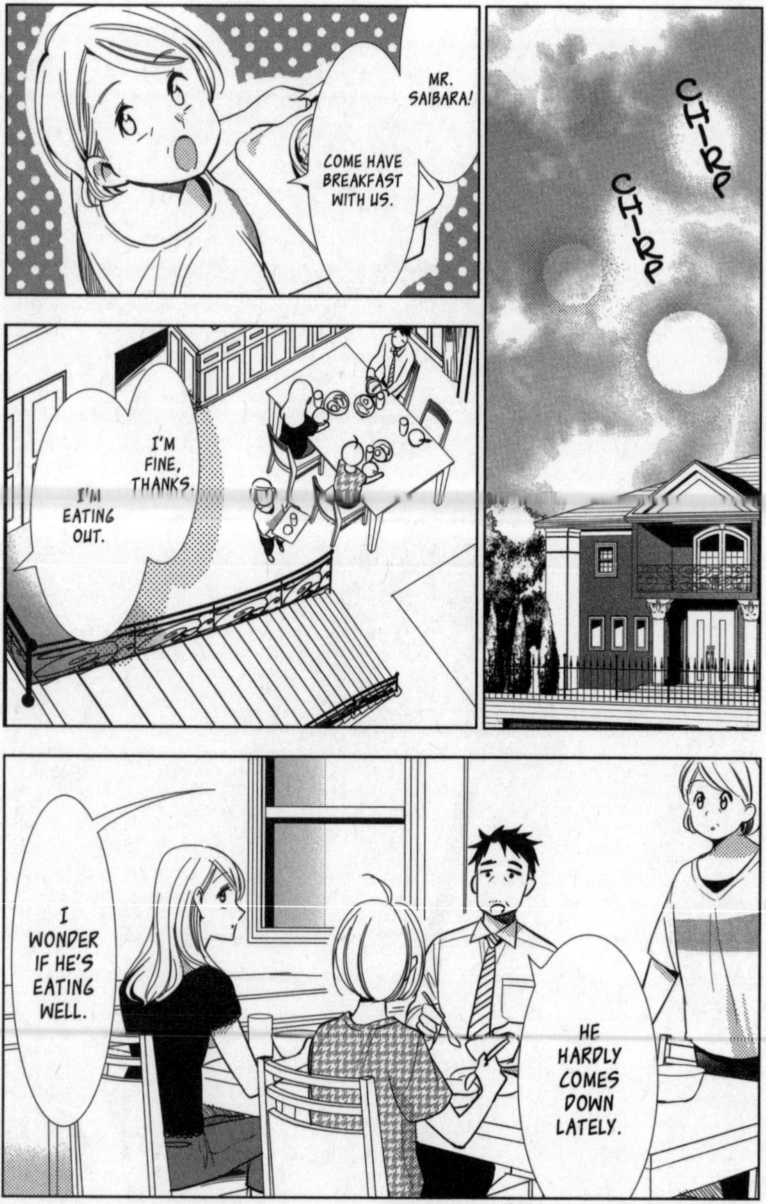
CHIRP
CHIRP
MR. SAIBARA!
COME HAVE BREAKFAST WITH US.
I'M FINE, THANKS.
I'M EATING OUT.
HE HARDLY COMES DOWN LATELY.
I WONDER IF HE'S EATING WELL.

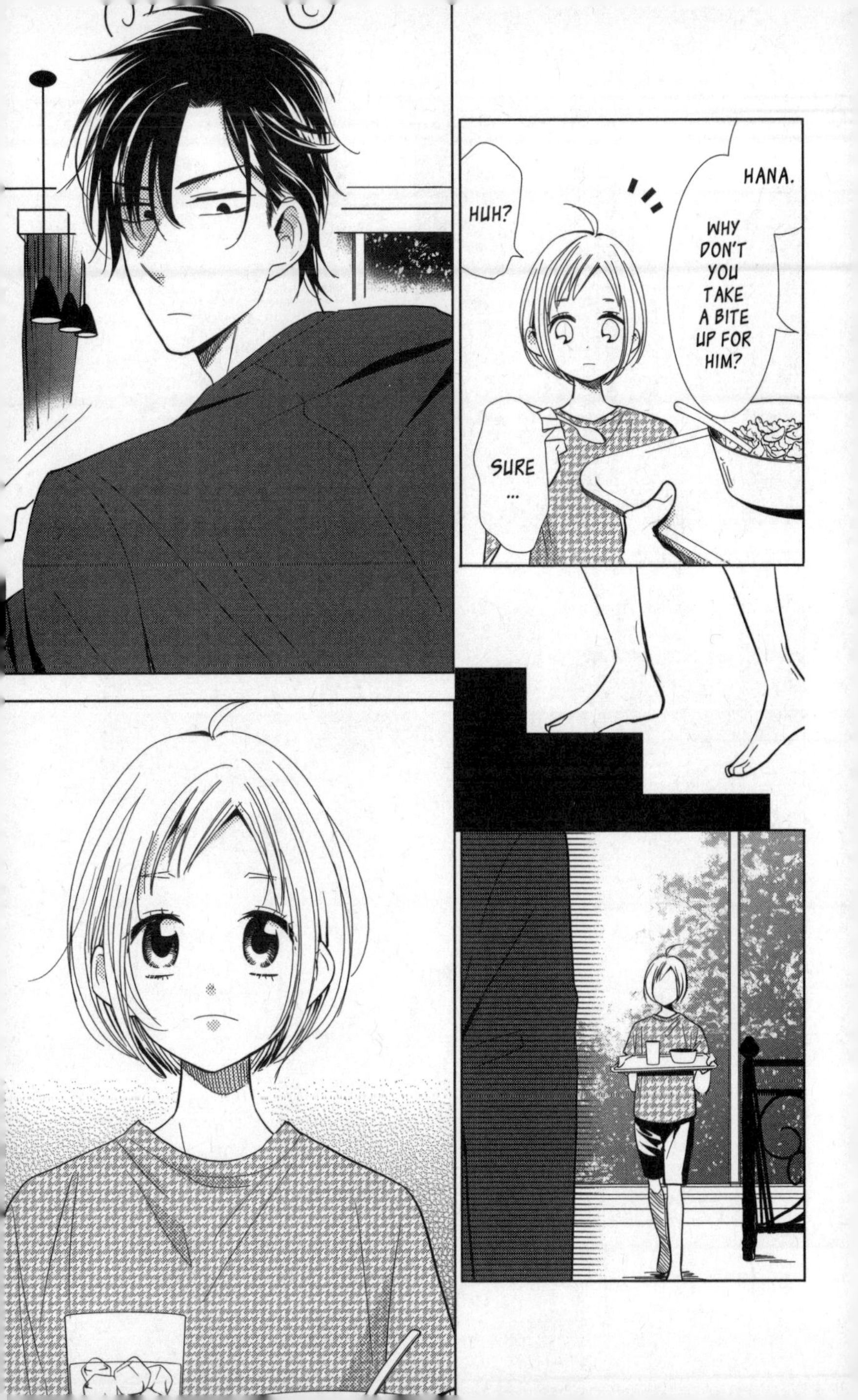
HANA.
WHY DON'T YOU TAKE A BITE UP FOR HIM?
HUH?
SURE ...

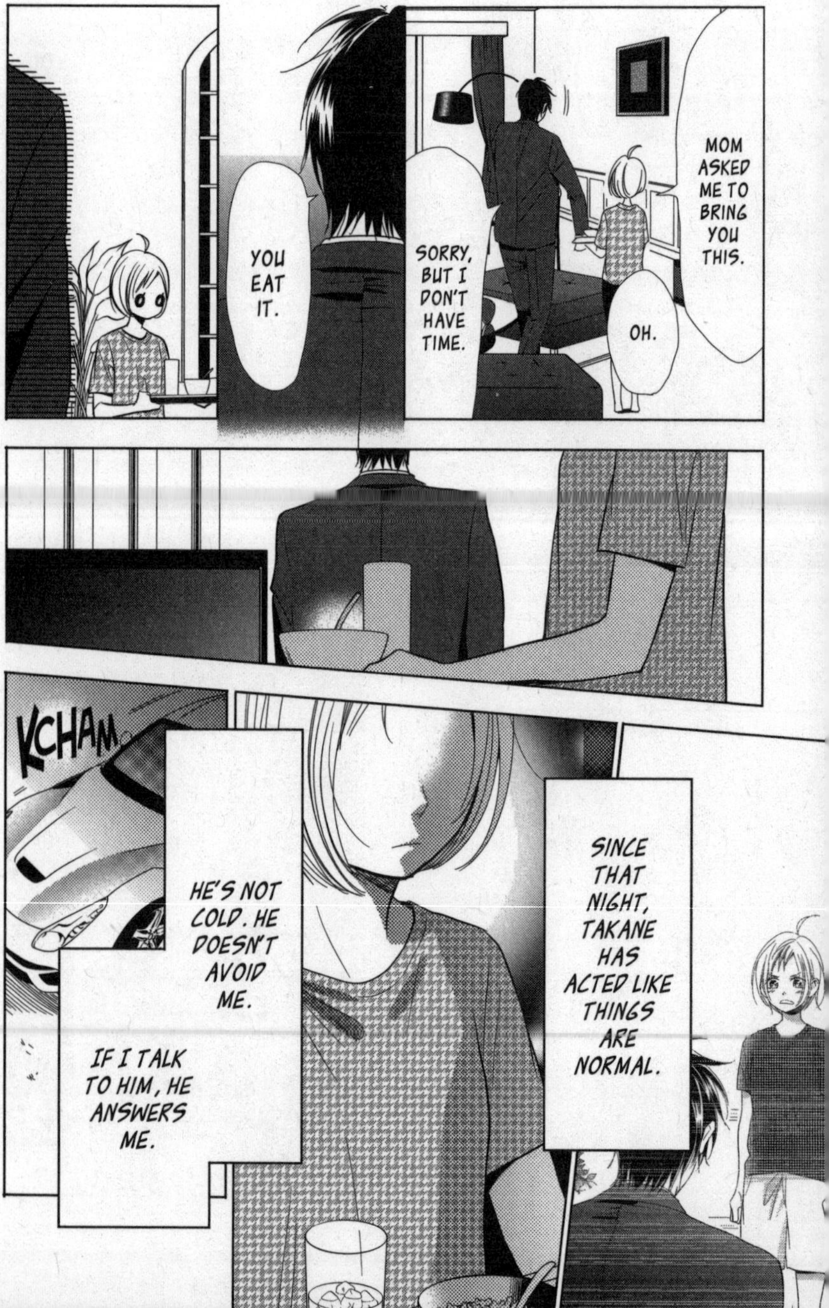
MOM ASKED ME TO BRING YOU THIS.
OH.
SORRY, BUT I DON'T HAVE TIME.
YOU EAT IT.
SINCE THAT NIGHT, TAKANE HAS ACTED LIKE THINGS ARE NORMAL.
HE'S NOT COLD. HE DOESN'T AVOID ME.
IF I TALK TO HIM, HE ANSWERS ME.
KCHAM

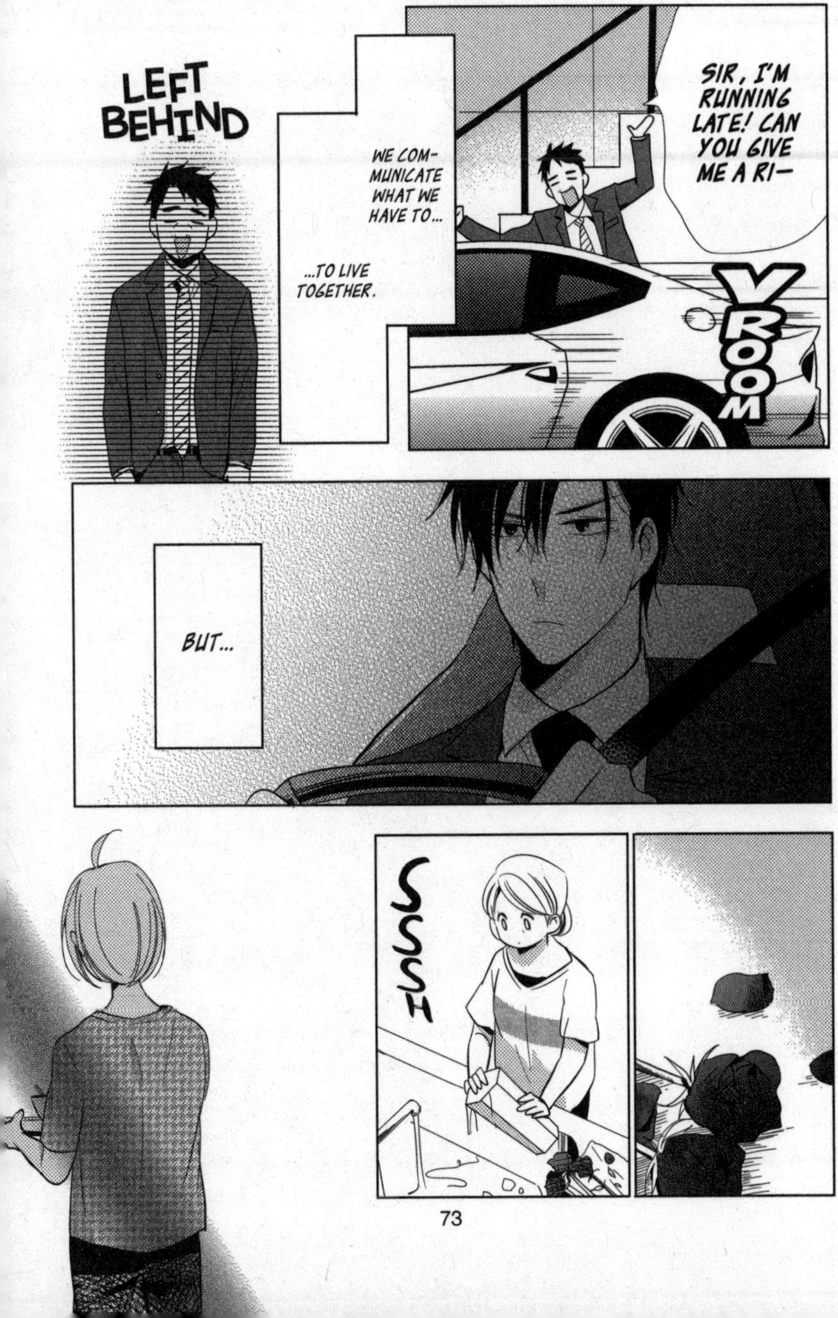
SIR, I'M RUNNING LATE! CAN YOU GIVE ME A RI—
VROOM
WE COM-MUNICATE WHAT WE HAVE TO...
...TO LIVE TOGETHER.
LEFT BEHIND
BUT...
SSSH

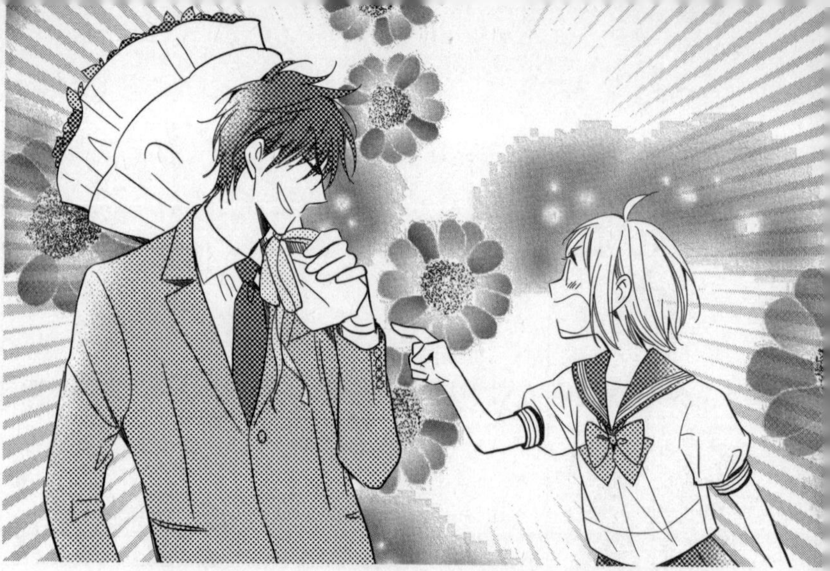
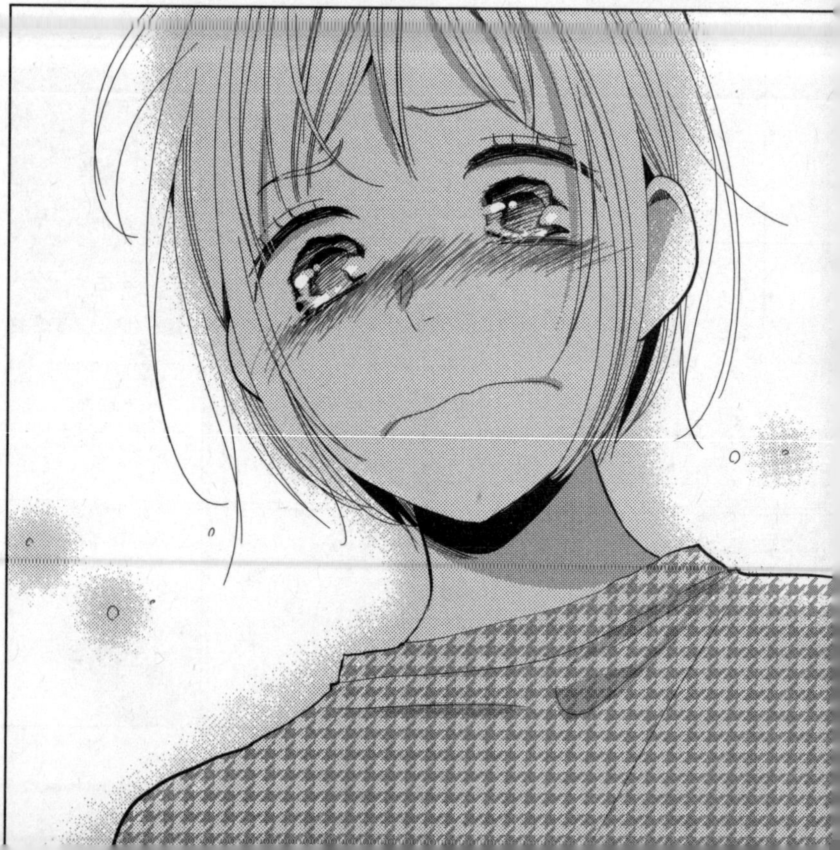

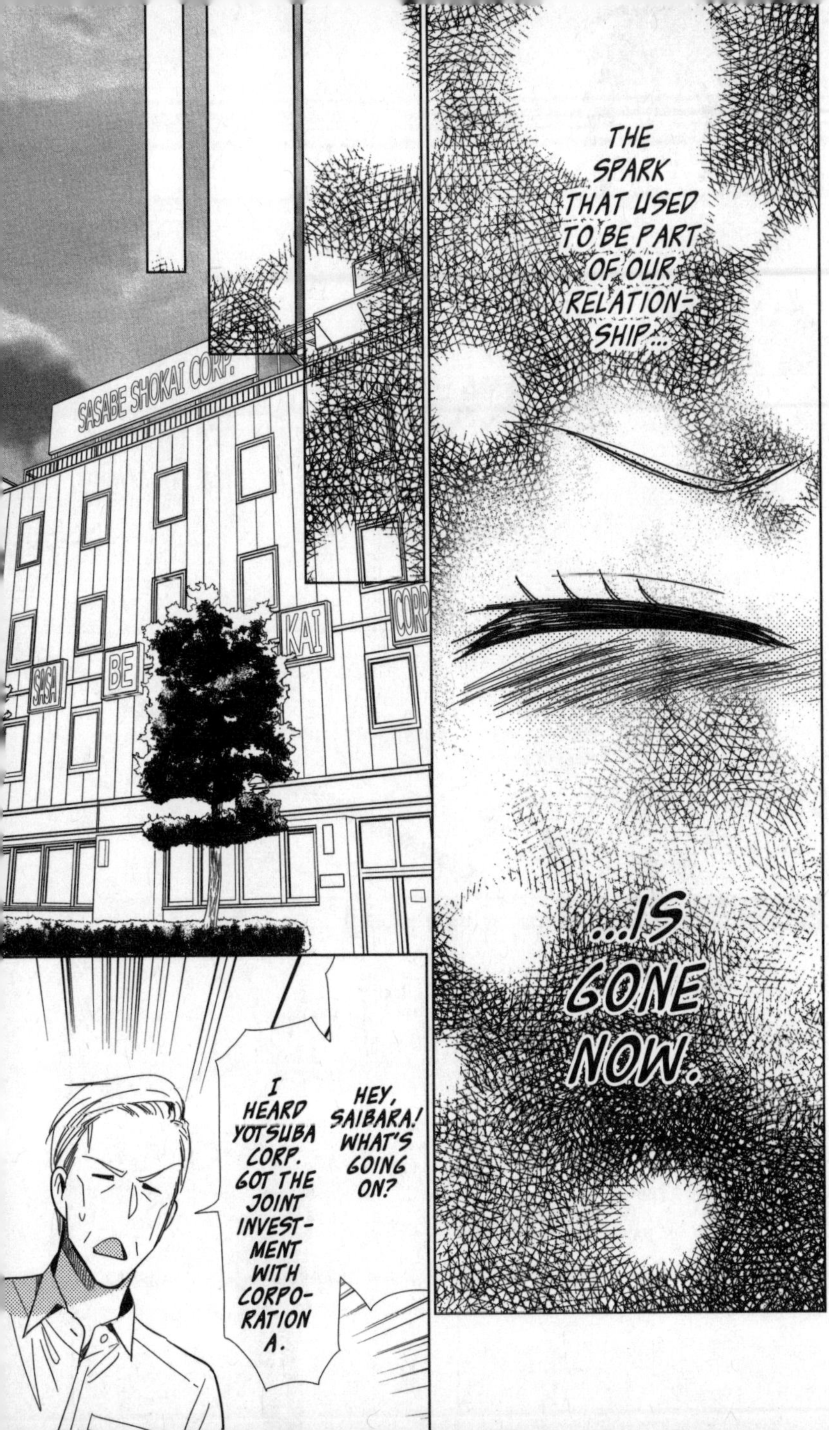
THE SPARK THAT USED TO BE PART OF OUR RELATION-SHIP...
...IS GONE NOW.
SASABE SHOKAI CORP.
SASA BE KAI CORP
HEY, SAIBARA! WHAT'S GOING ON?
I HEARD YOTSUBA CORP. GOT THE JOINT INVEST-MENT WITH CORPO-RATION A.

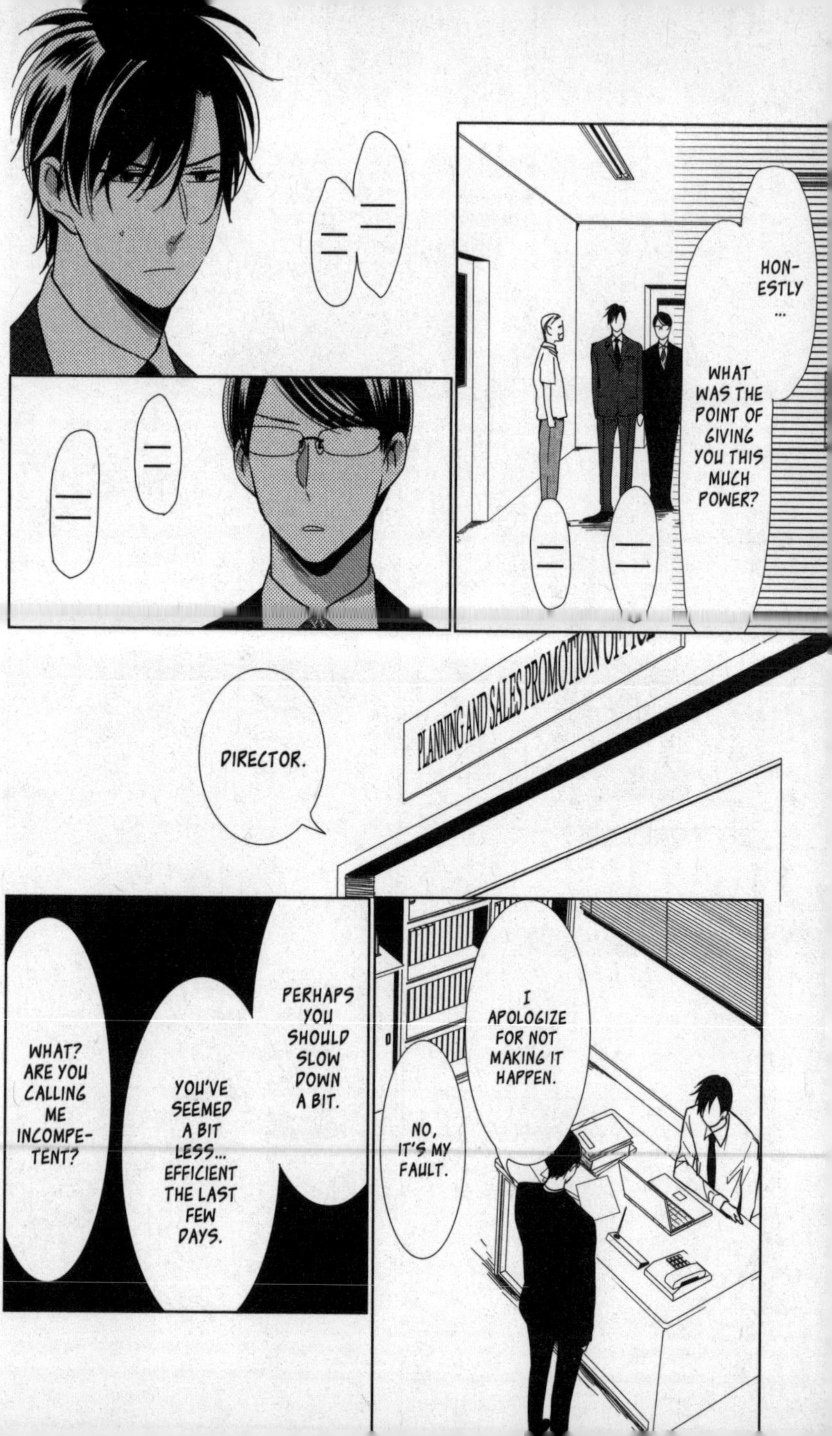

HONESTLY...
WHAT WAS THE POINT OF GIVING YOU THIS MUCH POWER?
——
——
——
——
——
——
PLANNING AND SALES PROMOTION OFFI
DIRECTOR.
I APOLOGIZE FOR NOT MAKING IT HAPPEN.
NO, IT'S MY FAULT.
PERHAPS YOU SHOULD SLOW DOWN A BIT.
YOU'VE SEEMED A BIT LESS... EFFICIENT THE LAST FEW DAYS.
WHAT? ARE YOU CALLING ME INCOMPETENT?

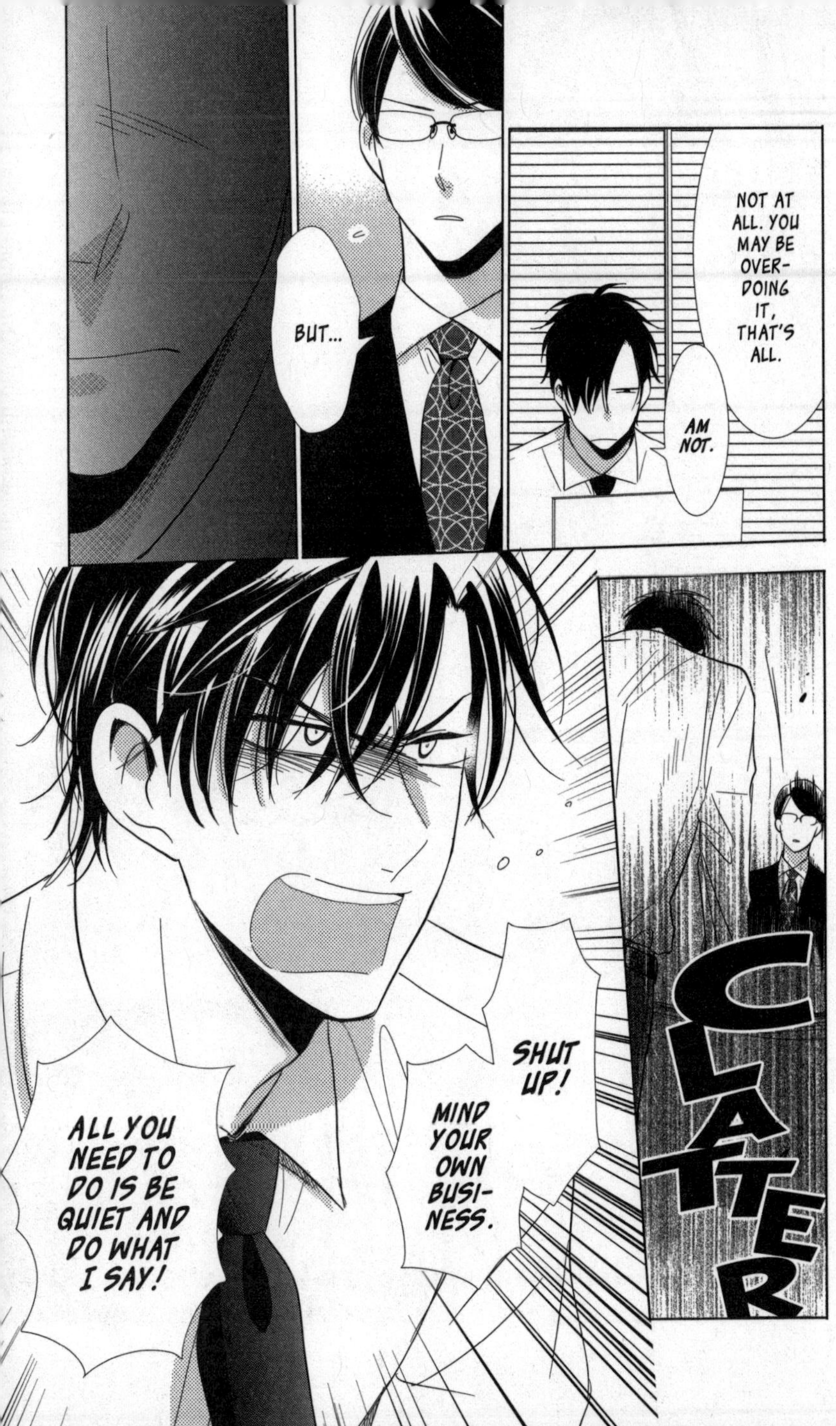
NOT AT ALL. YOU MAY BE OVER-DOING IT, THAT'S ALL.
AM NOT.
BUT...
CLATTER
SHUT UP!
MIND YOUR OWN BUSI-NESS.
ALL YOU NEED TO DO IS BE QUIET AND DO WHAT I SAY!

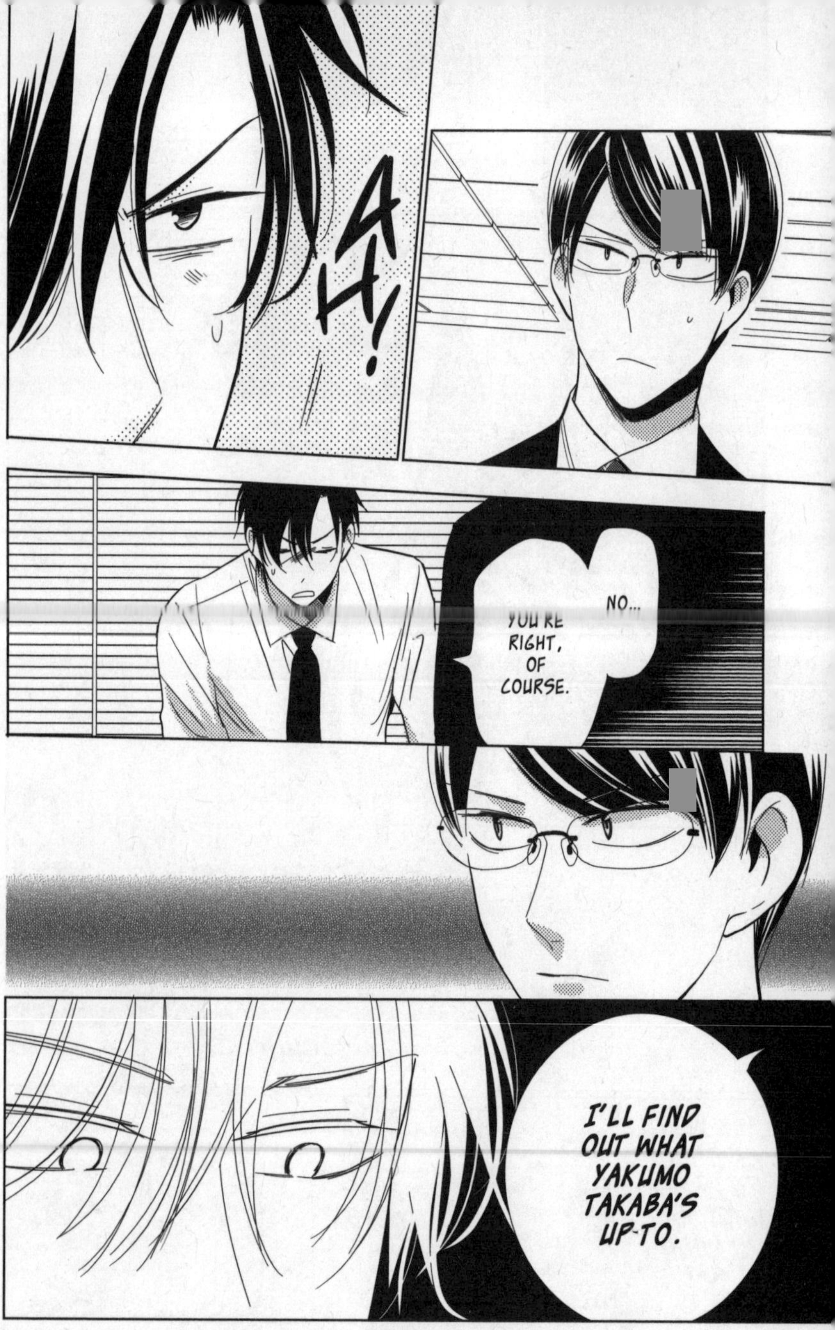
AH!
NO... YOU'RE RIGHT, OF COURSE.
I'LL FIND OUT WHAT YAKUMO TAKABA'S UP-TO.

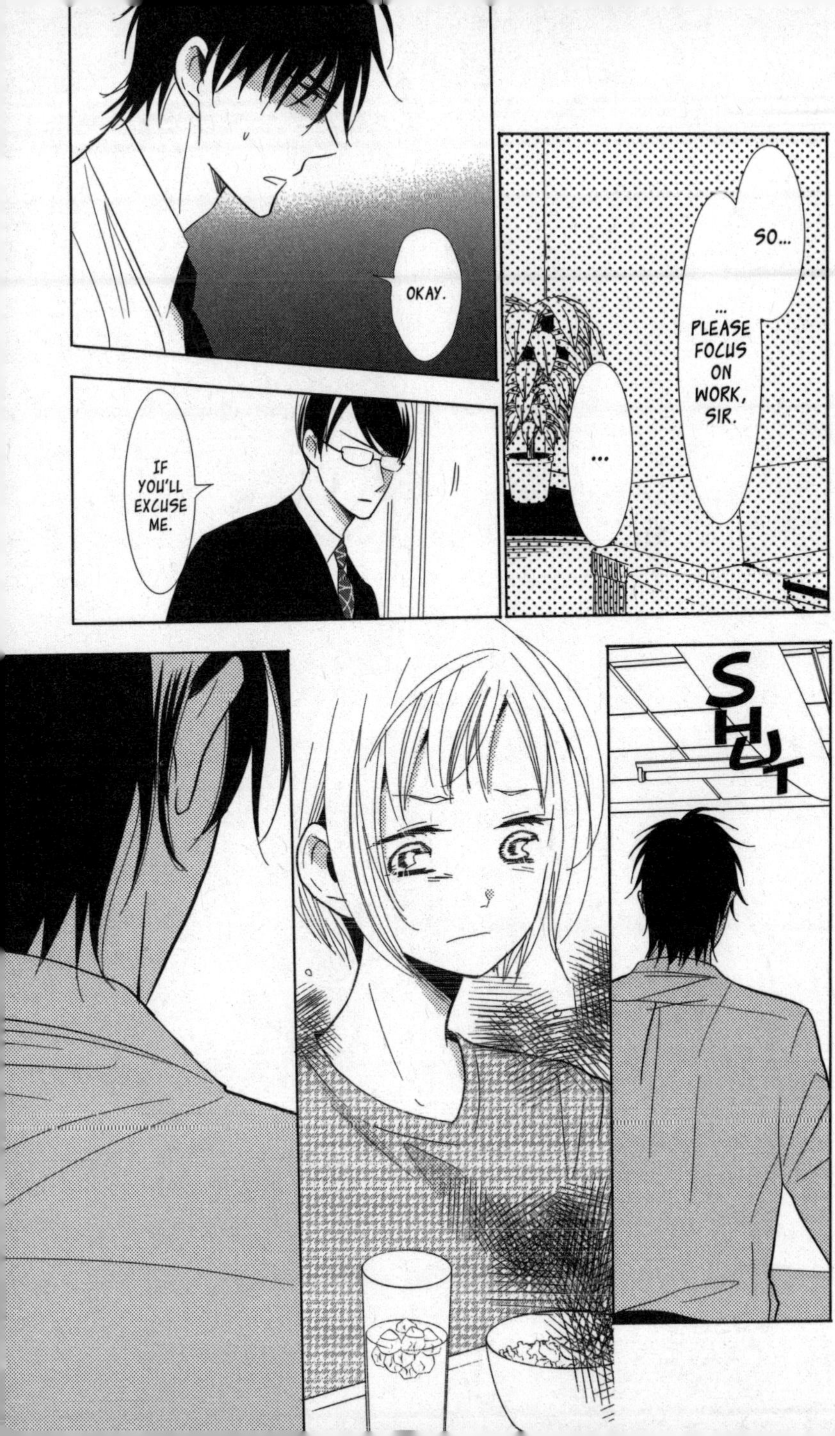
SO...
... PLEASE FOCUS ON WORK, SIR.
...
OKAY.
IF YOU'LL EXCUSE ME.
SHUT

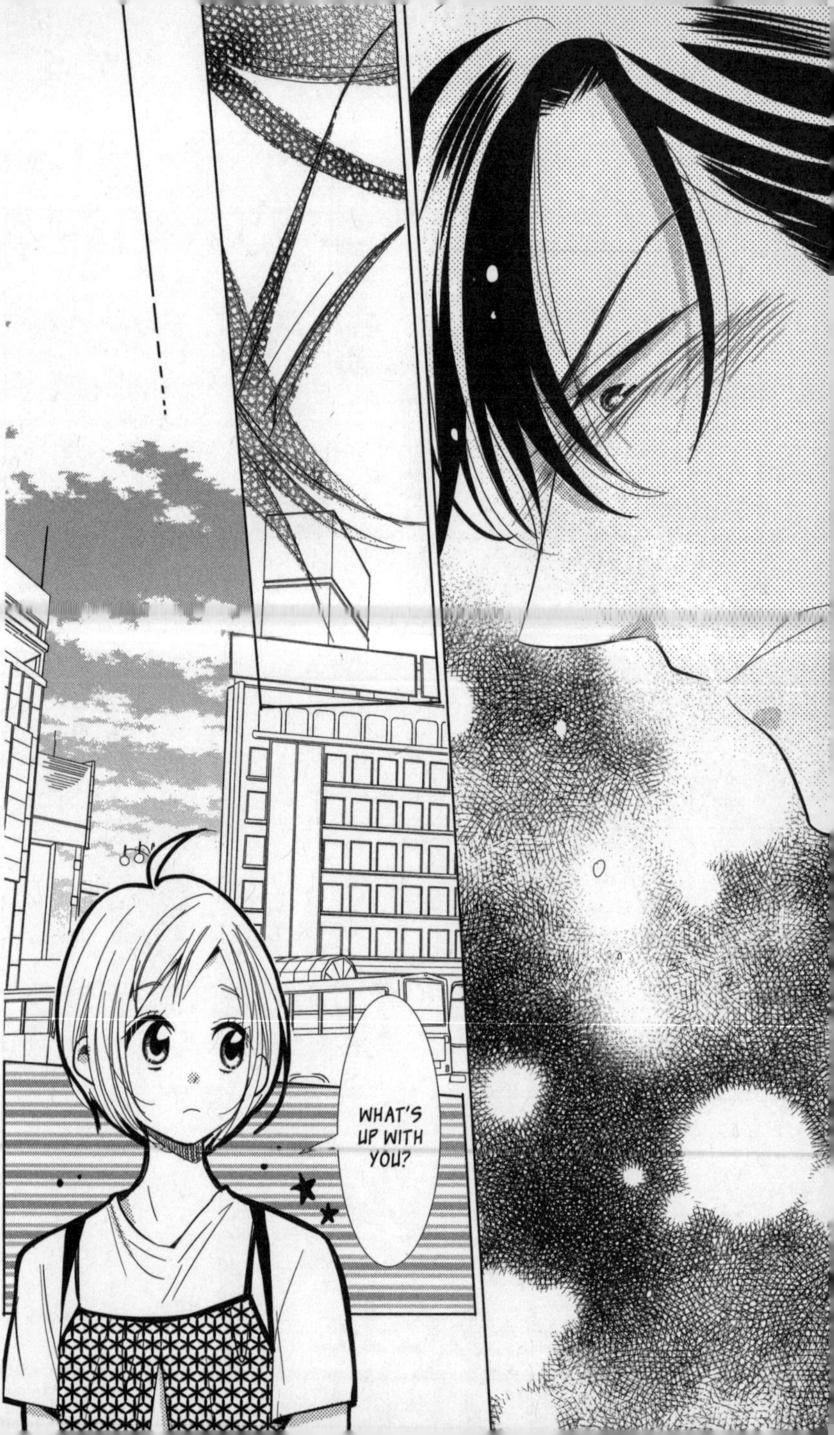
WHAT'S UP WITH YOU?

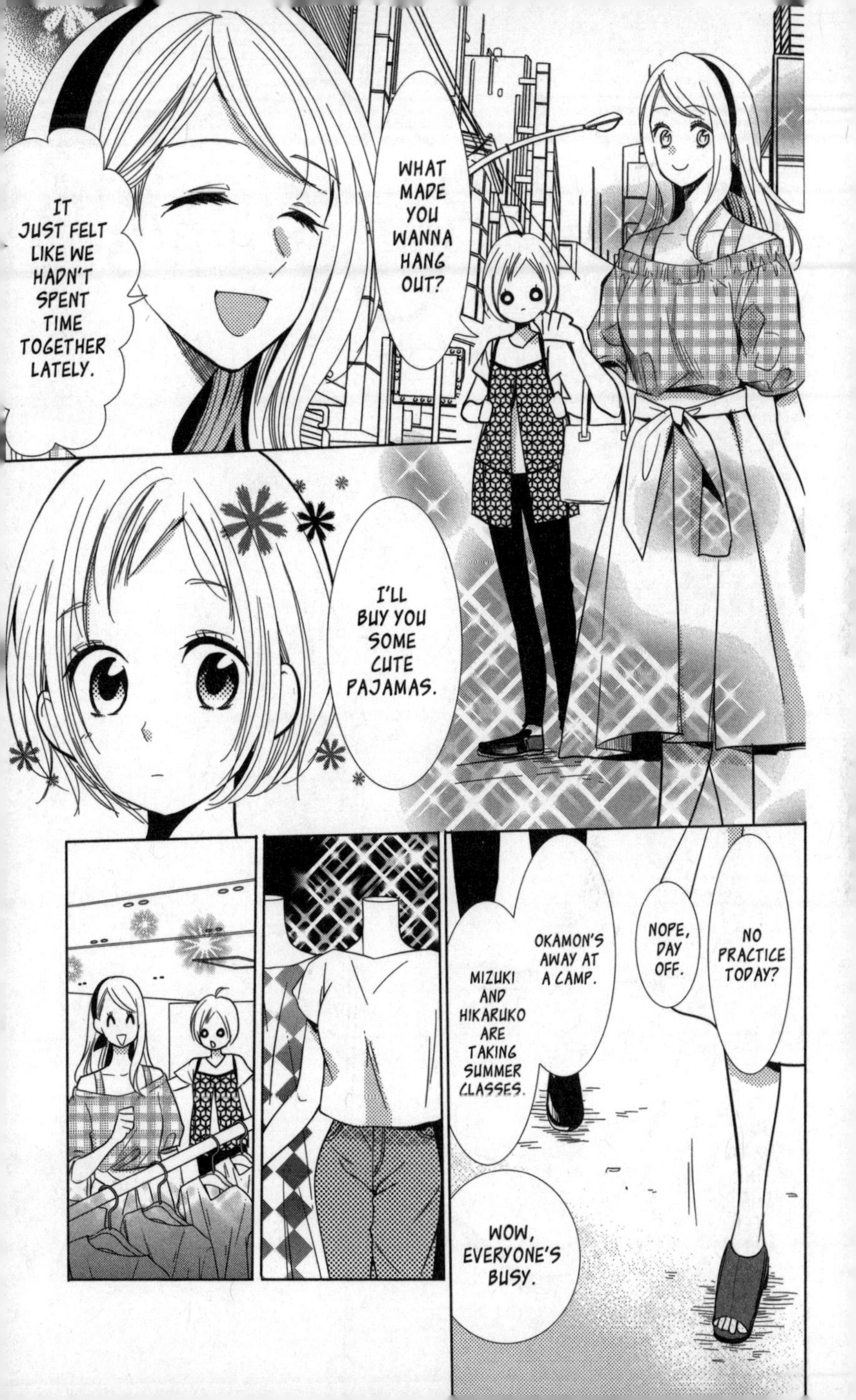
WHAT MADE YOU WANNA HANG OUT?
IT JUST FELT LIKE WE HADN'T SPENT TIME TOGETHER LATELY.
I'LL BUY YOU SOME CUTE PAJAMAS.
NO PRACTICE TODAY?
NOPE, DAY OFF.
OKAMON'S AWAY AT A CAMP.
MIZUKI AND HIKARUKO ARE TAKING SUMMER CLASSES.
WOW, EVERYONE'S BUSY.

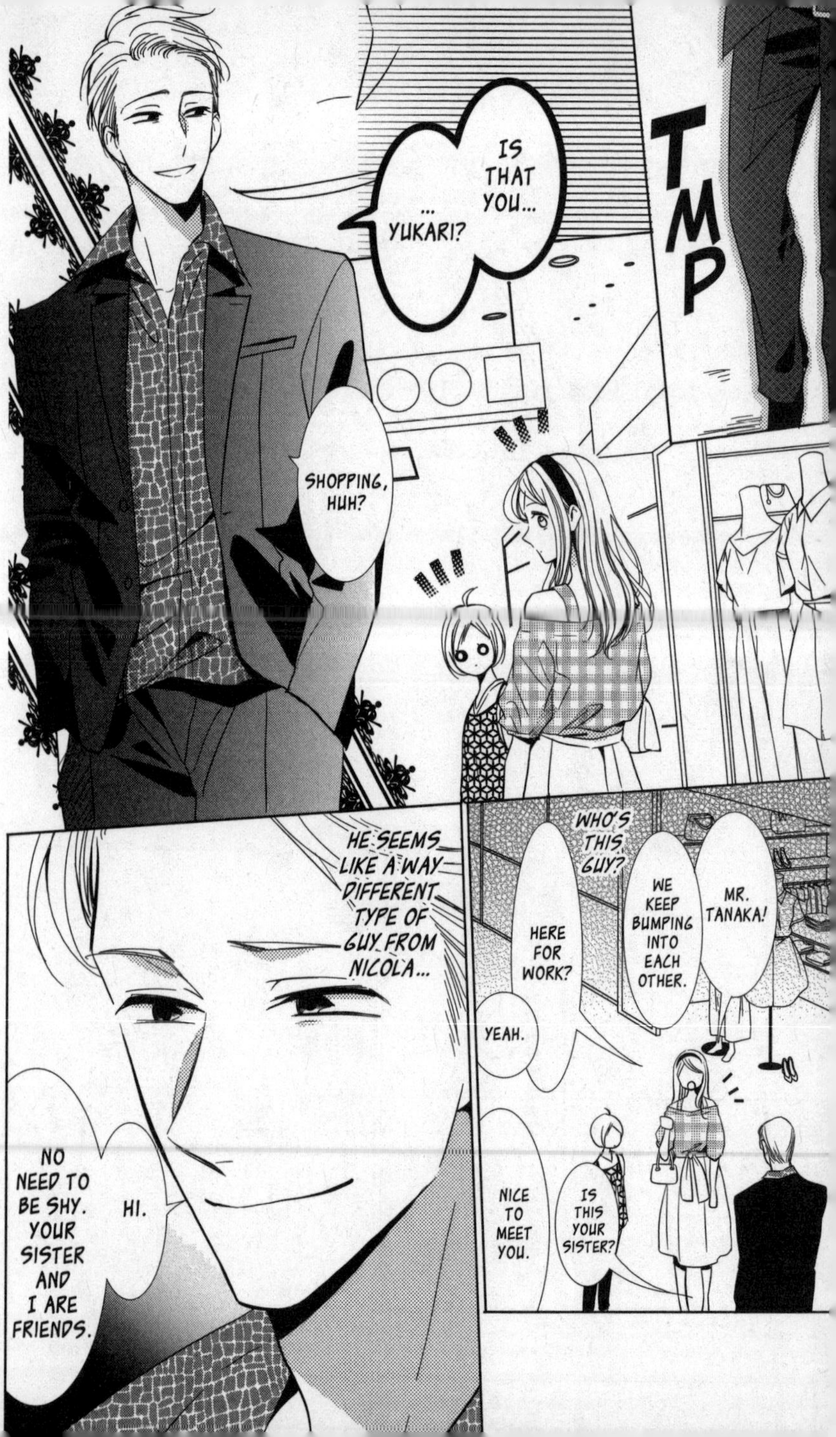
TMP
IS THAT YOU... ...YUKARI?
SHOPPING, HUH?
MR. TANAKA!
WE KEEP BUMPING INTO EACH OTHER.
WHO'S THIS GUY?
HERE FOR WORK?
YEAH.
IS THIS YOUR SISTER?
NICE TO MEET YOU.
HE SEEMS LIKE A WAY DIFFERENT TYPE OF GUY FROM NICOLA...
HI.
NO NEED TO BE SHY. YOUR SISTER AND I ARE FRIENDS.

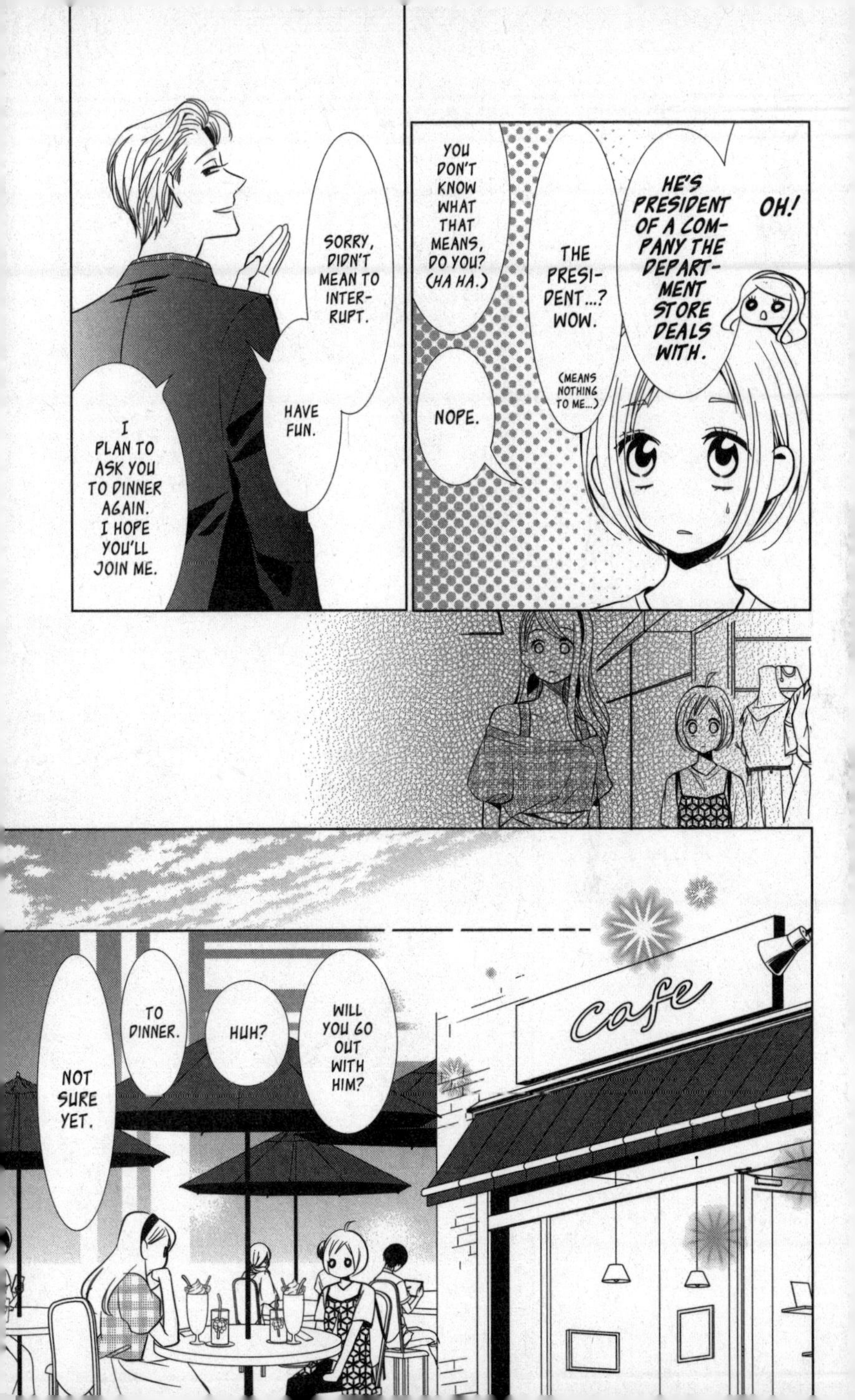
OH!
HE'S PRESIDENT OF A COMPANY THE DEPARTMENT STORE DEALS WITH.
THE PRESIDENT...? WOW.
(MEANS NOTHING TO ME...)
YOU DON'T KNOW WHAT THAT MEANS, DO YOU? (HA HA.)
NOPE.
SORRY, DIDN'T MEAN TO INTERRUPT.
HAVE FUN.
I PLAN TO ASK YOU TO DINNER AGAIN. I HOPE YOU'LL JOIN ME.
cafe
WILL YOU GO OUT WITH HIM?
HUH?
TO DINNER.
NOT SURE YET.

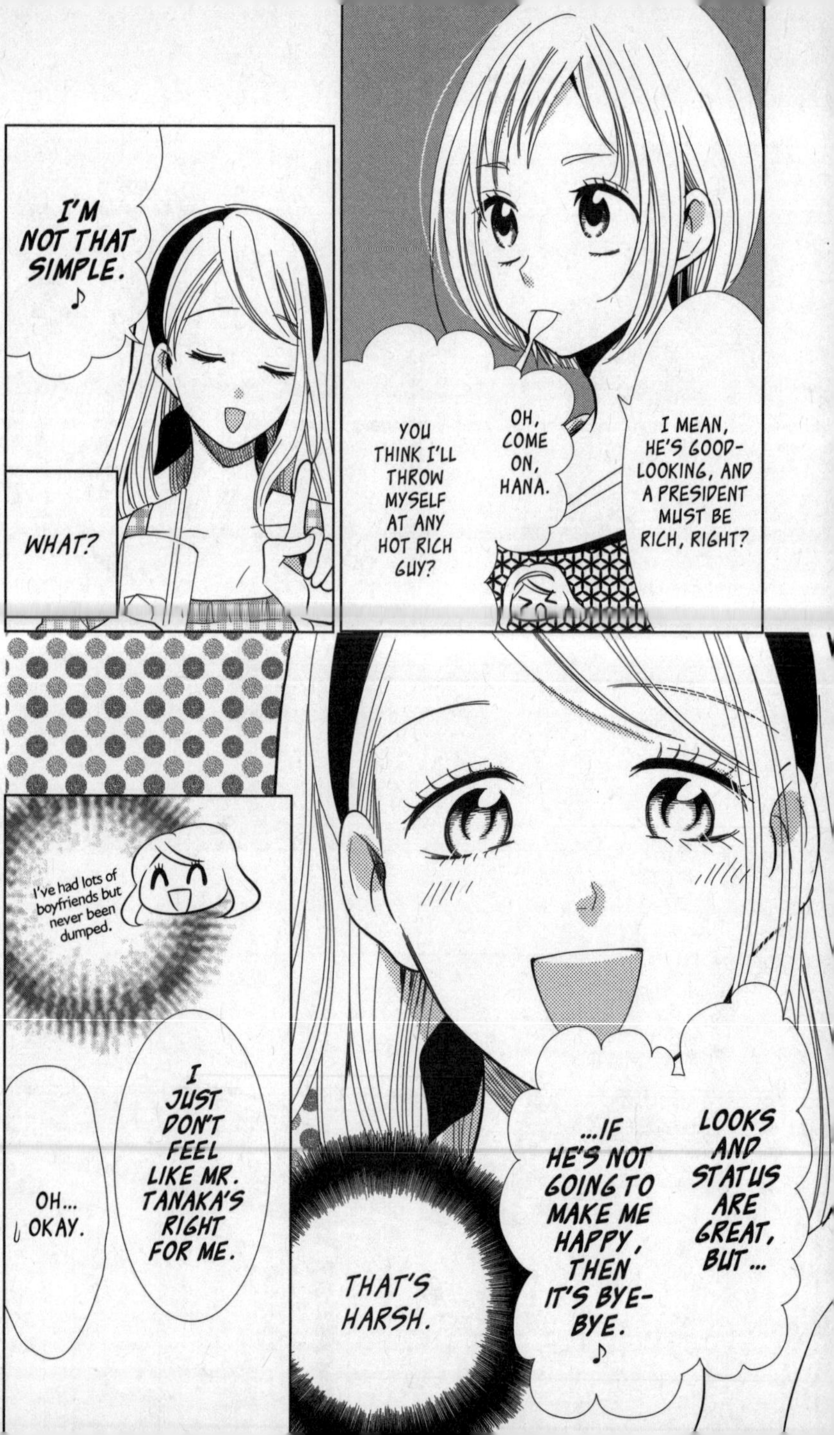
I MEAN, HE'S GOOD-LOOKING, AND A PRESIDENT MUST BE RICH, RIGHT?
OH, COME ON, HANA.
YOU THINK I'LL THROW MYSELF AT ANY HOT RICH GUY?
I'M NOT THAT SIMPLE. ♪
WHAT?
LOOKS AND STATUS ARE GREAT, BUT...
...IF HE'S NOT GOING TO MAKE ME HAPPY, THEN IT'S BYE-BYE. ♪
THAT'S HARSH.
I've had lots of boyfriends but never been dumped.
I JUST DON'T FEEL LIKE MR. TANAKA'S RIGHT FOR ME.
OH... OKAY.

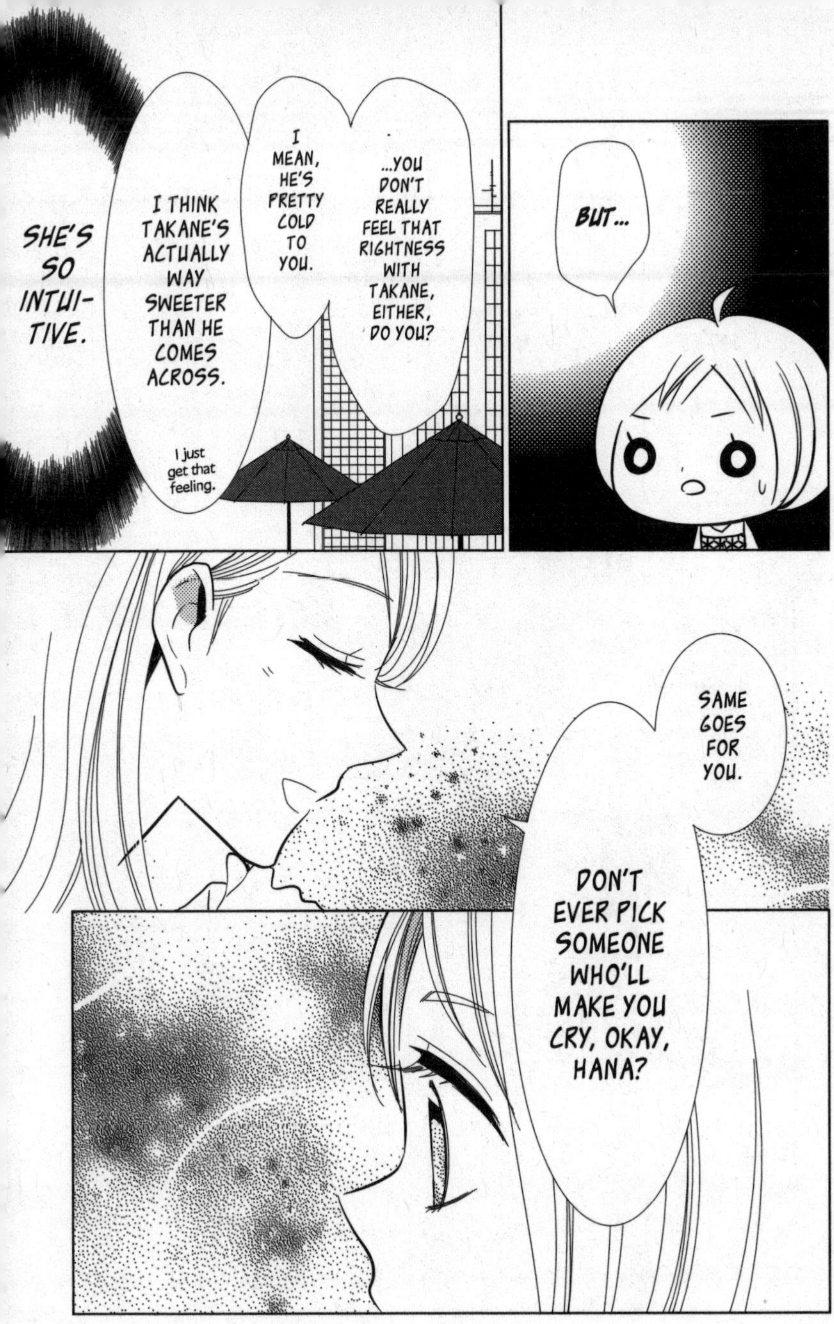
BUT...
...YOU DON'T REALLY FEEL THAT RIGHTNESS WITH TAKANE, EITHER, DO YOU?
I MEAN, HE'S PRETTY COLD TO YOU.
I THINK TAKANE'S ACTUALLY WAY SWEETER THAN HE COMES ACROSS.
I just get that feeling.
SHE'S SO INTUI-TIVE.
SAME GOES FOR YOU.
DON'T EVER PICK SOMEONE WHO'LL MAKE YOU CRY, OKAY, HANA?

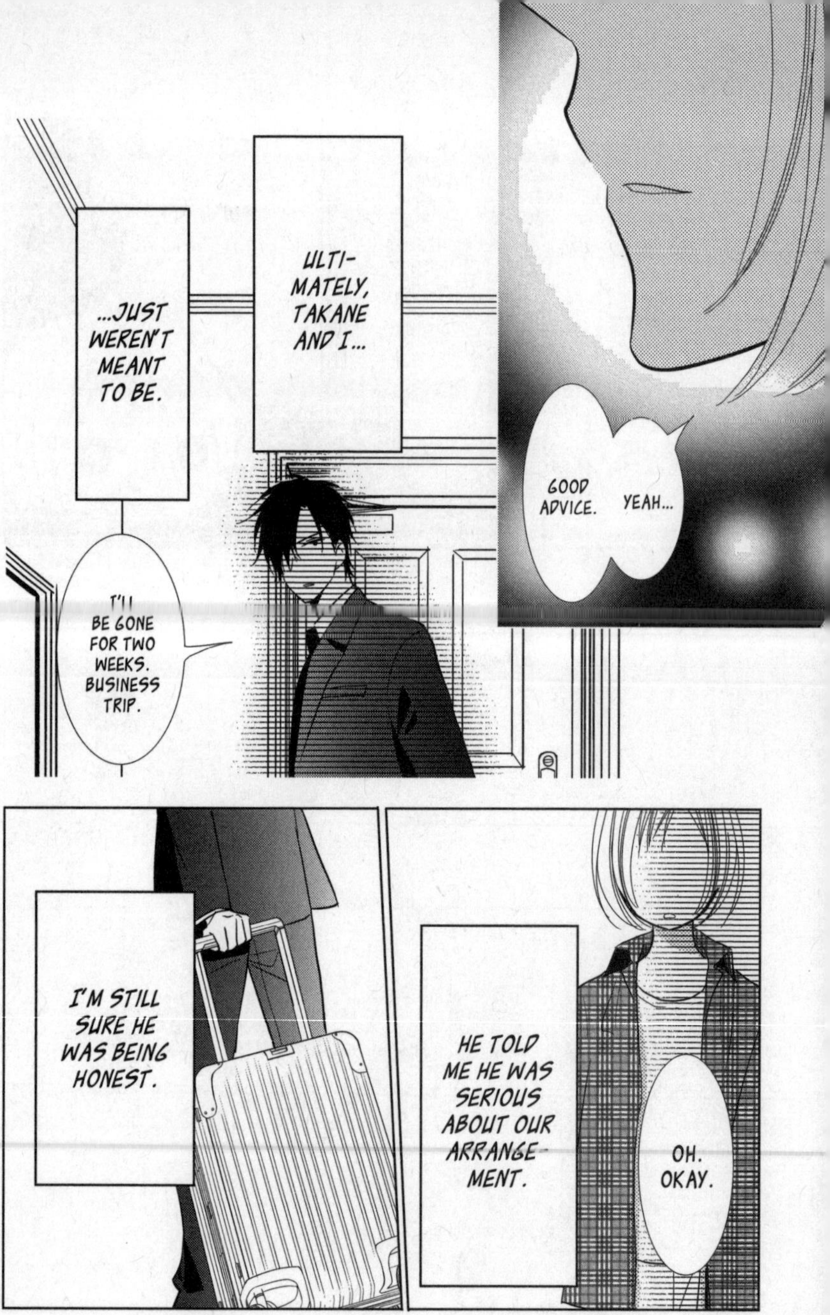
YEAH...
GOOD ADVICE.
ULTIMATELY, TAKANE AND I...
...JUST WEREN'T MEANT TO BE.
I'LL BE GONE FOR TWO WEEKS. BUSINESS TRIP.
HE TOLD ME HE WAS SERIOUS ABOUT OUR ARRANGEMENT.
OH. OKAY.
I'M STILL SURE HE WAS BEING HONEST.

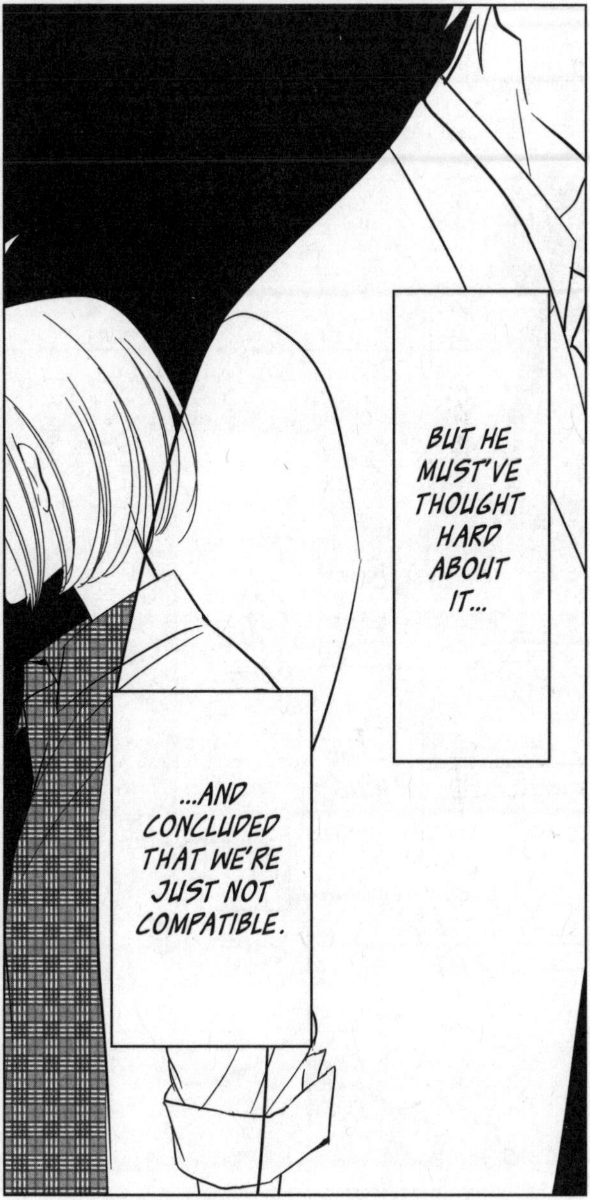
BUT HE MUST'VE THOUGHT HARD ABOUT IT...
...AND CONCLUDED THAT WE'RE JUST NOT COMPATIBLE.

FYI, the head editor is the one who comes up with the sales copy (in Japan), not the author.

They put so much time and effort into getting it right, and the copy all sounds so great that only publishing it once in the magazine is...

...a waste!

So here we go!

• Chapter 4 (in volume 1) •

A rich, handsome, high class man? Bring it on!

I'll accept this arranged marriage meeting partnership!

What's the point of an arranged marriage meeting, again?

This is the chapter 4 sales copy that marked the beginning of the series. Let's hear it for the sales copy!

• Chapter 6 (in volume 2) •

I'm looking for the wearer of this practical shoe, who obviously prioritizes function over beauty. Have you seen her?

Meet Prince Not-So-Charming!

It's too funny. (*Ha ha!*)

The frontispiece shows Prince Takane looking for Cinderella Hana.

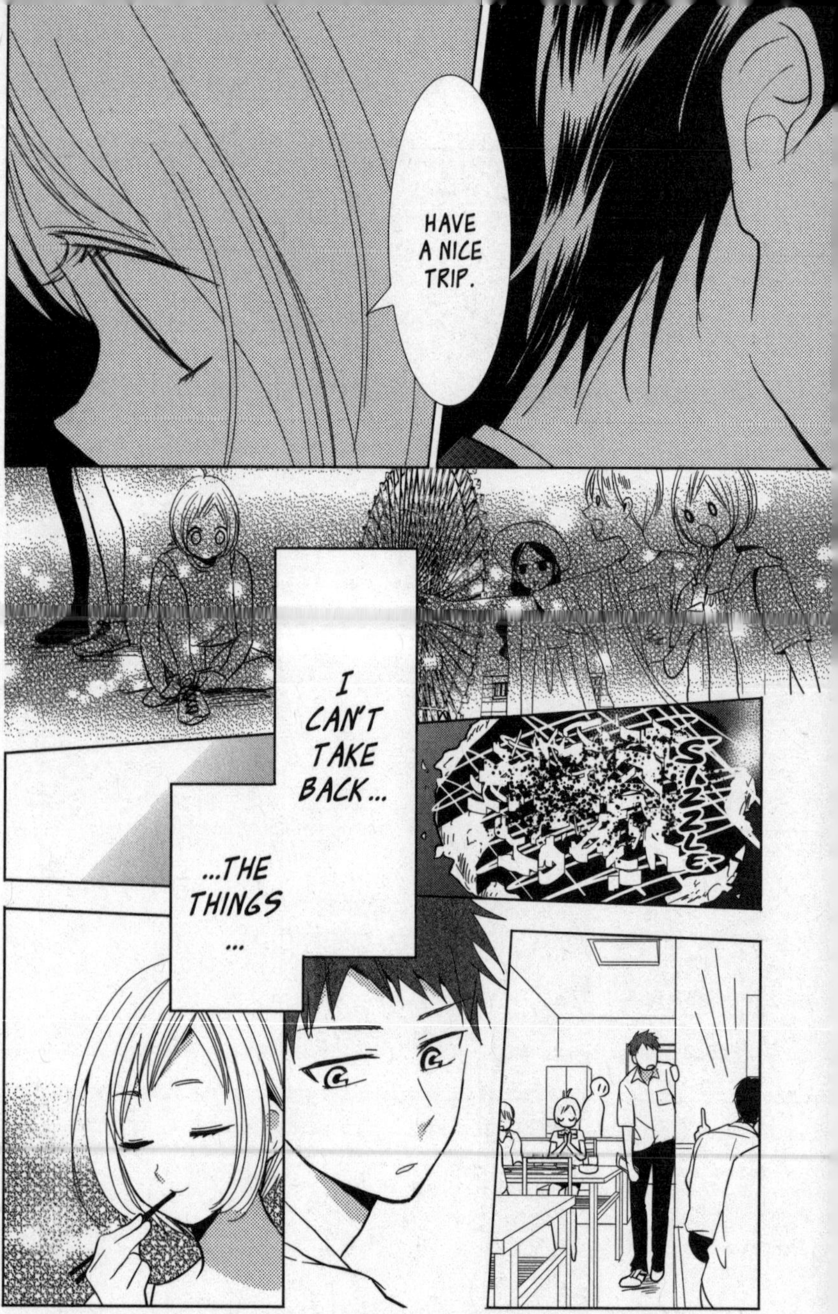
HAVE A NICE TRIP.
I CAN'T TAKE BACK...
SIZZLE
...THE THINGS ...

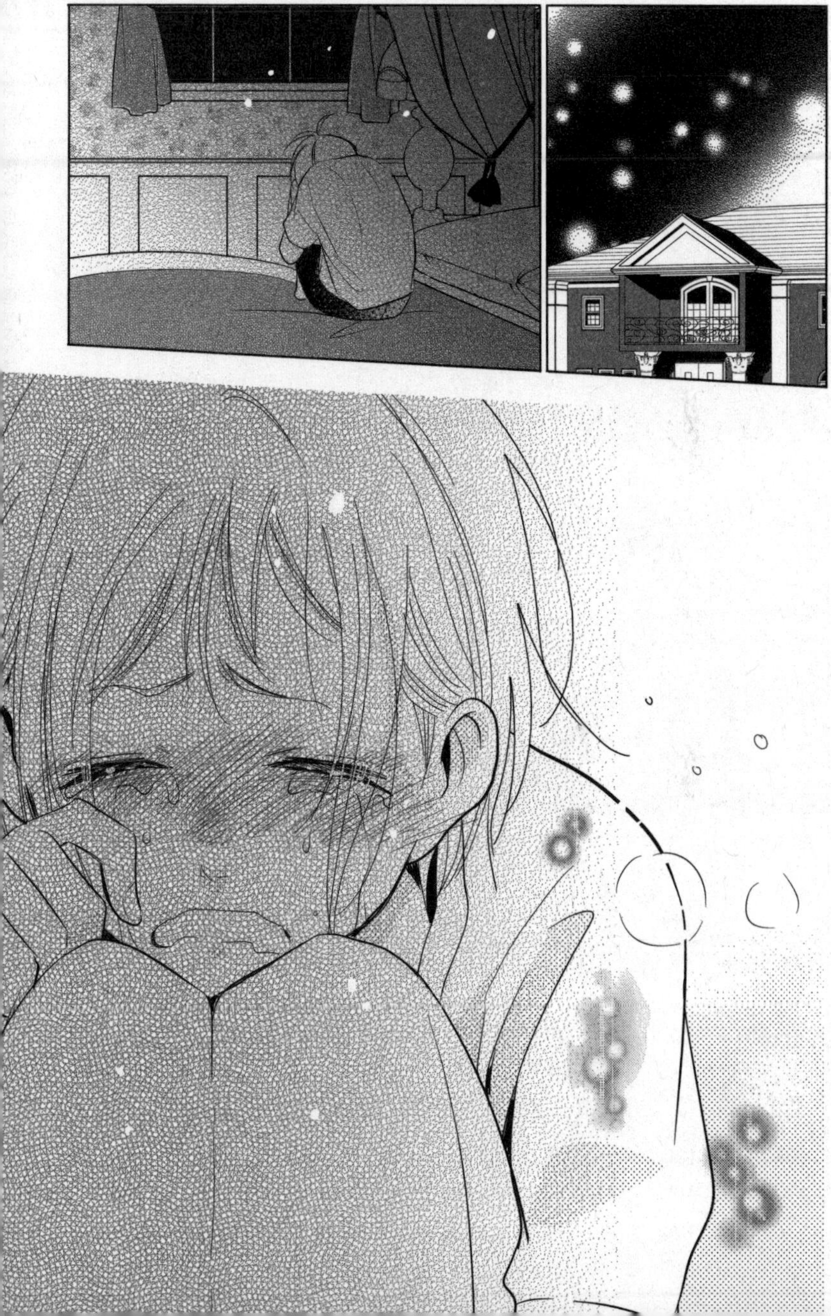

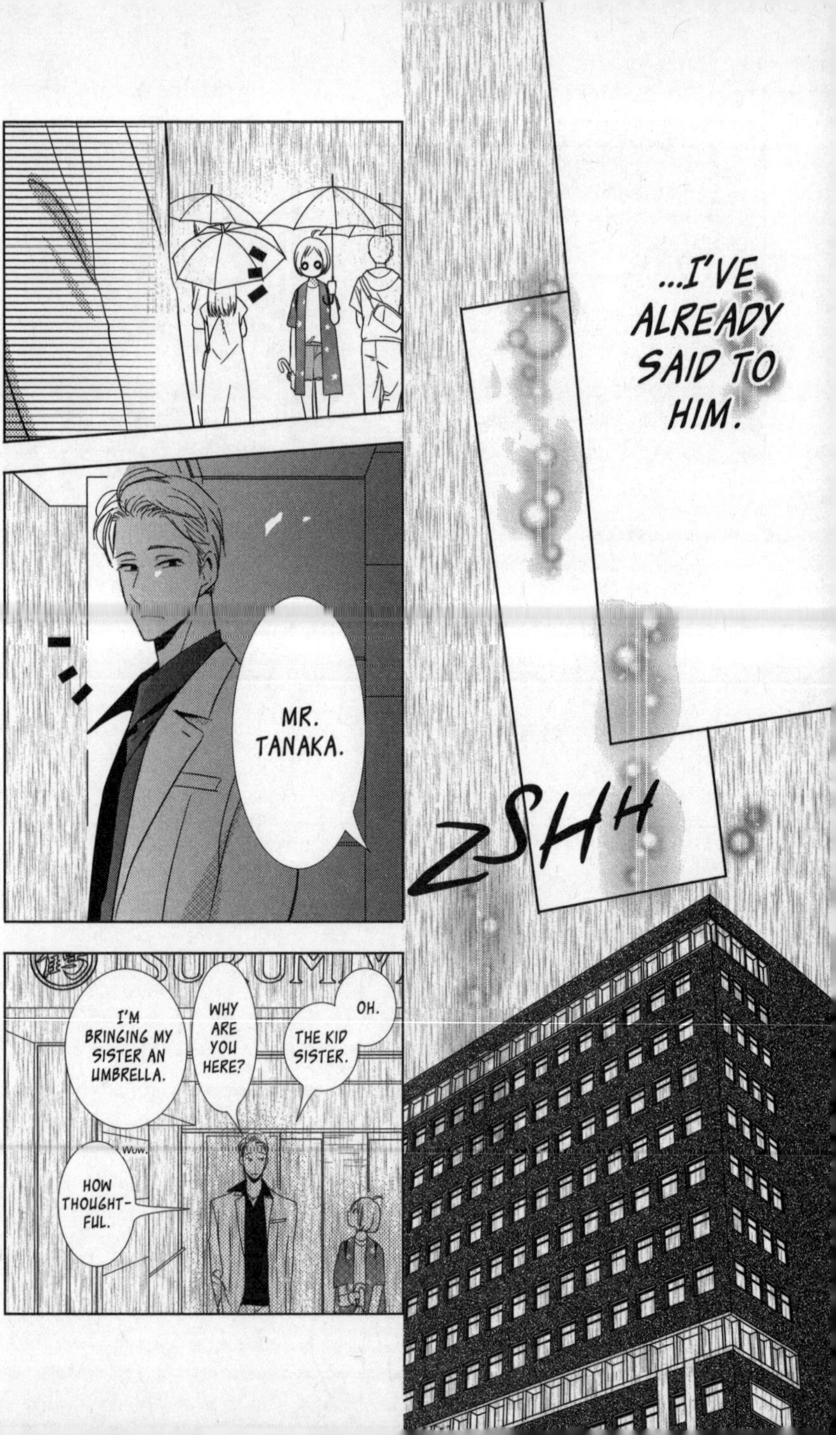
...I'VE ALREADY SAID TO HIM.
ZSHH
MR. TANAKA.
OH.
THE KID SISTER.
WHY ARE YOU HERE?
I'M BRINGING MY SISTER AN UMBRELLA.
WOW.
HOW THOUGHTFUL.

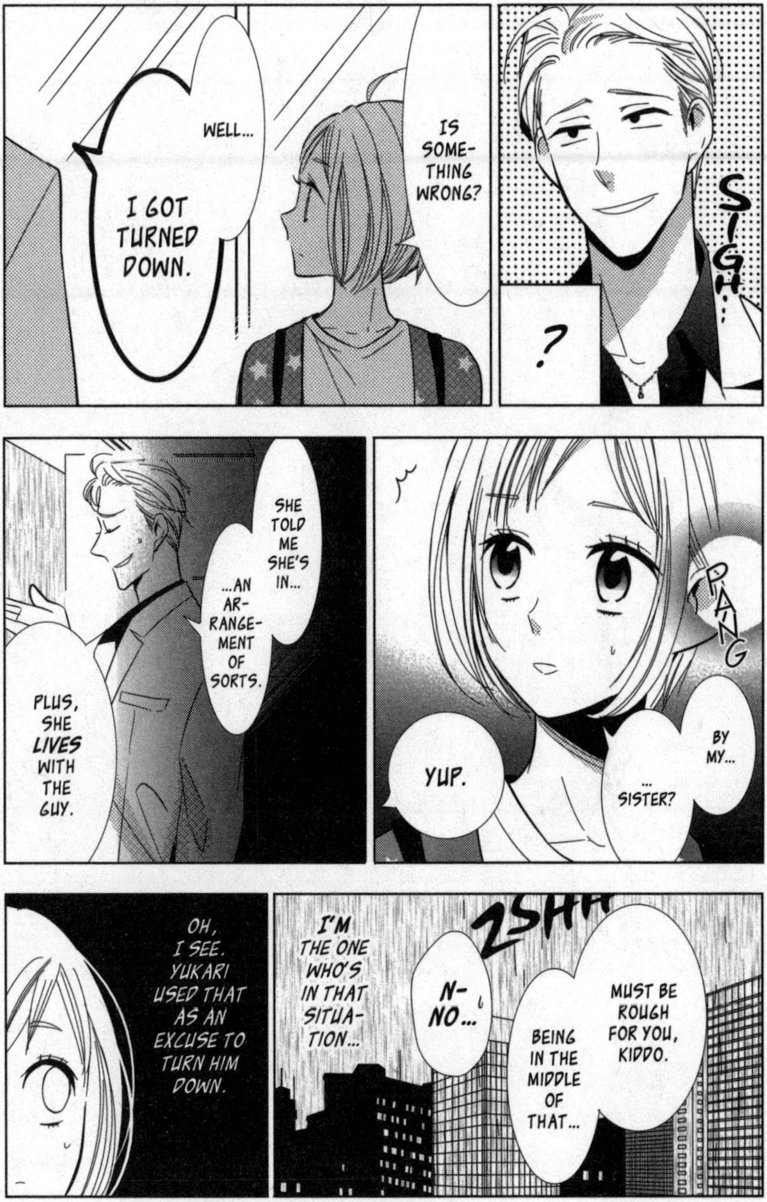
SIGH...
?
IS SOMETHING WRONG?
WELL...
I GOT TURNED DOWN.
PANG
BY MY...
...SISTER?
YUP.
SHE TOLD ME SHE'S IN...
...AN ARRANGEMENT OF SORTS.
PLUS, SHE *LIVES* WITH THE GUY.
ZSHA
MUST BE ROUGH FOR YOU, KIDDO.
BEING IN THE MIDDLE OF THAT...
N-NO...
I'M THE ONE WHO'S IN THAT SITUATION...
OH, I SEE. YUKARI USED THAT AS AN EXCUSE TO TURN HIM DOWN.

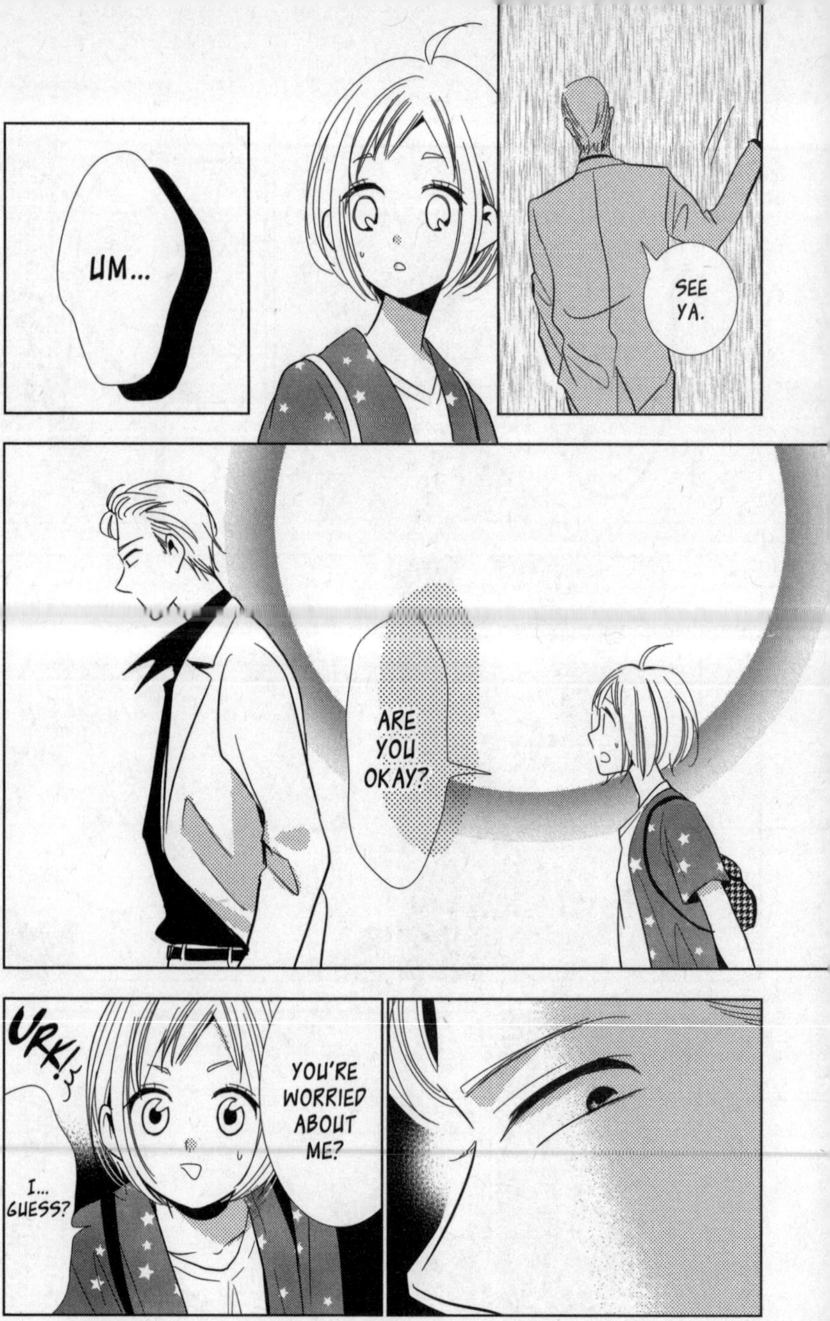
SEE YA.
UM...
ARE YOU OKAY?
YOU'RE WORRIED ABOUT ME?
URK!
I... GUESS?

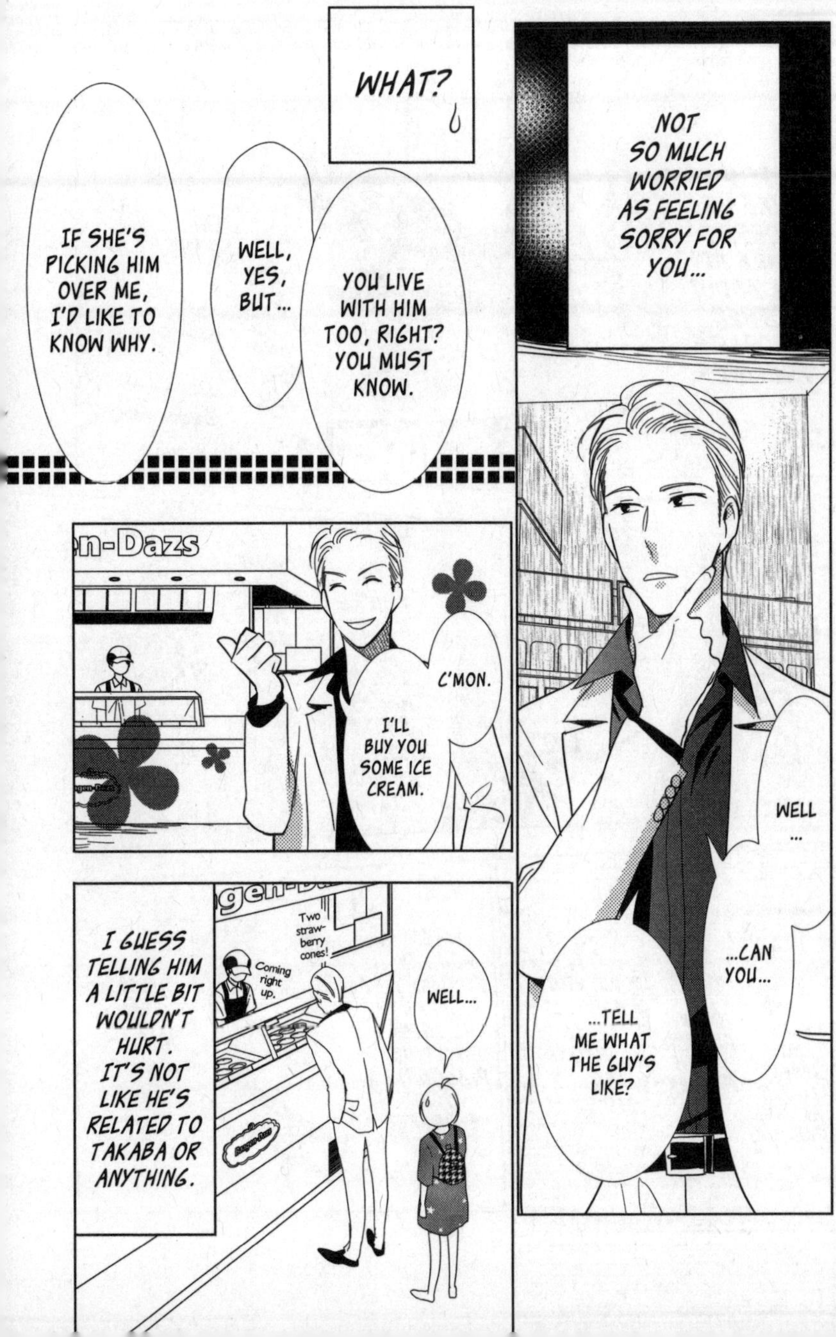
WHAT?
YOU LIVE WITH HIM TOO, RIGHT? YOU MUST KNOW.
WELL, YES, BUT...
IF SHE'S PICKING HIM OVER ME, I'D LIKE TO KNOW WHY.
NOT SO MUCH WORRIED AS FEELING SORRY FOR YOU...
WELL...
...CAN YOU...
...TELL ME WHAT THE GUY'S LIKE?
C'MON.
I'LL BUY YOU SOME ICE CREAM.
Two strawberry cones!
Coming right up.
WELL...
I GUESS TELLING HIM A LITTLE BIT WOULDN'T HURT. IT'S NOT LIKE HE'S RELATED TO TAKABA OR ANYTHING.

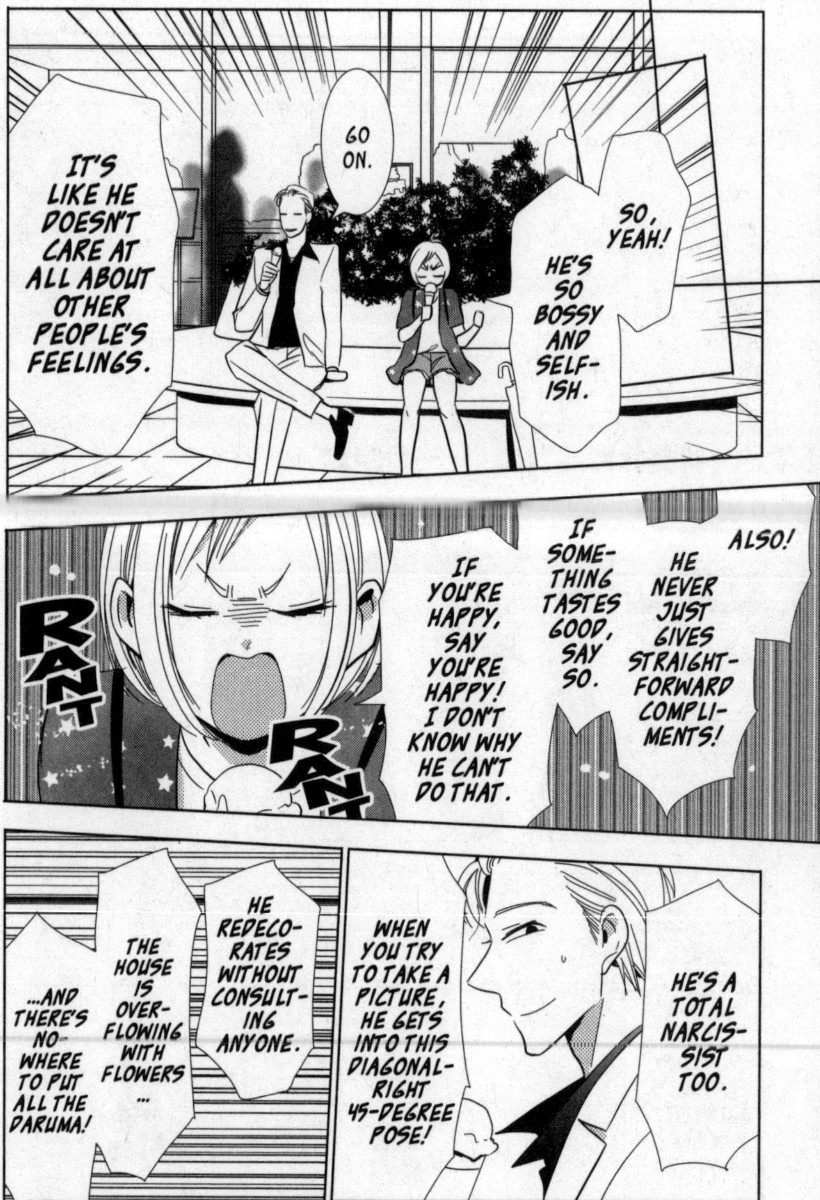
SO, YEAH!
HE'S SO BOSSY AND SELFISH.
GO ON.
IT'S LIKE HE DOESN'T CARE AT ALL ABOUT OTHER PEOPLE'S FEELINGS.
ALSO!
HE NEVER JUST GIVES STRAIGHT-FORWARD COMPLIMENTS!
IF SOMETHING TASTES GOOD, SAY SO.
IF YOU'RE HAPPY, SAY YOU'RE HAPPY! I DON'T KNOW WHY HE CAN'T DO THAT.
RANT
RANT
HE'S A TOTAL NARCISSIST TOO.
WHEN YOU TRY TO TAKE A PICTURE, HE GETS INTO THIS DIAGONAL-RIGHT 45-DEGREE POSE!
HE REDECORATES WITHOUT CONSULTING ANYONE.
THE HOUSE IS OVERFLOWING WITH FLOWERS...
...AND THERE'S NOWHERE TO PUT ALL THE DARUMA!

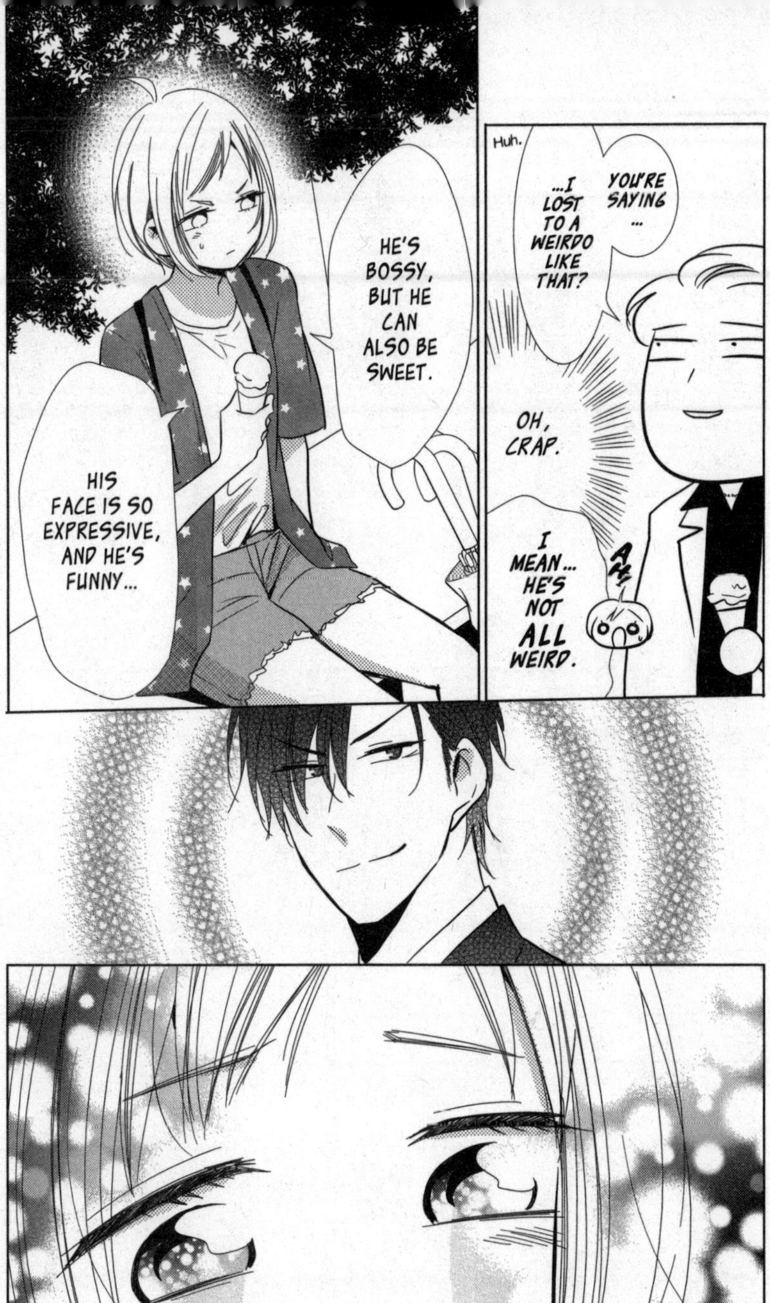
YOU'RE SAYING...
...I LOST TO A WEIRDO LIKE THAT?
Huh.
OH, CRAP.
AH!
I MEAN... HE'S NOT ALL WEIRD.
HE'S BOSSY, BUT HE CAN ALSO BE SWEET.
HIS FACE IS SO EXPRESSIVE, AND HE'S FUNNY...

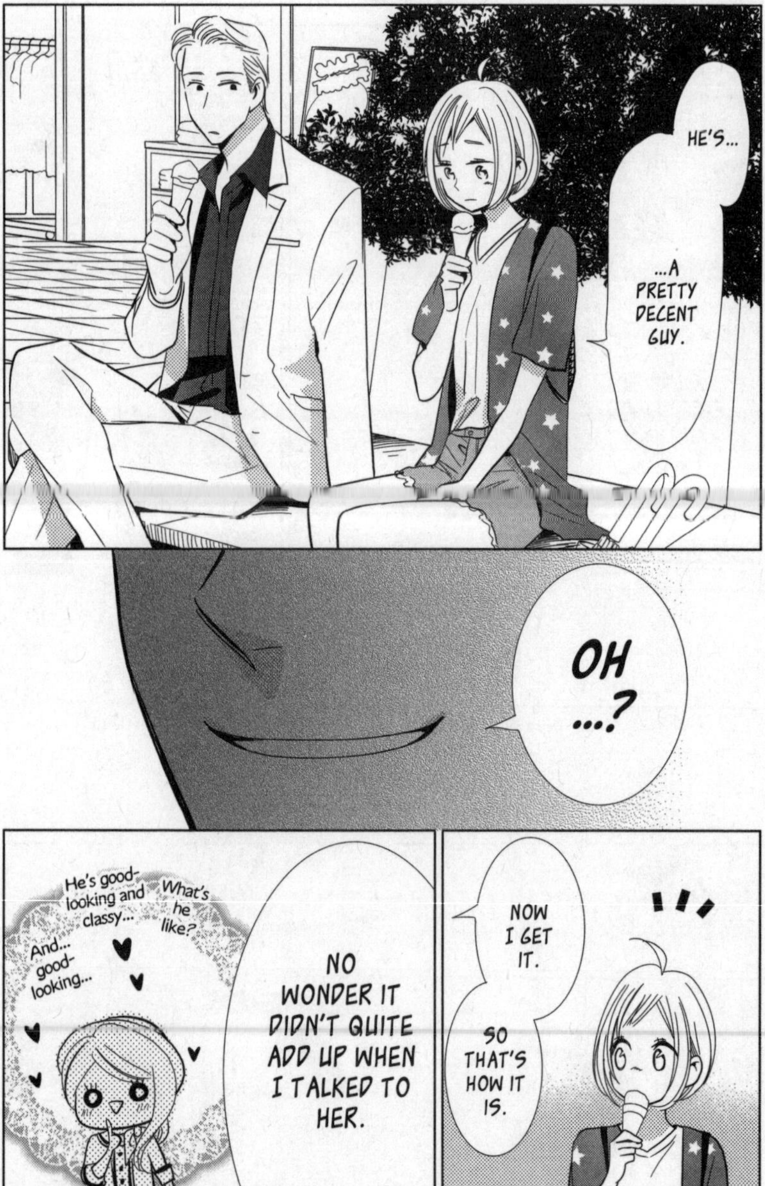
HE'S...
...A PRETTY DECENT GUY.
OH ...?
NOW I GET IT.
SO THAT'S HOW IT IS.
NO WONDER IT DIDN'T QUITE ADD UP WHEN I TALKED TO HER.
What's he like?
He's good-looking and classy...
And... good-looking...

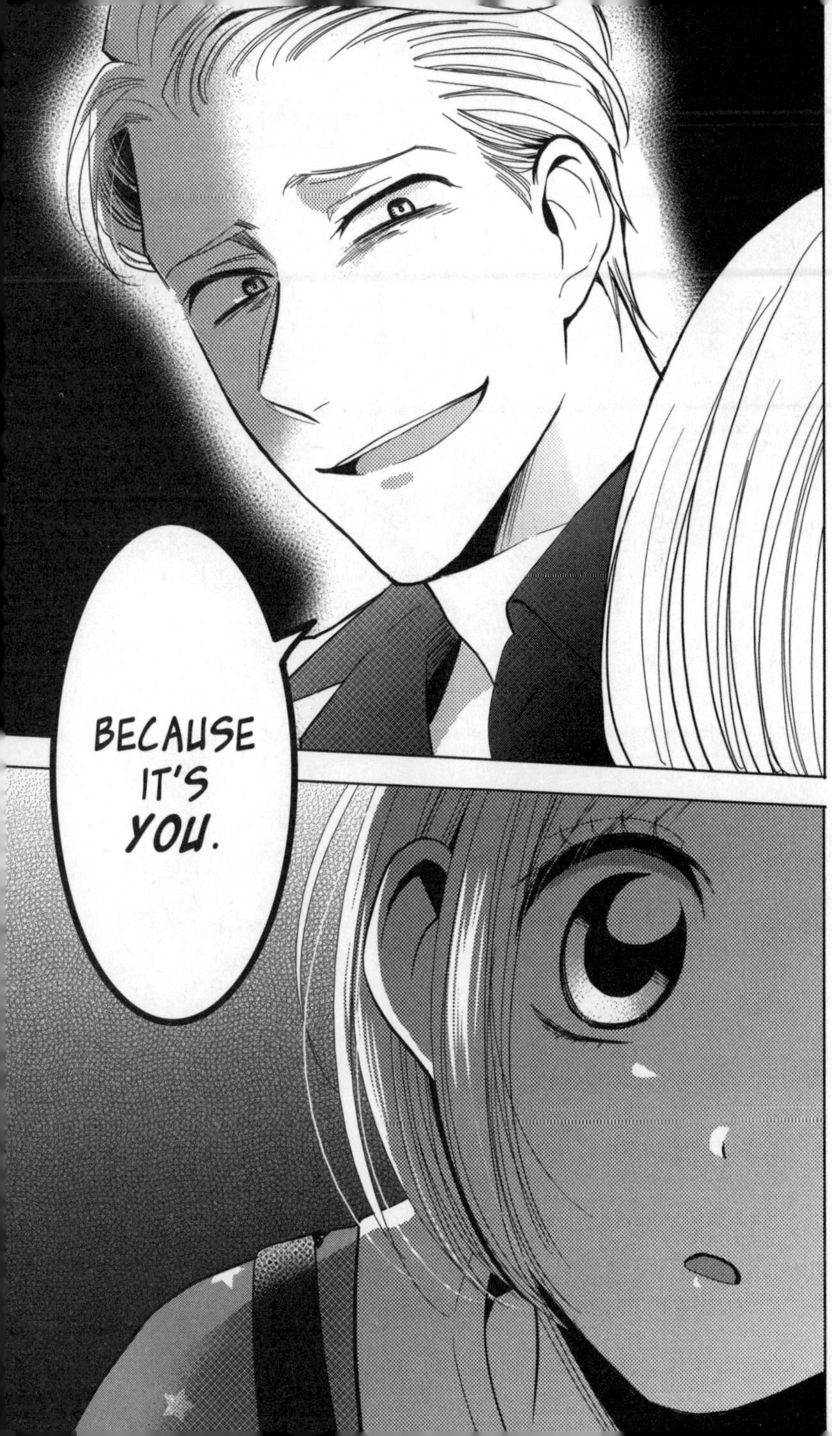
BECAUSE IT'S *YOU*.

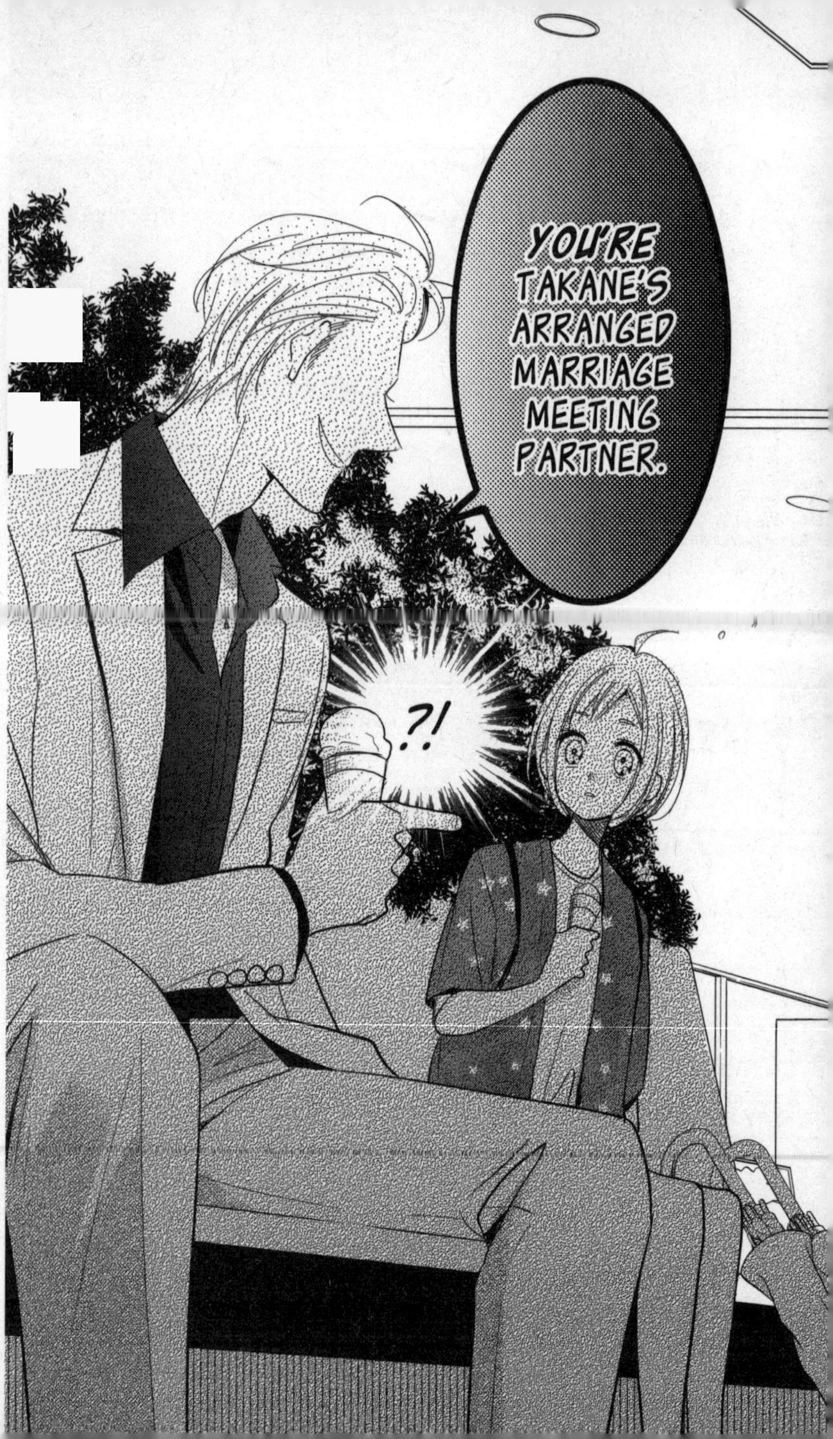
YOU'RE TAKANE'S ARRANGED MARRIAGE MEETING PARTNER.
?!

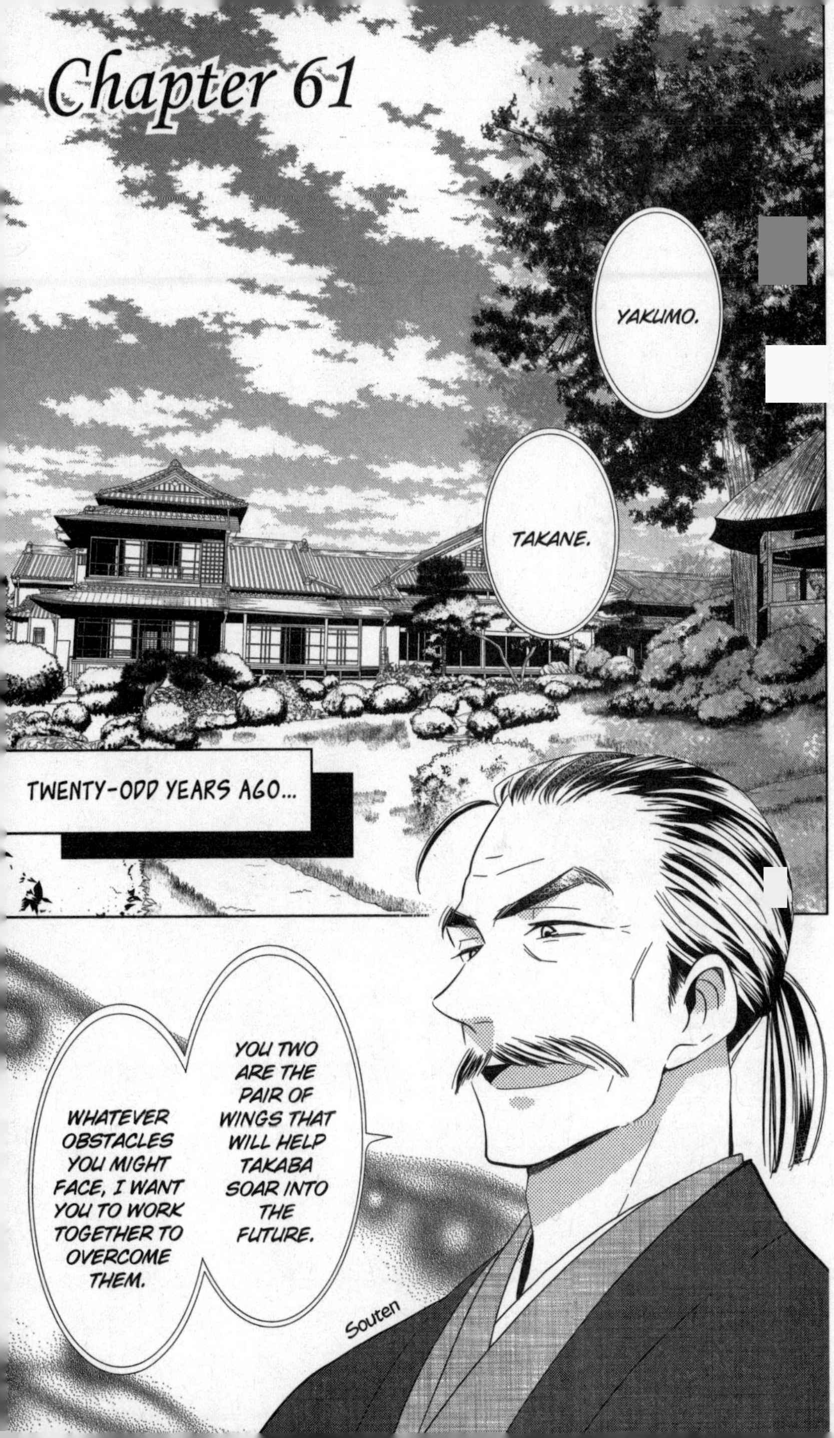
Chapter 61
YAKUMO.
TAKANE.
TWENTY-ODD YEARS AGO...
YOU TWO ARE THE PAIR OF WINGS THAT WILL HELP TAKABA SOAR INTO THE FUTURE.
WHATEVER OBSTACLES YOU MIGHT FACE, I WANT YOU TO WORK TOGETHER TO OVERCOME THEM.
Souten

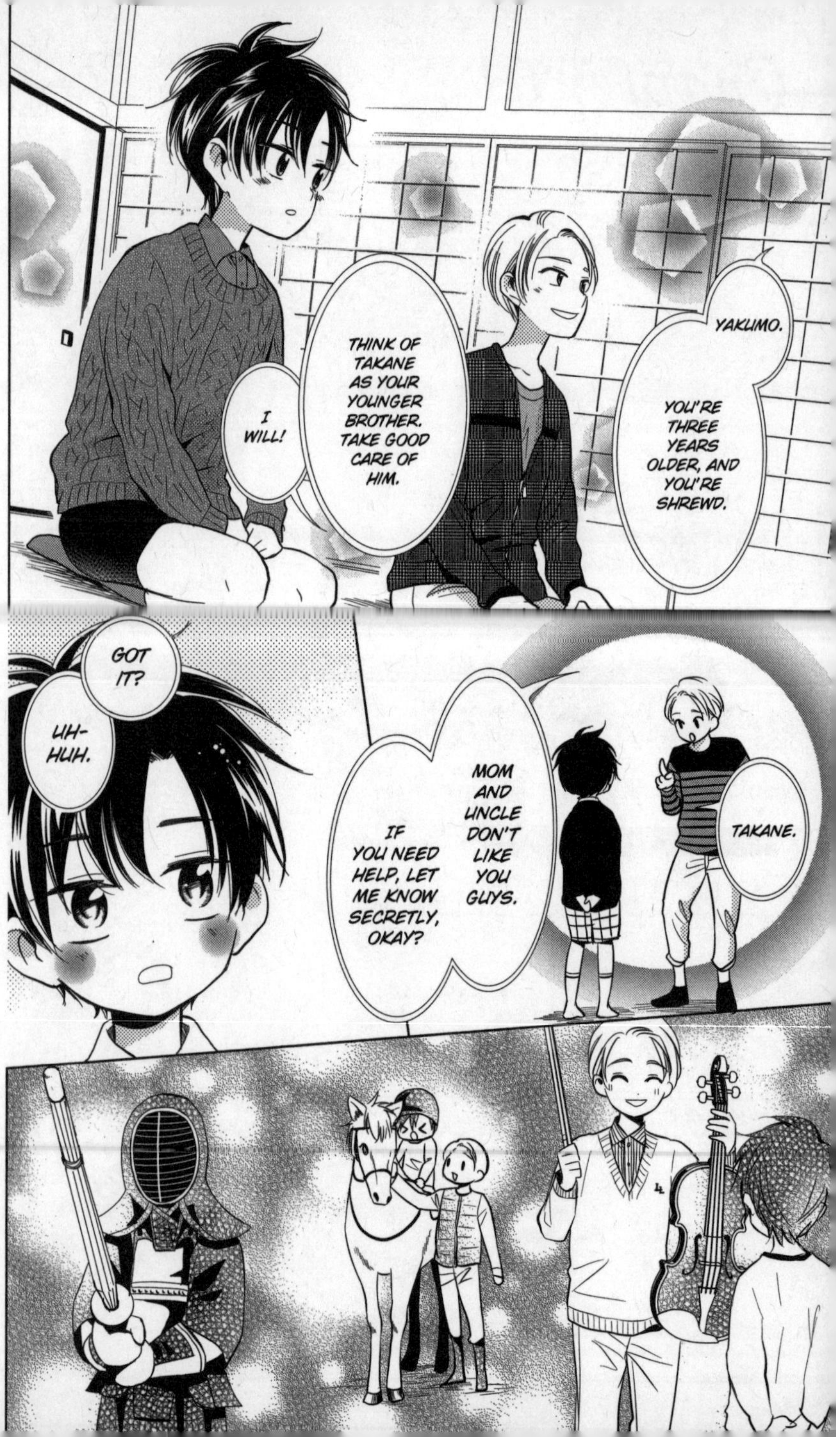
YAKUMO.
YOU'RE THREE YEARS OLDER, AND YOU'RE SHREWD.
THINK OF TAKANE AS YOUR YOUNGER BROTHER. TAKE GOOD CARE OF HIM.
I WILL!
TAKANE.
MOM AND UNCLE DON'T LIKE YOU GUYS.
IF YOU NEED HELP, LET ME KNOW SECRETLY, OKAY?
GOT IT?
UH-HUH.

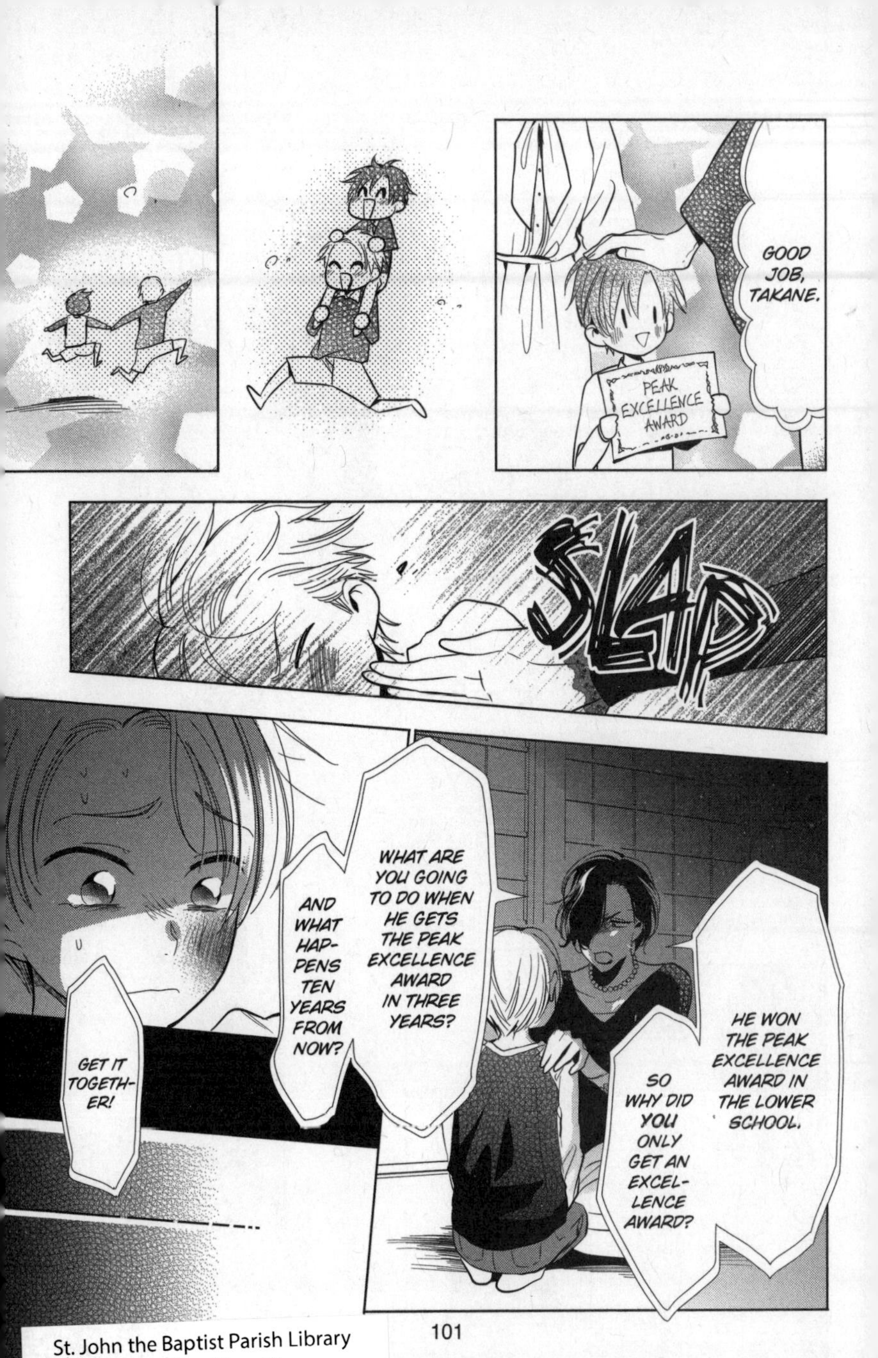
GOOD JOB, TAKANE.
PEAK EXCELLENCE AWARD
SLAP
HE WON THE PEAK EXCELLENCE AWARD IN THE LOWER SCHOOL.
SO WHY DID YOU ONLY GET AN EXCEL-LENCE AWARD?
WHAT ARE YOU GOING TO DO WHEN HE GETS THE PEAK EXCELLENCE AWARD IN THREE YEARS?
AND WHAT HAP-PENS TEN YEARS FROM NOW?
GET IT TOGETH-ER!

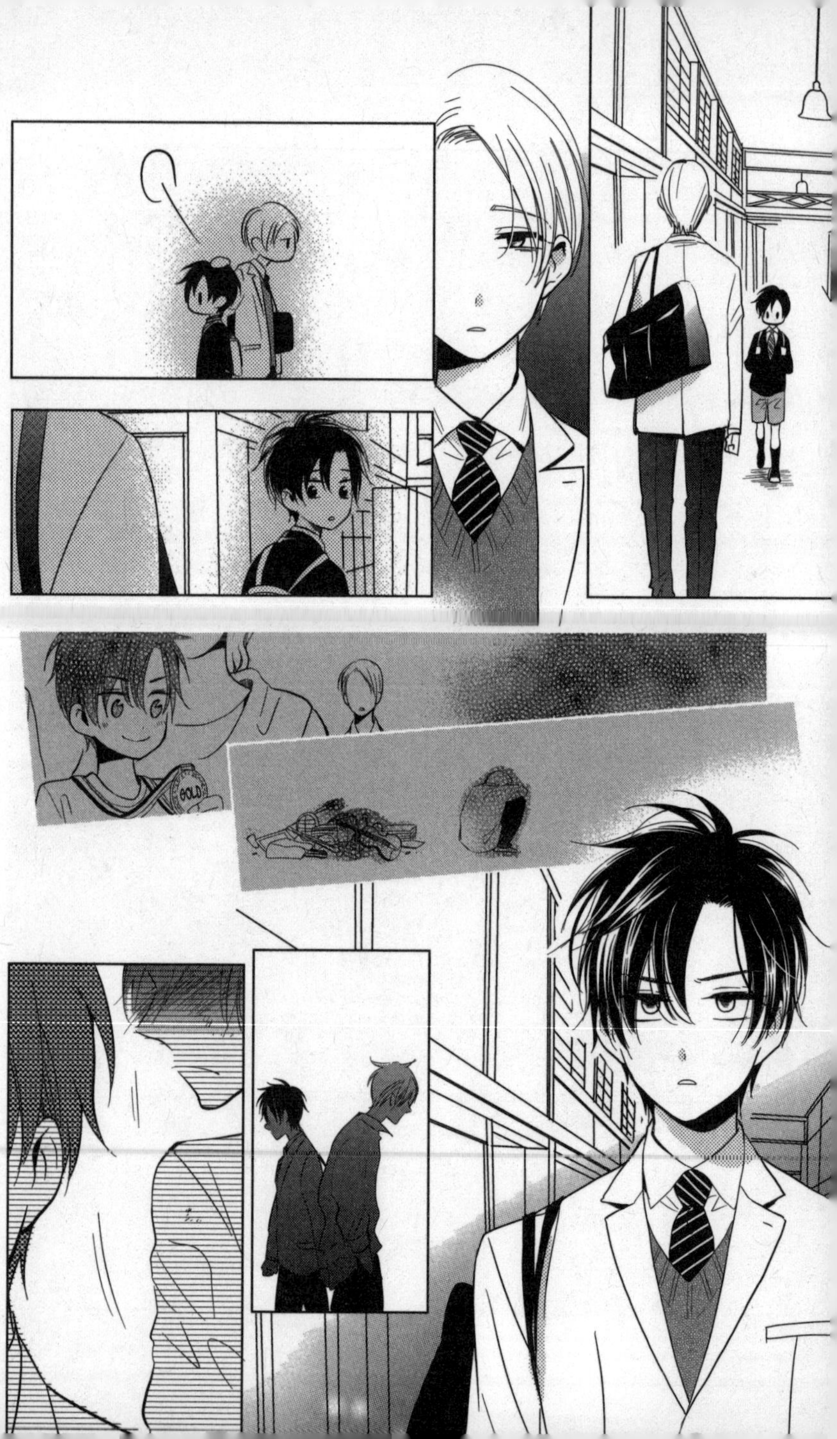
GOLD

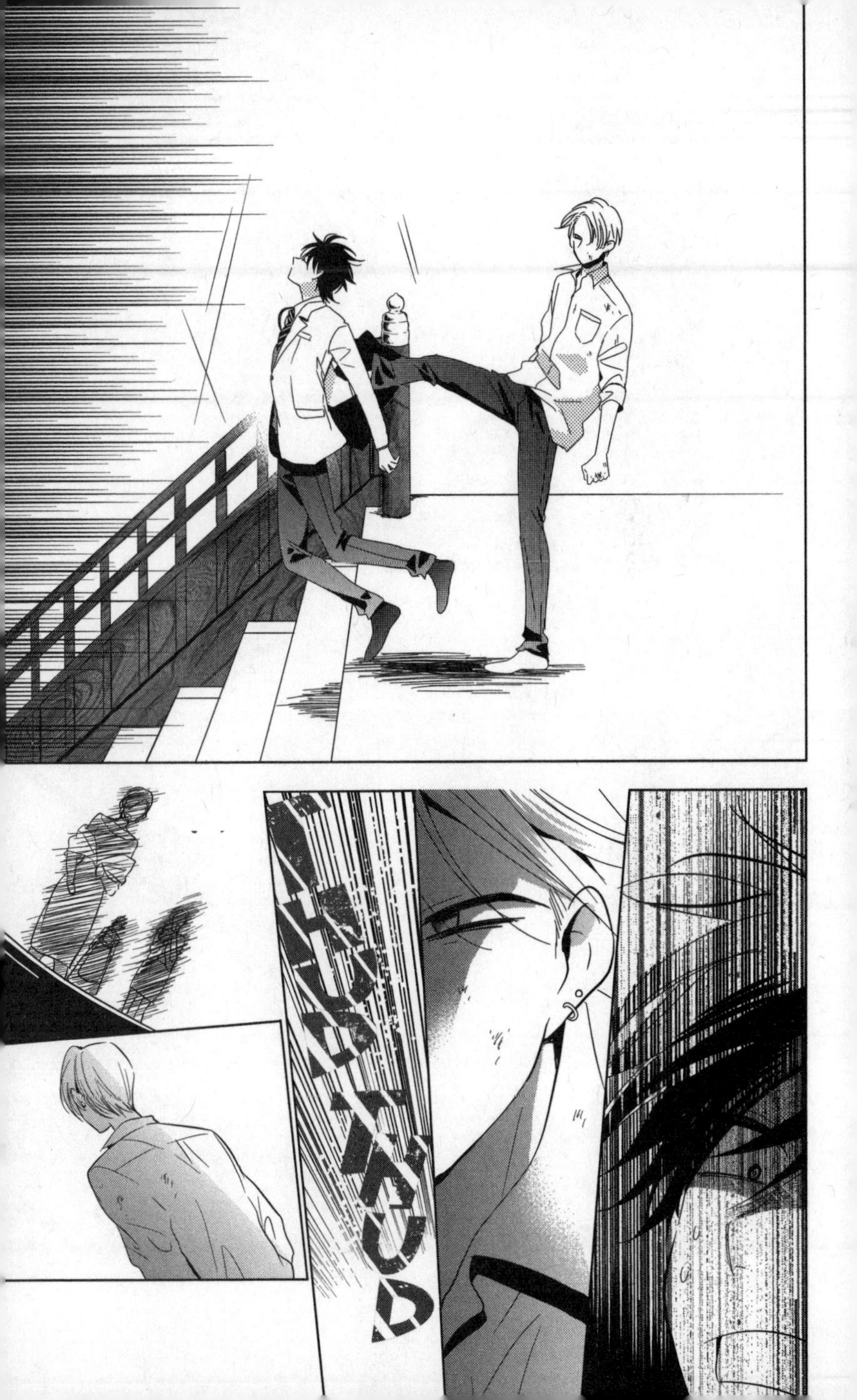

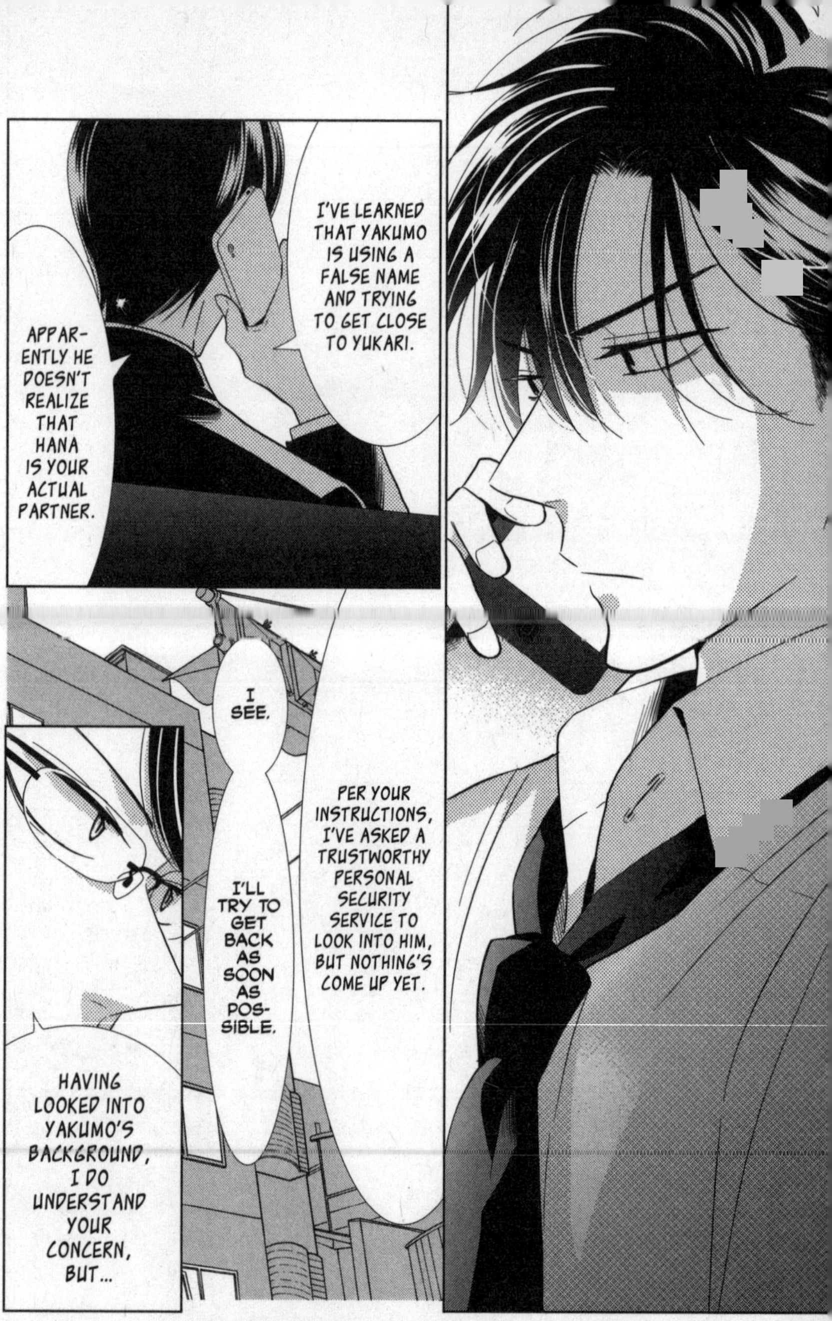
I'VE LEARNED THAT YAKUMO IS USING A FALSE NAME AND TRYING TO GET CLOSE TO YUKARI.
APPAR-ENTLY HE DOESN'T REALIZE THAT HANA IS YOUR ACTUAL PARTNER.
PER YOUR INSTRUCTIONS, I'VE ASKED A TRUSTWORTHY PERSONAL SECURITY SERVICE TO LOOK INTO HIM, BUT NOTHING'S COME UP YET.
I SEE.
I'LL TRY TO GET BACK AS SOON AS POS-SIBLE.
HAVING LOOKED INTO YAKUMO'S BACKGROUND, I DO UNDERSTAND YOUR CONCERN, BUT...

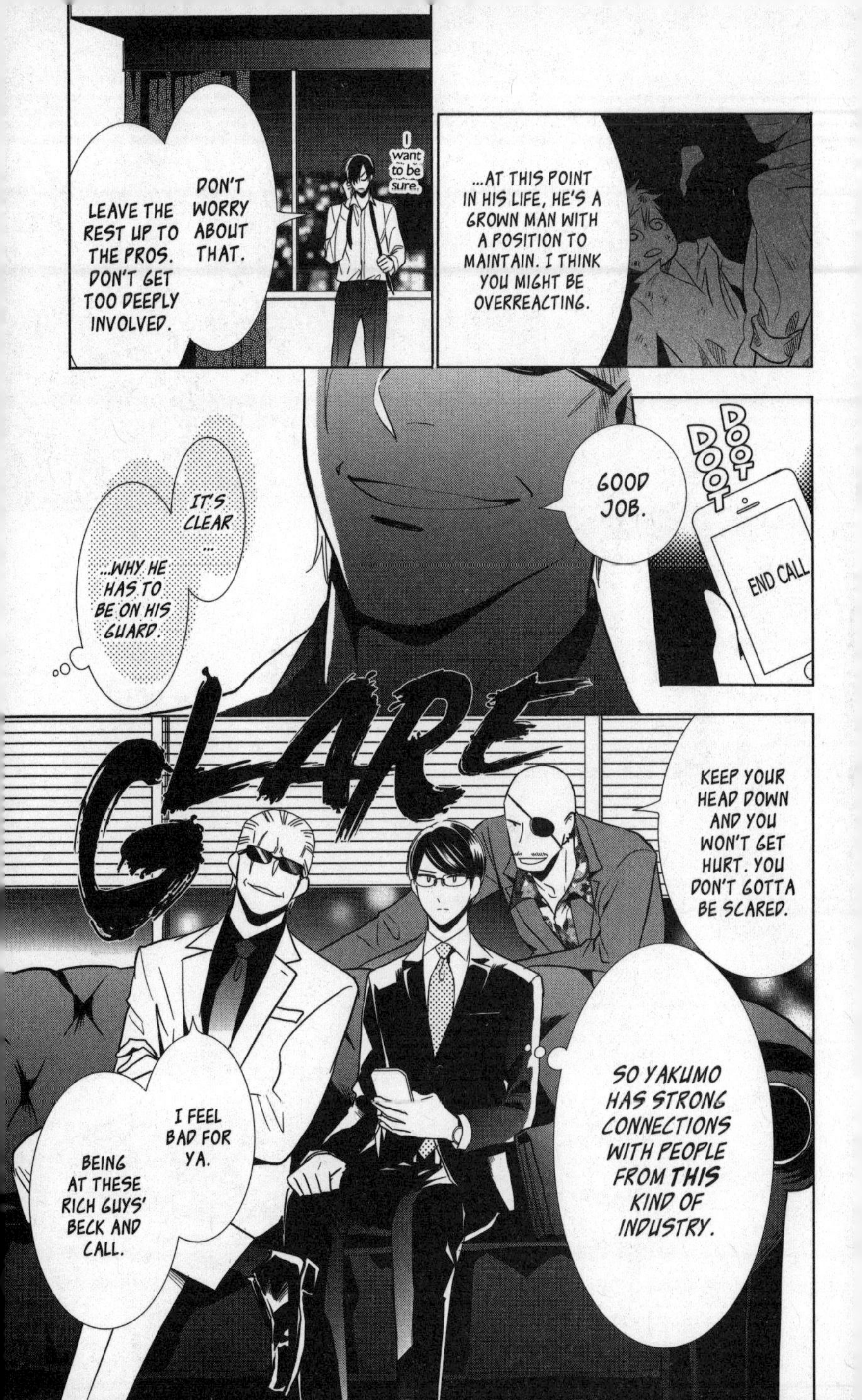
...AT THIS POINT IN HIS LIFE, HE'S A GROWN MAN WITH A POSITION TO MAINTAIN. I THINK YOU MIGHT BE OVERREACTING.
I want to be sure.
DON'T WORRY ABOUT THAT.
LEAVE THE REST UP TO THE PROS. DON'T GET TOO DEEPLY INVOLVED.
DOOT DOOT
END CALL
GOOD JOB.
IT'S CLEAR...
...WHY HE HAS TO BE ON HIS GUARD.
GLARE
KEEP YOUR HEAD DOWN AND YOU WON'T GET HURT. YOU DON'T GOTTA BE SCARED.
SO YAKUMO HAS STRONG CONNECTIONS WITH PEOPLE FROM THIS KIND OF INDUSTRY.
I FEEL BAD FOR YA.
BEING AT THESE RICH GUYS' BECK AND CALL.

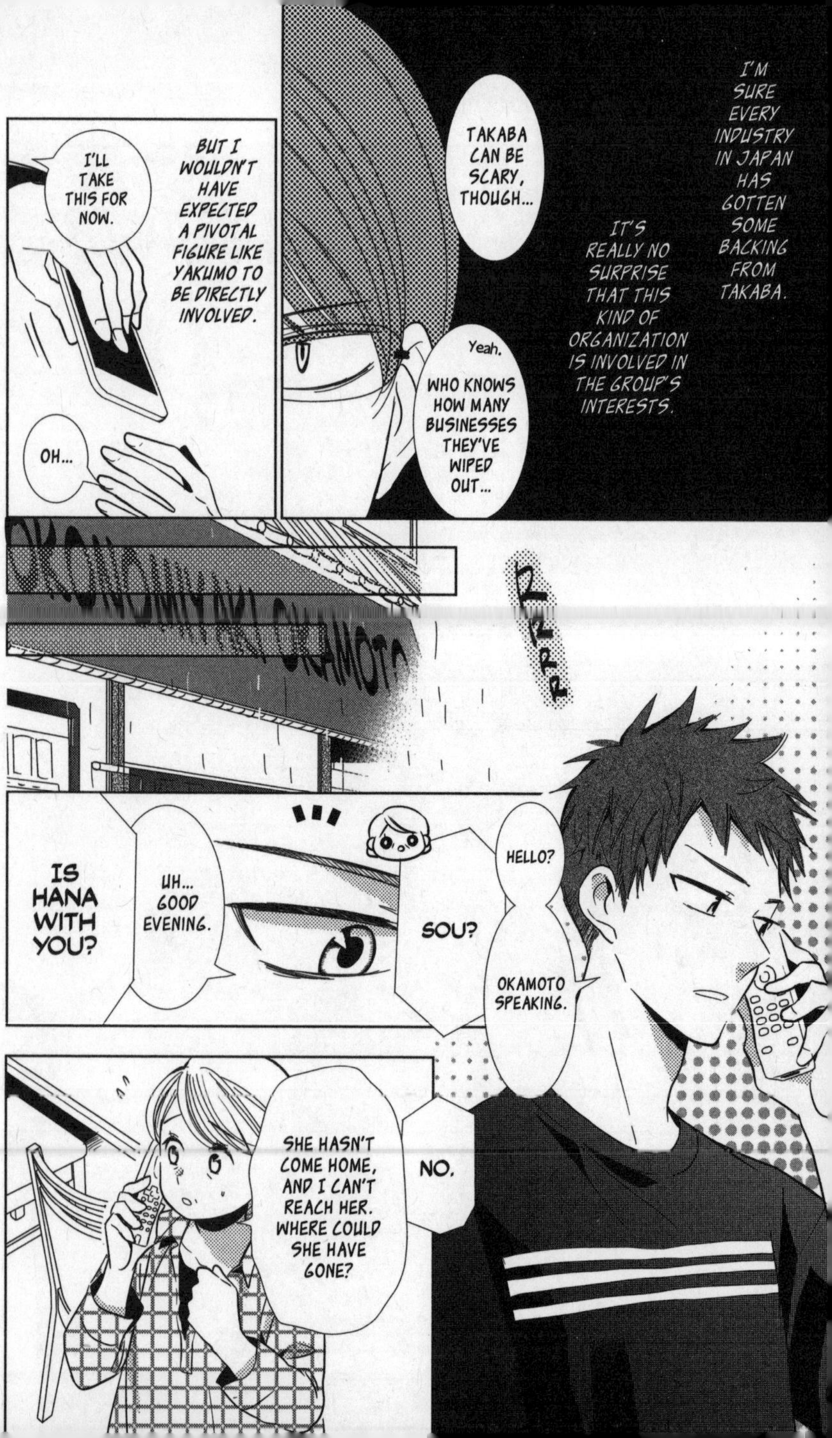

I'M SURE EVERY INDUSTRY IN JAPAN HAS GOTTEN SOME BACKING FROM TAKABA.
IT'S REALLY NO SURPRISE THAT THIS KIND OF ORGANIZATION IS INVOLVED IN THE GROUP'S INTERESTS.
TAKABA CAN BE SCARY, THOUGH...
Yeah.
WHO KNOWS HOW MANY BUSINESSES THEY'VE WIPED OUT...
BUT I WOULDN'T HAVE EXPECTED A PIVOTAL FIGURE LIKE YAKUMO TO BE DIRECTLY INVOLVED.
I'LL TAKE THIS FOR NOW.
OH...
RRRRR
HELLO?
OKAMOTO SPEAKING.
...
SOU?
UH... GOOD EVENING.
IS HANA WITH YOU?
NO.
SHE HASN'T COME HOME, AND I CAN'T REACH HER. WHERE COULD SHE HAVE GONE?

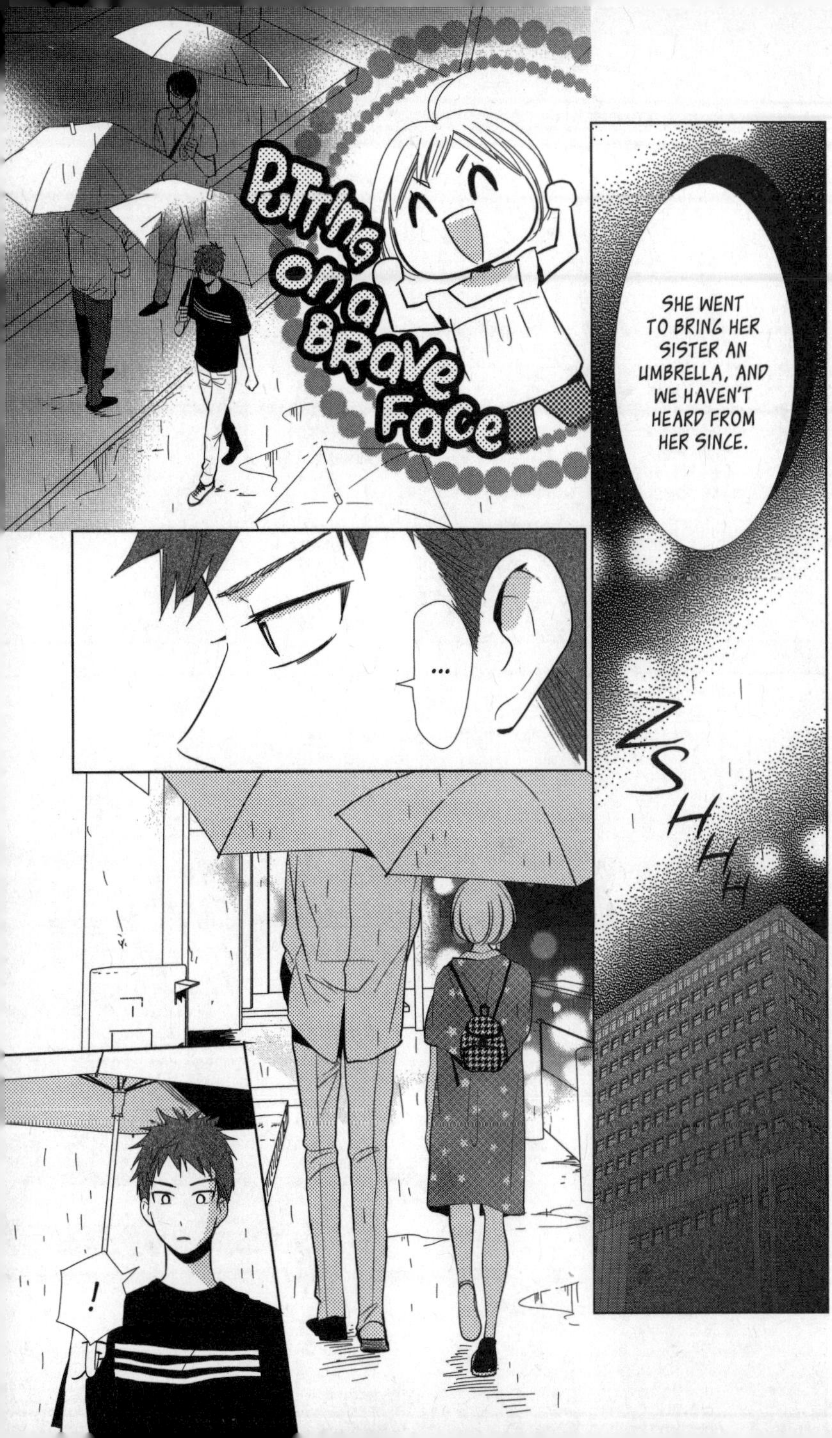
SHE WENT TO BRING HER SISTER AN UMBRELLA, AND WE HAVEN'T HEARD FROM HER SINCE.
ZSHHH
PUTTING ON A BRAVE FACE
...
!

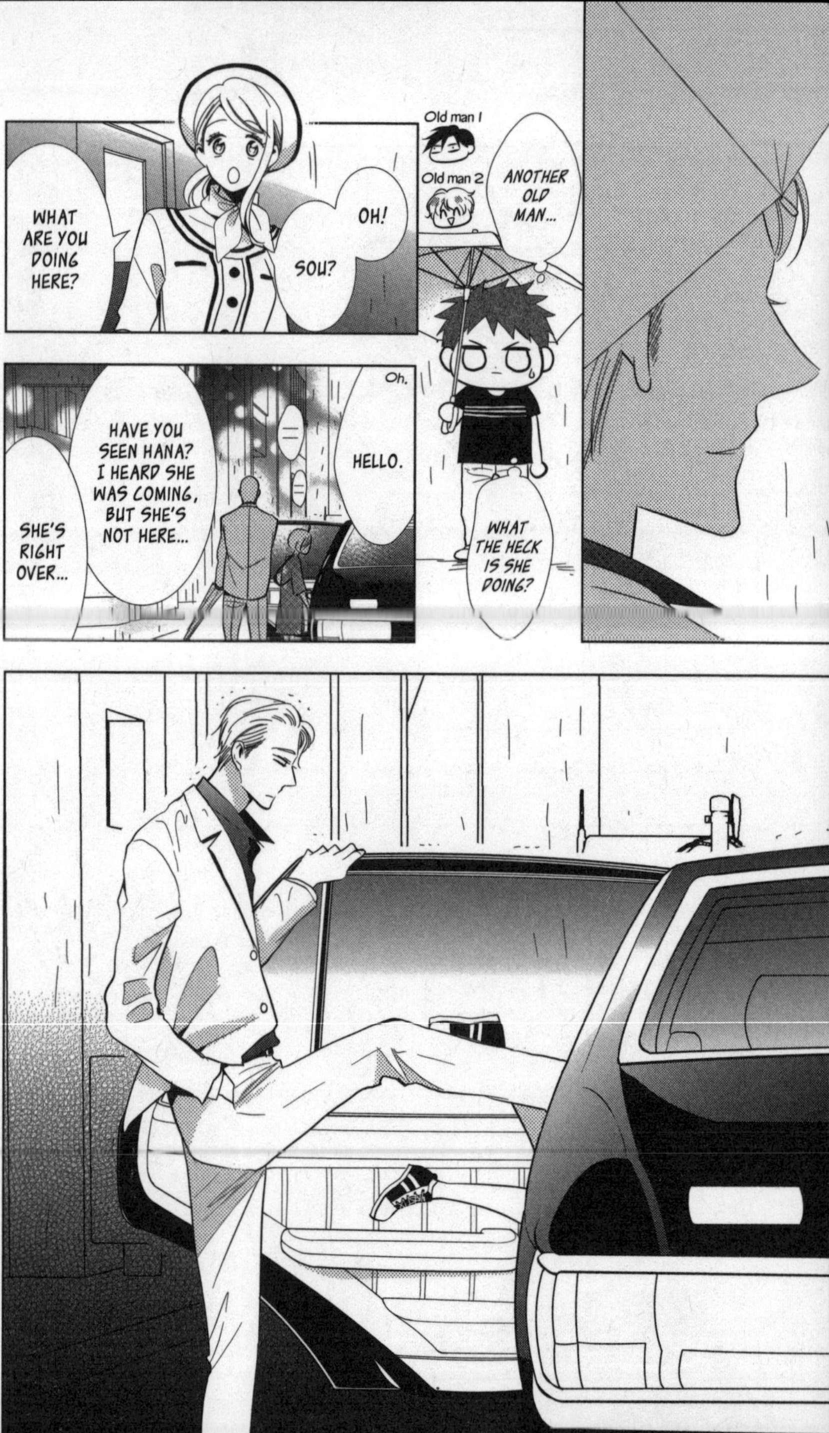
Old man 1
Old man 2
ANOTHER OLD MAN...
WHAT THE HECK IS SHE DOING?
OH!
SOU?
WHAT ARE YOU DOING HERE?
Oh.
HELLO.
HAVE YOU SEEN HANA? I HEARD SHE WAS COMING, BUT SHE'S NOT HERE...
SHE'S RIGHT OVER...

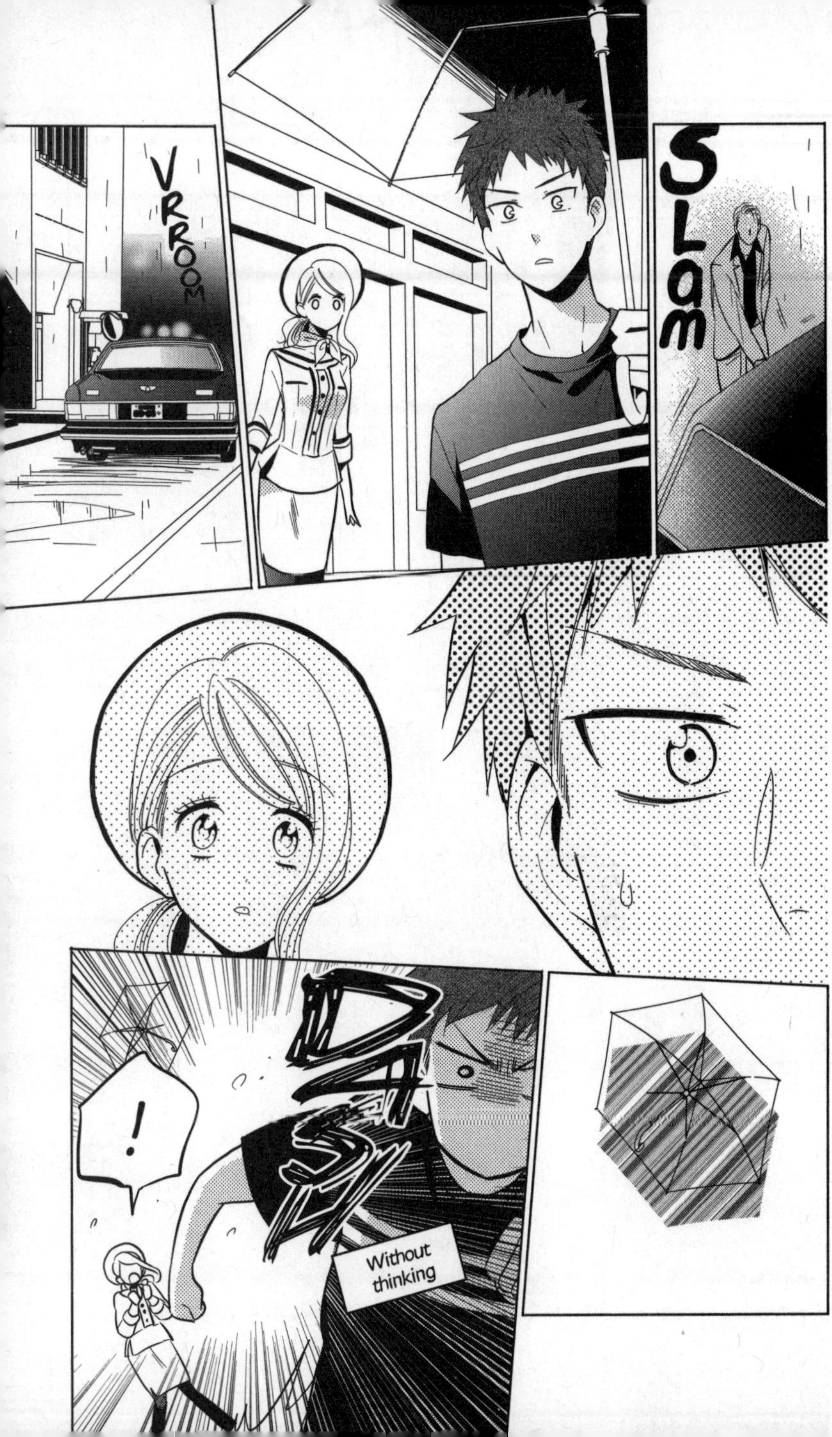
SLAM
VRROOM
DASH
!
Without thinking

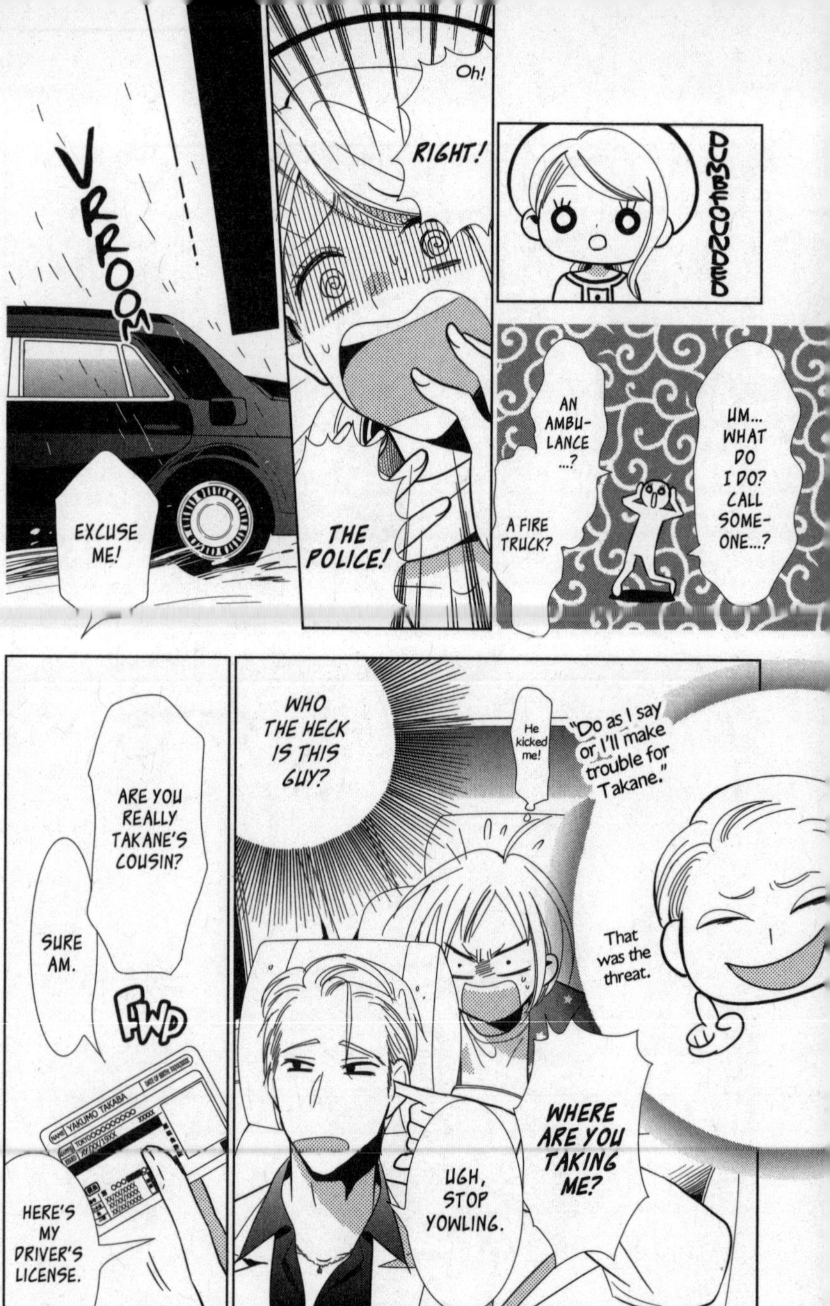
DUMBFOUNDED
UM... WHAT DO I DO? CALL SOME-ONE...?
AN AMBU-LANCE ...?
A FIRE TRUCK?
Oh!
RIGHT!
THE POLICE!
VRROOM
EXCUSE ME!
"Do as I say or I'll make trouble for Takane."
He kicked me!
WHO THE HECK IS THIS GUY?
That was the threat.
WHERE ARE YOU TAKING ME?
UGH, STOP YOWLING.
ARE YOU REALLY TAKANE'S COUSIN?
SURE AM.
FWP
HERE'S MY DRIVER'S LICENSE.

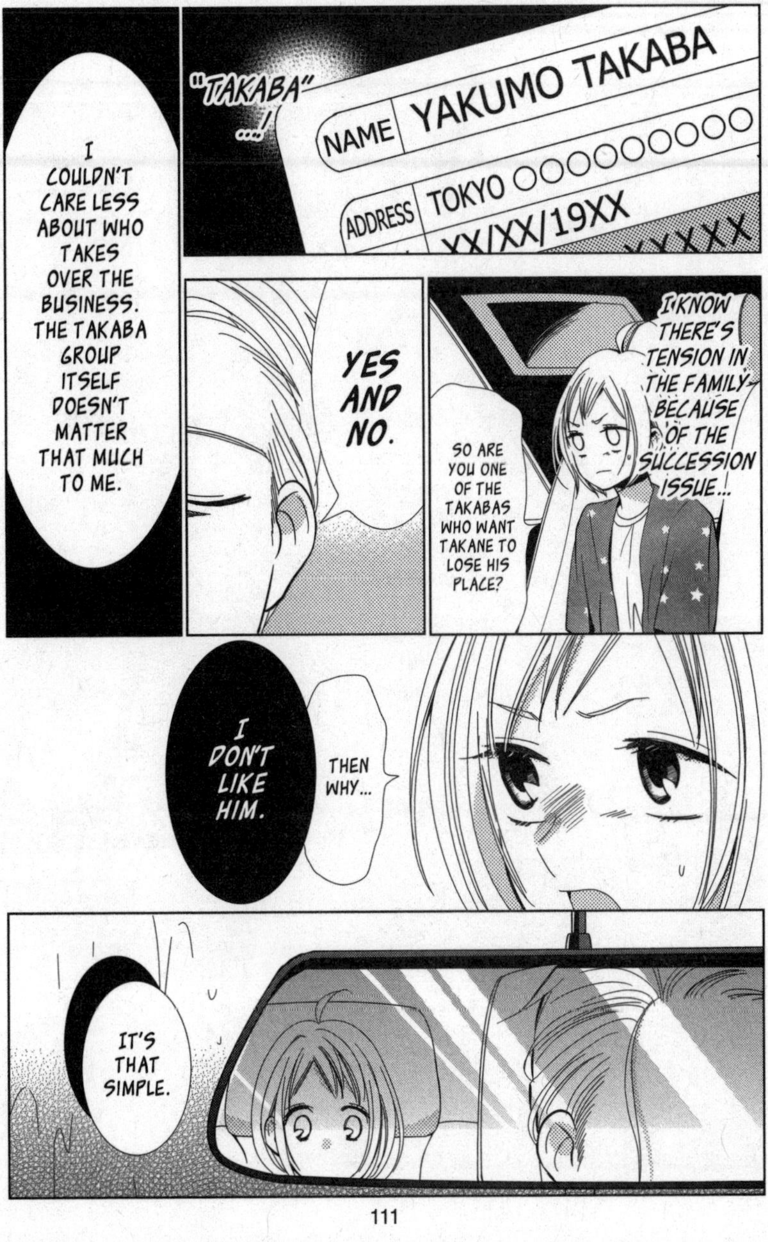
YAKUMO TAKABA
NAME
TOKYO ○○○○○○○○○○
ADDRESS
XX/XX/19XX
XXXXX
"TAKABA" ...!
I COULDN'T CARE LESS ABOUT WHO TAKES OVER THE BUSINESS. THE TAKABA GROUP ITSELF DOESN'T MATTER THAT MUCH TO ME.
I KNOW THERE'S TENSION IN THE FAMILY BECAUSE OF THE SUCCESSION ISSUE...
SO ARE YOU ONE OF THE TAKABAS WHO WANT TAKANE TO LOSE HIS PLACE?
YES AND NO.
THEN WHY...
I DON'T LIKE HIM.
IT'S THAT SIMPLE.

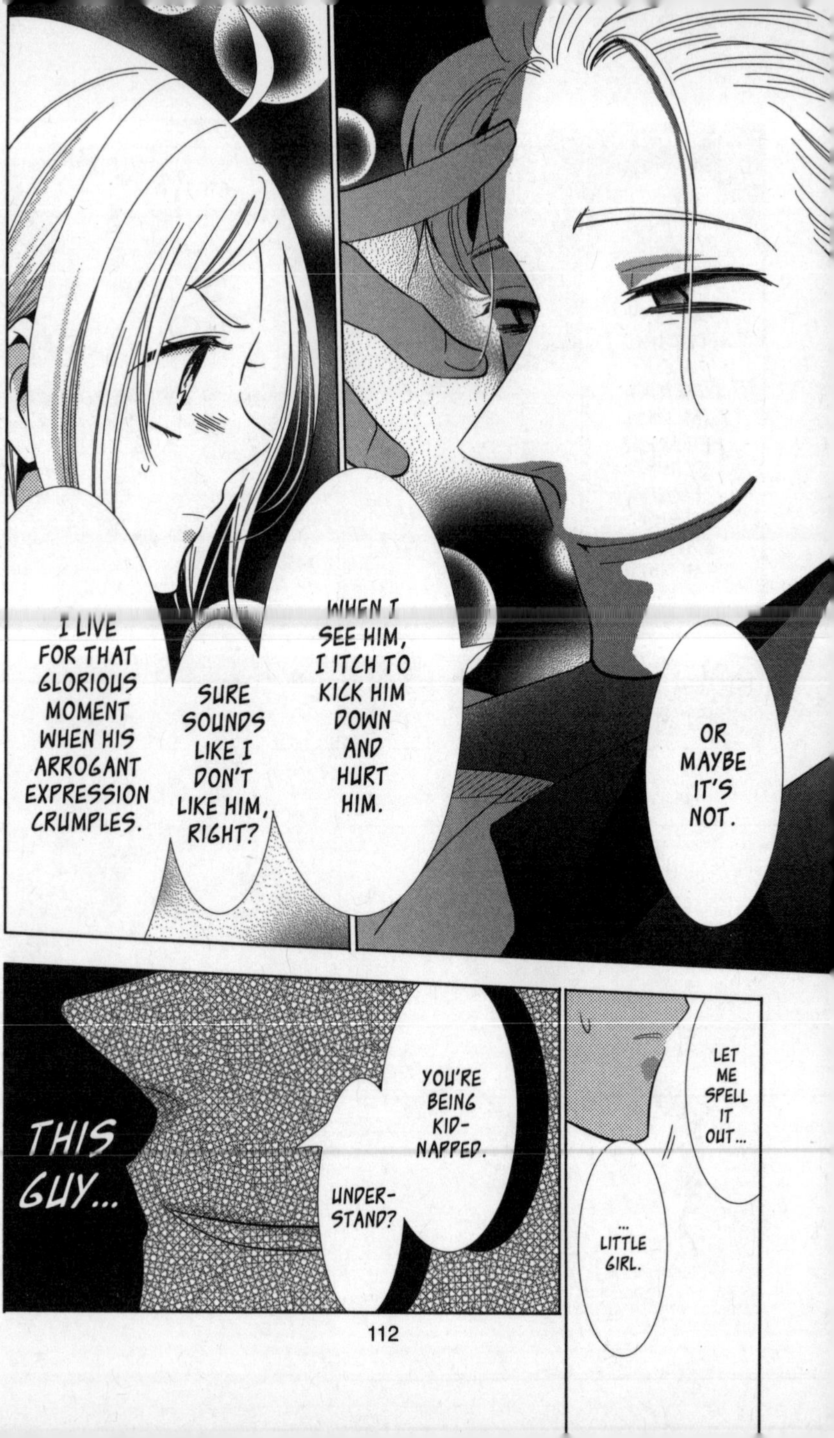
WHEN I SEE HIM, I ITCH TO KICK HIM DOWN AND HURT HIM.
SURE SOUNDS LIKE I DON'T LIKE HIM, RIGHT?
I LIVE FOR THAT GLORIOUS MOMENT WHEN HIS ARROGANT EXPRESSION CRUMPLES.
OR MAYBE IT'S NOT.
LET ME SPELL IT OUT...
...LITTLE GIRL.
YOU'RE BEING KID-NAPPED.
UNDER-STAND?
THIS GUY...

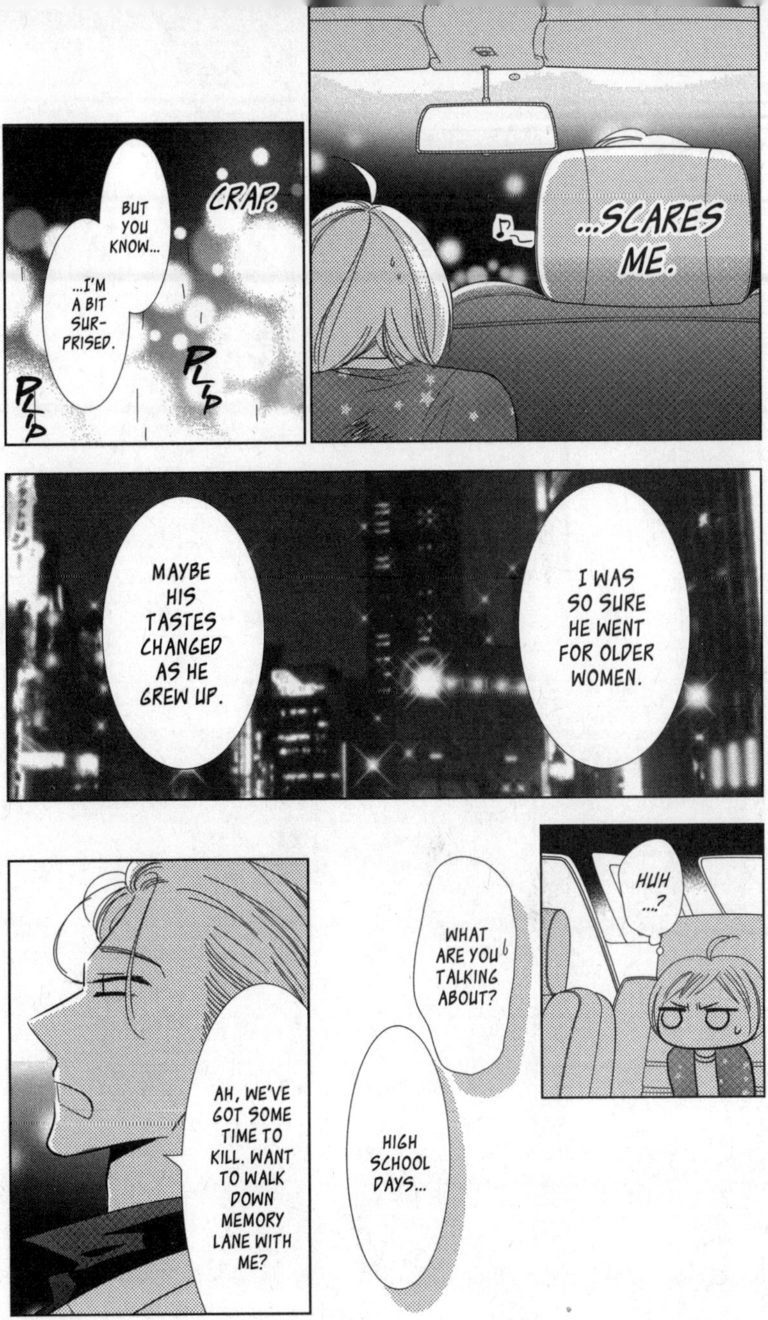
...SCARES ME.
CRAP.
BUT YOU KNOW...
...I'M A BIT SUR-PRISED.
PLIP
PLIP
I WAS SO SURE HE WENT FOR OLDER WOMEN.
MAYBE HIS TASTES CHANGED AS HE GREW UP.
HUH ...?
WHAT ARE YOU TALKING ABOUT?
HIGH SCHOOL DAYS...
AH, WE'VE GOT SOME TIME TO KILL. WANT TO WALK DOWN MEMORY LANE WITH ME?

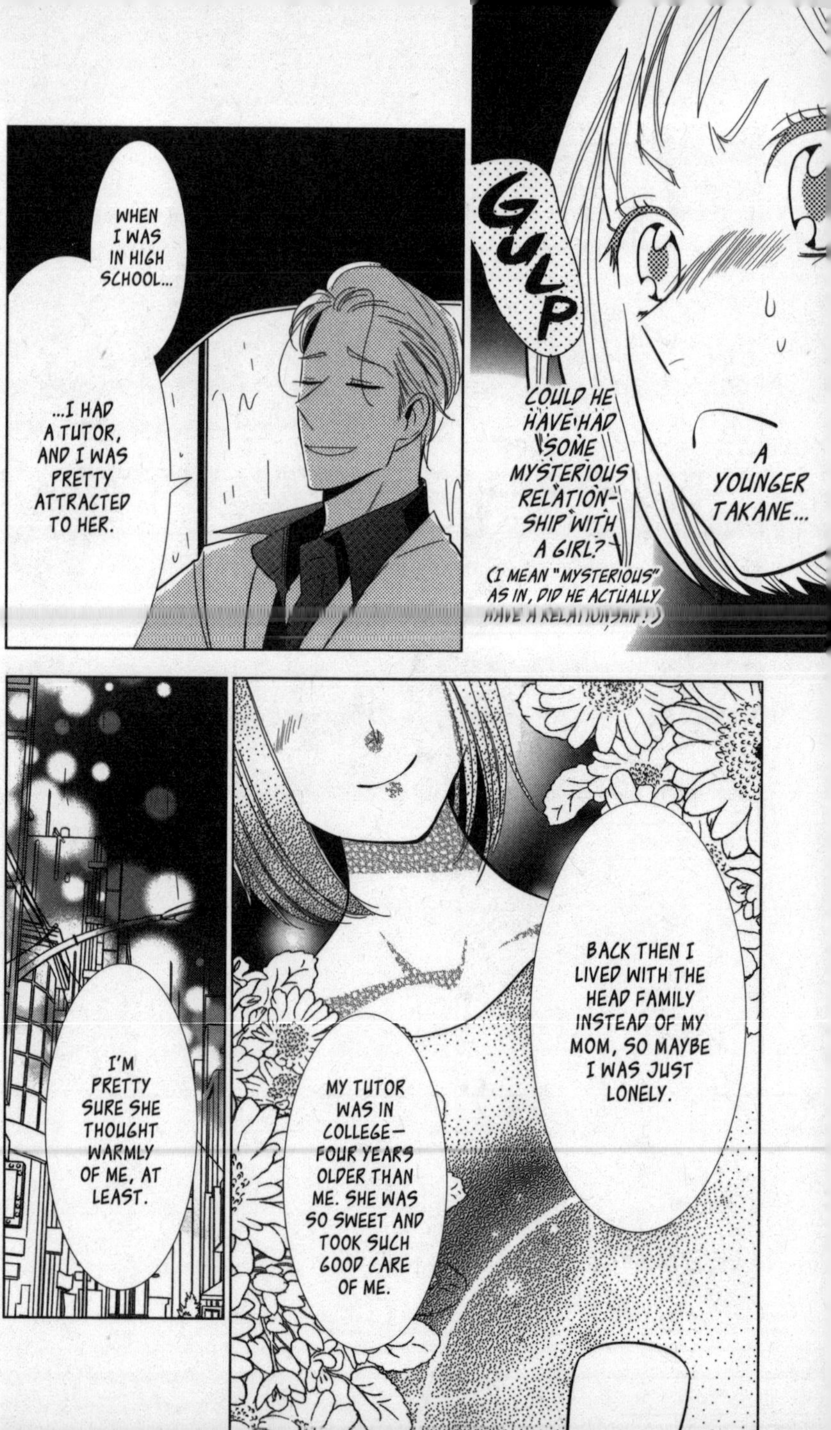
GULP
A YOUNGER TAKANE...
COULD HE HAVE HAD SOME MYSTERIOUS RELATIONSHIP WITH A GIRL?
(I MEAN "MYSTERIOUS" AS IN, DID HE ACTUALLY HAVE A RELATIONSHIP!)
WHEN I WAS IN HIGH SCHOOL...
...I HAD A TUTOR, AND I WAS PRETTY ATTRACTED TO HER.
BACK THEN I LIVED WITH THE HEAD FAMILY INSTEAD OF MY MOM, SO MAYBE I WAS JUST LONELY.
MY TUTOR WAS IN COLLEGE—FOUR YEARS OLDER THAN ME. SHE WAS SO SWEET AND TOOK SUCH GOOD CARE OF ME.
I'M PRETTY SURE SHE THOUGHT WARMLY OF ME, AT LEAST.

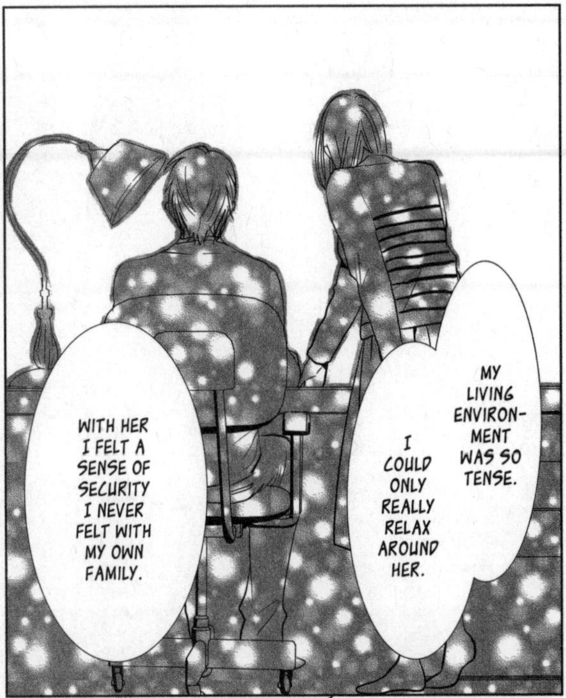
MY LIVING ENVIRONMENT WAS SO TENSE.
I COULD ONLY REALLY RELAX AROUND HER.
WITH HER I FELT A SENSE OF SECURITY I NEVER FELT WITH MY OWN FAMILY.

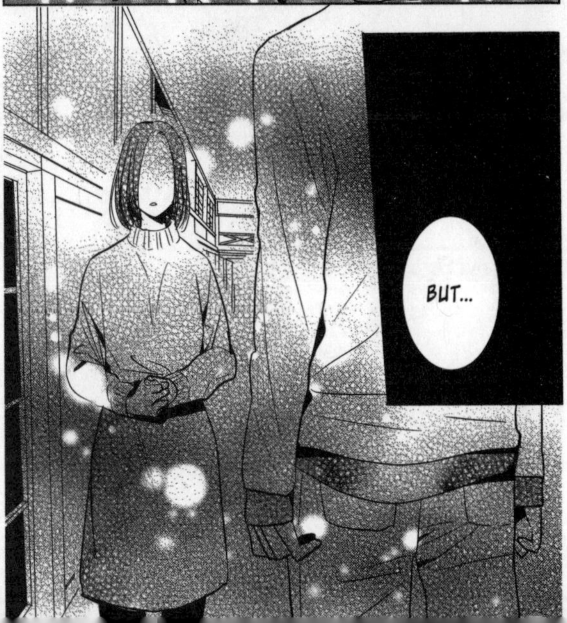
BUT...

Chapter 11
(in volume 3)

1 + 1 = Double the charm

But don't forget, it's double the trouble too!

Text on an illustration of Takane and Nicola together.

Chapter 18
(in volume 4)

It's not that I don't need them. I just don't want them going to waste.

The illustration was of Hana sharing her roses with Okamon.

That's right. She just doesn't want to waste them.

Chapter 22
(in volume 5)

So you can't believe what I say? In that case, trust in your charm.

Featured an extreme close-up of Nicola.
It's a classic Nicola line, and a great one at that! Don't think "I'm not good enough" or "I just can't."

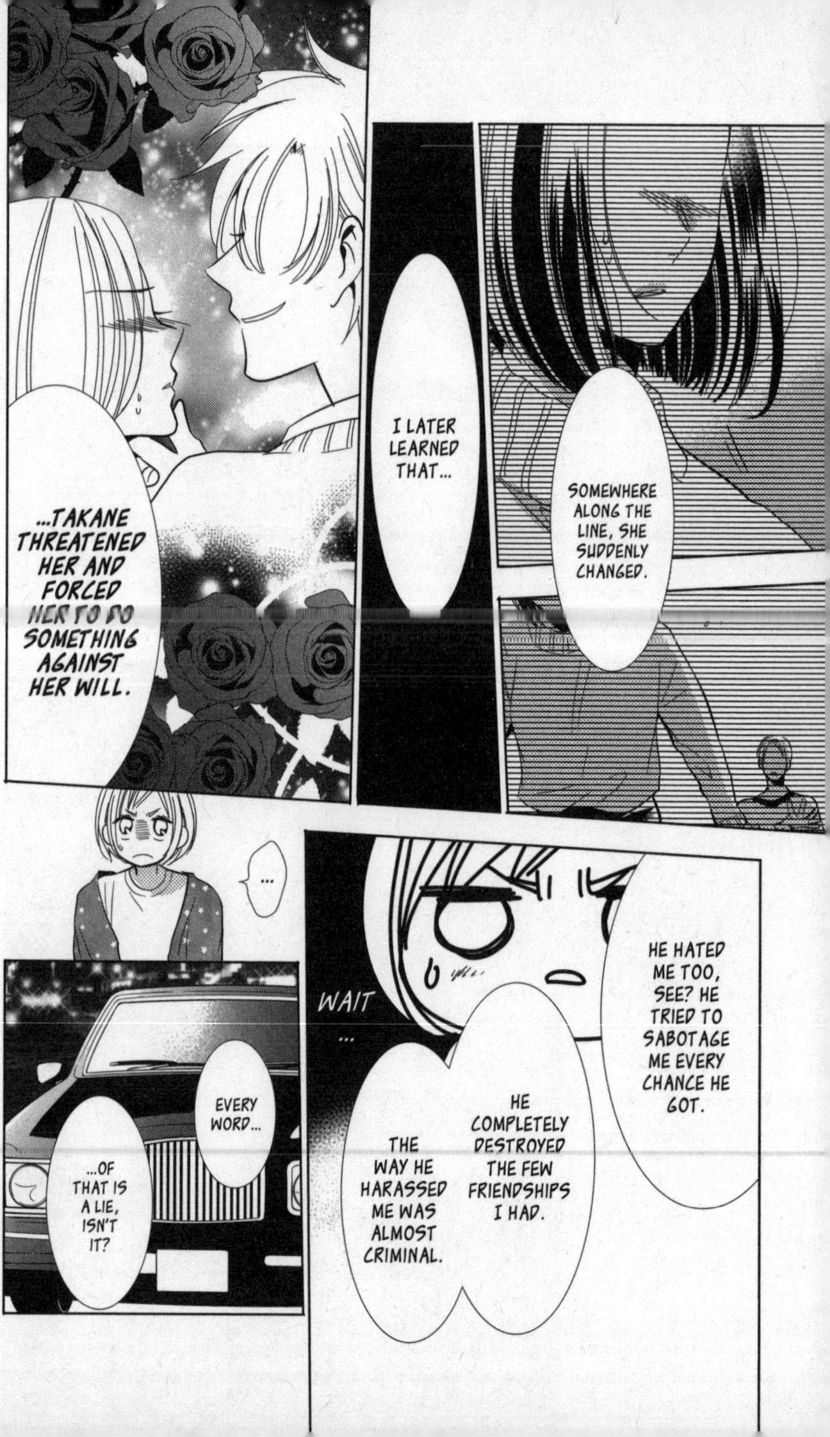
SOMEWHERE ALONG THE LINE, SHE SUDDENLY CHANGED.
I LATER LEARNED THAT...
...TAKANE THREATENED HER AND FORCED HER TO DO SOMETHING AGAINST HER WILL.
HE HATED ME TOO, SEE? HE TRIED TO SABOTAGE ME EVERY CHANCE HE GOT.
HE COMPLETELY DESTROYED THE FEW FRIENDSHIPS I HAD.
THE WAY HE HARASSED ME WAS ALMOST CRIMINAL.
WAIT...
...
EVERY WORD...
...OF THAT IS A LIE, ISN'T IT?

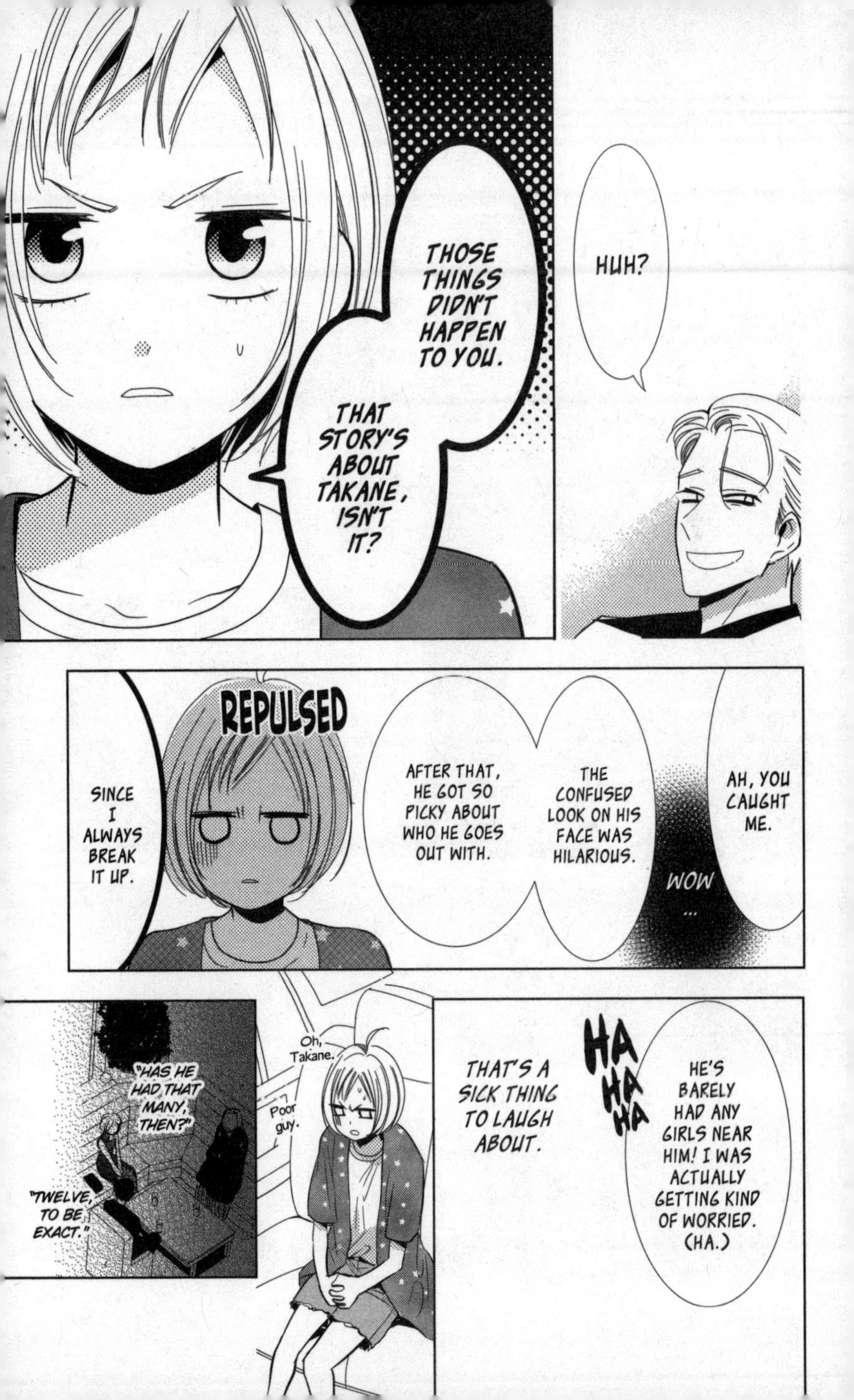
HUH?
THOSE THINGS DIDN'T HAPPEN TO YOU.
THAT STORY'S ABOUT TAKANE, ISN'T IT?
AH, YOU CAUGHT ME.
WOW...
THE CONFUSED LOOK ON HIS FACE WAS HILARIOUS.
AFTER THAT, HE GOT SO PICKY ABOUT WHO HE GOES OUT WITH.
REPULSED
SINCE I ALWAYS BREAK IT UP.
HE'S BARELY HAD ANY GIRLS NEAR HIM! I WAS ACTUALLY GETTING KIND OF WORRIED. (HA.)
HA HA HA
THAT'S A SICK THING TO LAUGH ABOUT.
Oh, Takane.
Poor guy.
"HAS HE HAD THAT MANY, THEN?"
"TWELVE, TO BE EXACT."

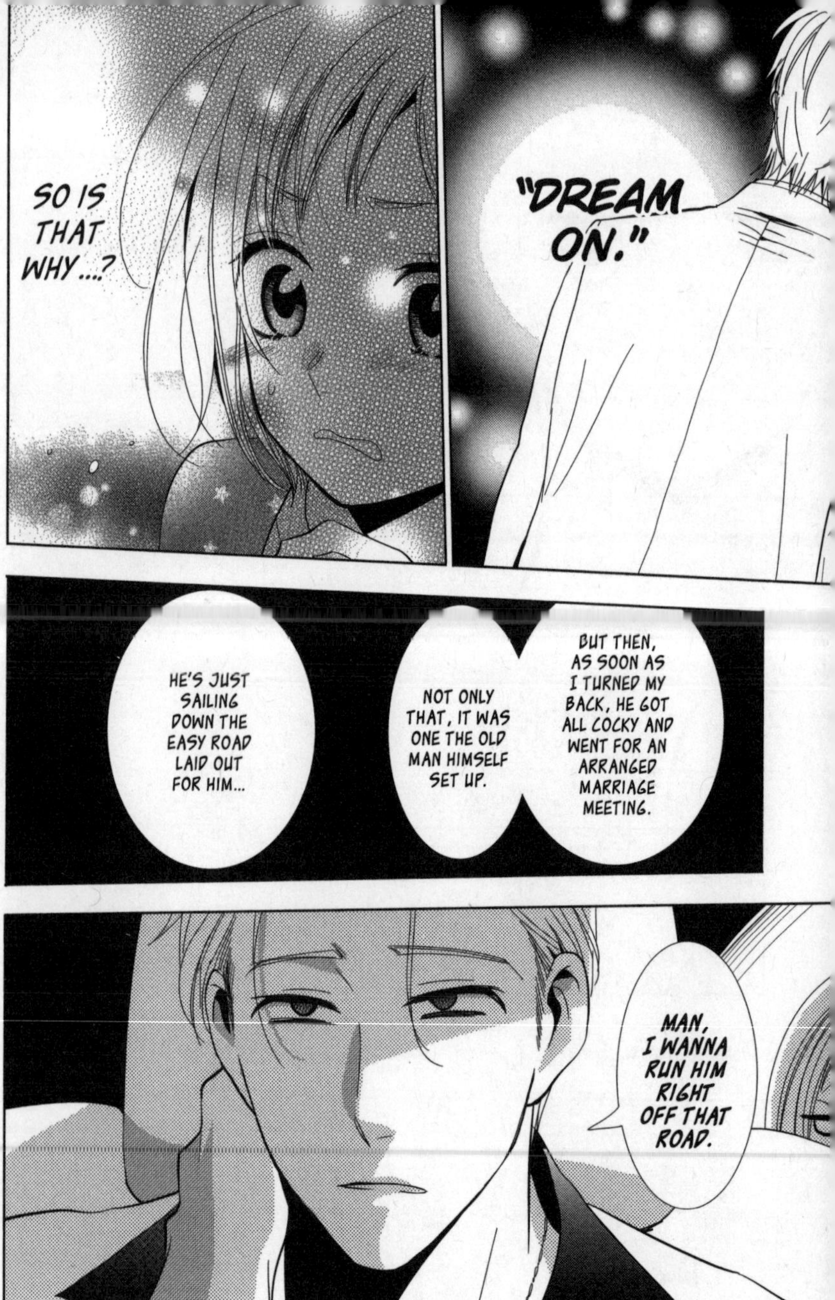
"DREAM ON."
SO IS THAT WHY...?
BUT THEN, AS SOON AS I TURNED MY BACK, HE GOT ALL COCKY AND WENT FOR AN ARRANGED MARRIAGE MEETING.
NOT ONLY THAT, IT WAS ONE THE OLD MAN HIMSELF SET UP.
HE'S JUST SAILING DOWN THE EASY ROAD LAID OUT FOR HIM...
MAN, I WANNA RUN HIM RIGHT OFF THAT ROAD.

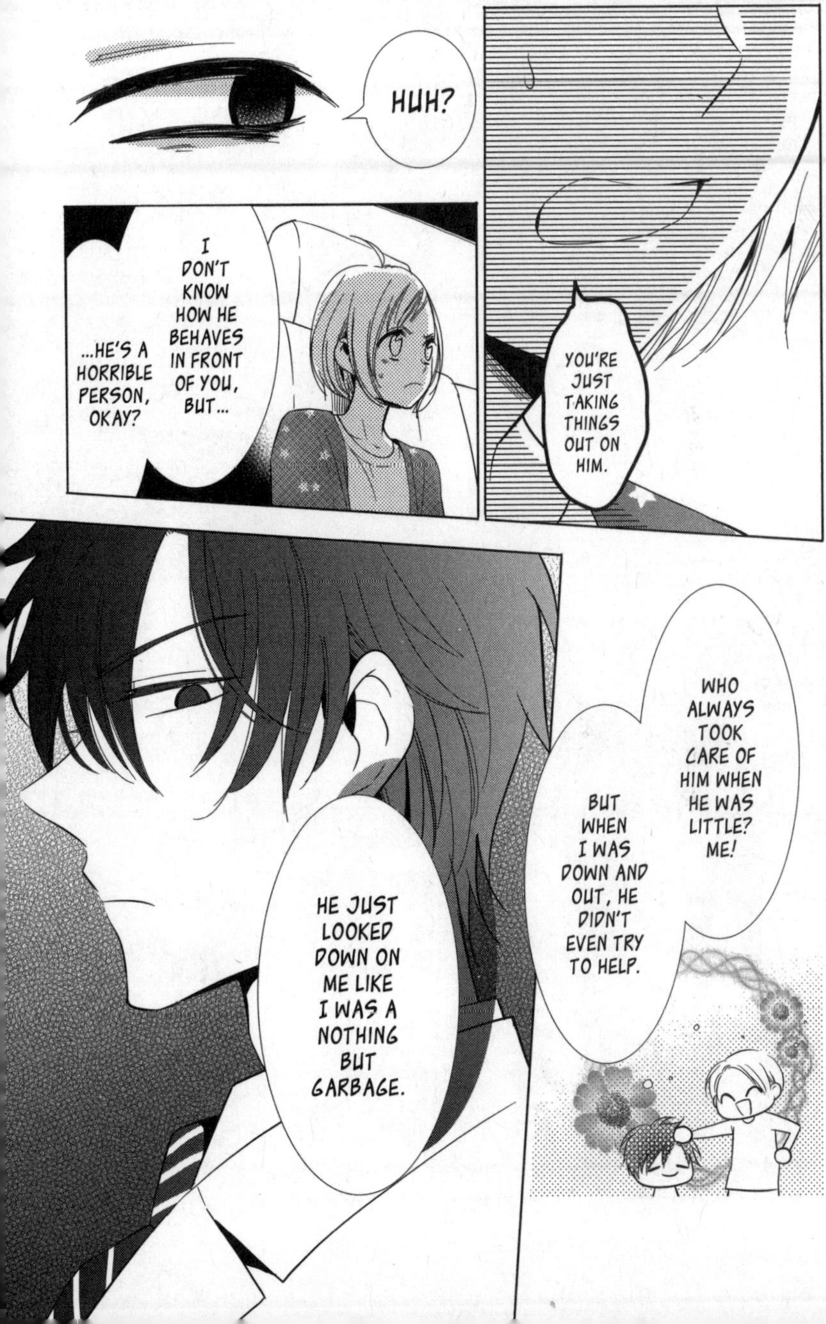
YOU'RE JUST TAKING THINGS OUT ON HIM.
HUH?
I DON'T KNOW HOW HE BEHAVES IN FRONT OF YOU, BUT...
...HE'S A HORRIBLE PERSON, OKAY?
WHO ALWAYS TOOK CARE OF HIM WHEN HE WAS LITTLE? ME!
BUT WHEN I WAS DOWN AND OUT, HE DIDN'T EVEN TRY TO HELP.
HE JUST LOOKED DOWN ON ME LIKE I WAS A NOTHING BUT GARBAGE.

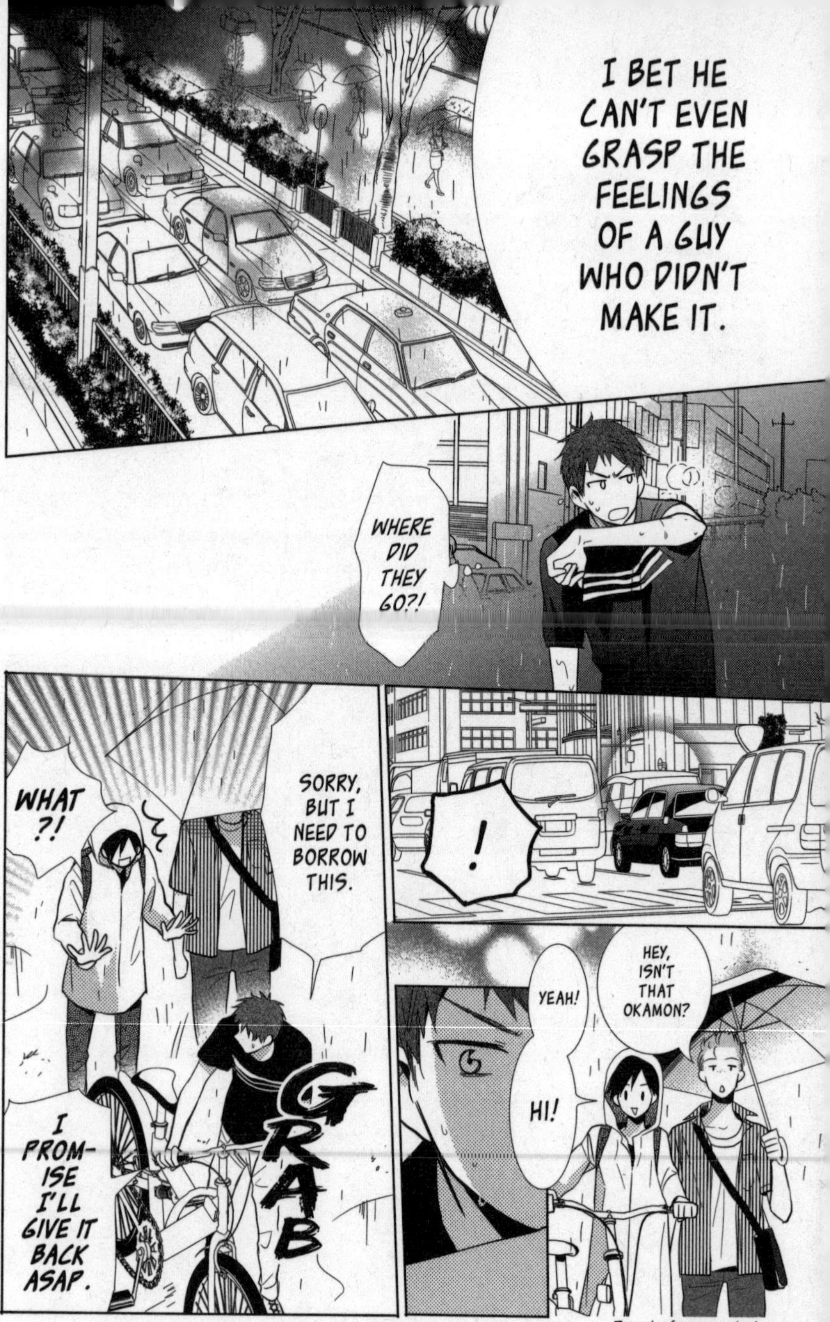
I BET HE CAN'T EVEN GRASP THE FEELINGS OF A GUY WHO DIDN'T MAKE IT.
WHERE DID THEY GO?!
!
HEY, ISN'T THAT OKAMON?
YEAH!
HI!
SORRY, BUT I NEED TO BORROW THIS.
WHAT?!
GRAB
I PROMISE I'LL GIVE IT BACK ASAP.
Returning from cram school

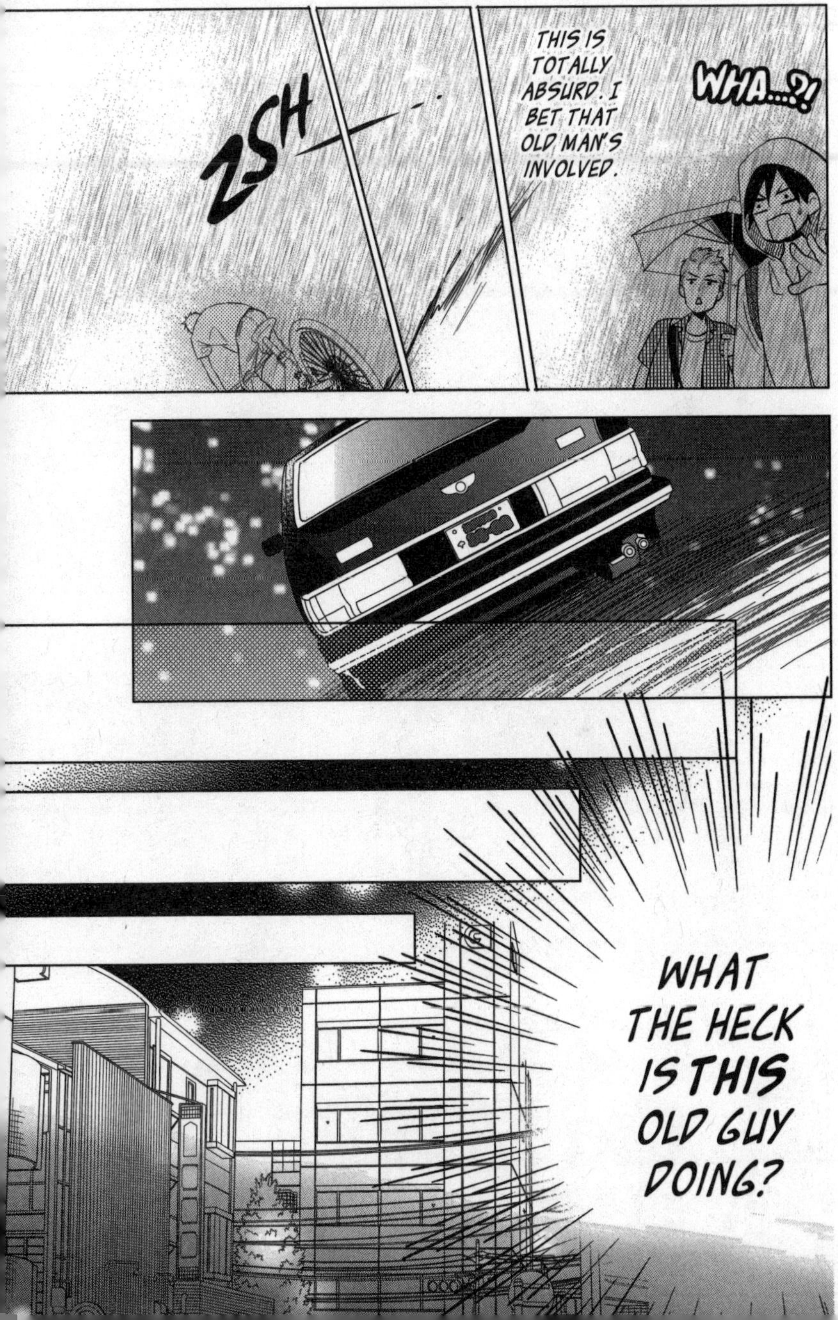
WHA...?!
THIS IS TOTALLY ABSURD. I BET THAT OLD MAN'S INVOLVED.
ZSH
WHAT THE HECK IS THIS OLD GUY DOING?

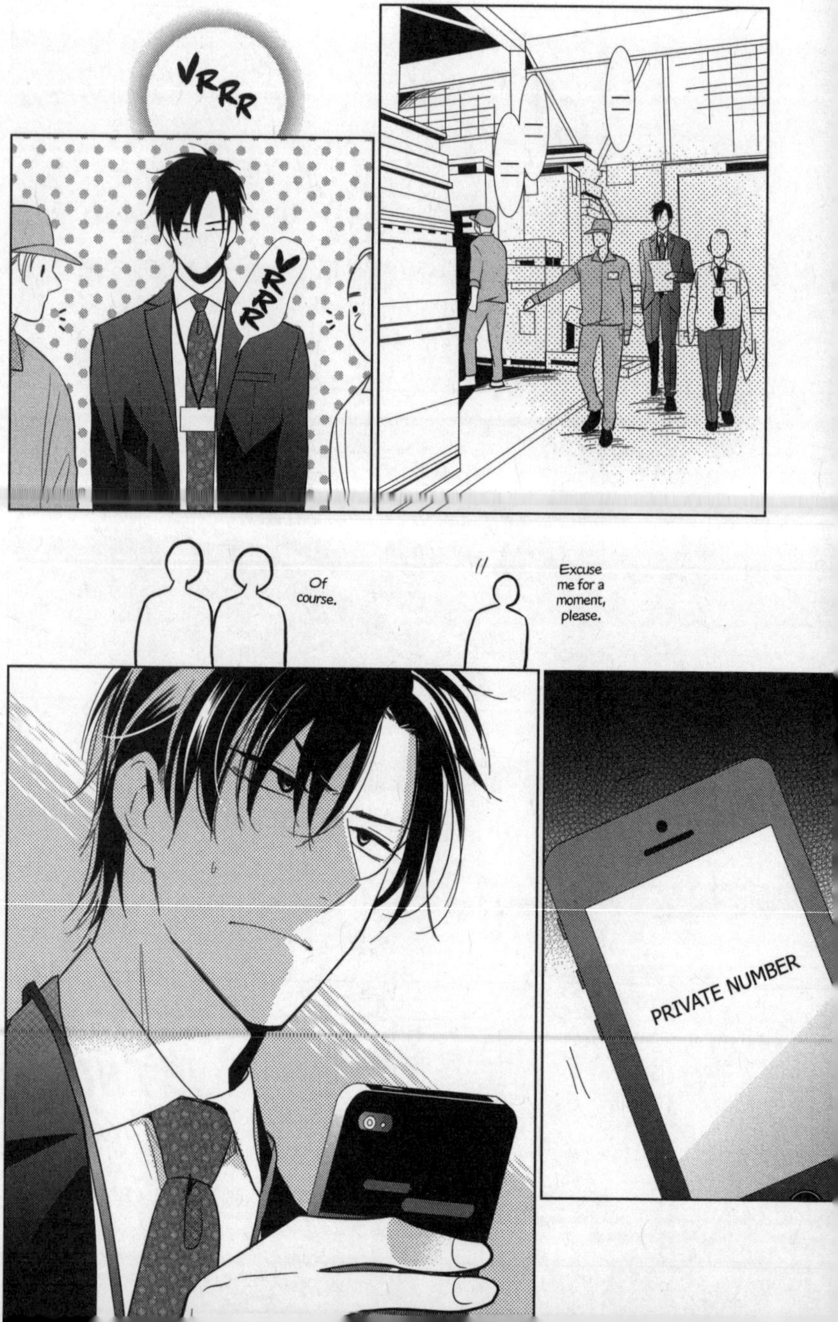
VRRR
VRRR
Excuse me for a moment, please.
Of course.
PRIVATE NUMBER

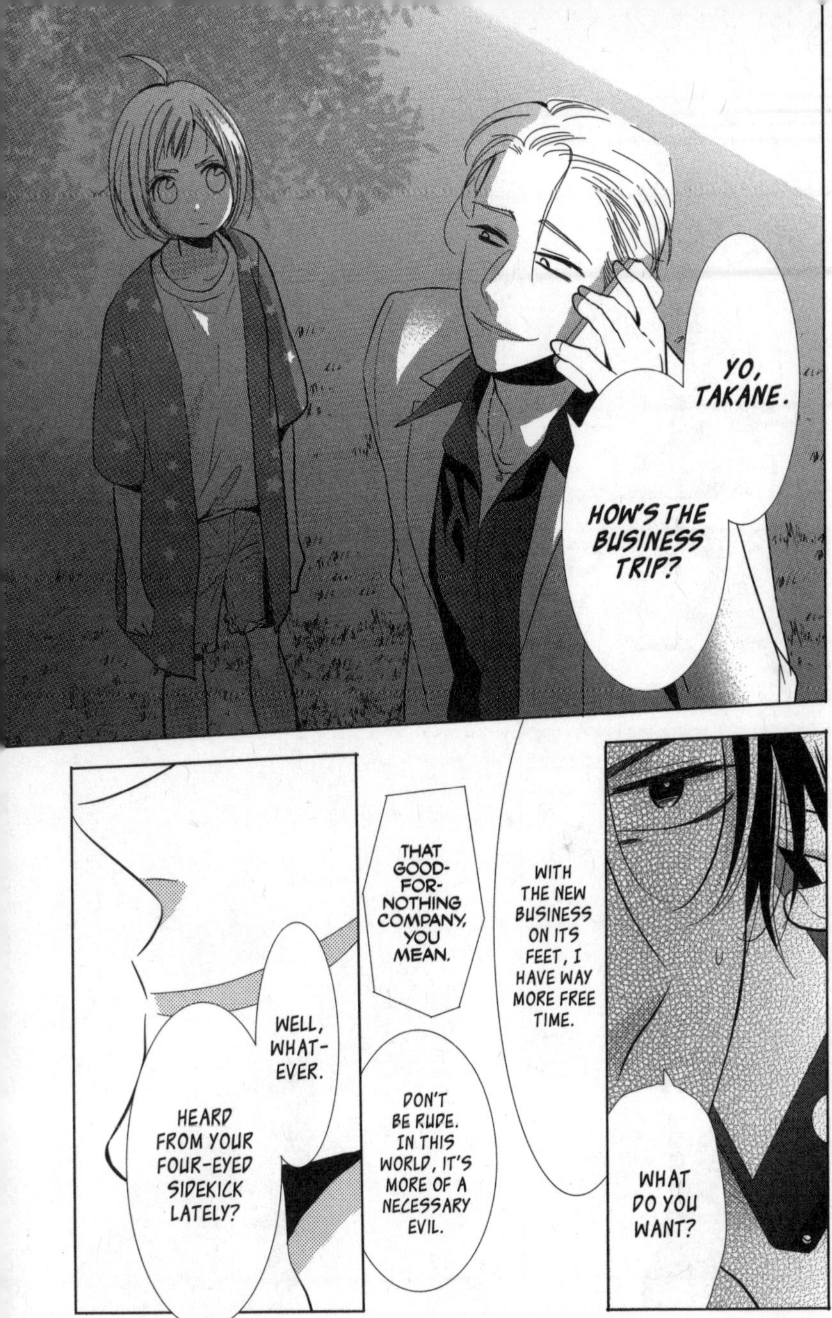
YO, TAKANE.
HOW'S THE BUSINESS TRIP?
WHAT DO YOU WANT?
WITH THE NEW BUSINESS ON ITS FEET, I HAVE WAY MORE FREE TIME.
THAT GOOD-FOR-NOTHING COMPANY, YOU MEAN.
DON'T BE RUDE. IN THIS WORLD, IT'S MORE OF A NECESSARY EVIL.
WELL, WHATEVER.
HEARD FROM YOUR FOUR-EYED SIDEKICK LATELY?

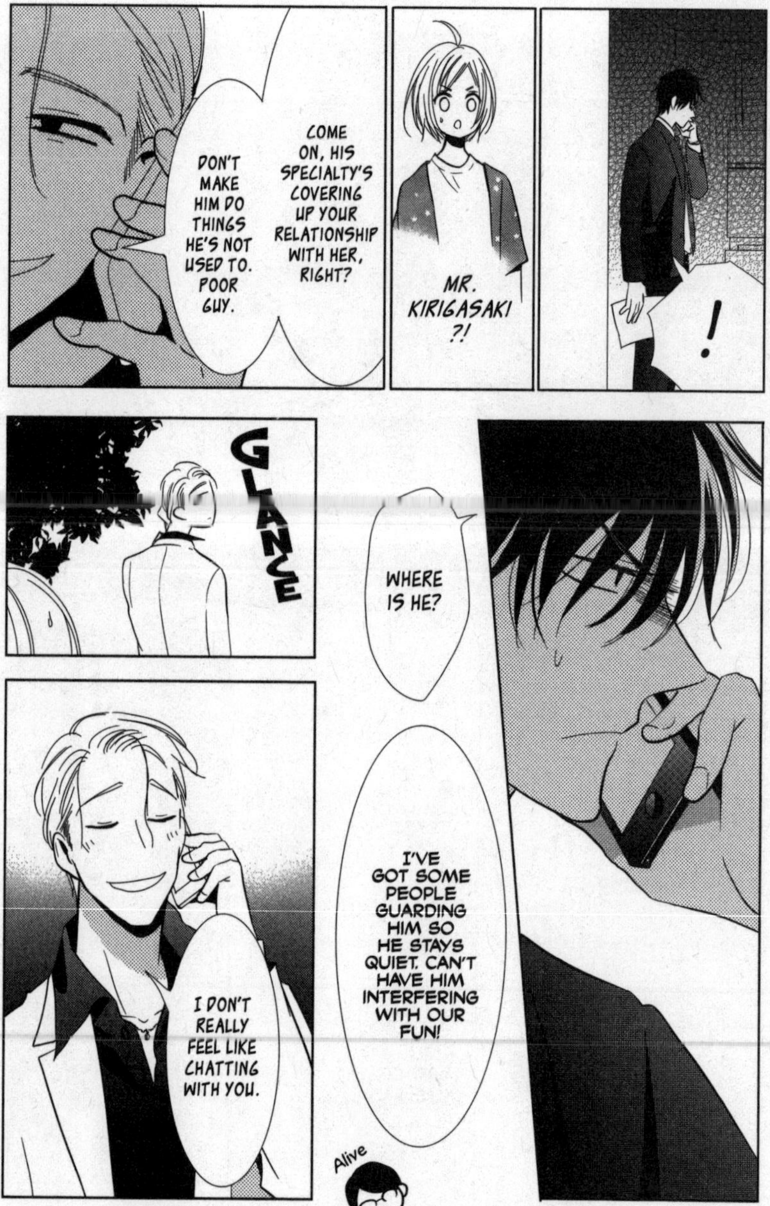
!
MR. KIRIGASAKI ?!
COME ON, HIS SPECIALTY'S COVERING UP YOUR RELATIONSHIP WITH HER, RIGHT?
DON'T MAKE HIM DO THINGS HE'S NOT USED TO. POOR GUY.
WHERE IS HE?
I'VE GOT SOME PEOPLE GUARDING HIM SO HE STAYS QUIET. CAN'T HAVE HIM INTERFERING WITH OUR FUN!
GLANCE
I DON'T REALLY FEEL LIKE CHATTING WITH YOU.
Alive

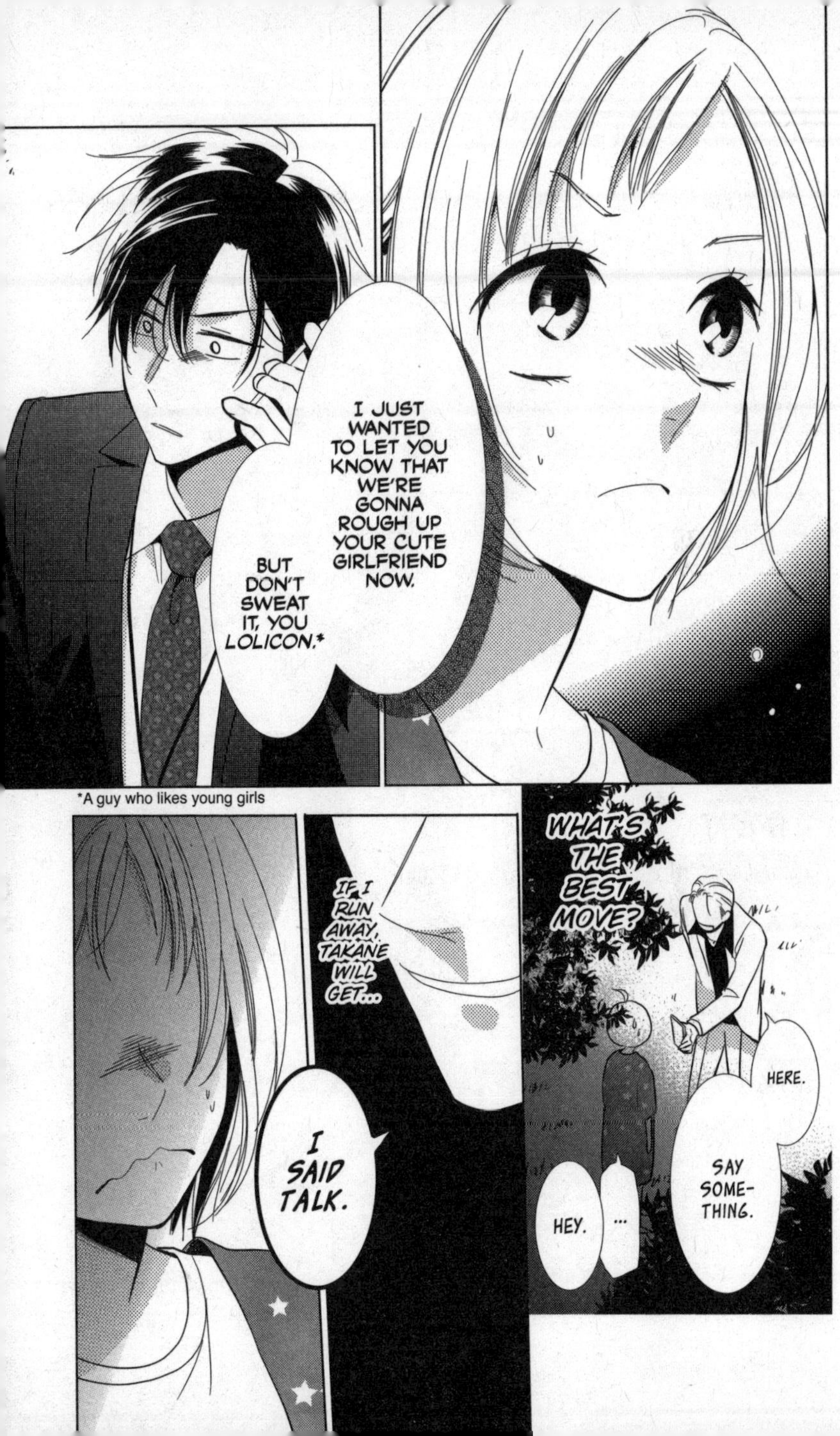
I JUST WANTED TO LET YOU KNOW THAT WE'RE GONNA ROUGH UP YOUR CUTE GIRLFRIEND NOW.
BUT DON'T SWEAT IT, YOU LOLICON.*
WHAT'S THE BEST MOVE?
HERE.
SAY SOME-THING.
...
HEY.
IF I RUN AWAY, TAKANE WILL GET...
I SAID TALK.

*A guy who likes young girls

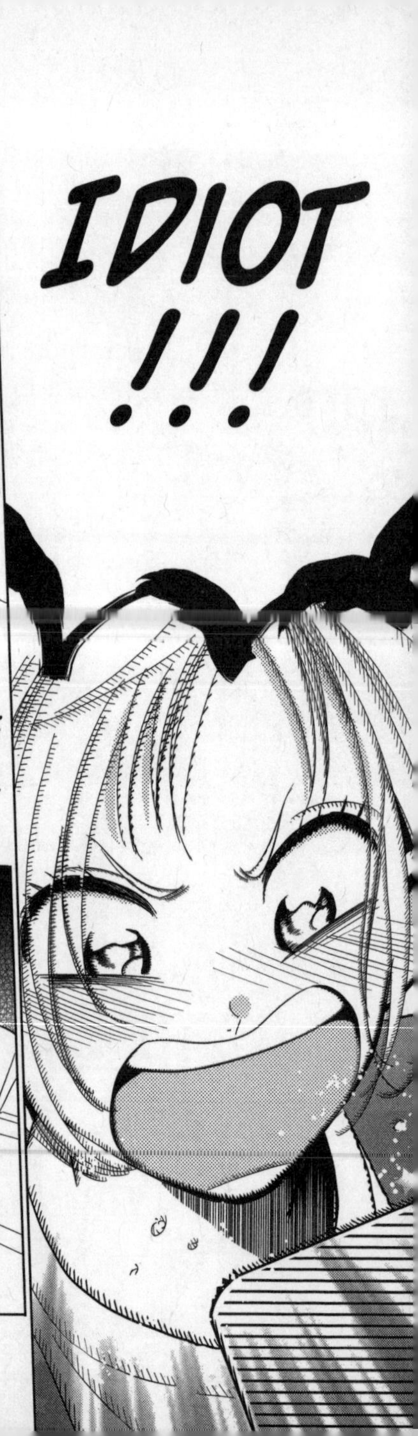
IDIOT !!!

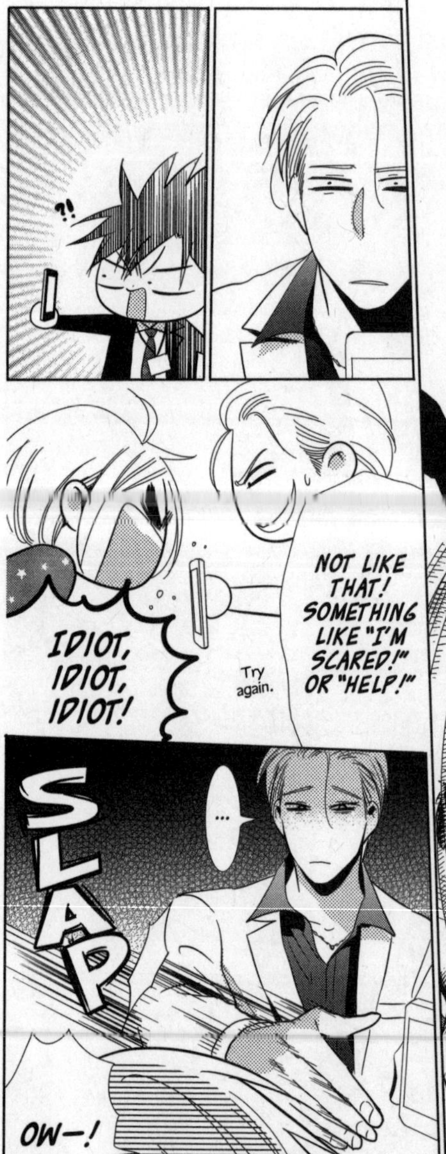
?!
NOT LIKE THAT! SOMETHING LIKE "I'M SCARED!" OR "HELP!"
Try again.
IDIOT, IDIOT, IDIOT!
...
SLAP
OW—!

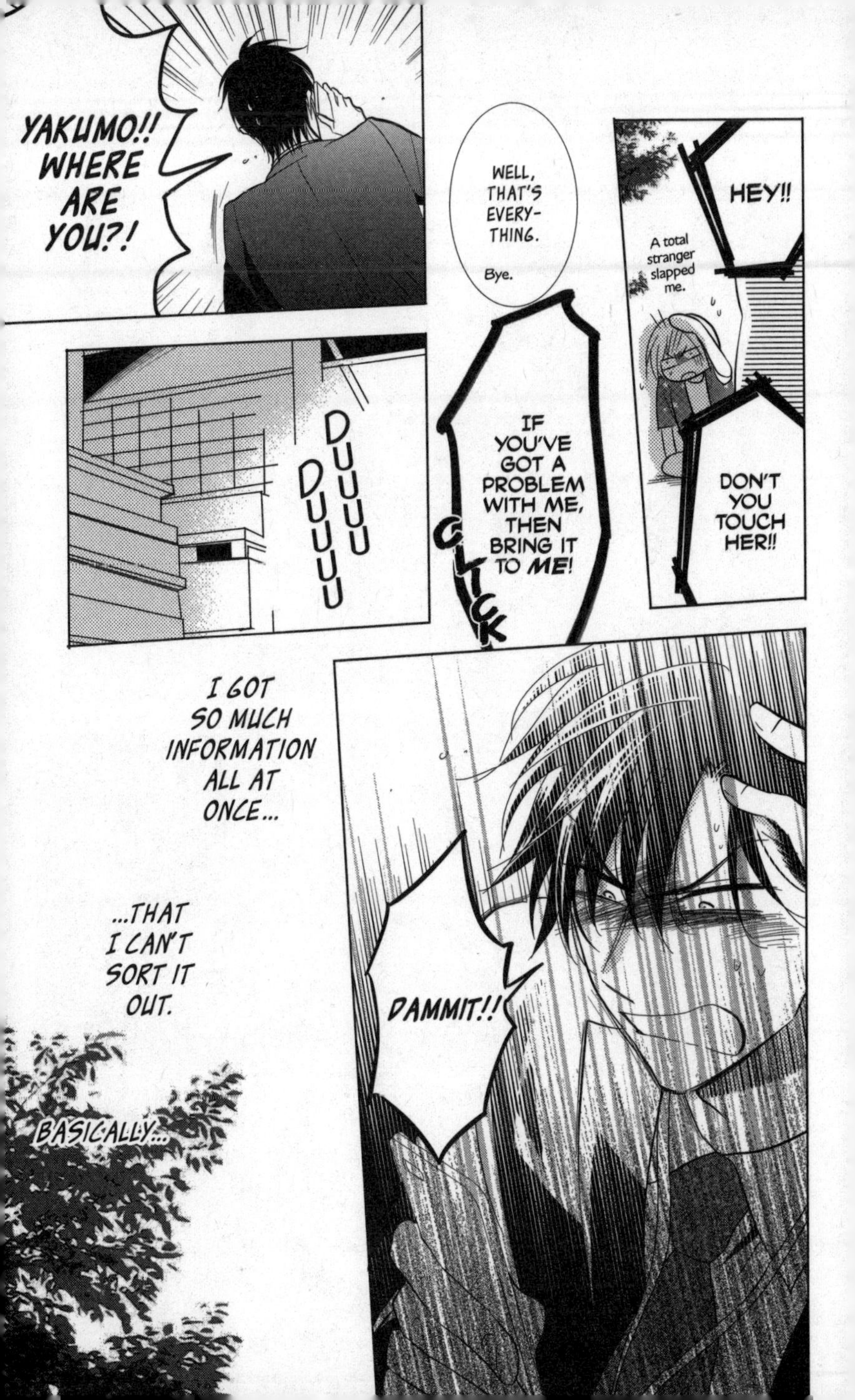

YAKUMO!! WHERE ARE YOU?!
WELL, THAT'S EVERY-THING.
Bye.
CLICK
DUUUU DUUUUU
HEY!!
A total stranger slapped me.
DON'T YOU TOUCH HER!!
IF YOU'VE GOT A PROBLEM WITH ME, THEN BRING IT TO *ME*!
I GOT SO MUCH INFORMATION ALL AT ONCE...
...THAT I CAN'T SORT IT OUT.
DAMMIT!!
BASICALLY...

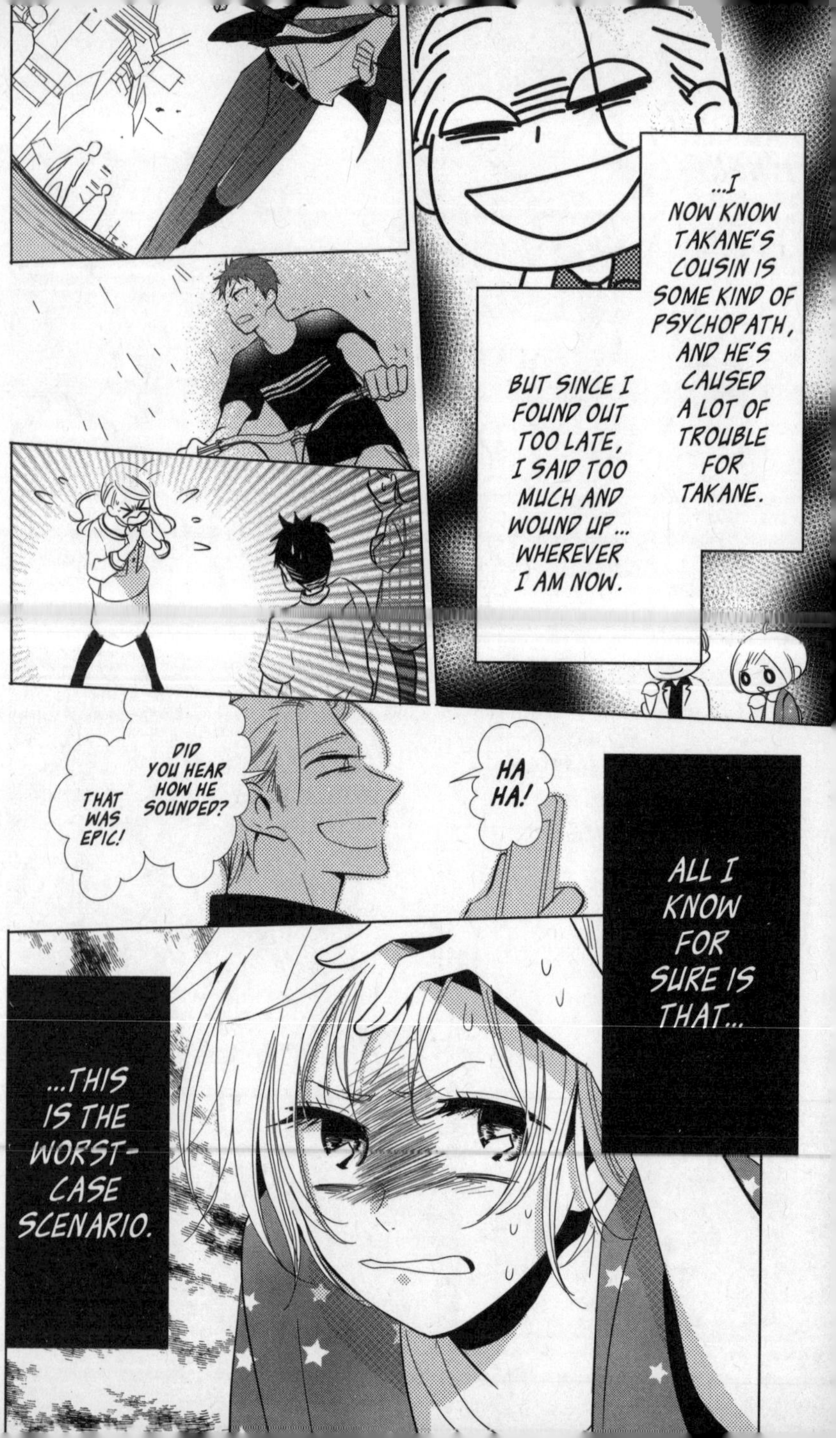
...I NOW KNOW TAKANE'S COUSIN IS SOME KIND OF PSYCHOPATH, AND HE'S CAUSED A LOT OF TROUBLE FOR TAKANE.
BUT SINCE I FOUND OUT TOO LATE, I SAID TOO MUCH AND WOUND UP... WHEREVER I AM NOW.
HA HA!
DID YOU HEAR HOW HE SOUNDED?
THAT WAS EPIC!
ALL I KNOW FOR SURE IS THAT...
...THIS IS THE WORST-CASE SCENARIO.

Chapter 62

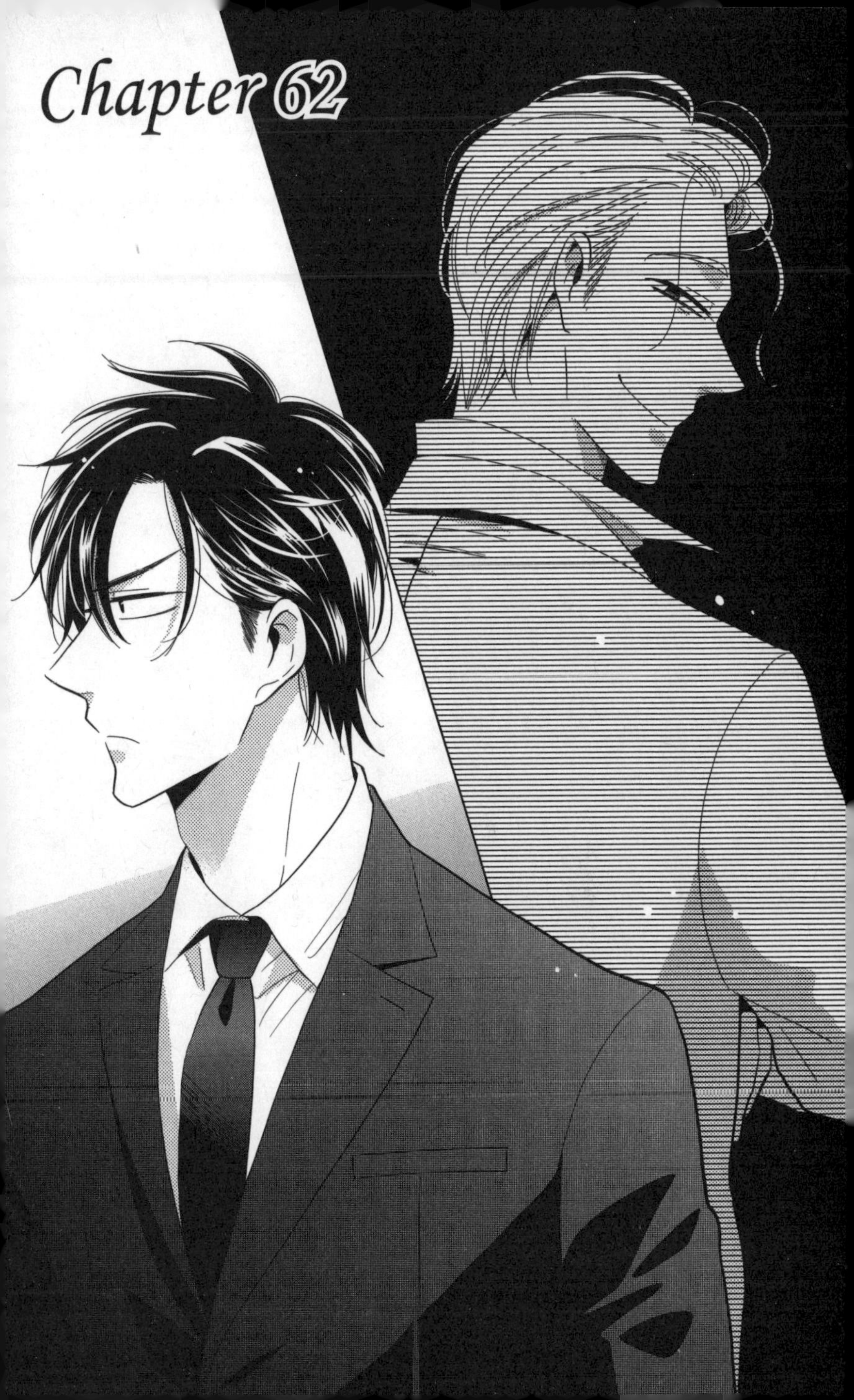

HOW ABOUT YOU AND I HAVE SOME FUN?

ALL RIGHT!

HUH?

HOLD IT RIGHT THERE!

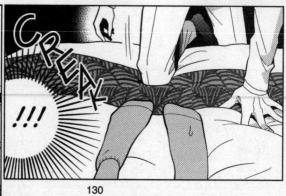

CREAK

!!!

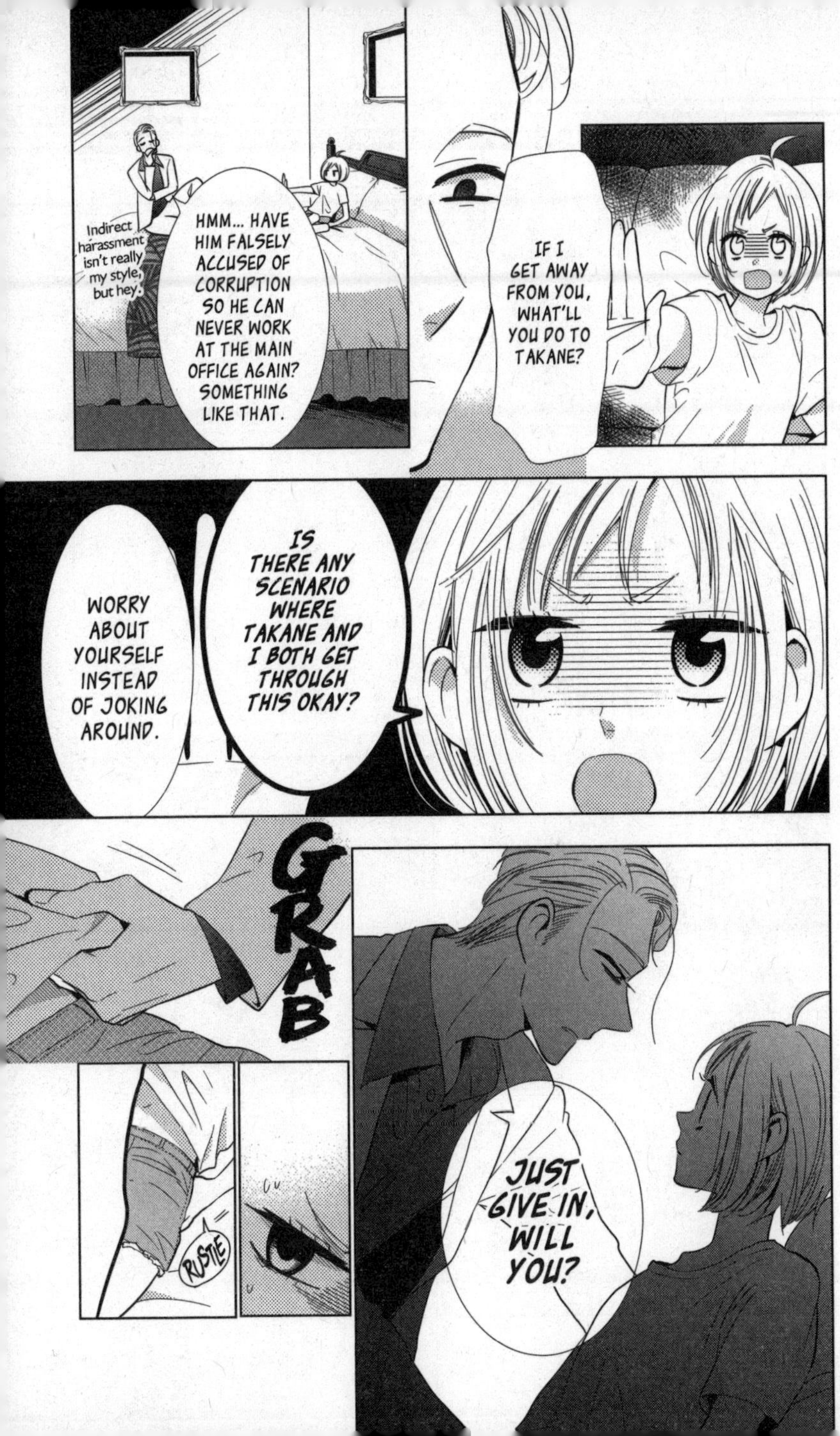
IF I GET AWAY FROM YOU, WHAT'LL YOU DO TO TAKANE?
HMM... HAVE HIM FALSELY ACCUSED OF CORRUPTION SO HE CAN NEVER WORK AT THE MAIN OFFICE AGAIN? SOMETHING LIKE THAT.
Indirect harassment isn't really my style, but hey.
IS THERE ANY SCENARIO WHERE TAKANE AND I BOTH GET THROUGH THIS OKAY?
WORRY ABOUT YOURSELF INSTEAD OF JOKING AROUND.
JUST GIVE IN, WILL YOU?
GRAB
RUSTLE

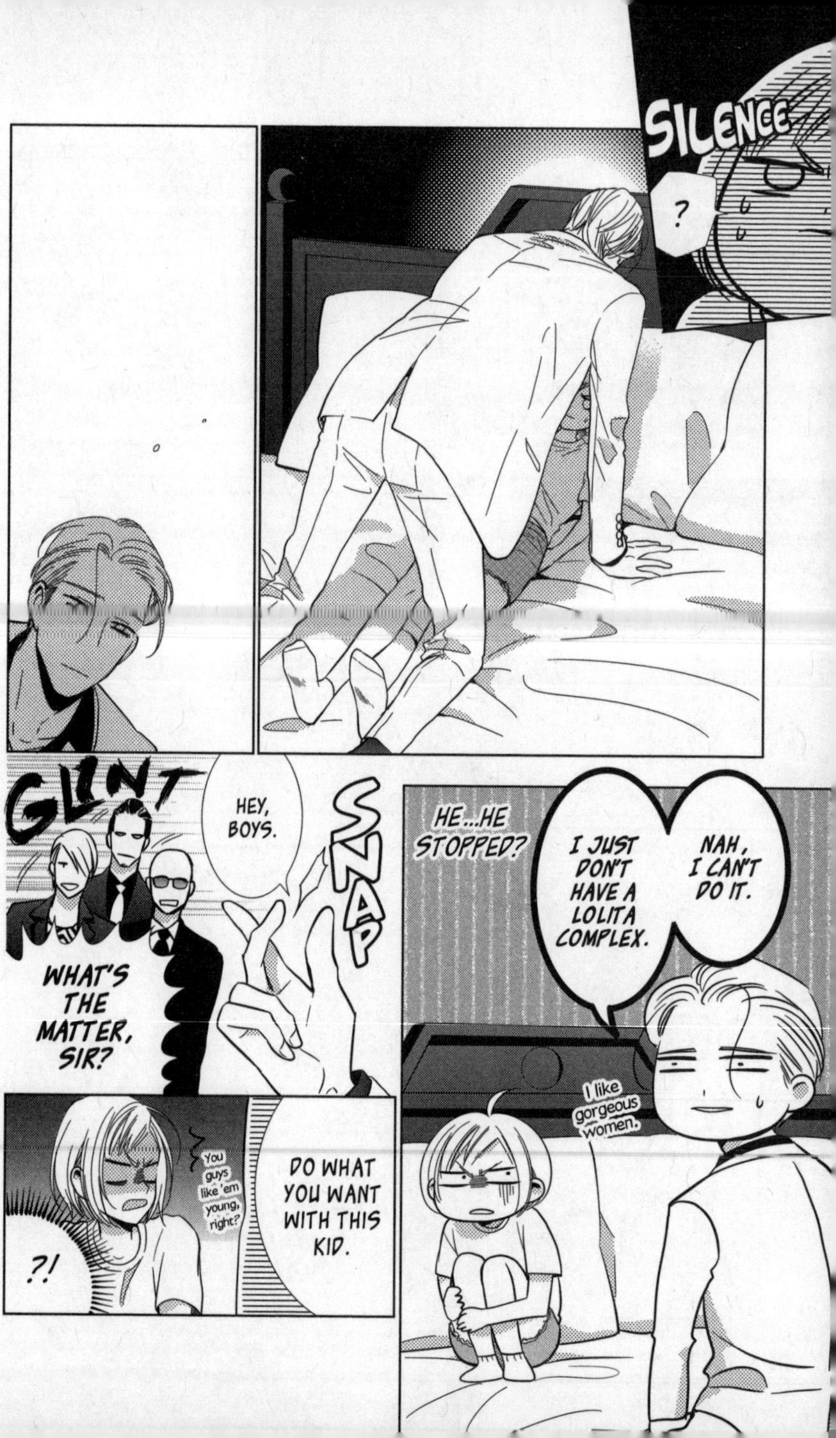
SILENCE
?
NAH, I CAN'T DO IT.
I JUST DON'T HAVE A LOLITA COMPLEX.
HE...HE STOPPED?
I like gorgeous women.
SNAP
HEY, BOYS.
GLINT
WHAT'S THE MATTER, SIR?
DO WHAT YOU WANT WITH THIS KID.
You guys like 'em young, right?
?!

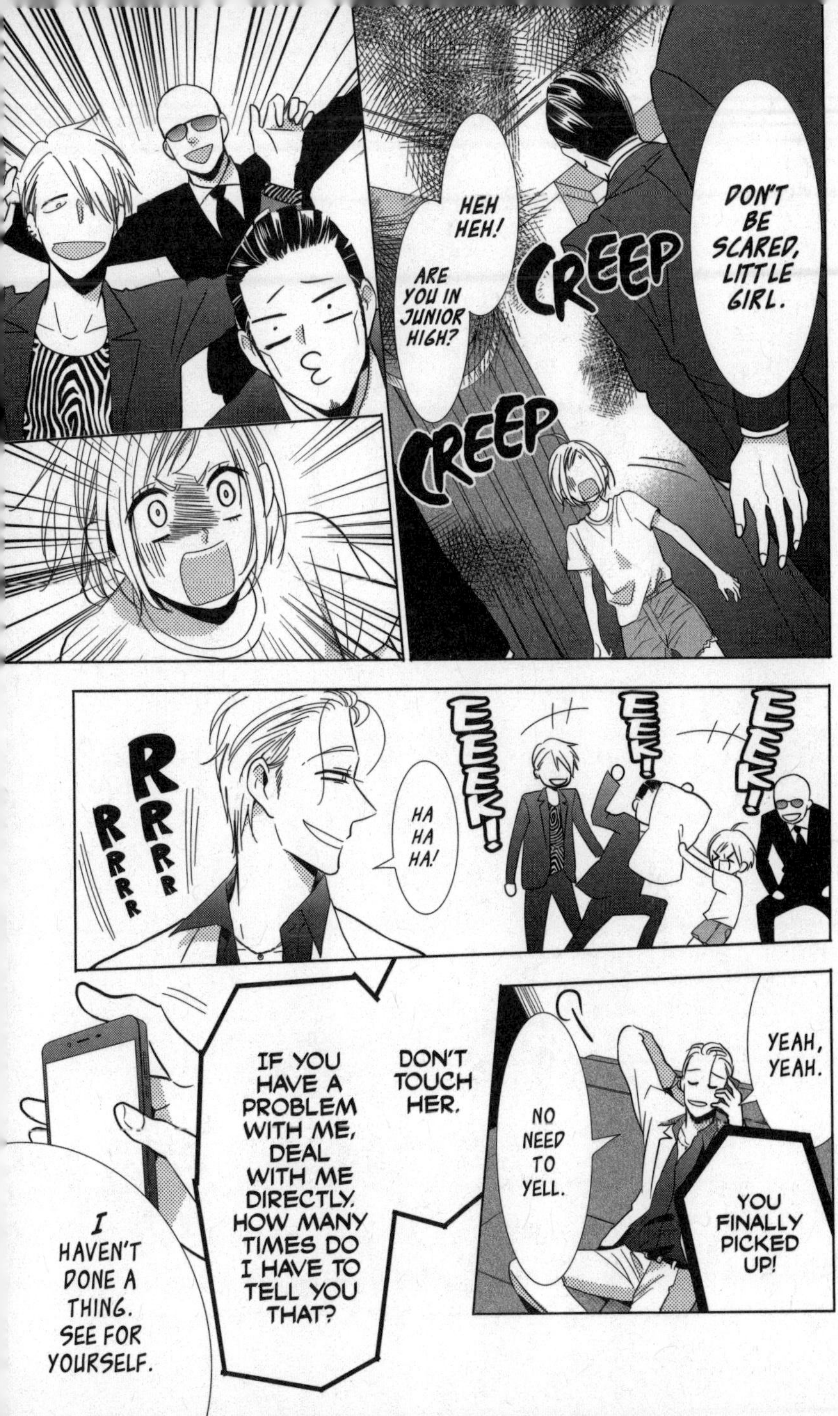
DON'T BE SCARED, LITTLE GIRL.
CREEP
HEH HEH!
ARE YOU IN JUNIOR HIGH?
CREEP
EEEK!
EEK!
EEEEK!
HA HA HA!
RRRRR
RRRR
YEAH, YEAH.
YOU FINALLY PICKED UP!
NO NEED TO YELL.
DON'T TOUCH HER.
IF YOU HAVE A PROBLEM WITH ME, DEAL WITH ME DIRECTLY. HOW MANY TIMES DO I HAVE TO TELL YOU THAT?
I HAVEN'T DONE A THING. SEE FOR YOURSELF.

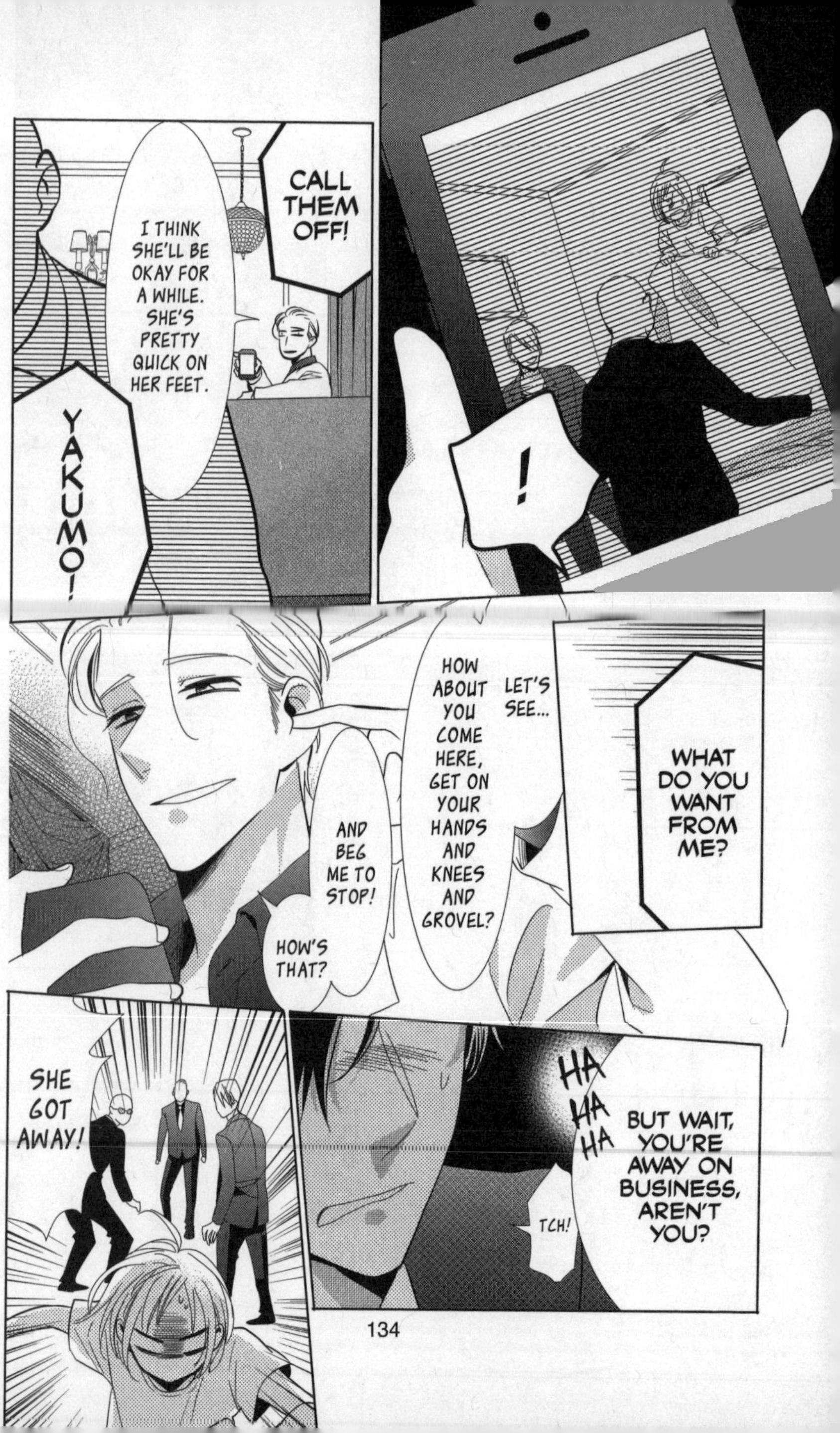
!
CALL THEM OFF!
I THINK SHE'LL BE OKAY FOR A WHILE. SHE'S PRETTY QUICK ON HER FEET.
YAKUMO!
WHAT DO YOU WANT FROM ME?
LET'S SEE...
HOW ABOUT YOU COME HERE, GET ON YOUR HANDS AND KNEES AND GROVEL?
AND BEG ME TO STOP!
HOW'S THAT?
HA HA HA
BUT WAIT, YOU'RE AWAY ON BUSINESS, AREN'T YOU?
TCH!
SHE GOT AWAY!

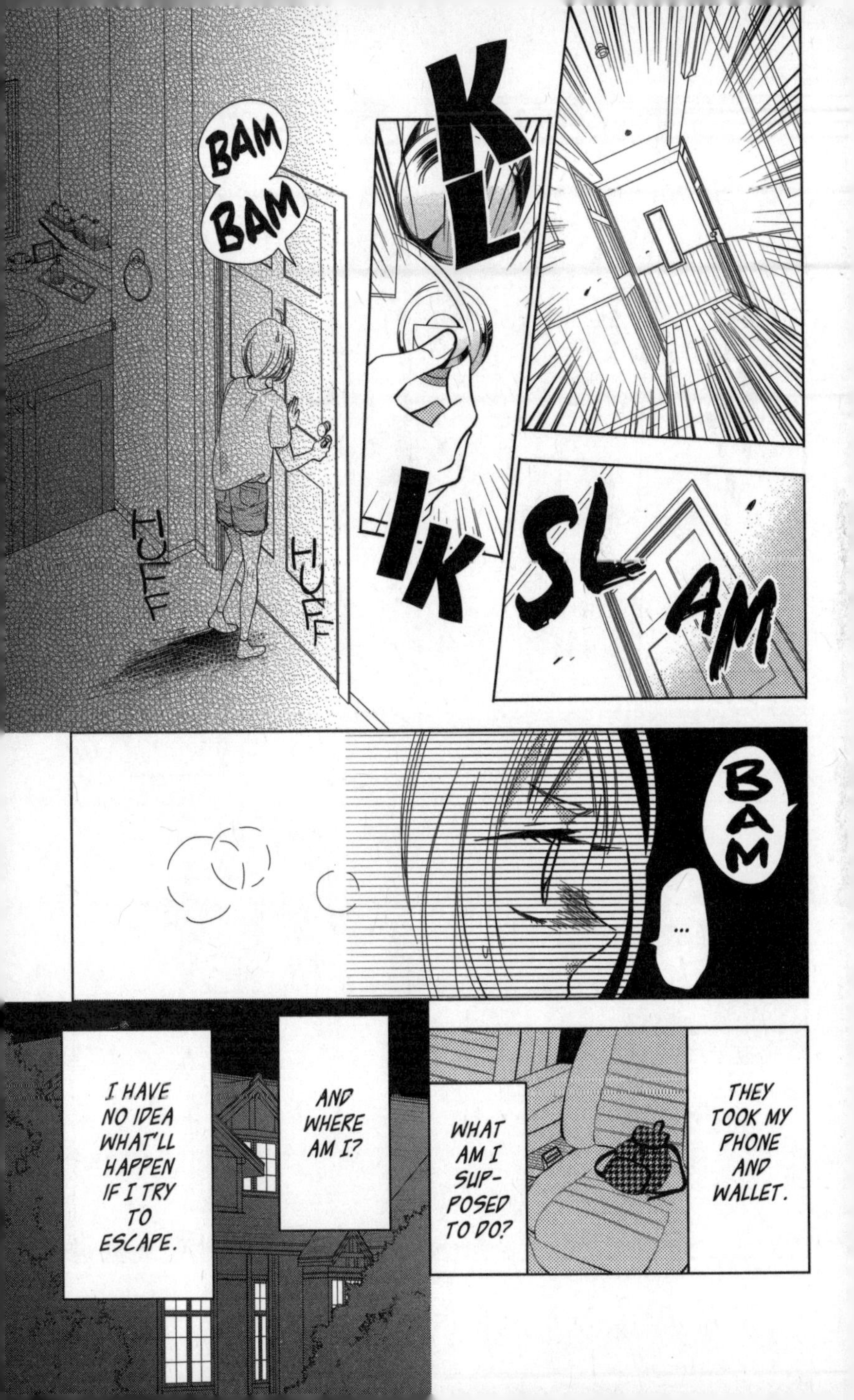
SLAM
KLIK
BAM BAM
HUFF
HUFF
BAM
...
THEY TOOK MY PHONE AND WALLET.
WHAT AM I SUP-POSED TO DO?
AND WHERE AM I?
I HAVE NO IDEA WHAT'LL HAPPEN IF I TRY TO ESCAPE.

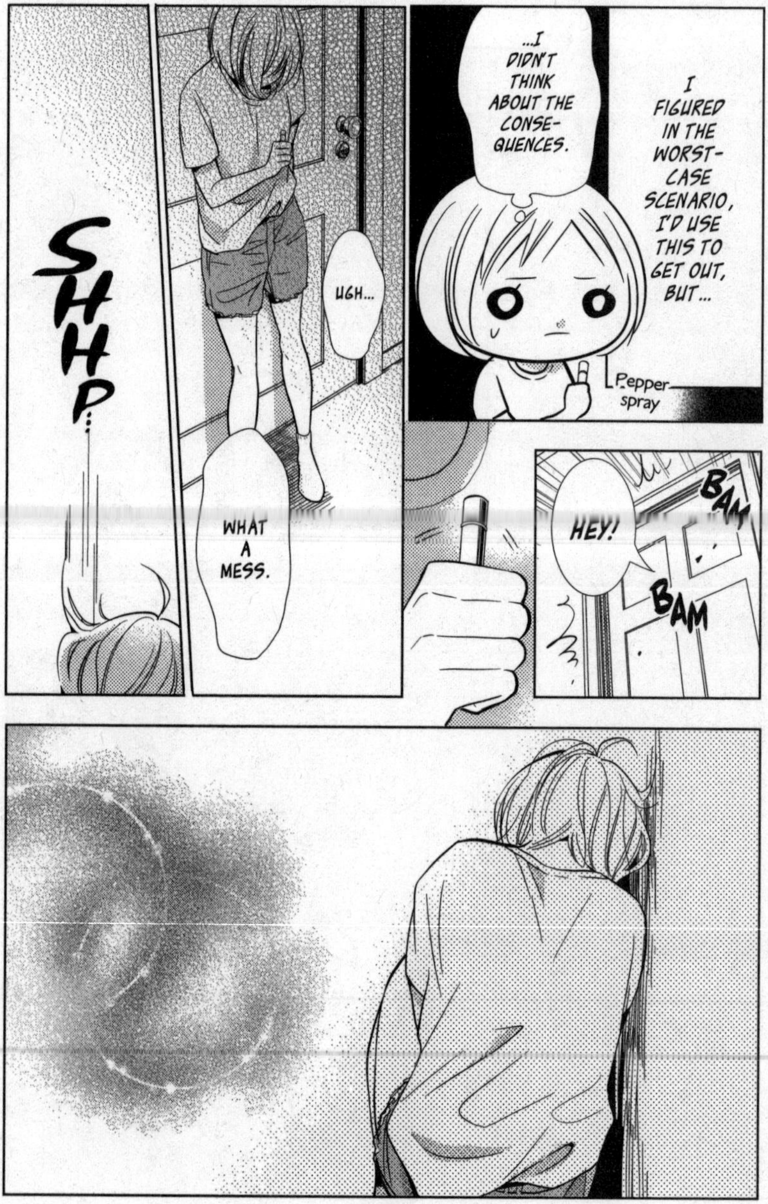
I figured in the worst-case scenario, I'd use this to get out, but...
...I didn't think about the consequences.
Pepper spray
Hey!
BAM BAM
Ugh...
What a mess.
SHHP...

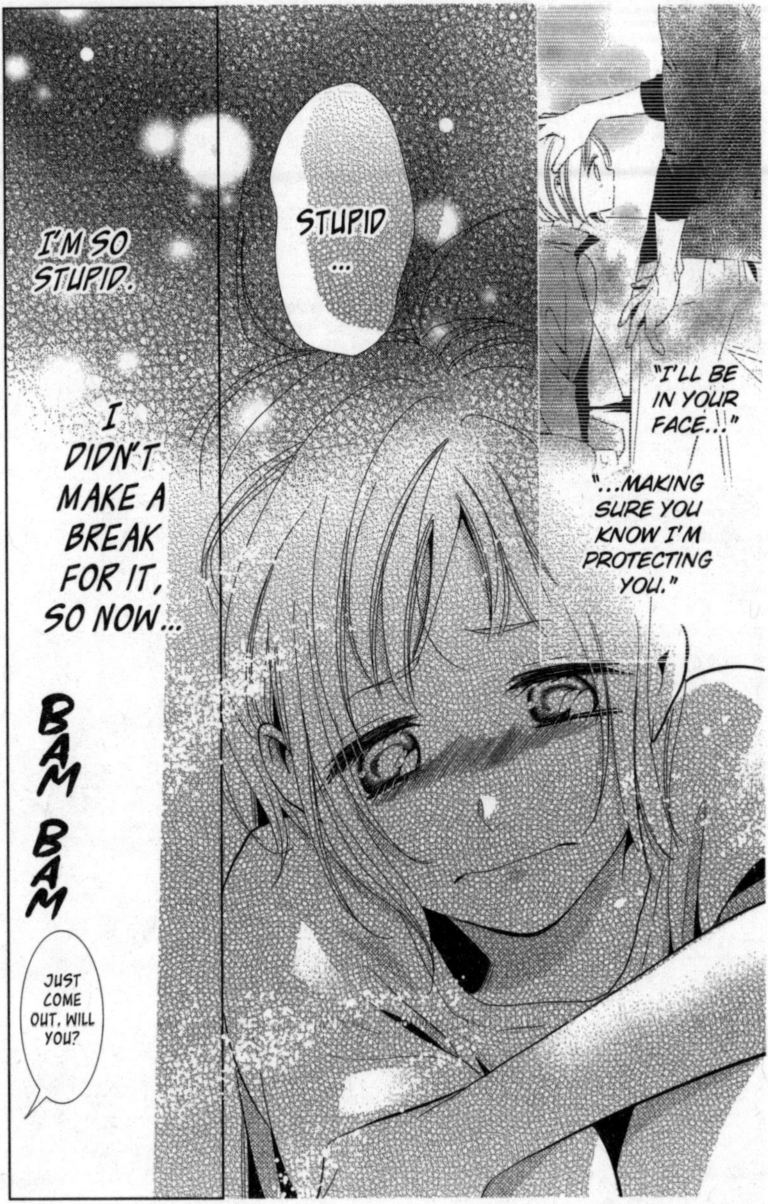
"I'LL BE IN YOUR FACE..."
"...MAKING SURE YOU KNOW I'M PROTECTING YOU."
STUPID ...
I'M SO STUPID.
I DIDN'T MAKE A BREAK FOR IT, SO NOW...
BAM BAM
JUST COME OUT, WILL YOU?

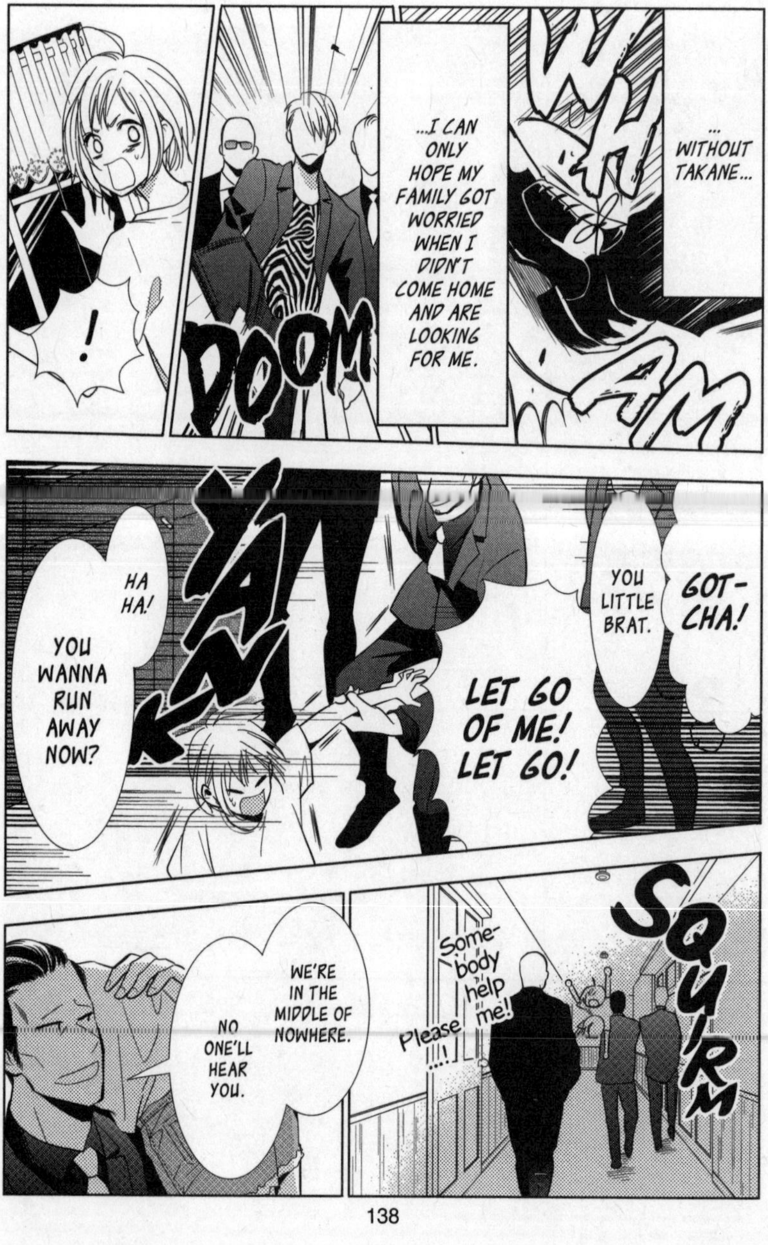
WHAM
...WITHOUT TAKANE...
...I CAN ONLY HOPE MY FAMILY GOT WORRIED WHEN I DIDN'T COME HOME AND ARE LOOKING FOR ME.
DOOM
!
GOT-CHA!
YOU LITTLE BRAT.
LET GO OF ME! LET GO!
YANK
HA HA!
YOU WANNA RUN AWAY NOW?
SQUIRM
Some-body help me!
Please...!
WE'RE IN THE MIDDLE OF NOWHERE.
NO ONE'LL HEAR YOU.

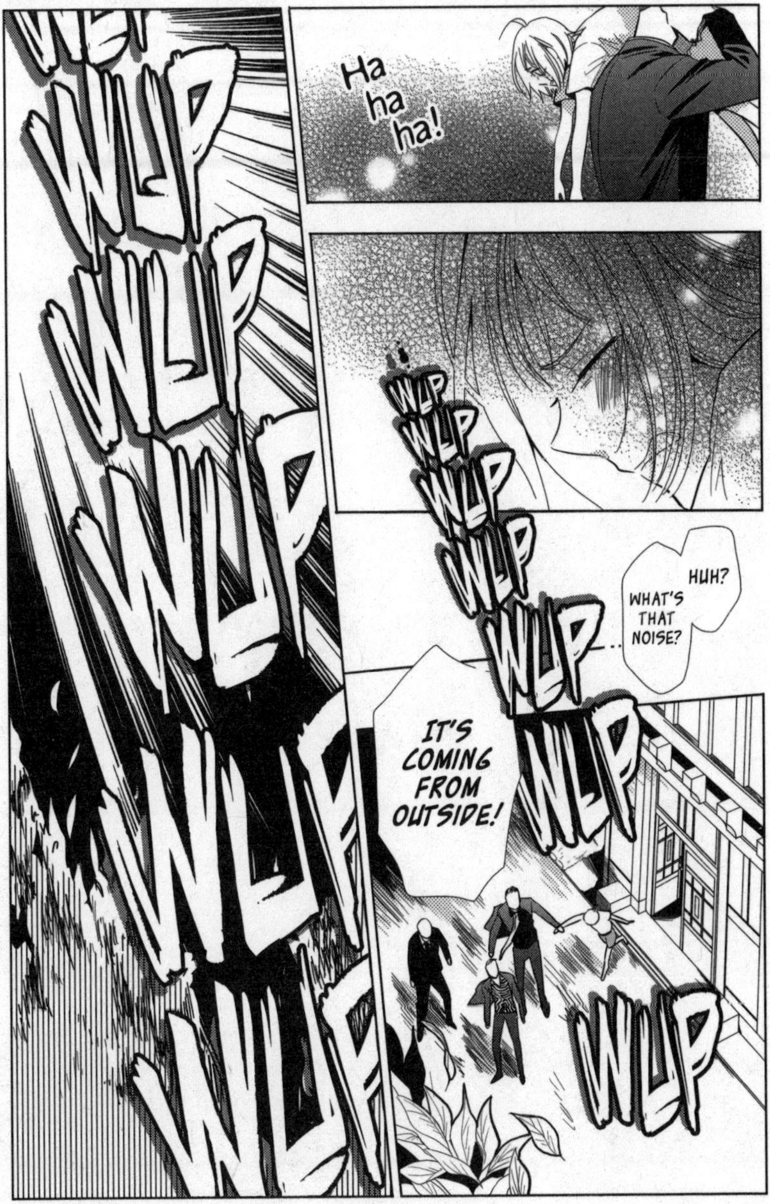
Ha ha ha!
WLP WLP WLP WLP WLP
HUH? WHAT'S THAT NOISE?
IT'S COMING FROM OUTSIDE!
WLP
WLP
WLP WLP WLP WLP WLP

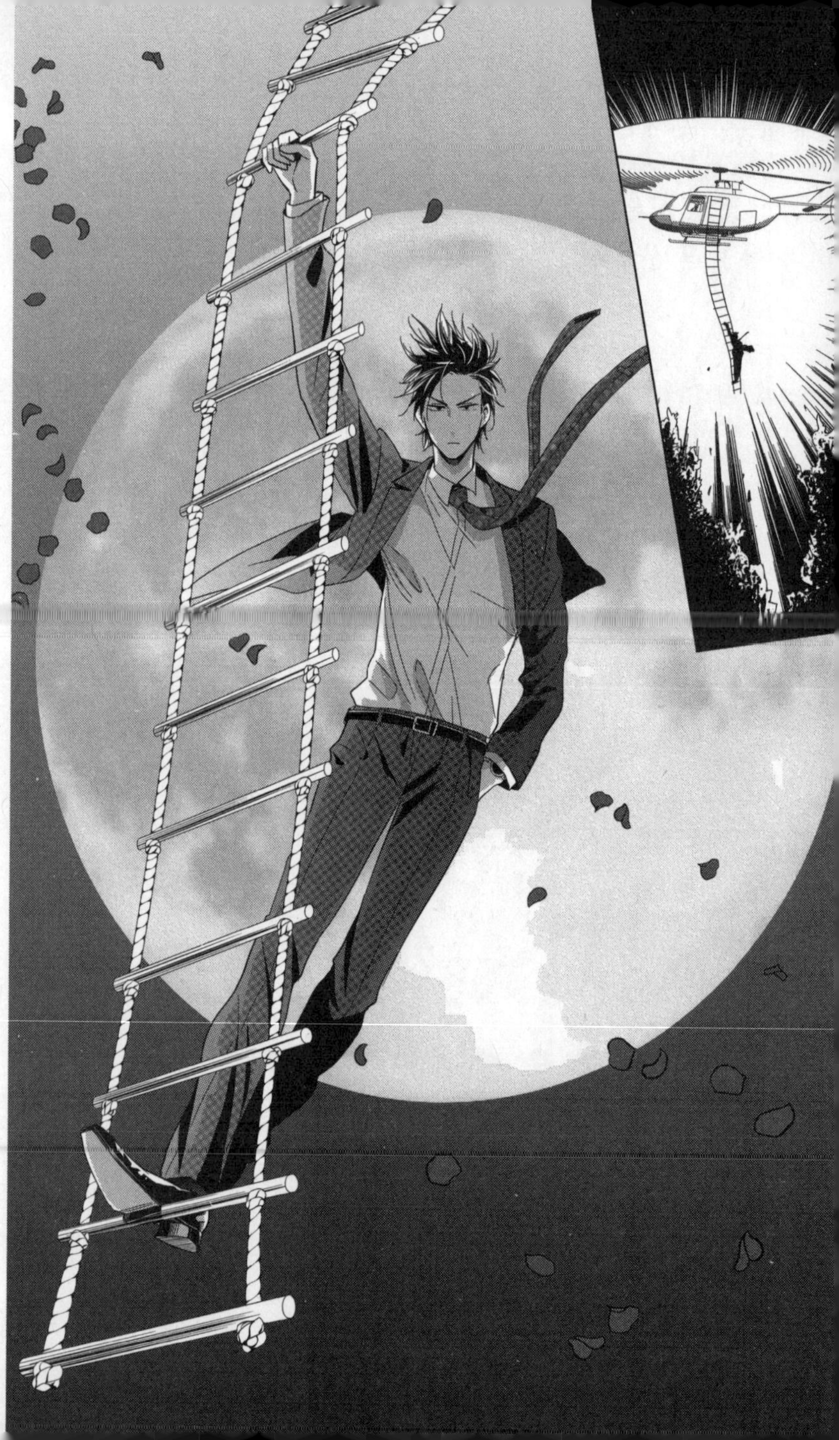

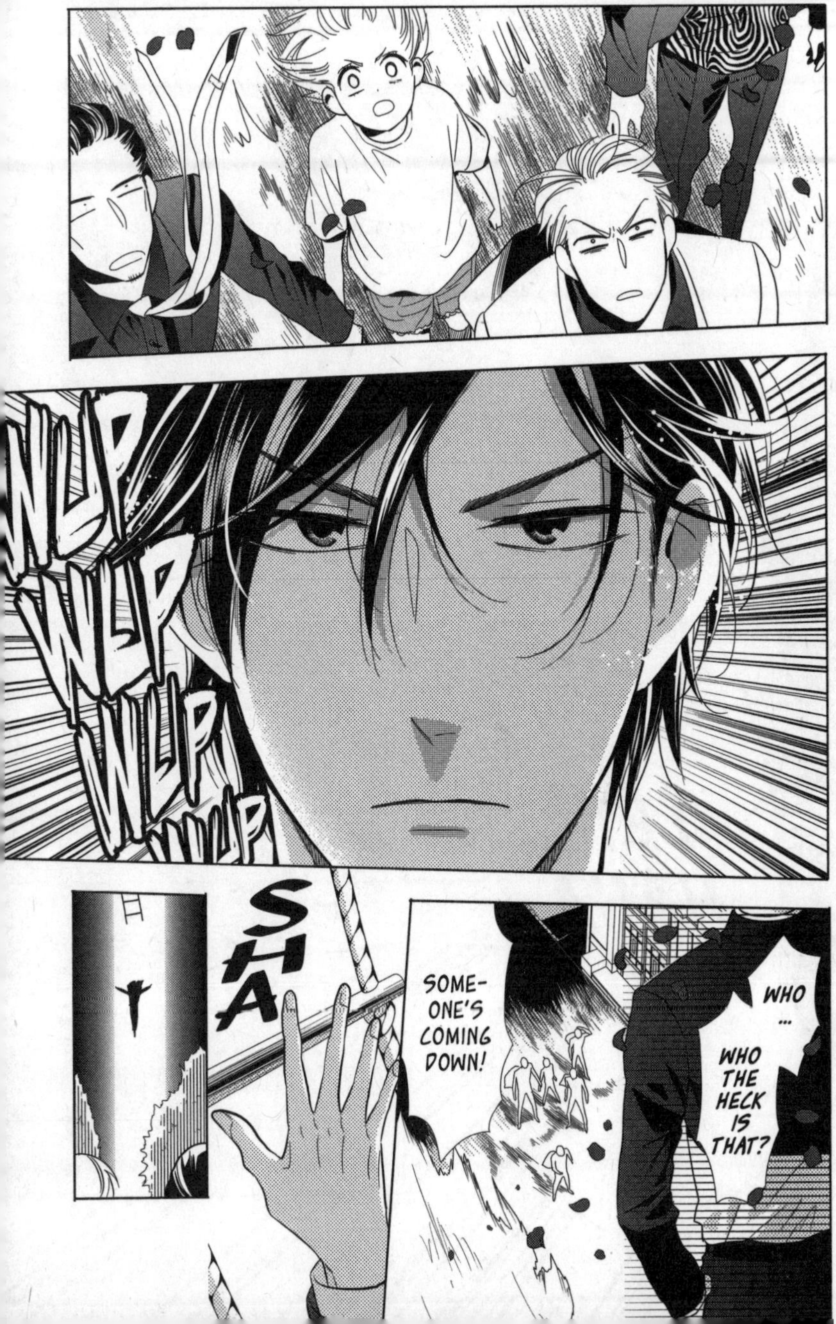

WLIP WLIP WLIP WLIP
WHO ... WHO THE HECK IS THAT?
SOME-ONE'S COMING DOWN!
SHA

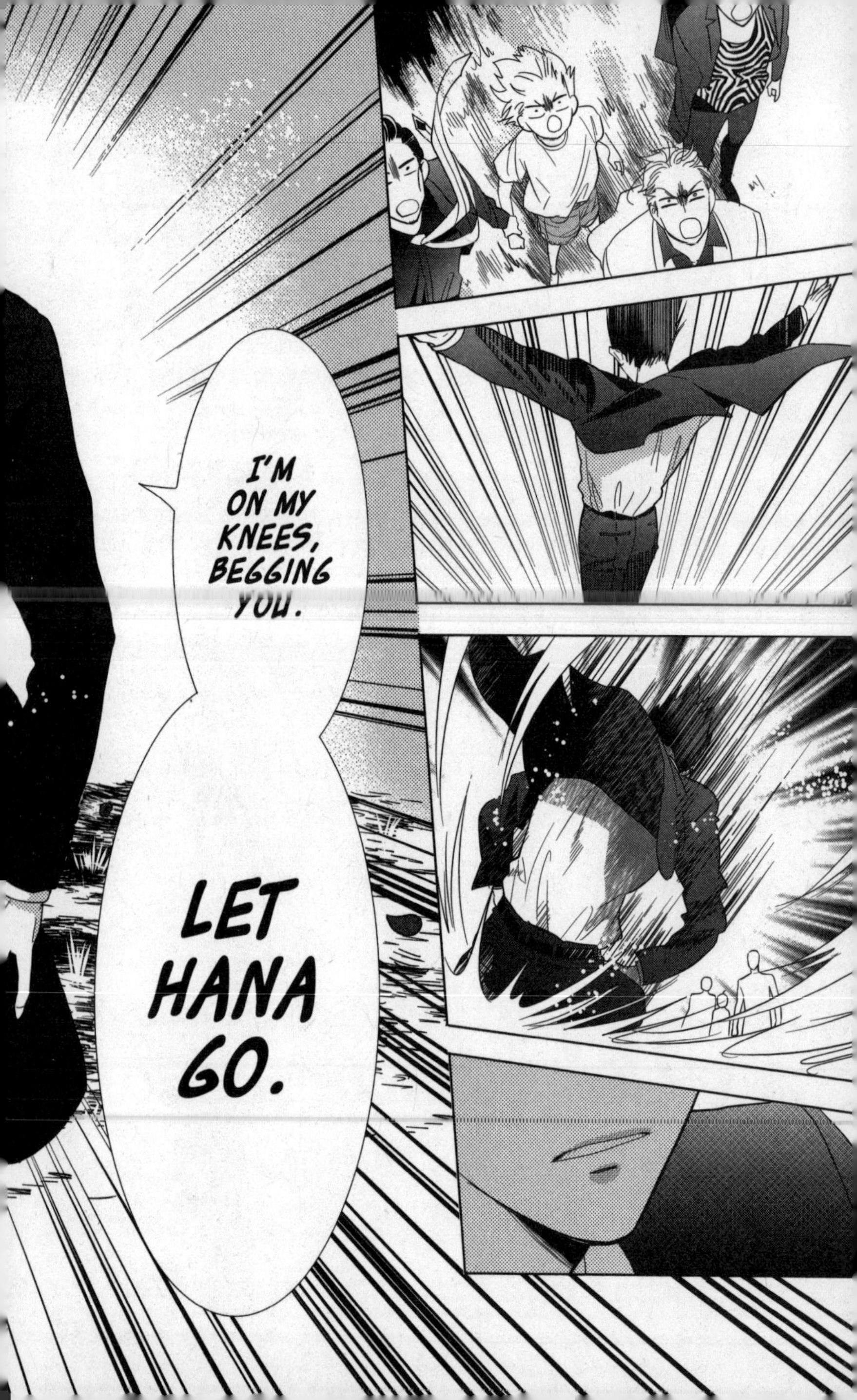
I'M ON MY KNEES, BEGGING YOU.
LET HANA GO.

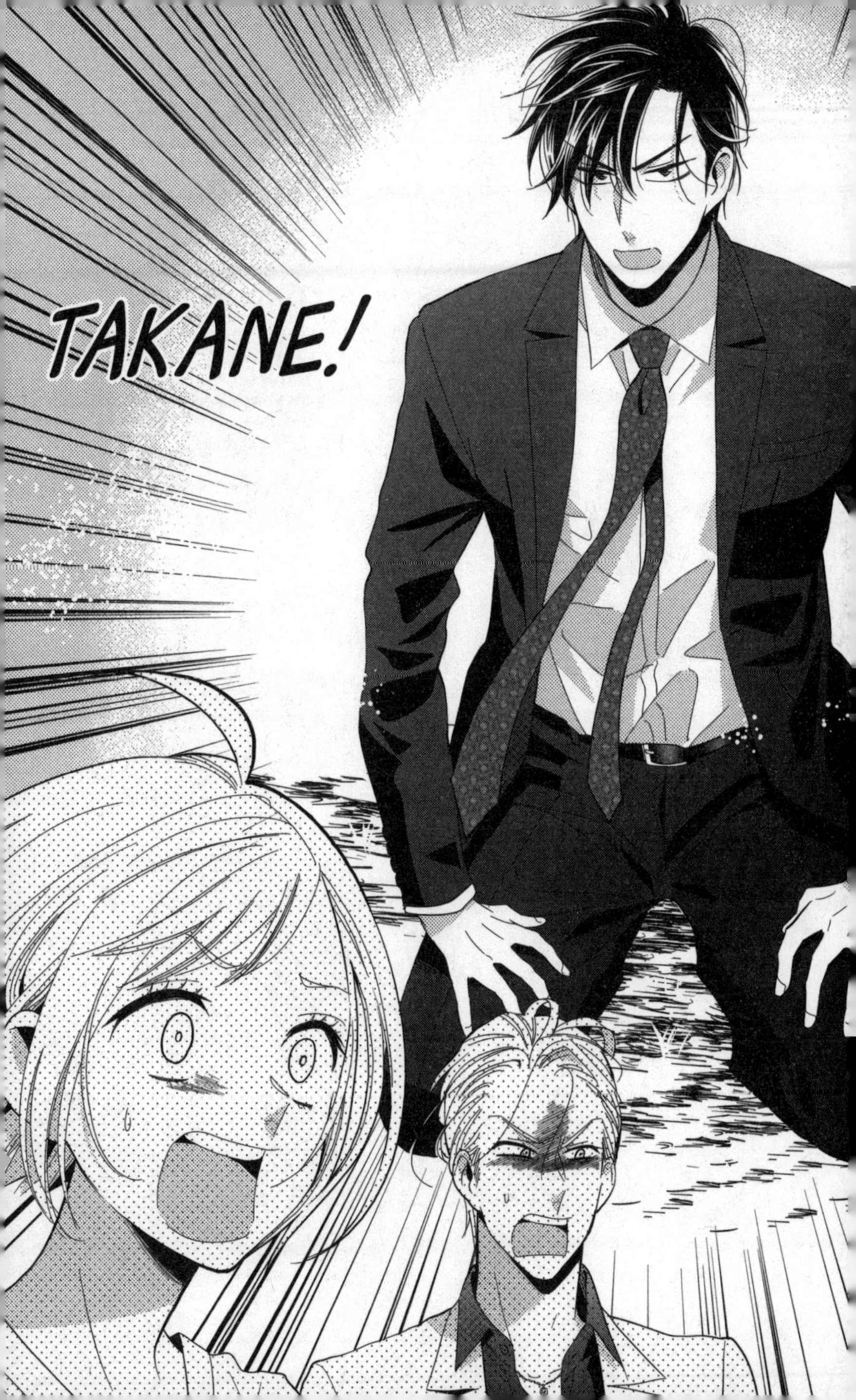
TAKANE!

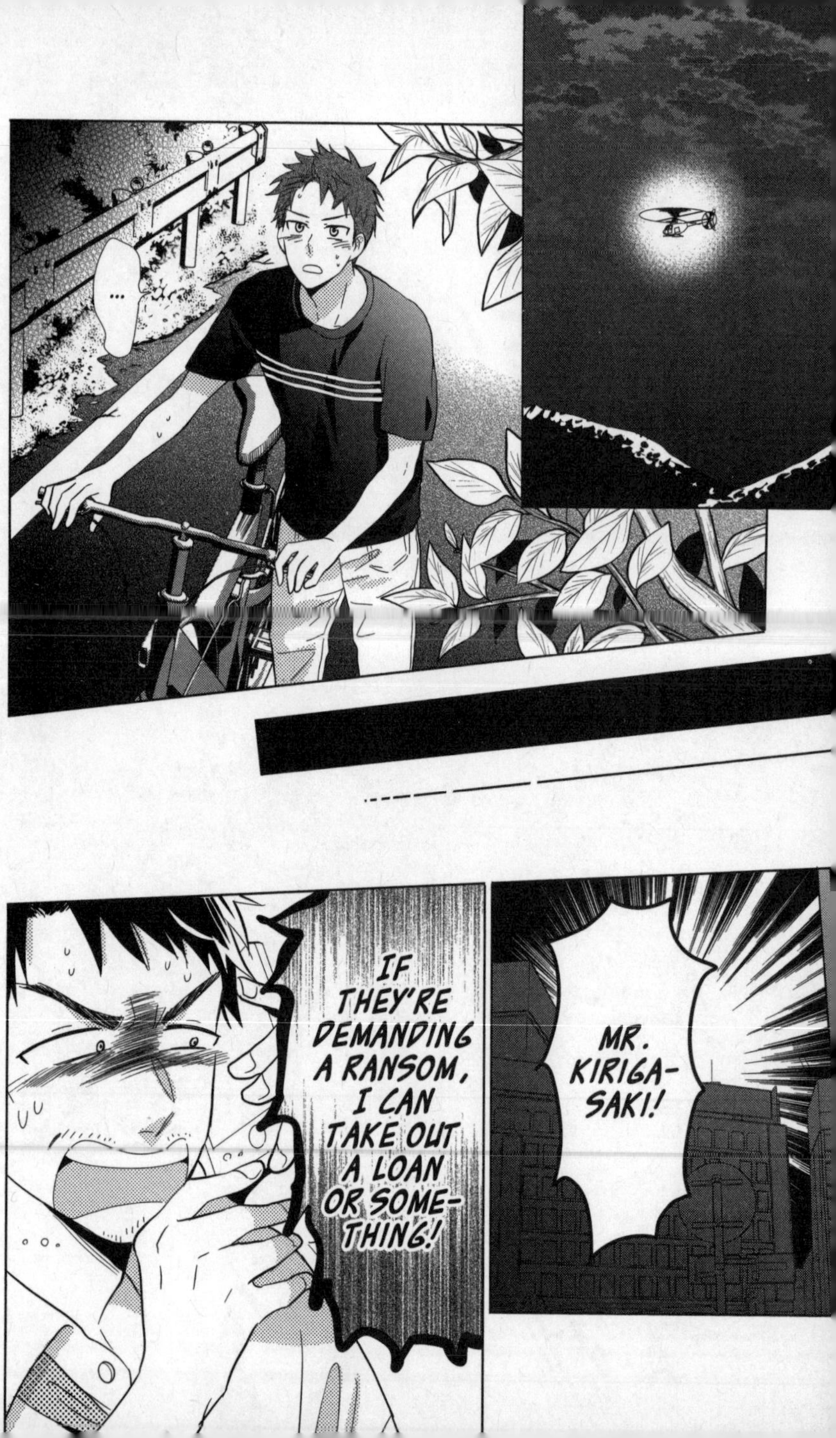
...
MR. KIRIGA-SAKI!
IF THEY'RE DEMANDING A RANSOM, I CAN TAKE OUT A LOAN OR SOME-THING!

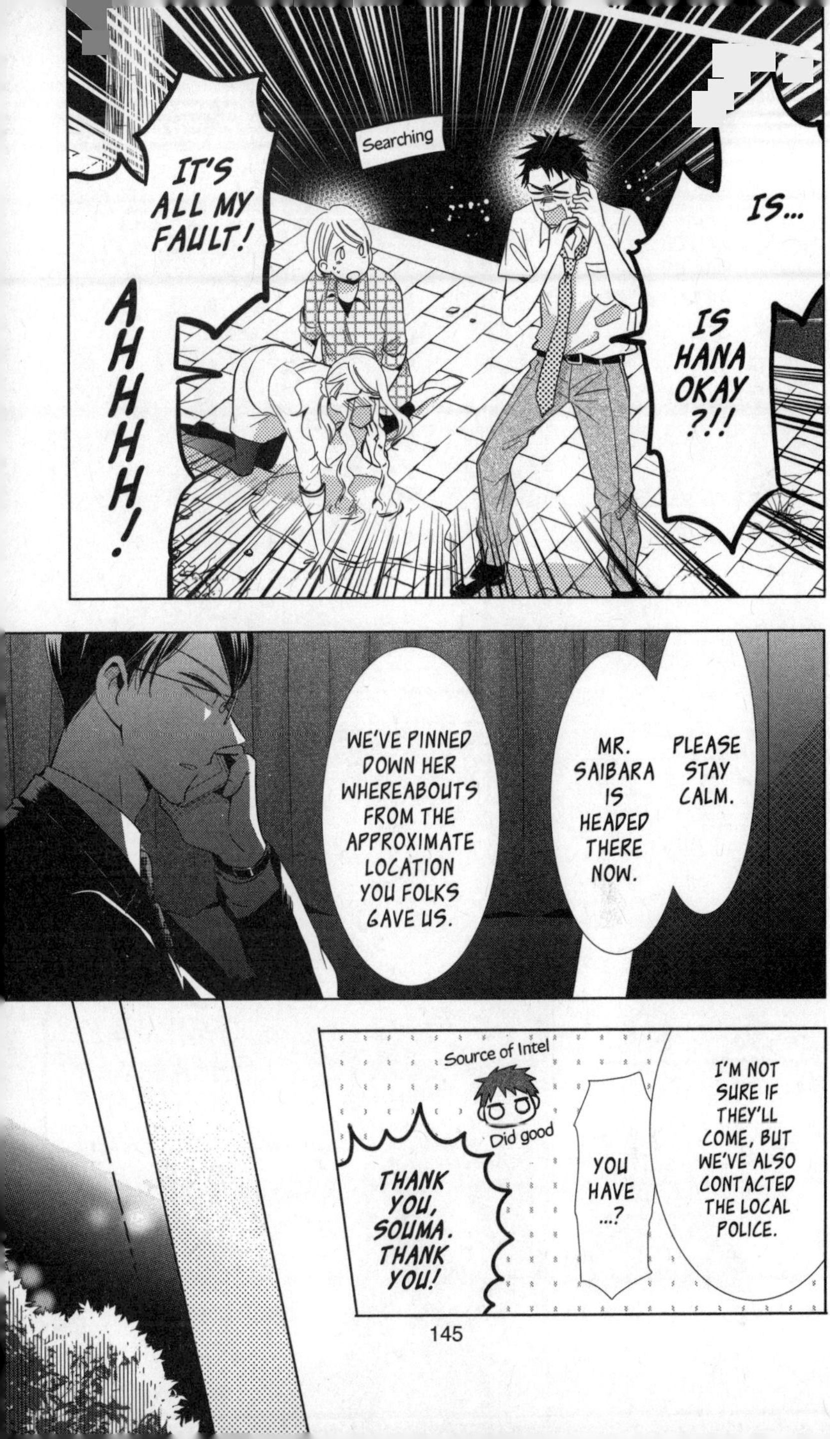
IS...
IS HANA OKAY?!!
Searching
IT'S ALL MY FAULT!
AHHHHH!
PLEASE STAY CALM.
MR. SAIBARA IS HEADED THERE NOW.
WE'VE PINNED DOWN HER WHEREABOUTS FROM THE APPROXIMATE LOCATION YOU FOLKS GAVE US.
I'M NOT SURE IF THEY'LL COME, BUT WE'VE ALSO CONTACTED THE LOCAL POLICE.
YOU HAVE ...?
Source of Intel
Did good
THANK YOU, SOUMA. THANK YOU!

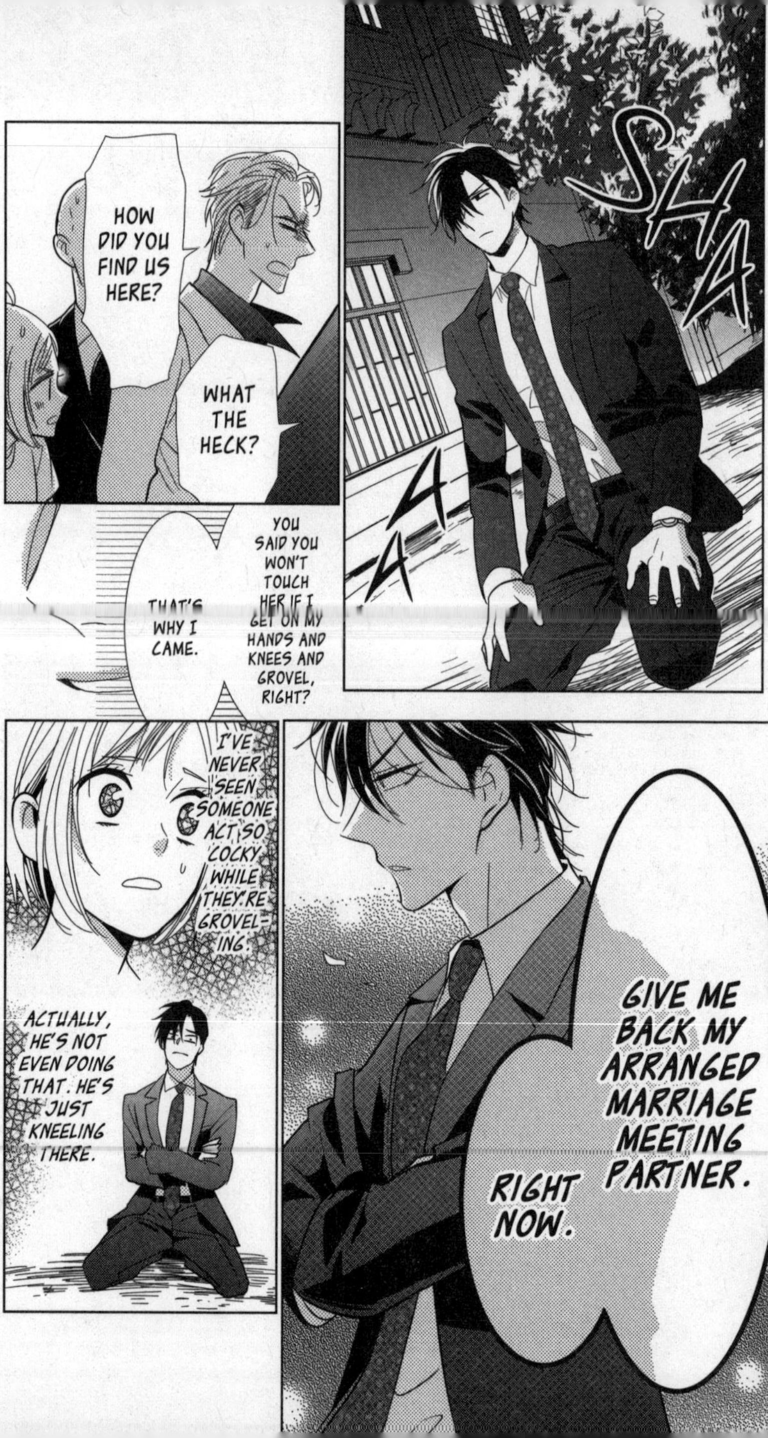
SHA
HOW DID YOU FIND US HERE?
WHAT THE HECK?
YOU SAID YOU WON'T TOUCH HER IF I GET ON MY HANDS AND KNEES AND GROVEL, RIGHT?
THAT'S WHY I CAME.
GIVE ME BACK MY ARRANGED MARRIAGE MEETING PARTNER.
RIGHT NOW.
I'VE NEVER SEEN SOMEONE ACT SO COCKY WHILE THEY'RE GROVELING.
ACTUALLY, HE'S NOT EVEN DOING THAT. HE'S JUST KNEELING THERE.

Chapter 33
(in volume 6)

It feels like something's missing if the only thing above me is snow.

As the snow falls, she reflects on her feelings for Takane, who's now dejected and penniless. A heartbreaking moment.

Chapter 37
(in volume 7)

Takane: "Three won't cut it. I need at least seven stars!" ★

Hana: "So you like ladybugs after all!" ★

The illustration shows a pompous Takane acting like a world-class chef.

This line refers to the previous chapter, chapter 36, where they talk about the seven spots on a ladybug.

Chapter 42
(in volume 8)

A runner in the lead will get left behind if they stop making progress.

Parodies "The Tortoise and the Hare." This is the chapter where Hana decides to make Takane fall for her.

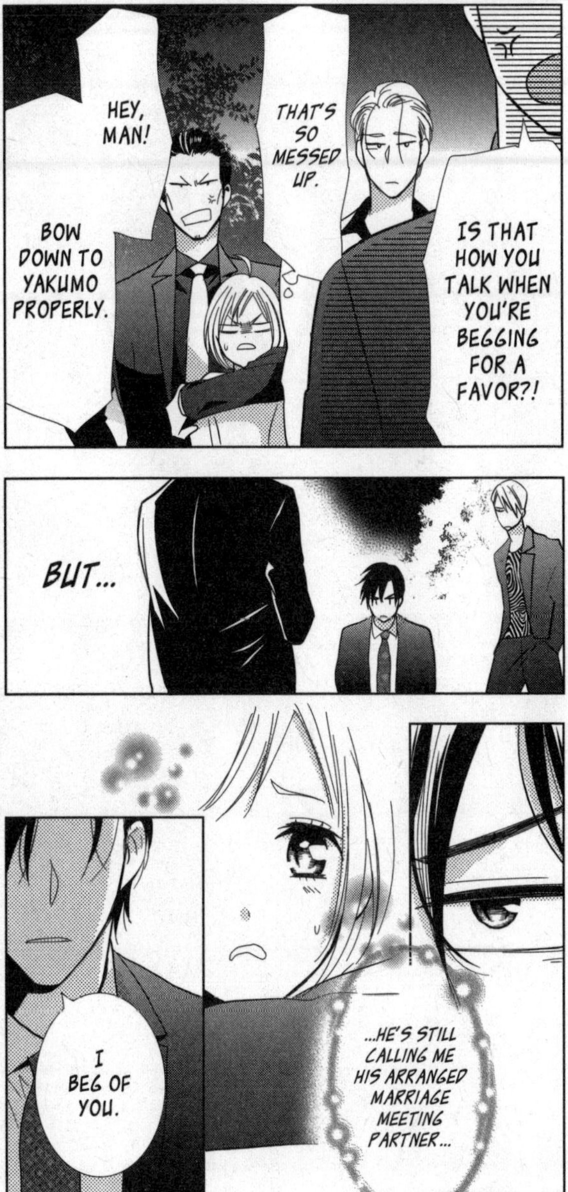
IS THAT HOW YOU TALK WHEN YOU'RE BEGGING FOR A FAVOR?!
THAT'S SO MESSED UP.
HEY, MAN!
BOW DOWN TO YAKUMO PROPERLY.
BUT...
I BEG OF YOU.
...HE'S STILL CALLING ME HIS ARRANGED MARRIAGE MEETING PARTNER...

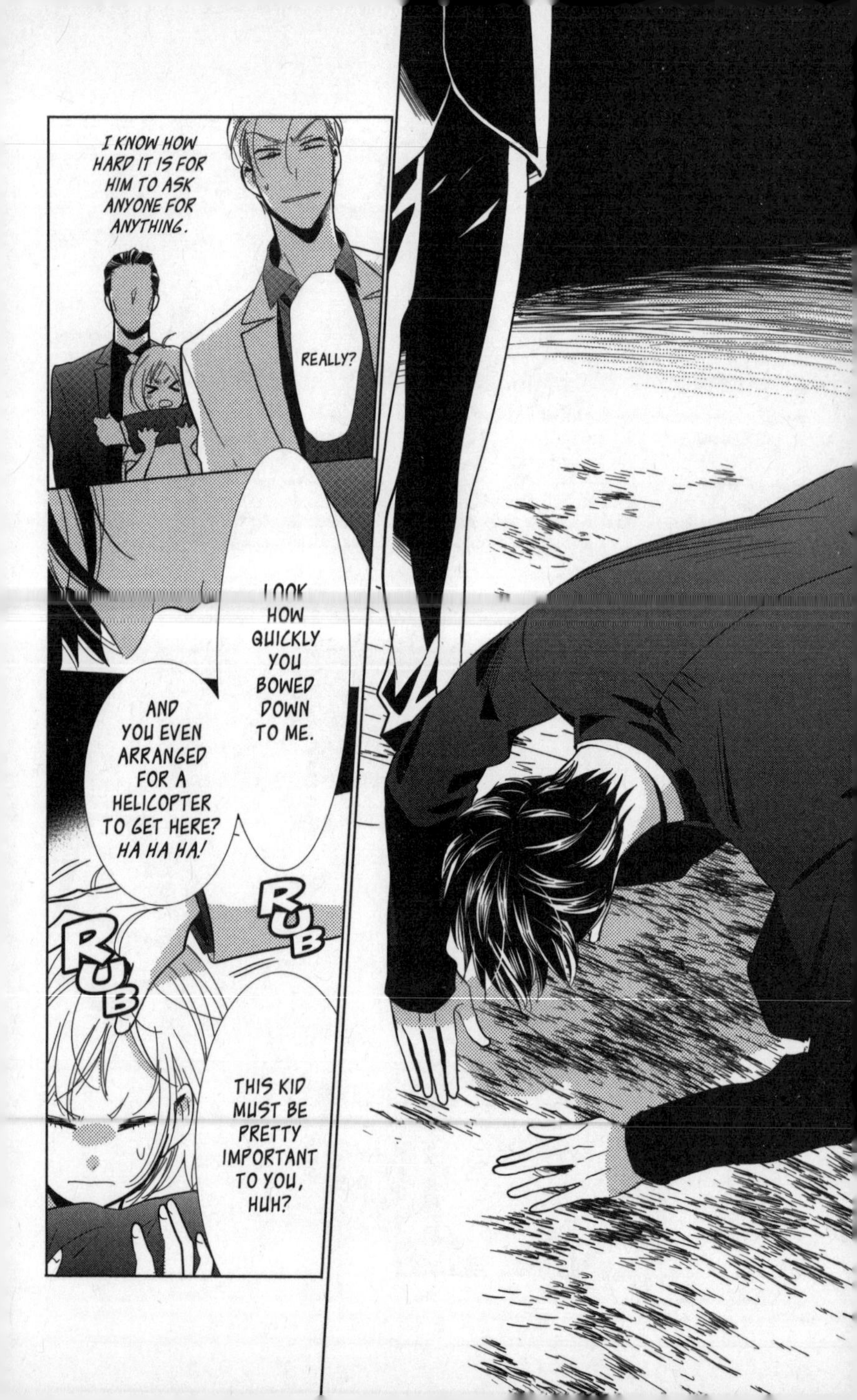
I KNOW HOW HARD IT IS FOR HIM TO ASK ANYONE FOR ANYTHING.
REALLY?
LOOK HOW QUICKLY YOU BOWED DOWN TO ME.
AND YOU EVEN ARRANGED FOR A HELICOPTER TO GET HERE? HA HA HA!
RUB
RUB
THIS KID MUST BE PRETTY IMPORTANT TO YOU, HUH?

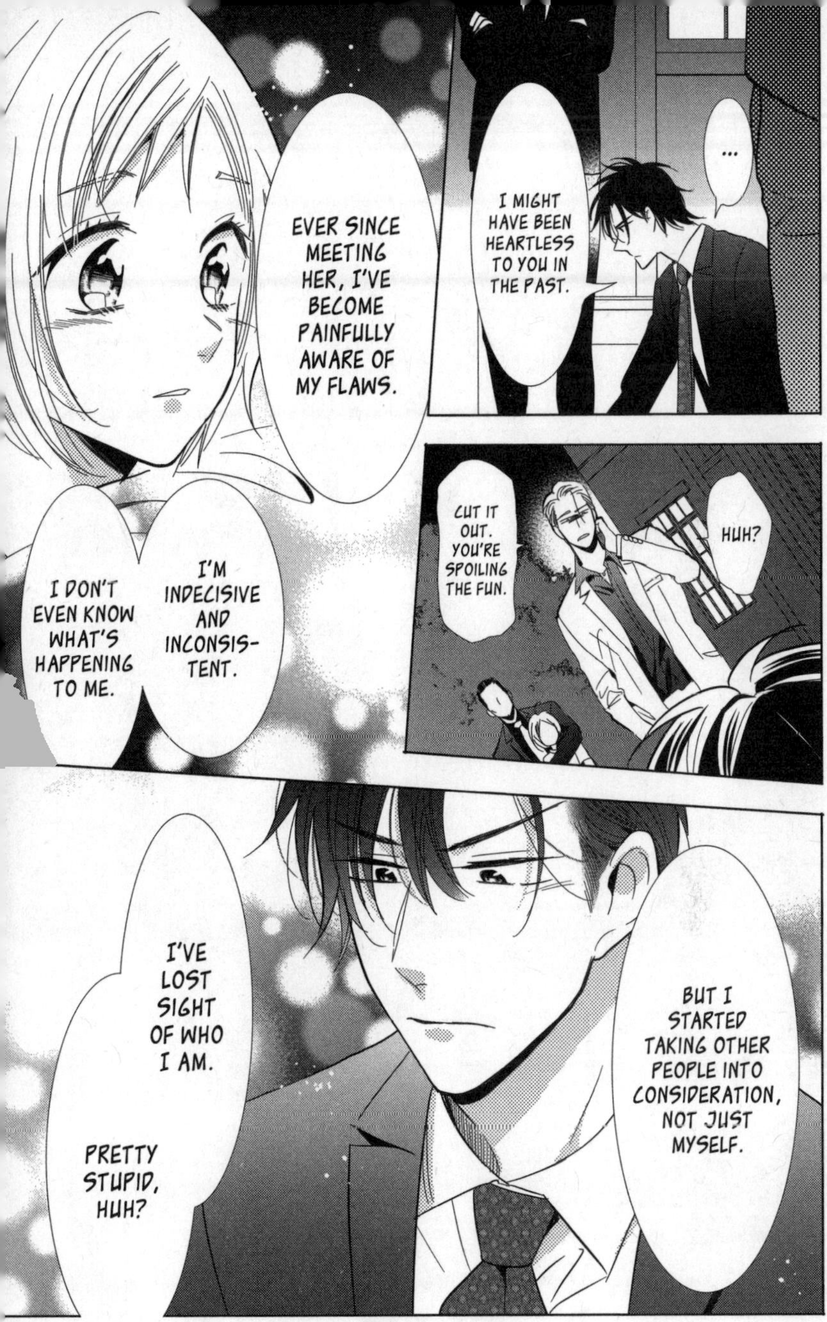
...
I MIGHT HAVE BEEN HEARTLESS TO YOU IN THE PAST.
HUH?
CUT IT OUT. YOU'RE SPOILING THE FUN.
EVER SINCE MEETING HER, I'VE BECOME PAINFULLY AWARE OF MY FLAWS.
I'M INDECISIVE AND INCONSIS-TENT.
I DON'T EVEN KNOW WHAT'S HAPPENING TO ME.
BUT I STARTED TAKING OTHER PEOPLE INTO CONSIDERATION, NOT JUST MYSELF.
I'VE LOST SIGHT OF WHO I AM.
PRETTY STUPID, HUH?

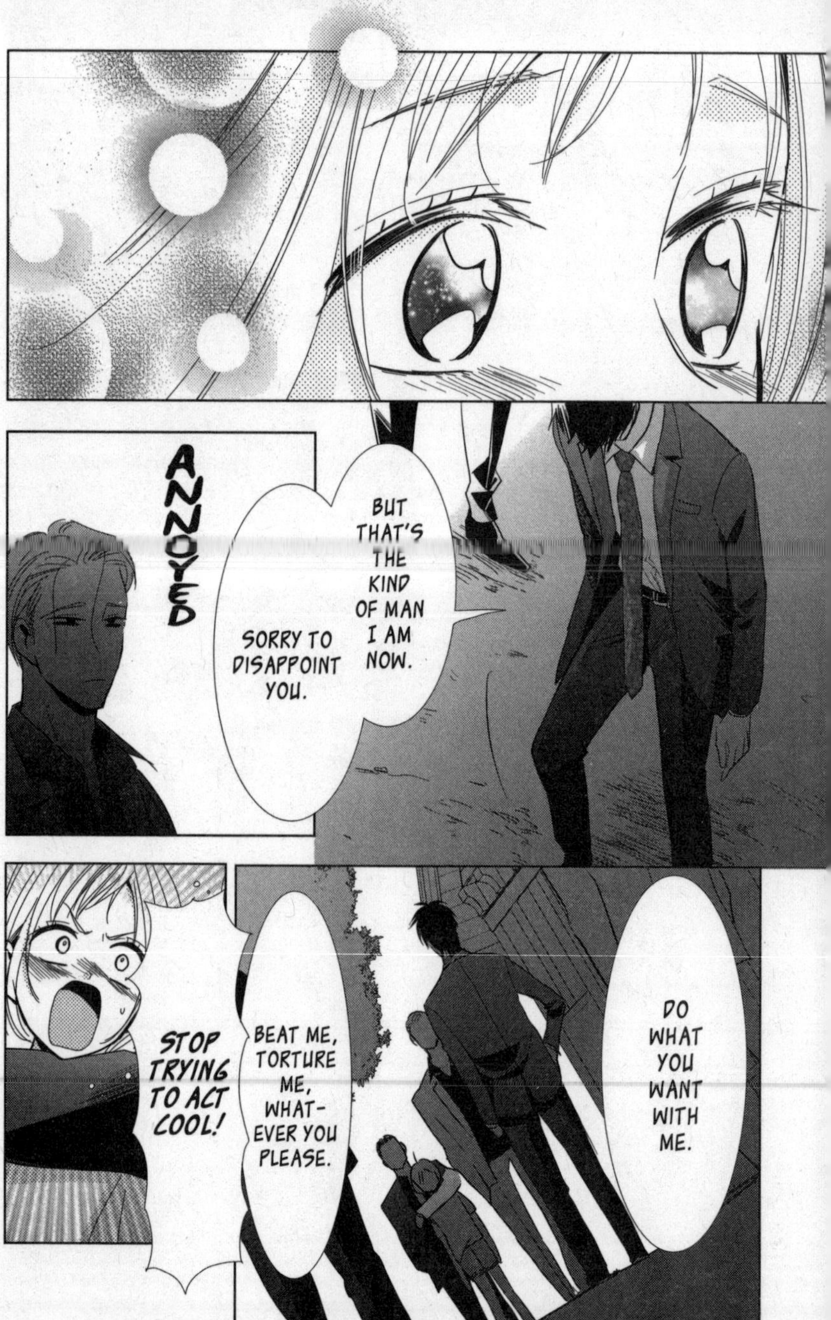
BUT THAT'S THE KIND OF MAN I AM NOW.
SORRY TO DISAPPOINT YOU.
ANNOYED
DO WHAT YOU WANT WITH ME.
BEAT ME, TORTURE ME, WHAT-EVER YOU PLEASE.
STOP TRYING TO ACT COOL!

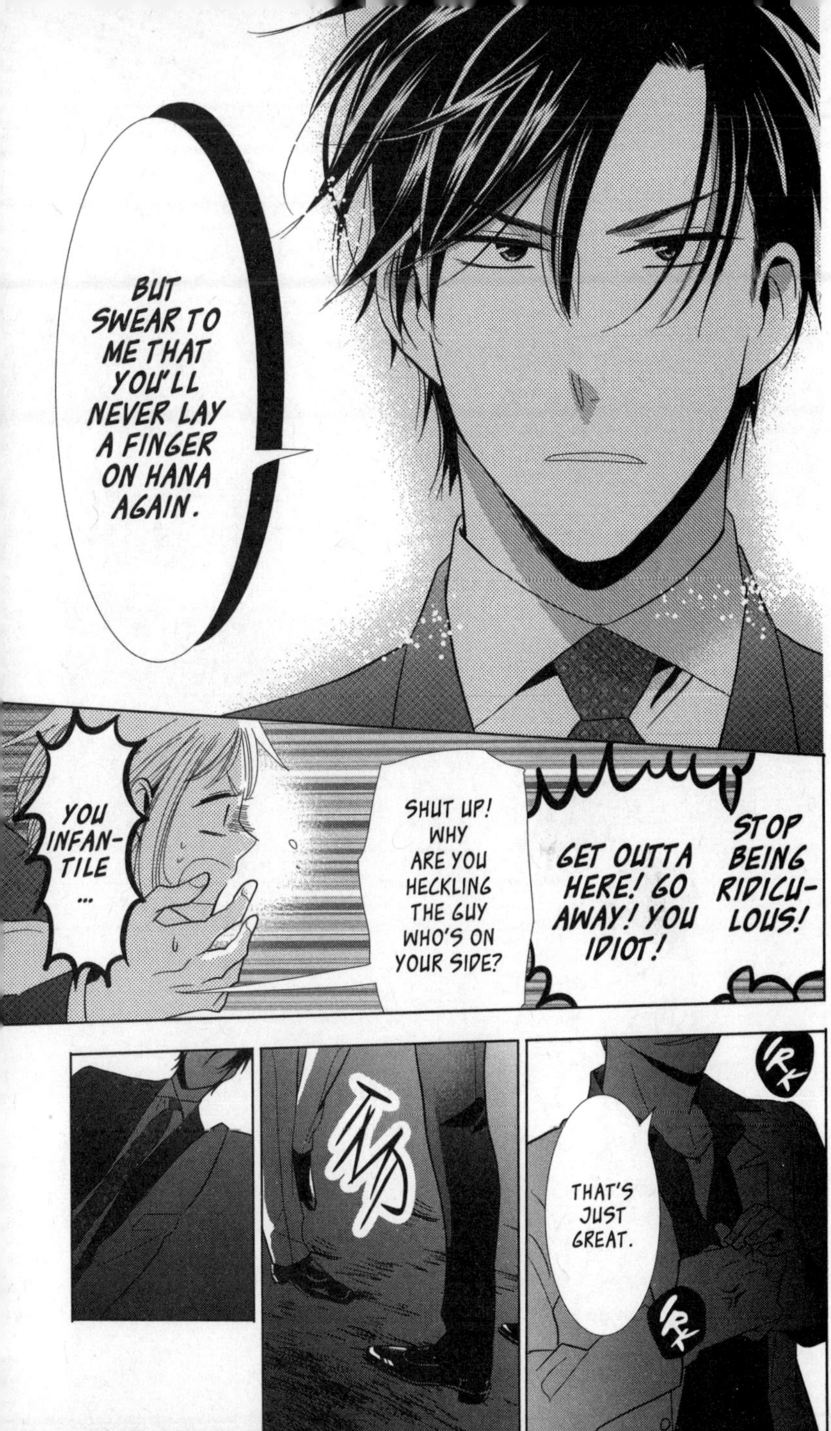
BUT SWEAR TO ME THAT YOU'LL NEVER LAY A FINGER ON HANA AGAIN.
STOP BEING RIDICULOUS!
GET OUTTA HERE! GO AWAY! YOU IDIOT!
SHUT UP! WHY ARE YOU HECKLING THE GUY WHO'S ON YOUR SIDE?
YOU INFANTILE...
IRK
THAT'S JUST GREAT.
IRK

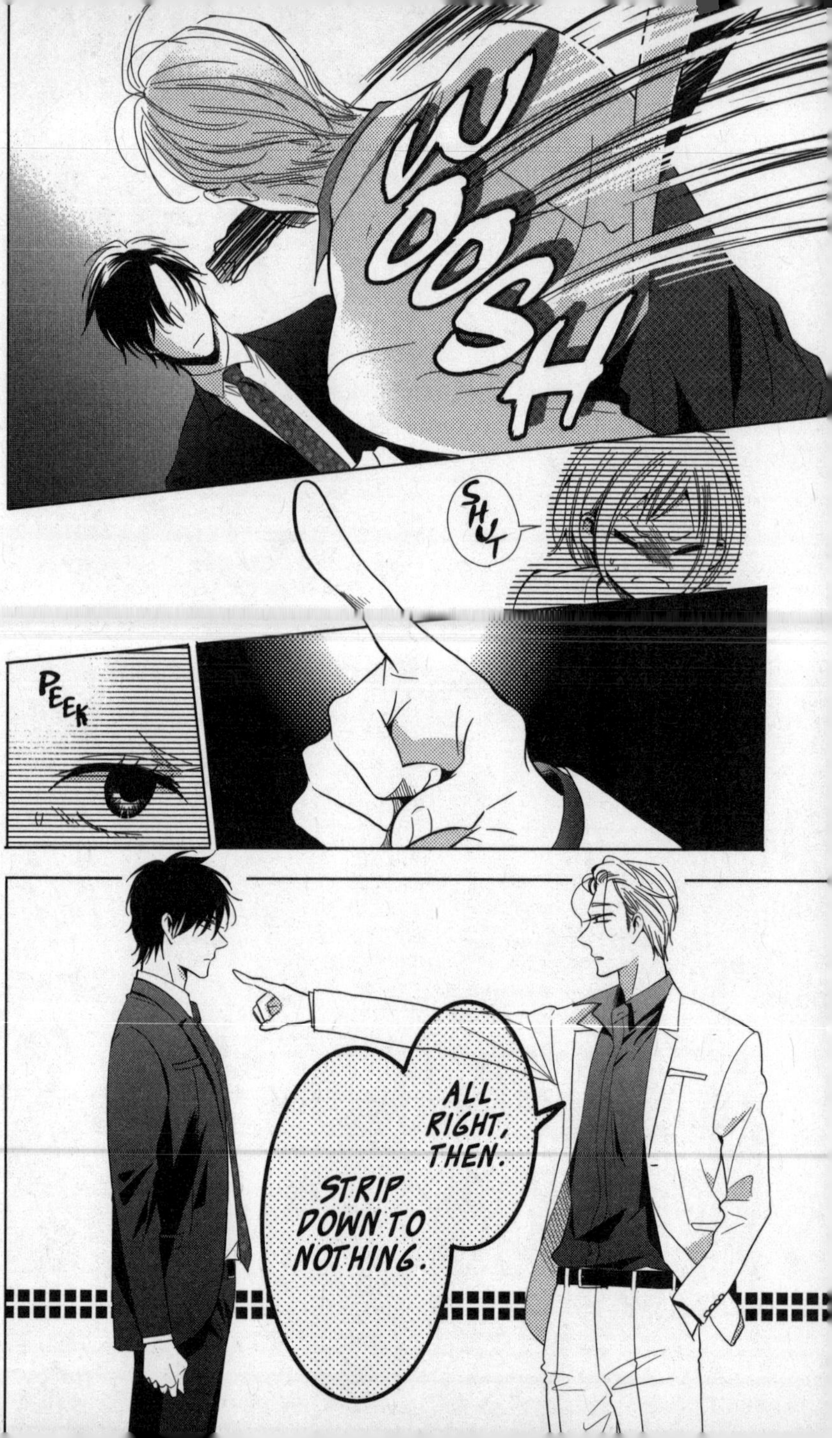
WOOSH
SHUT
PEEK
ALL RIGHT, THEN.
STRIP DOWN TO NOTHING.

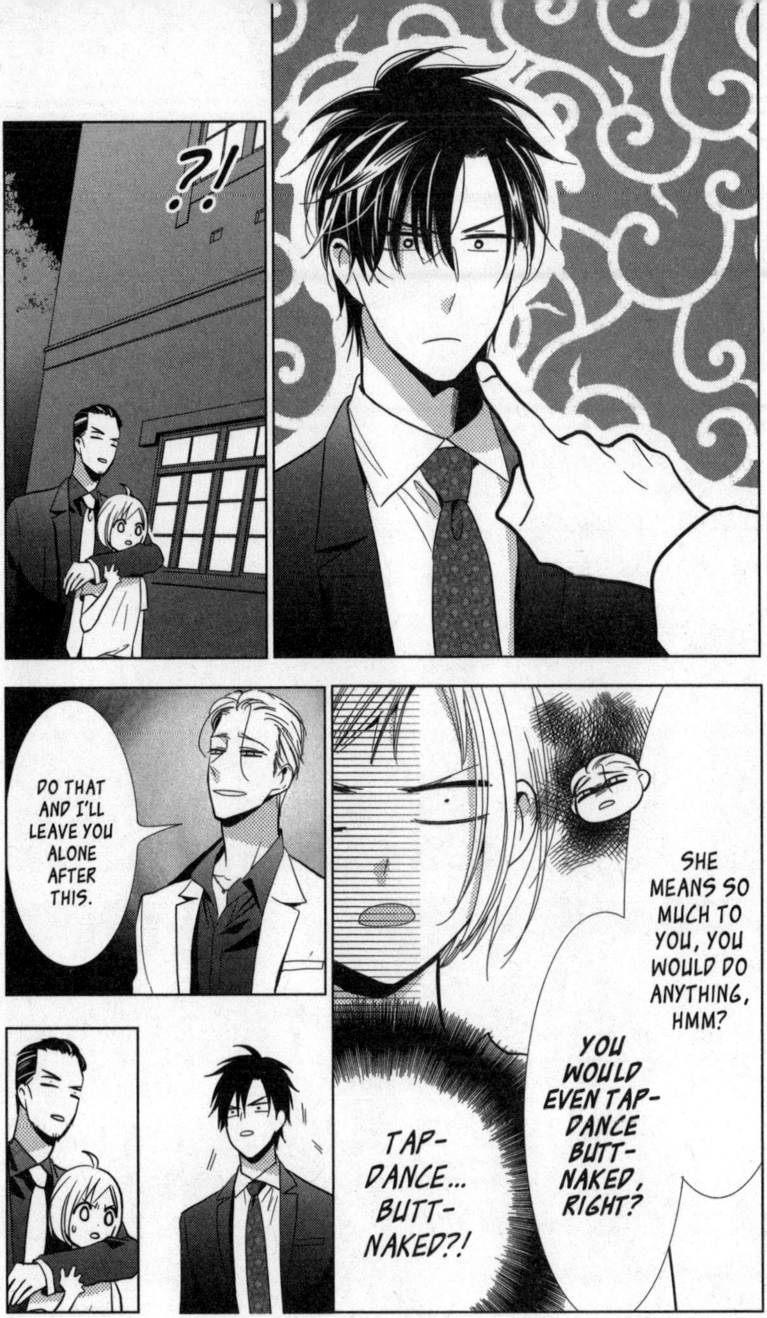
?!
SHE MEANS SO MUCH TO YOU, YOU WOULD DO ANYTHING, HMM?
YOU WOULD EVEN TAP-DANCE BUTT-NAKED, RIGHT?
TAP-DANCE... BUTT-NAKED?!
DO THAT AND I'LL LEAVE YOU ALONE AFTER THIS.

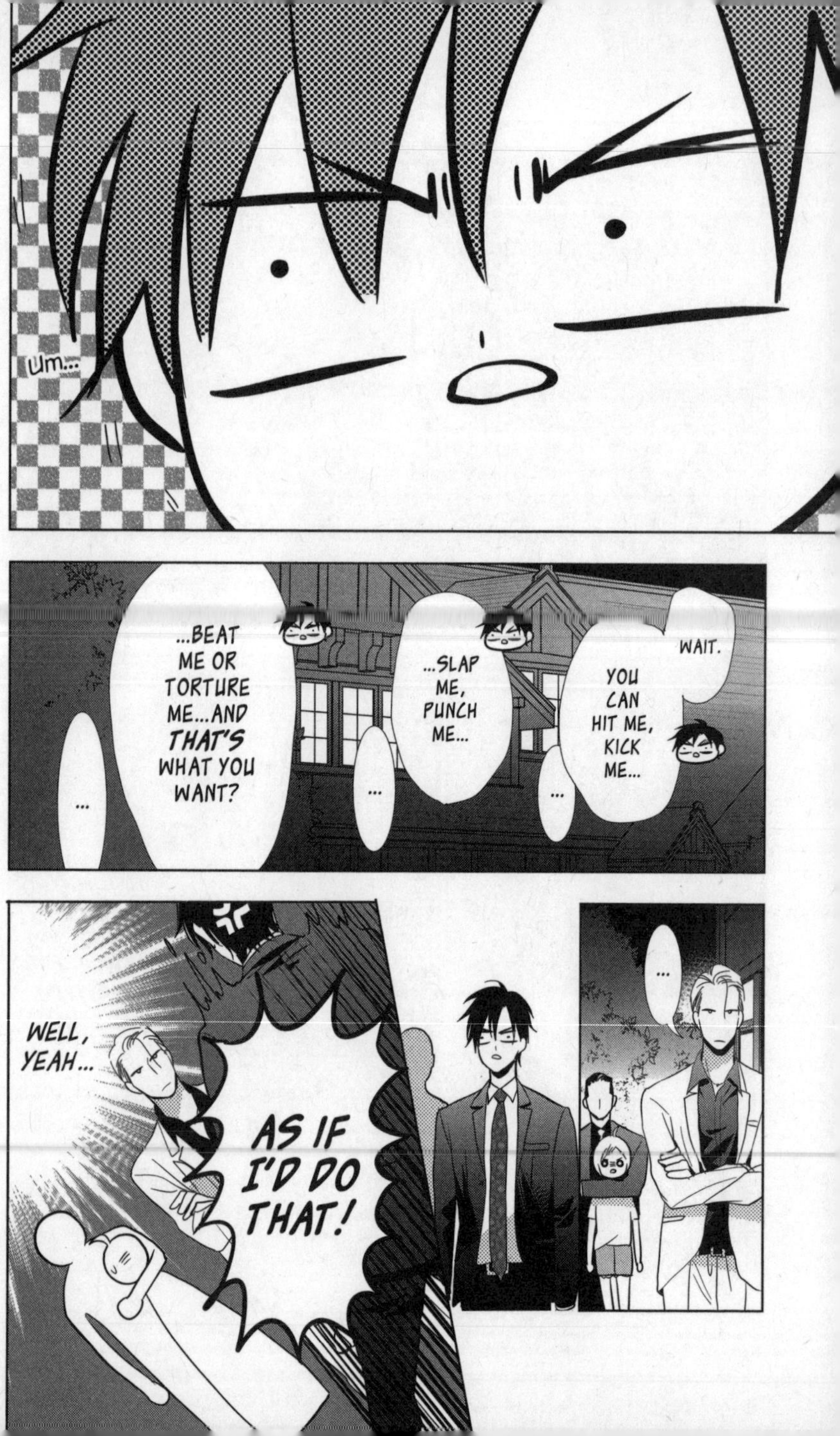
Um...
WAIT.
YOU CAN HIT ME, KICK ME...
...
...SLAP ME, PUNCH ME...
...
...BEAT ME OR TORTURE ME...AND THAT'S WHAT YOU WANT?
...
...
WELL, YEAH...
AS IF I'D DO THAT!

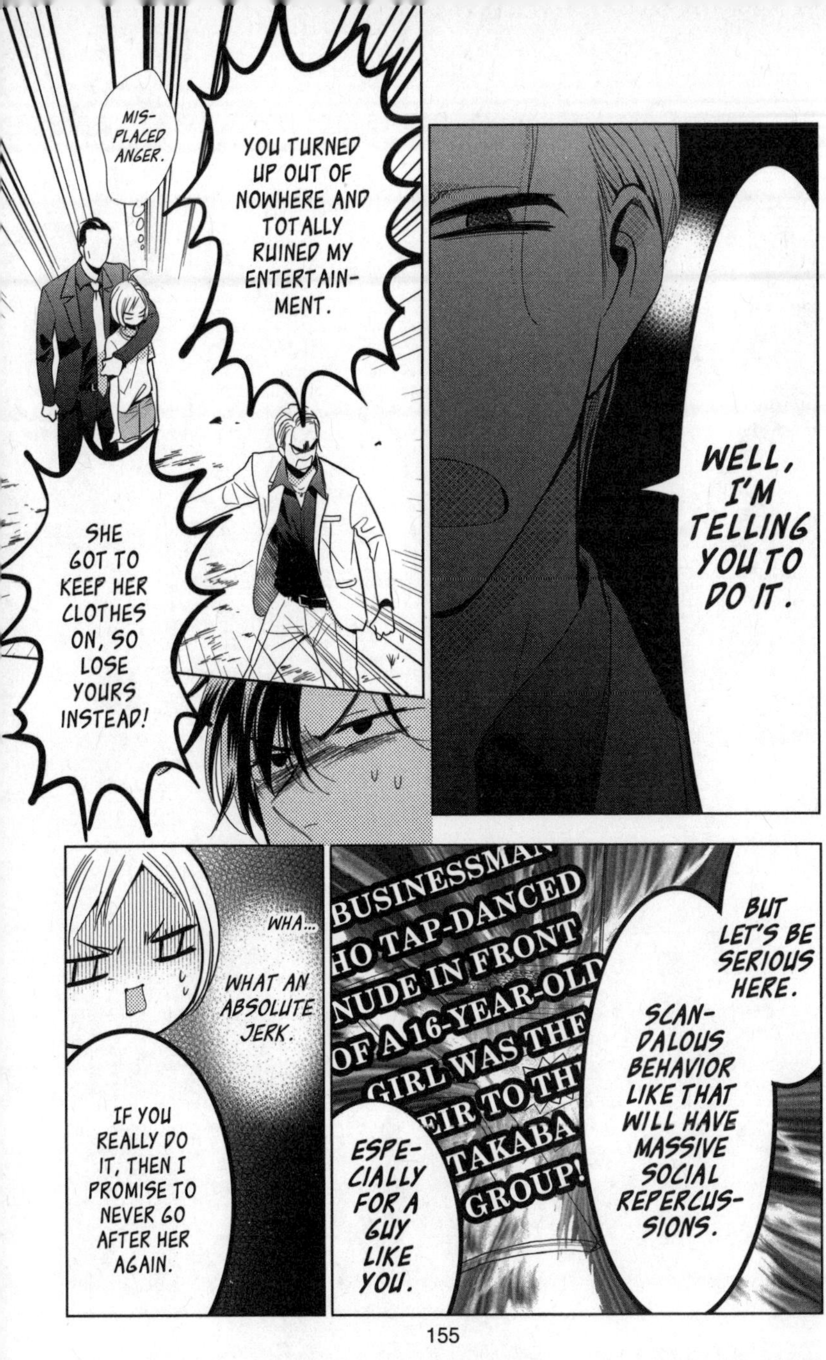
WELL, I'M TELLING YOU TO DO IT.
YOU TURNED UP OUT OF NOWHERE AND TOTALLY RUINED MY ENTERTAIN-MENT.
MIS-PLACED ANGER.
SHE GOT TO KEEP HER CLOTHES ON, SO LOSE YOURS INSTEAD!
BUT LET'S BE SERIOUS HERE.
SCAN-DALOUS BEHAVIOR LIKE THAT WILL HAVE MASSIVE SOCIAL REPERCUS-SIONS.
BUSINESSMAN HO TAP-DANCED NUDE IN FRONT OF A 16-YEAR-OLD GIRL WAS THE EIR TO TH TAKABA GROUP!
ESPE-CIALLY FOR A GUY LIKE YOU.
WHA...
WHAT AN ABSOLUTE JERK.
IF YOU REALLY DO IT, THEN I PROMISE TO NEVER GO AFTER HER AGAIN.

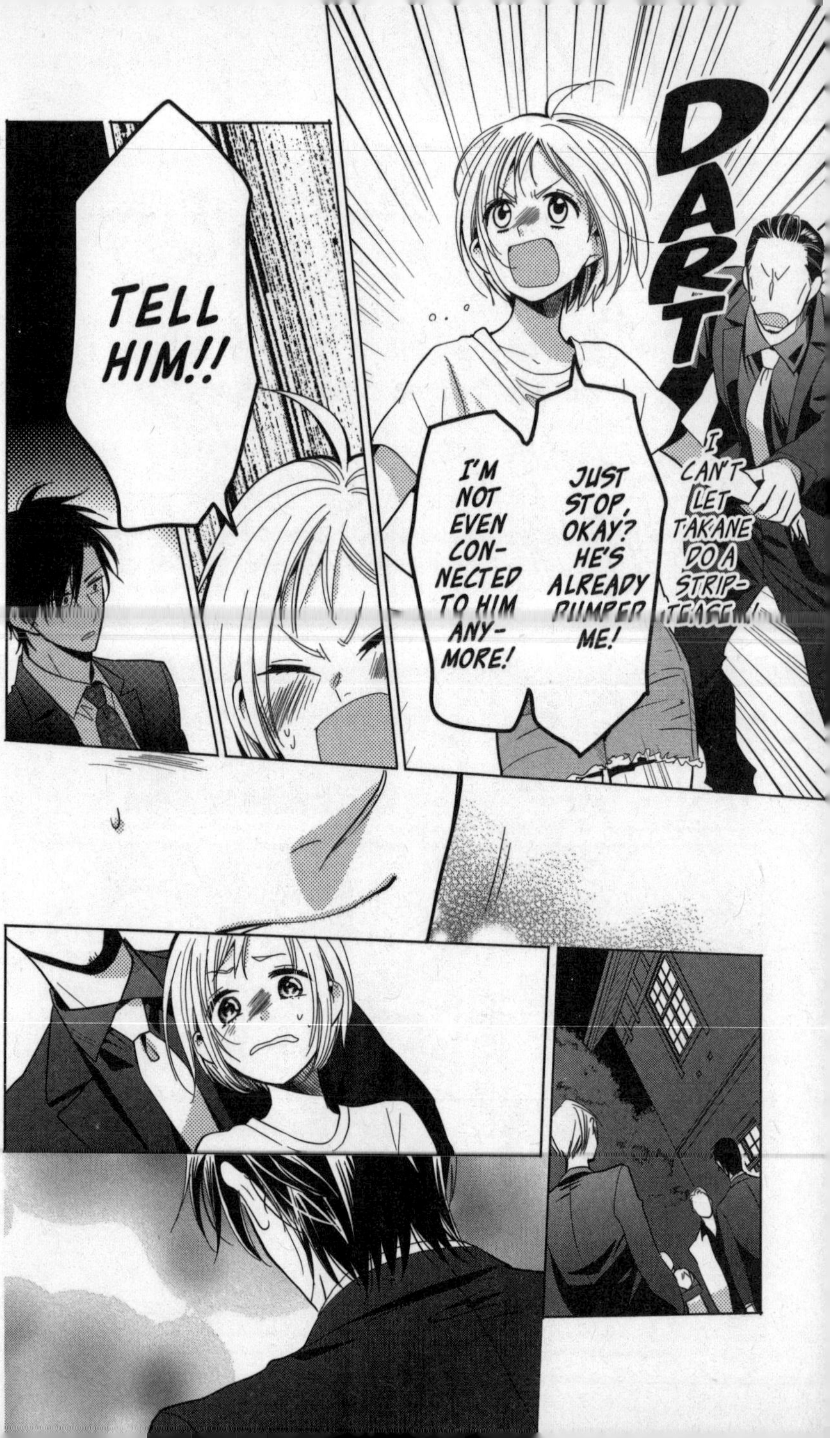
DART
I CAN'T LET TAKANE DO A STRIP-TEASE!
JUST STOP, OKAY? HE'S ALREADY DUMPED ME!
I'M NOT EVEN CONNECTED TO HIM ANYMORE!
TELL HIM!!

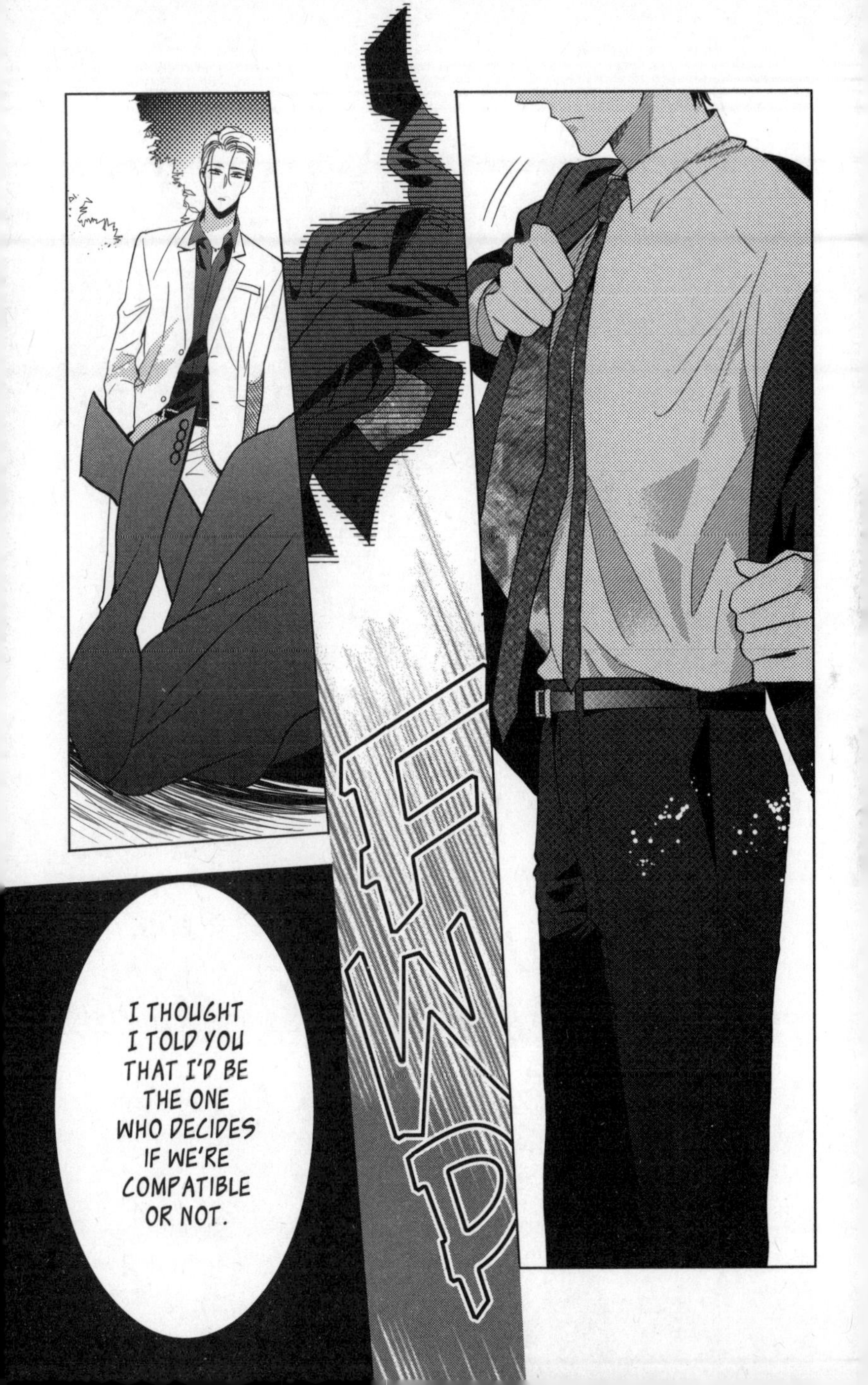
ZIP
I THOUGHT I TOLD YOU THAT I'D BE THE ONE WHO DECIDES IF WE'RE COMPATIBLE OR NOT.

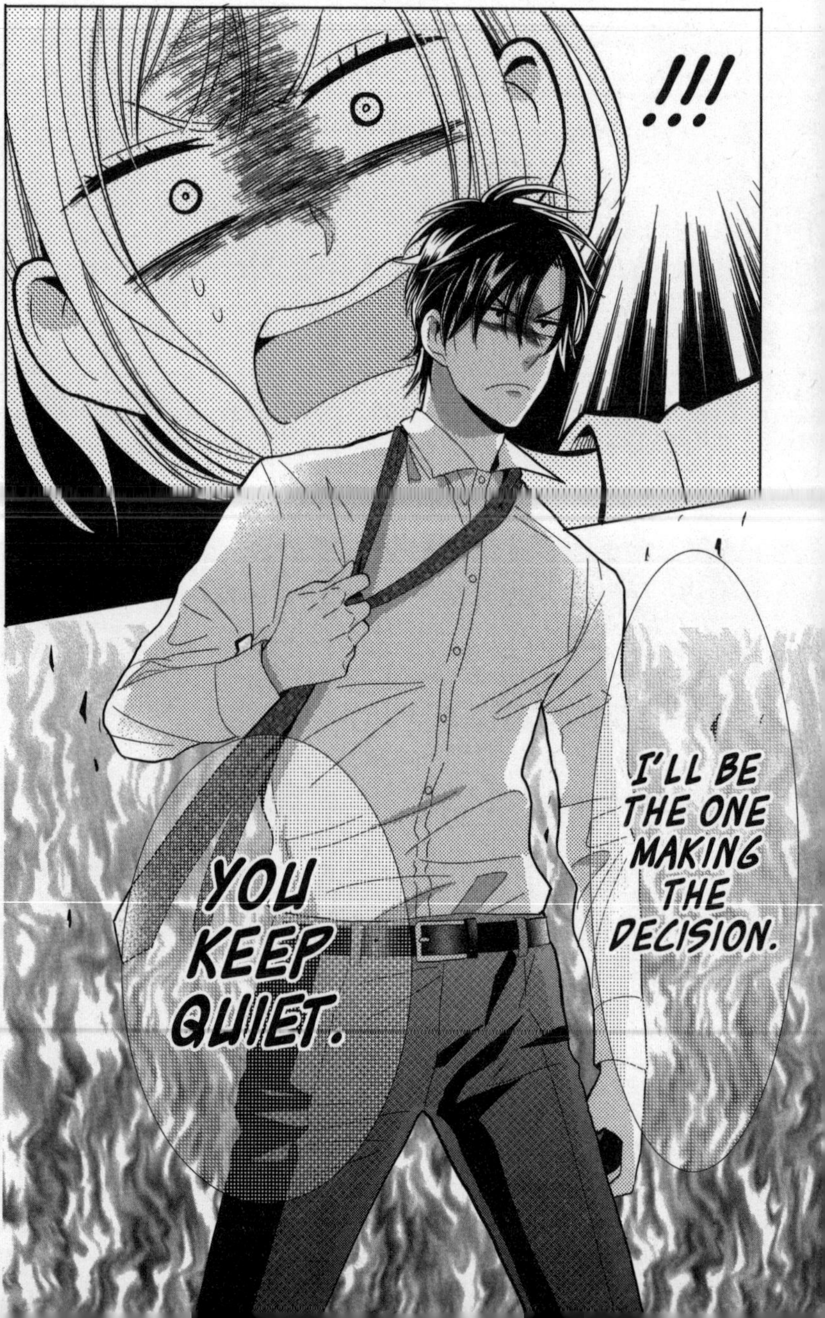
!!!
I'LL BE THE ONE MAKING THE DECISION.
YOU KEEP QUIET.

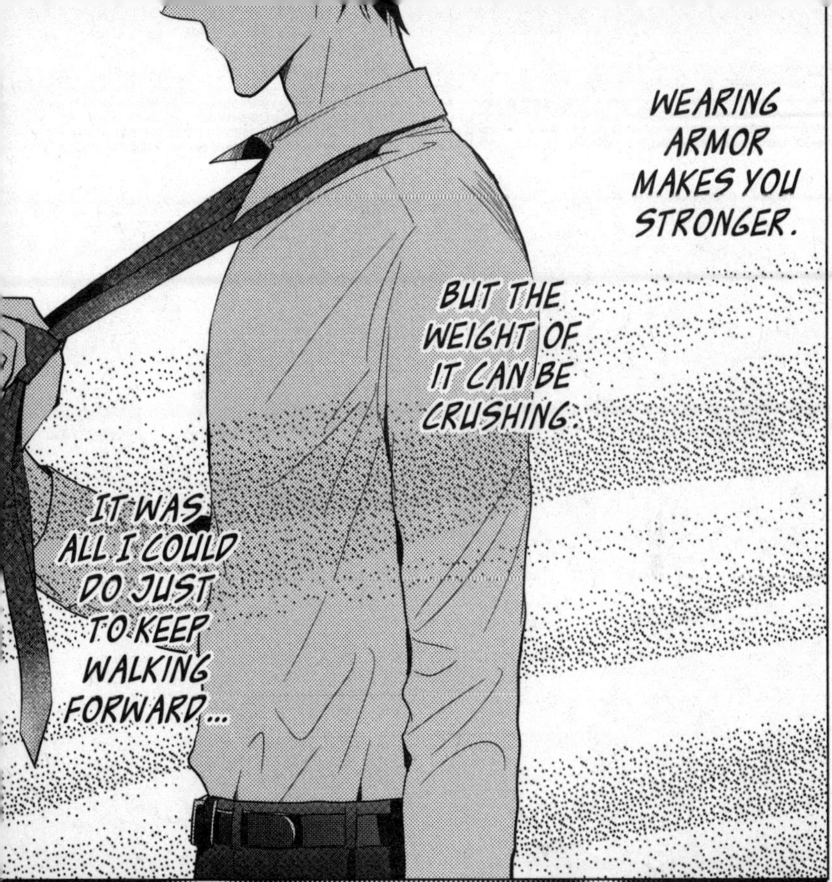
WEARING ARMOR MAKES YOU STRONGER.
BUT THE WEIGHT OF IT CAN BE CRUSHING.
IT WAS ALL I COULD DO JUST TO KEEP WALKING FORWARD...
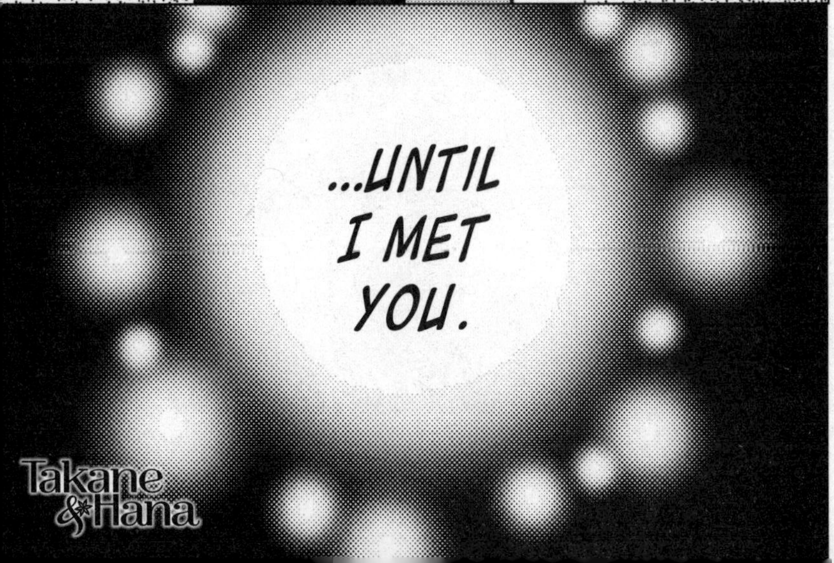
...UNTIL I MET YOU.

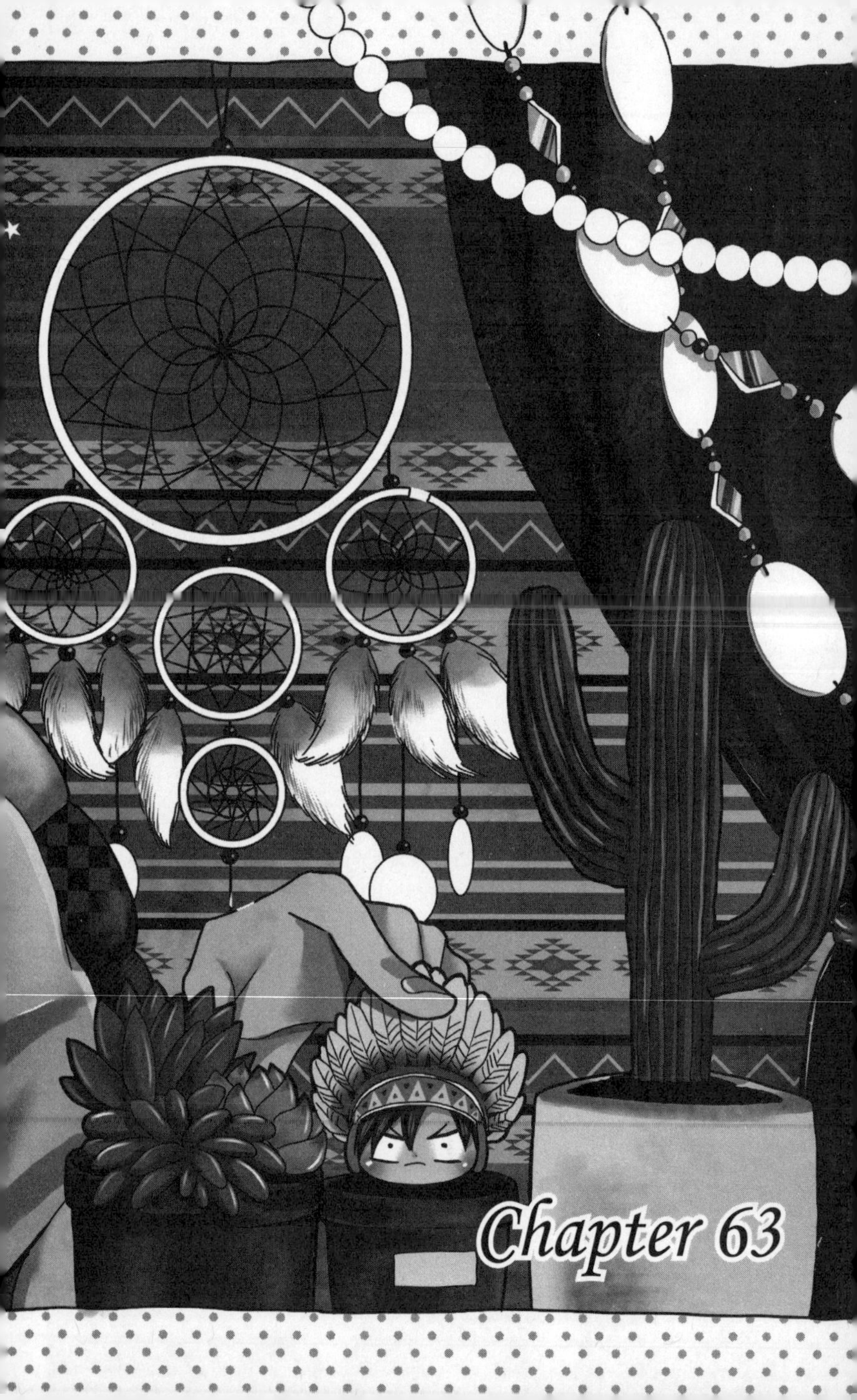
Chapter 63

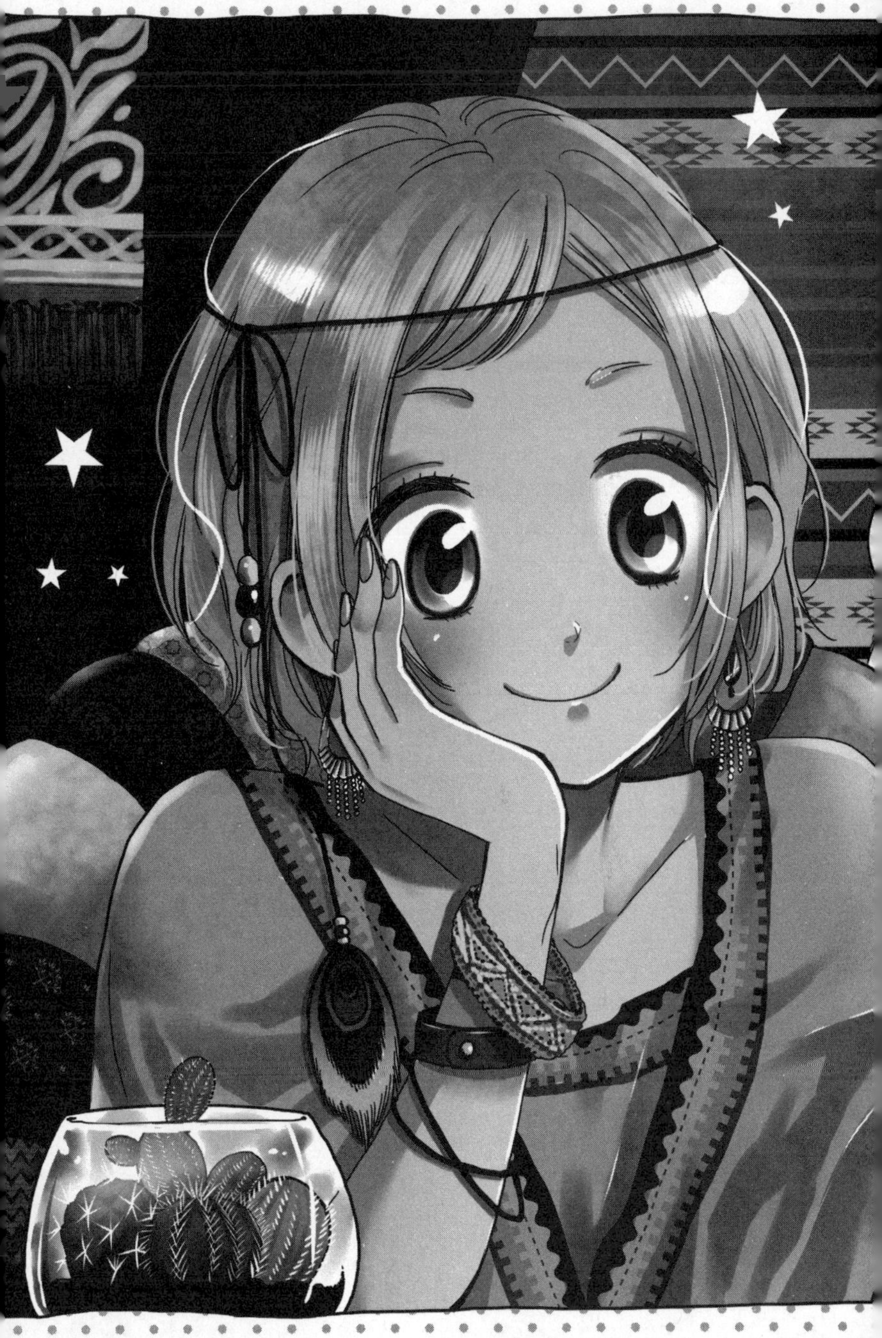

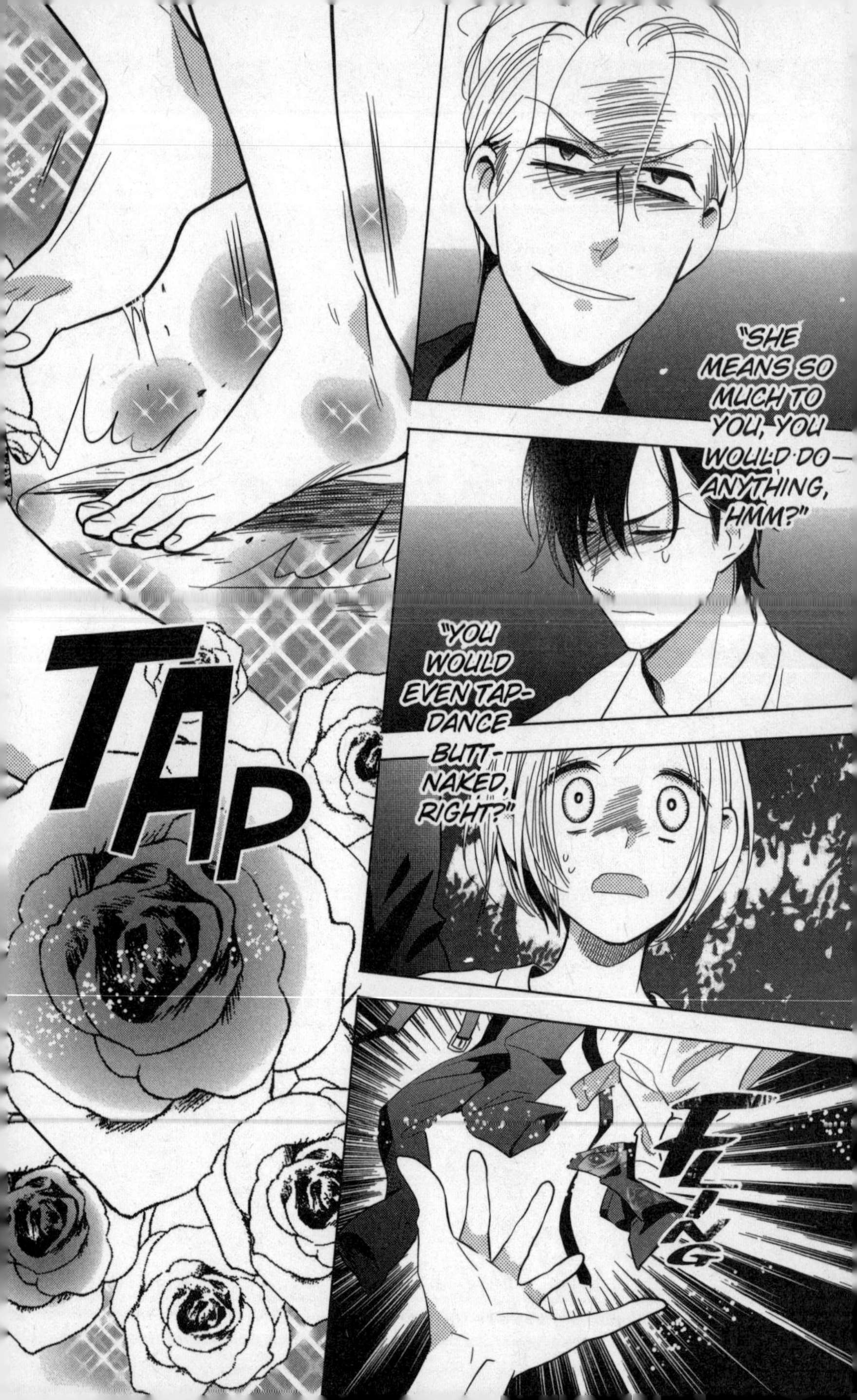
"SHE MEANS SO MUCH TO YOU, YOU WOULD DO ANYTHING, HMM?"
"YOU WOULD EVEN TAP-DANCE BUTT-NAKED, RIGHT?"
FLING
TAP

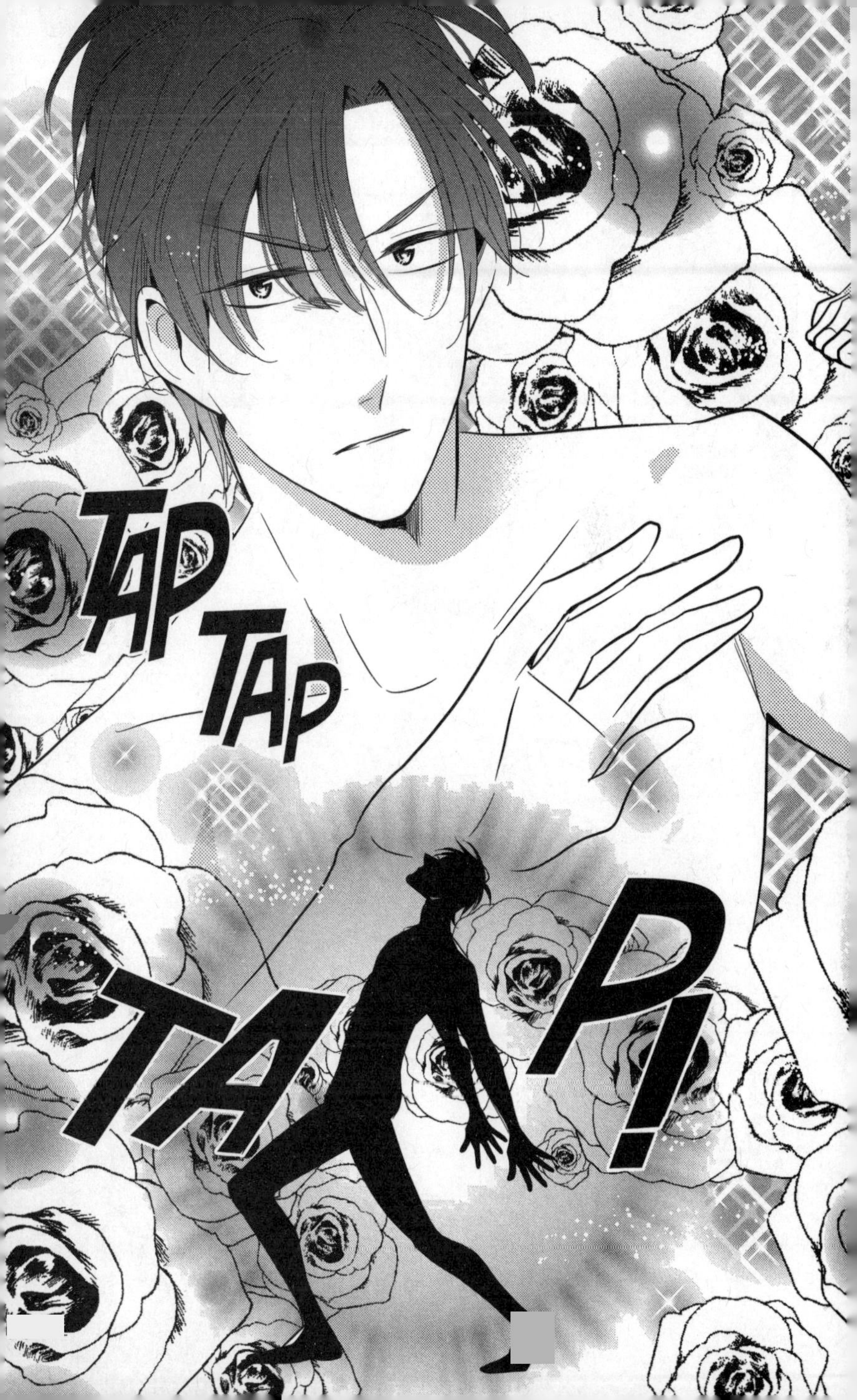
TAP
TAP
TAP!

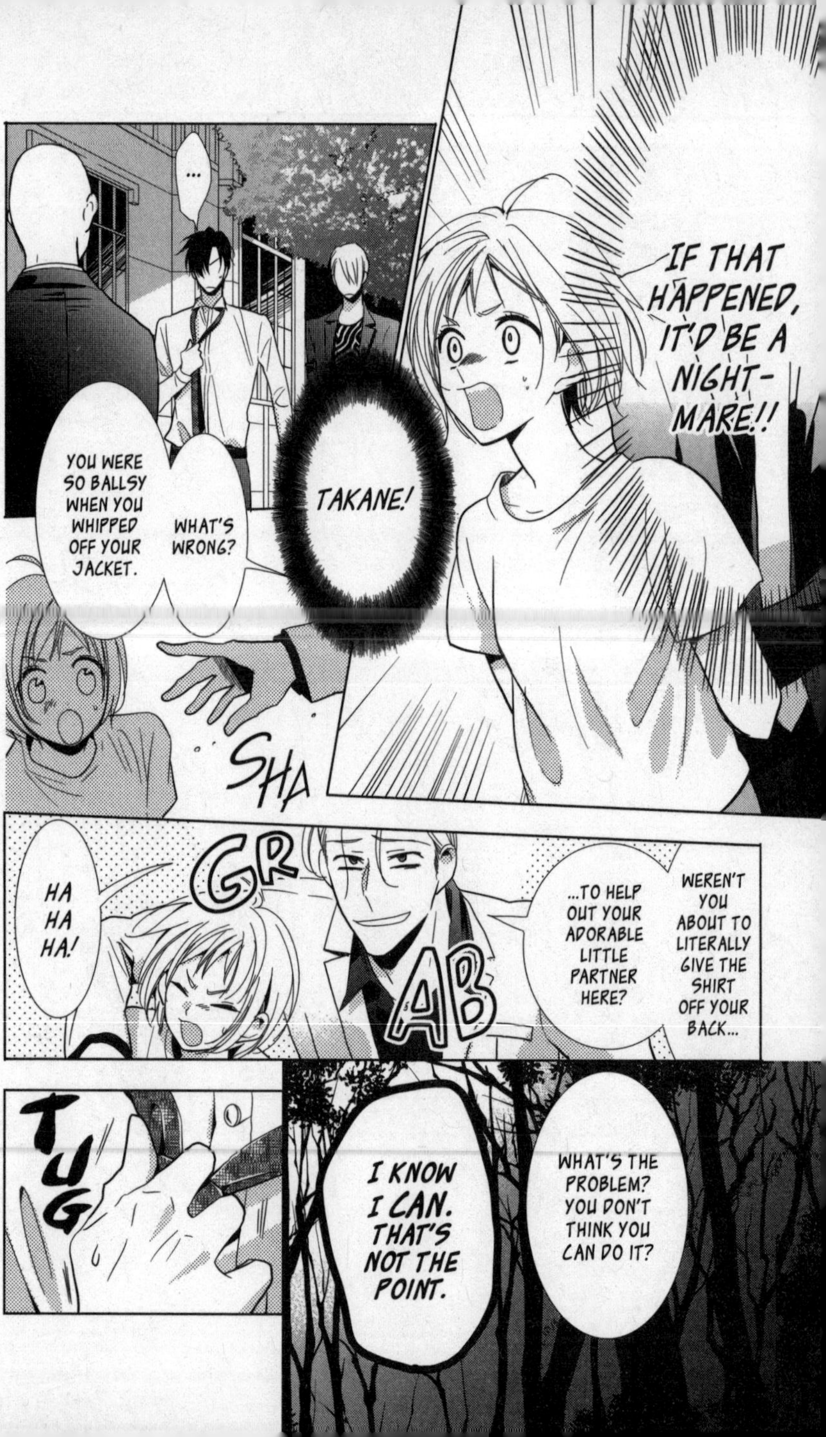
IF THAT HAPPENED, IT'D BE A NIGHT-MARE!!
...
TAKANE!
WHAT'S WRONG?
YOU WERE SO BALLSY WHEN YOU WHIPPED OFF YOUR JACKET.
SHA
WEREN'T YOU ABOUT TO LITERALLY GIVE THE SHIRT OFF YOUR BACK...
...TO HELP OUT YOUR ADORABLE LITTLE PARTNER HERE?
GRAB
HA HA HA!
WHAT'S THE PROBLEM? YOU DON'T THINK YOU CAN DO IT?
I KNOW I CAN. THAT'S NOT THE POINT.
TUG

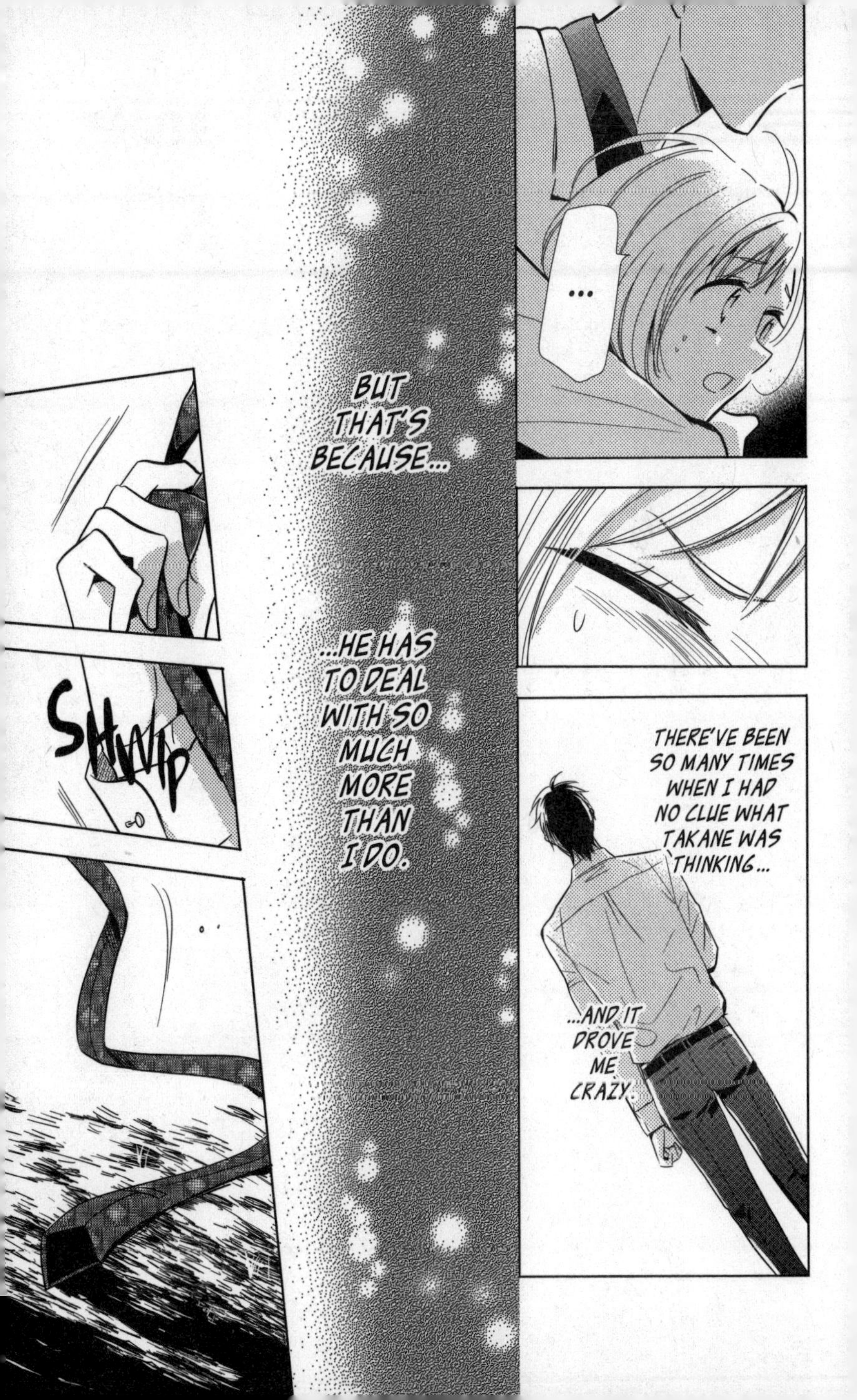
...
THERE'VE BEEN SO MANY TIMES WHEN I HAD NO CLUE WHAT TAKANE WAS THINKING...
...AND IT DROVE ME CRAZY.
BUT THAT'S BECAUSE...
...HE HAS TO DEAL WITH SO MUCH MORE THAN I DO.
SHWIP

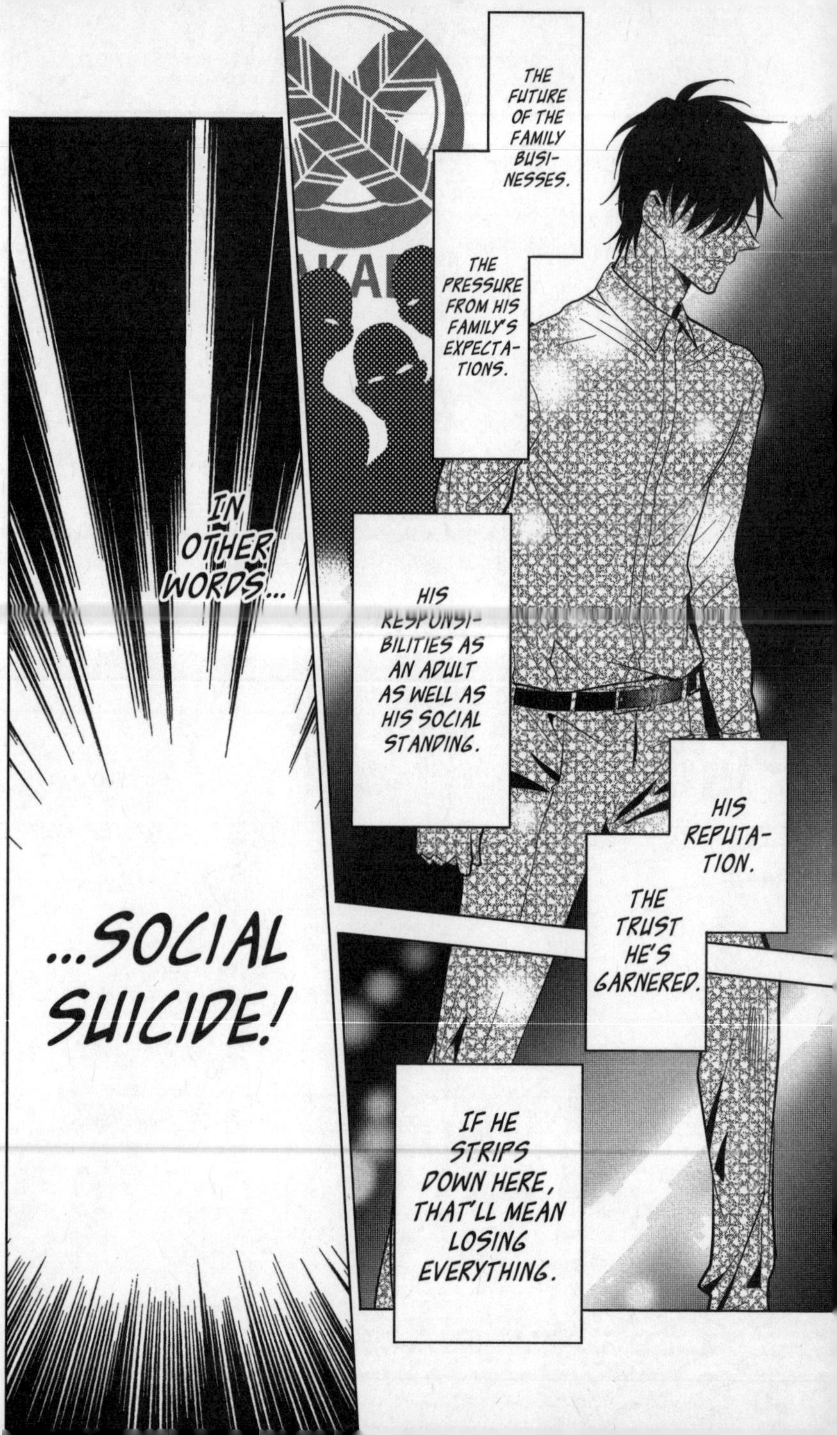
THE FUTURE OF THE FAMILY BUSINESSES.
THE PRESSURE FROM HIS FAMILY'S EXPECTATIONS.
HIS RESPONSIBILITIES AS AN ADULT AS WELL AS HIS SOCIAL STANDING.
HIS REPUTATION.
THE TRUST HE'S GARNERED.
IF HE STRIPS DOWN HERE, THAT'LL MEAN LOSING EVERYTHING.
IN OTHER WORDS...
...SOCIAL SUICIDE!

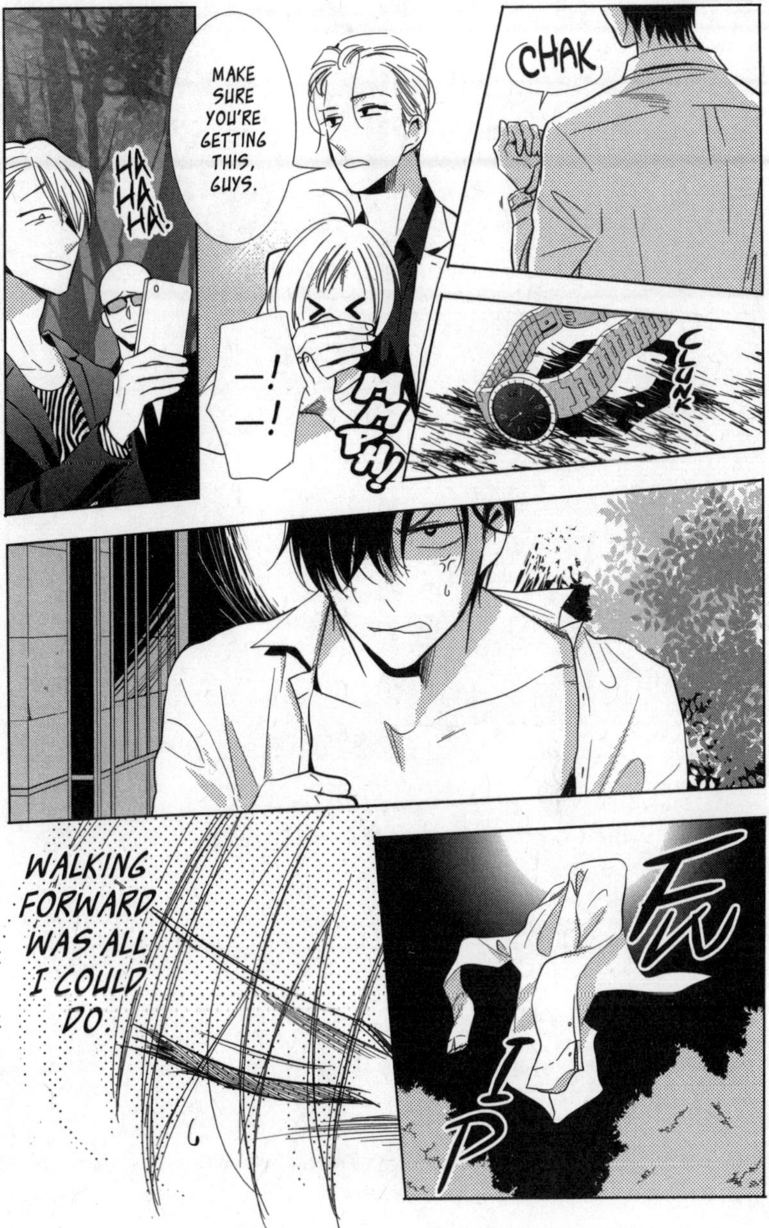
CHAK
CLUNK
MAKE SURE YOU'RE GETTING THIS, GUYS.
—! —!
MMPH!
HA HA HA!
FWIP
WALKING FORWARD WAS ALL I COULD DO.

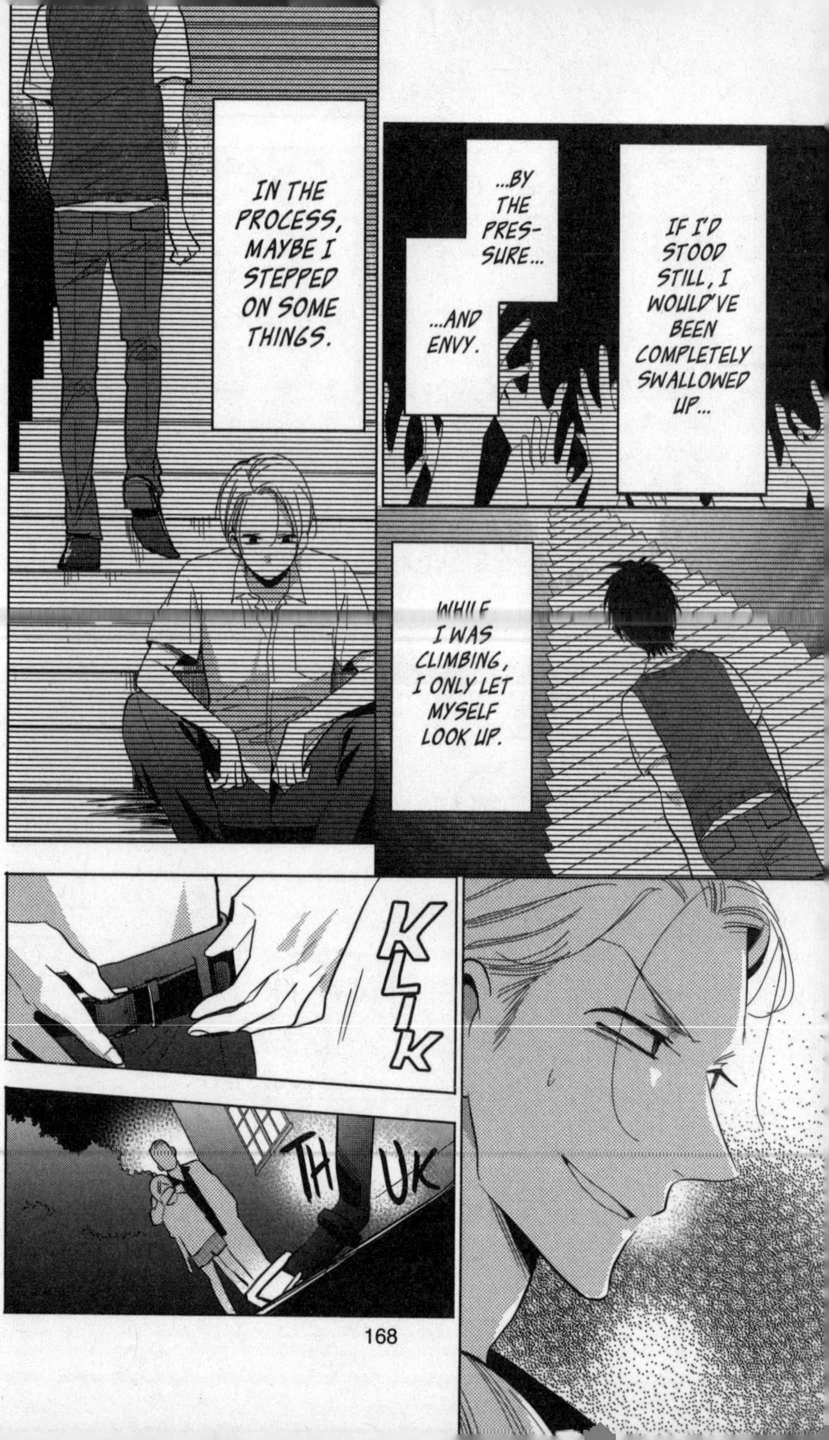
IF I'D STOOD STILL, I WOULD'VE BEEN COMPLETELY SWALLOWED UP...
...BY THE PRES-SURE...
...AND ENVY.
WHILE I WAS CLIMBING, I ONLY LET MYSELF LOOK UP.
IN THE PROCESS, MAYBE I STEPPED ON SOME THINGS.
KLIK
THUK

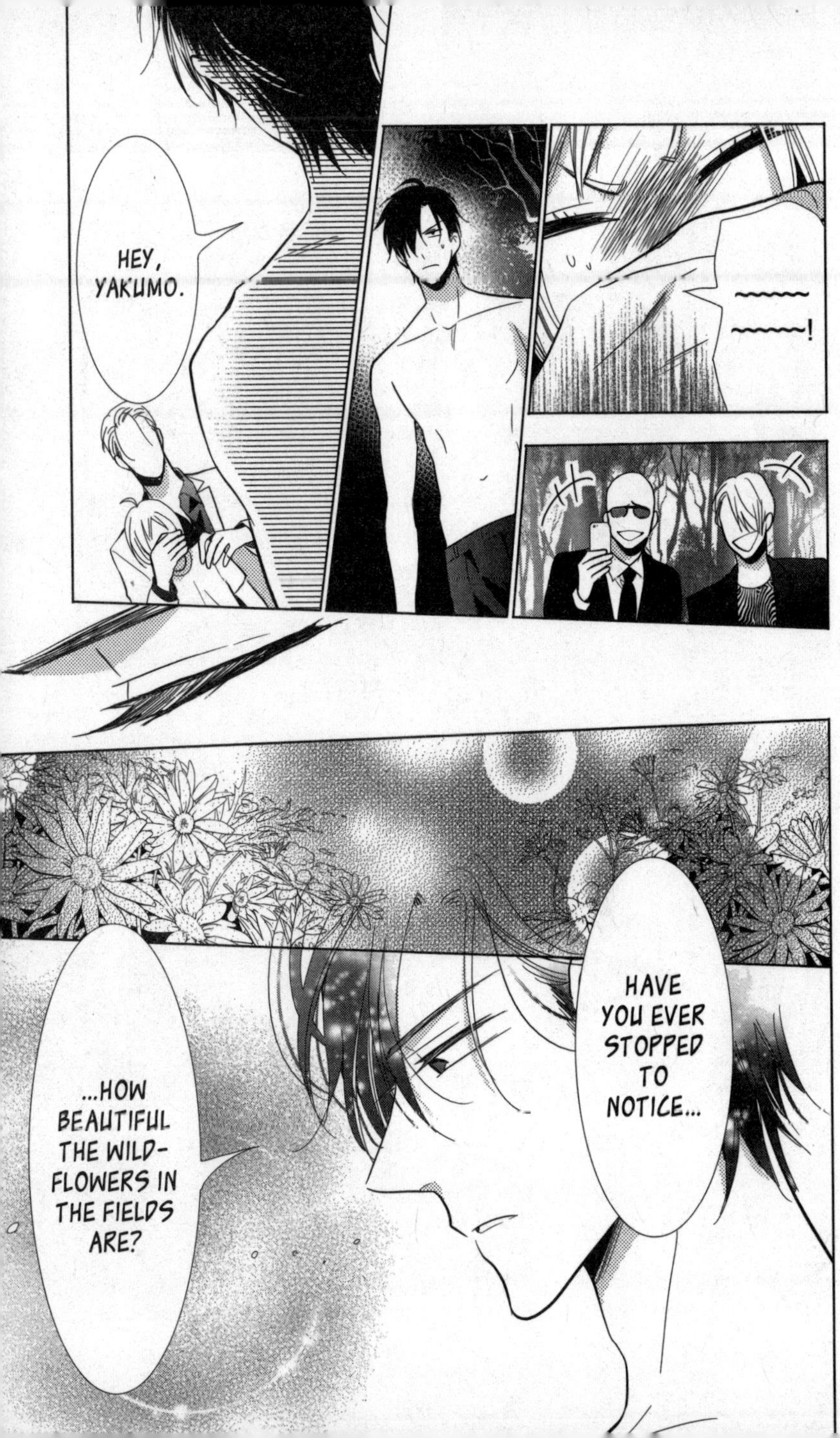
~~~~~
~~~~~!
HEY, YAKUMO.
HAVE YOU EVER STOPPED TO NOTICE...
...HOW BEAUTIFUL THE WILD-FLOWERS IN THE FIELDS ARE?

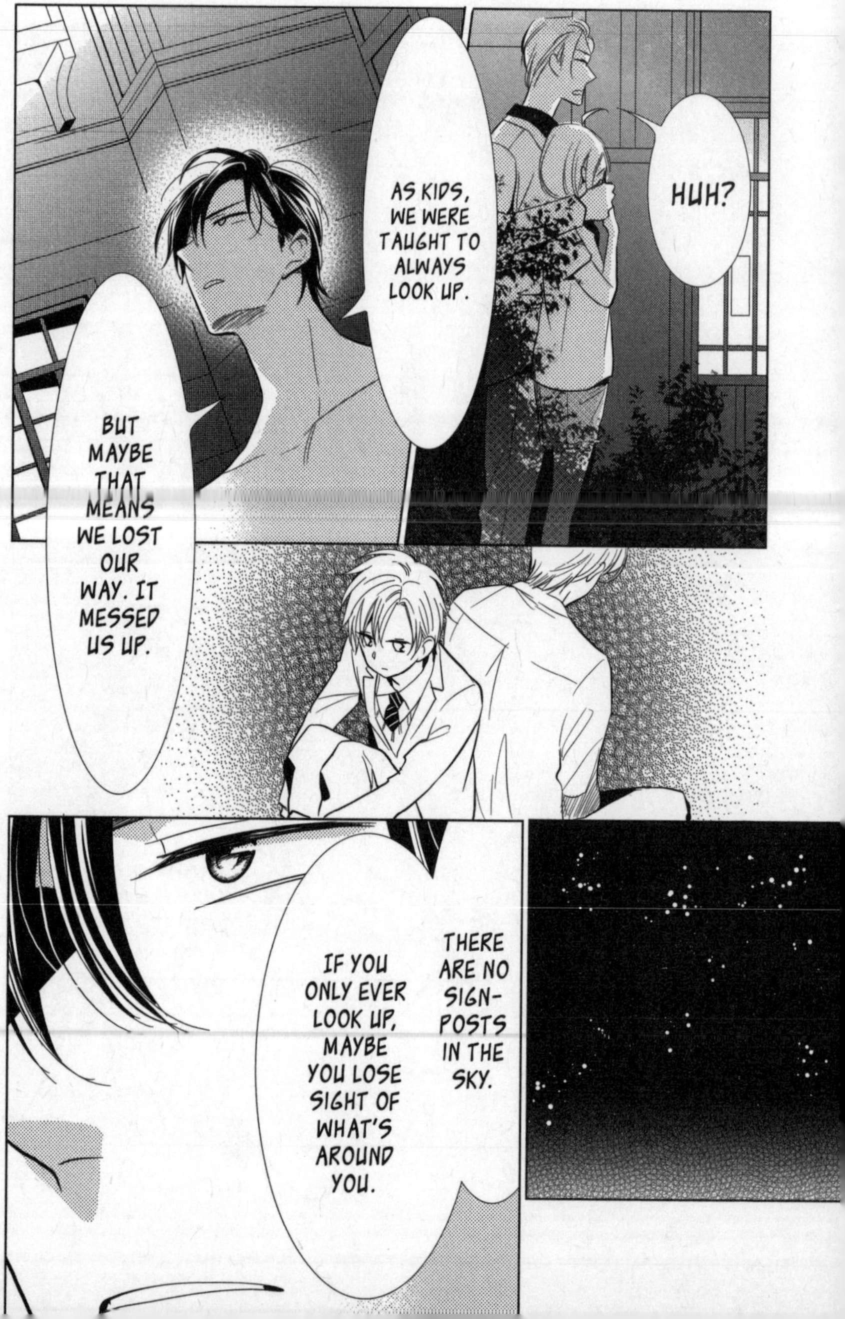
HUH?
AS KIDS, WE WERE TAUGHT TO ALWAYS LOOK UP.
BUT MAYBE THAT MEANS WE LOST OUR WAY. IT MESSED US UP.
THERE ARE NO SIGN-POSTS IN THE SKY.
IF YOU ONLY EVER LOOK UP, MAYBE YOU LOSE SIGHT OF WHAT'S AROUND YOU.

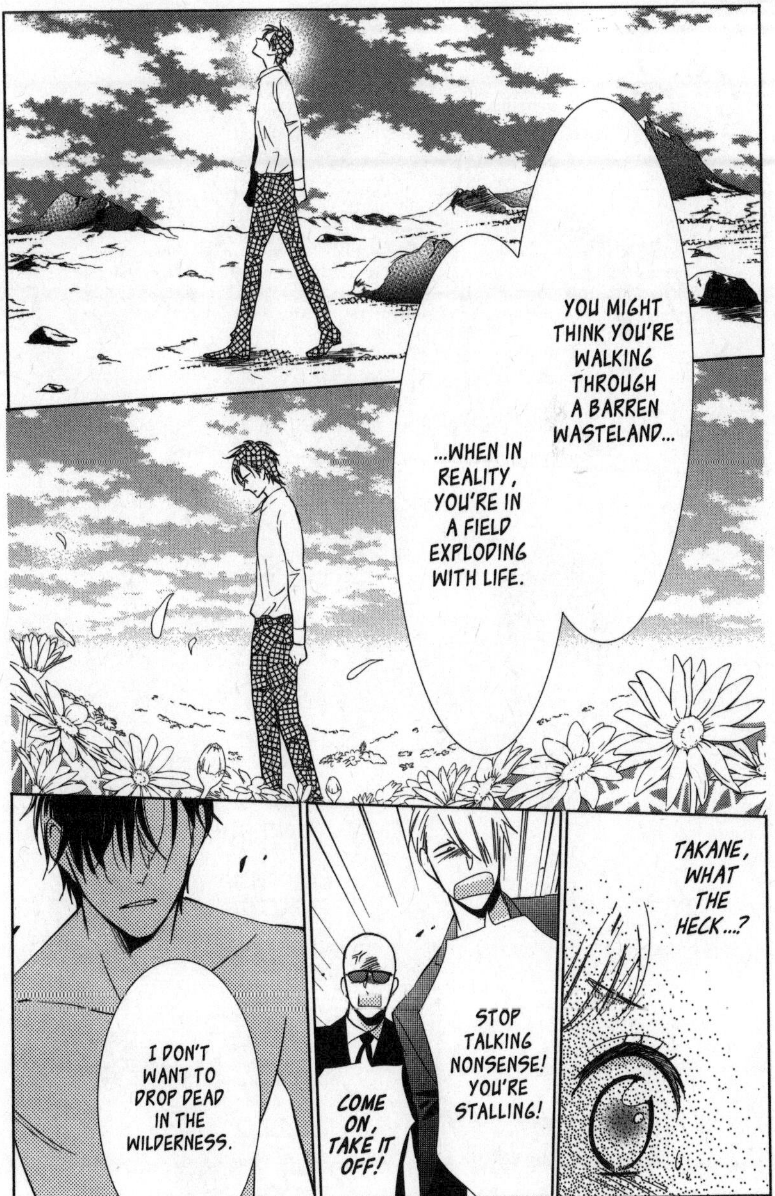
YOU MIGHT THINK YOU'RE WALKING THROUGH A BARREN WASTELAND...
...WHEN IN REALITY, YOU'RE IN A FIELD EXPLODING WITH LIFE.
TAKANE, WHAT THE HECK...?
STOP TALKING NONSENSE! YOU'RE STALLING!
COME ON, TAKE IT OFF!
I DON'T WANT TO DROP DEAD IN THE WILDERNESS.

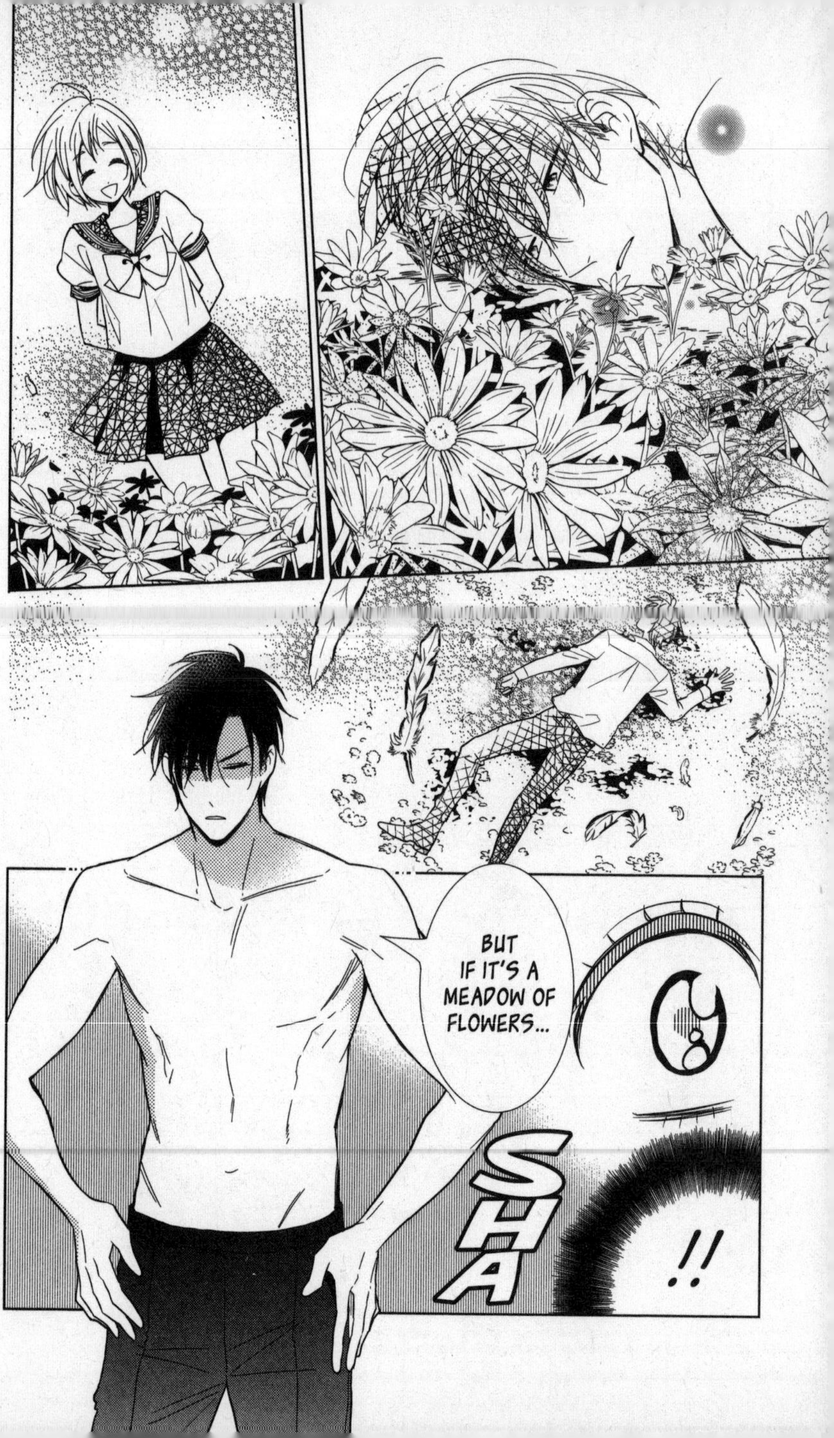
BUT IF IT'S A MEADOW OF FLOWERS...
SHA
!!

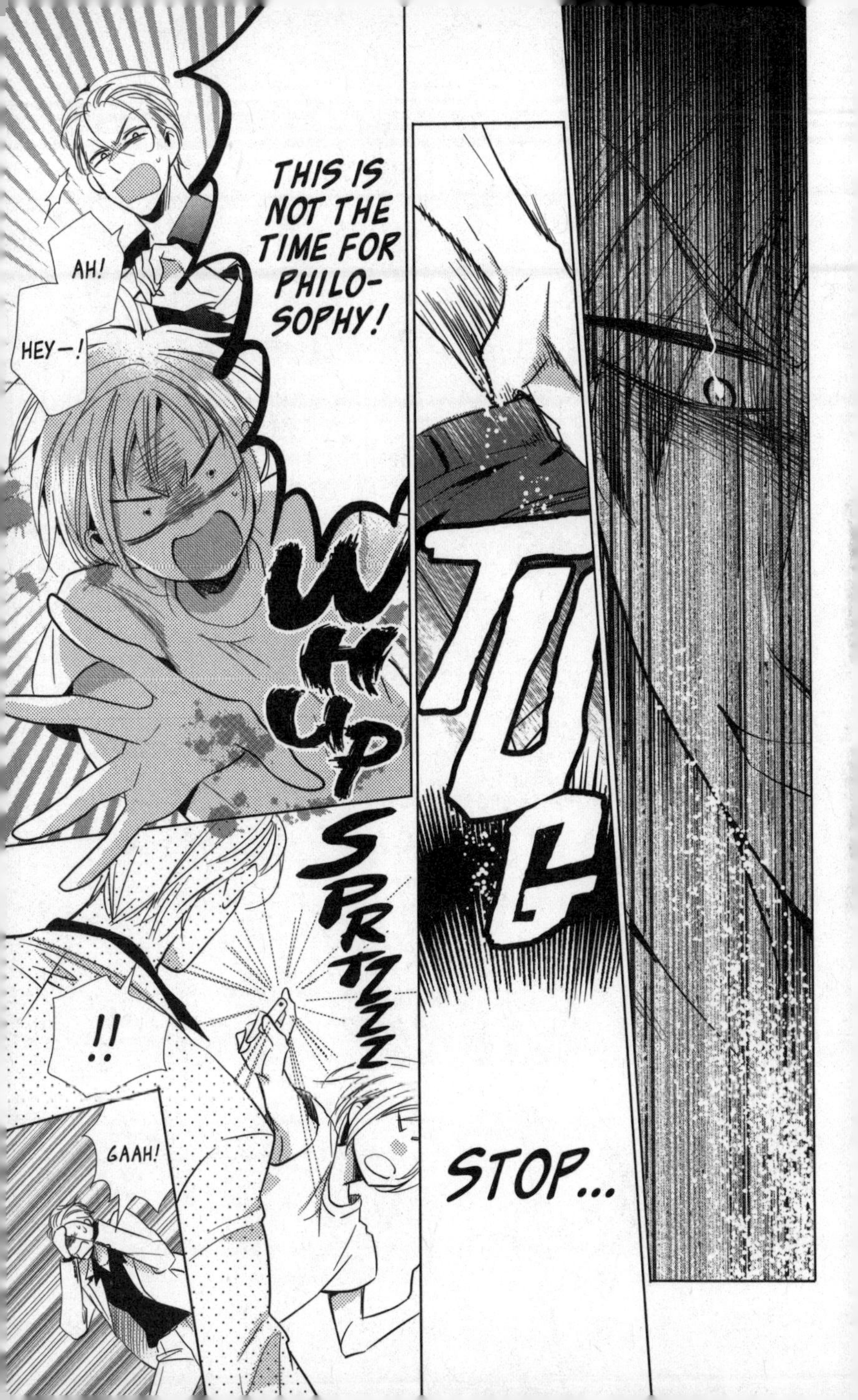
STOP...
TUG
THIS IS NOT THE TIME FOR PHILOSOPHY!
AH!
HEY—!
WHUP
SPRTZZZZ
!!
GAAH!

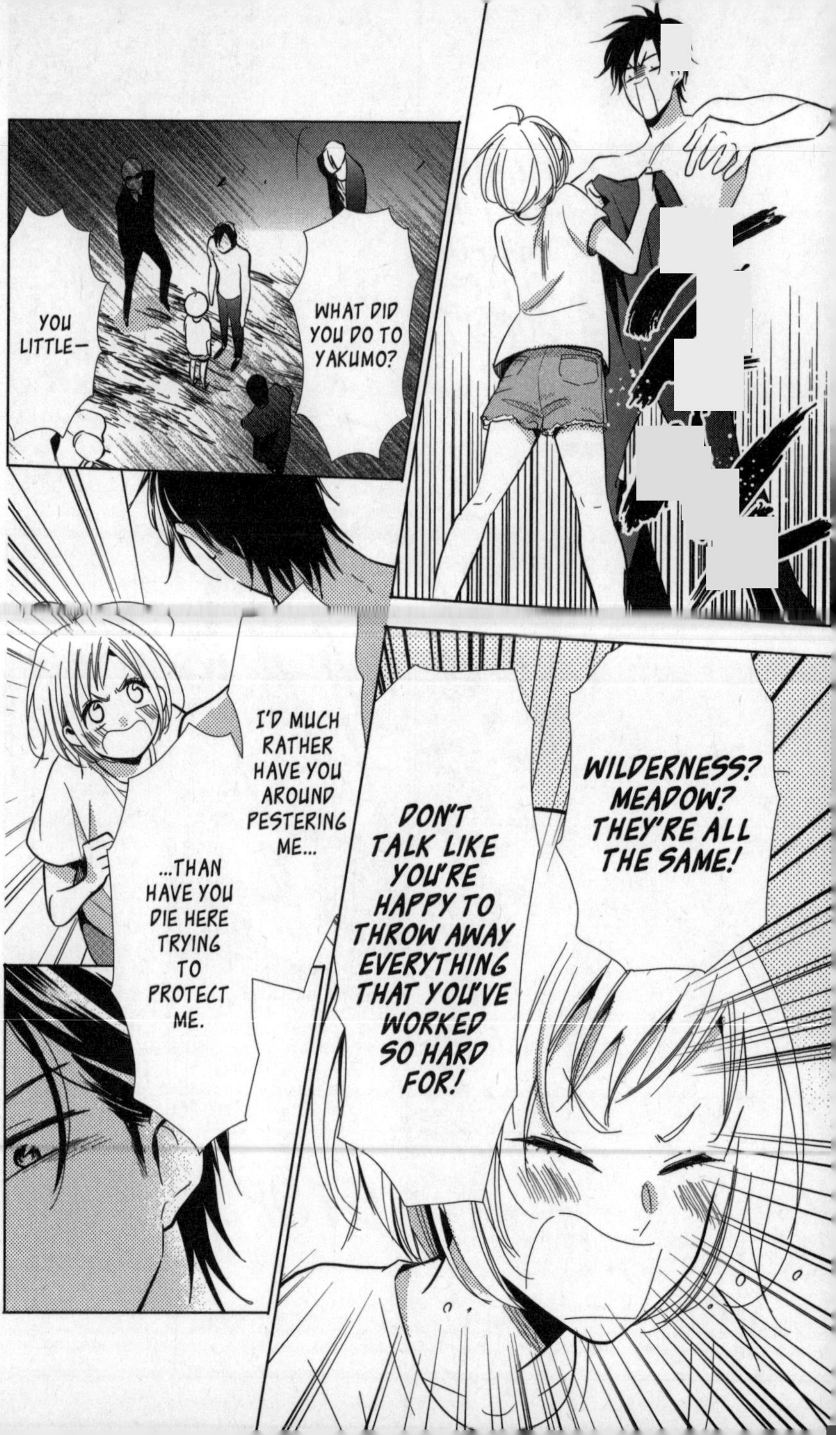
WHAT DID YOU DO TO YAKUMO?
YOU LITTLE—
WILDERNESS? MEADOW? THEY'RE ALL THE SAME!
DON'T TALK LIKE YOU'RE HAPPY TO THROW AWAY EVERYTHING THAT YOU'VE WORKED SO HARD FOR!
I'D MUCH RATHER HAVE YOU AROUND PESTERING ME...
...THAN HAVE YOU DIE HERE TRYING TO PROTECT ME.

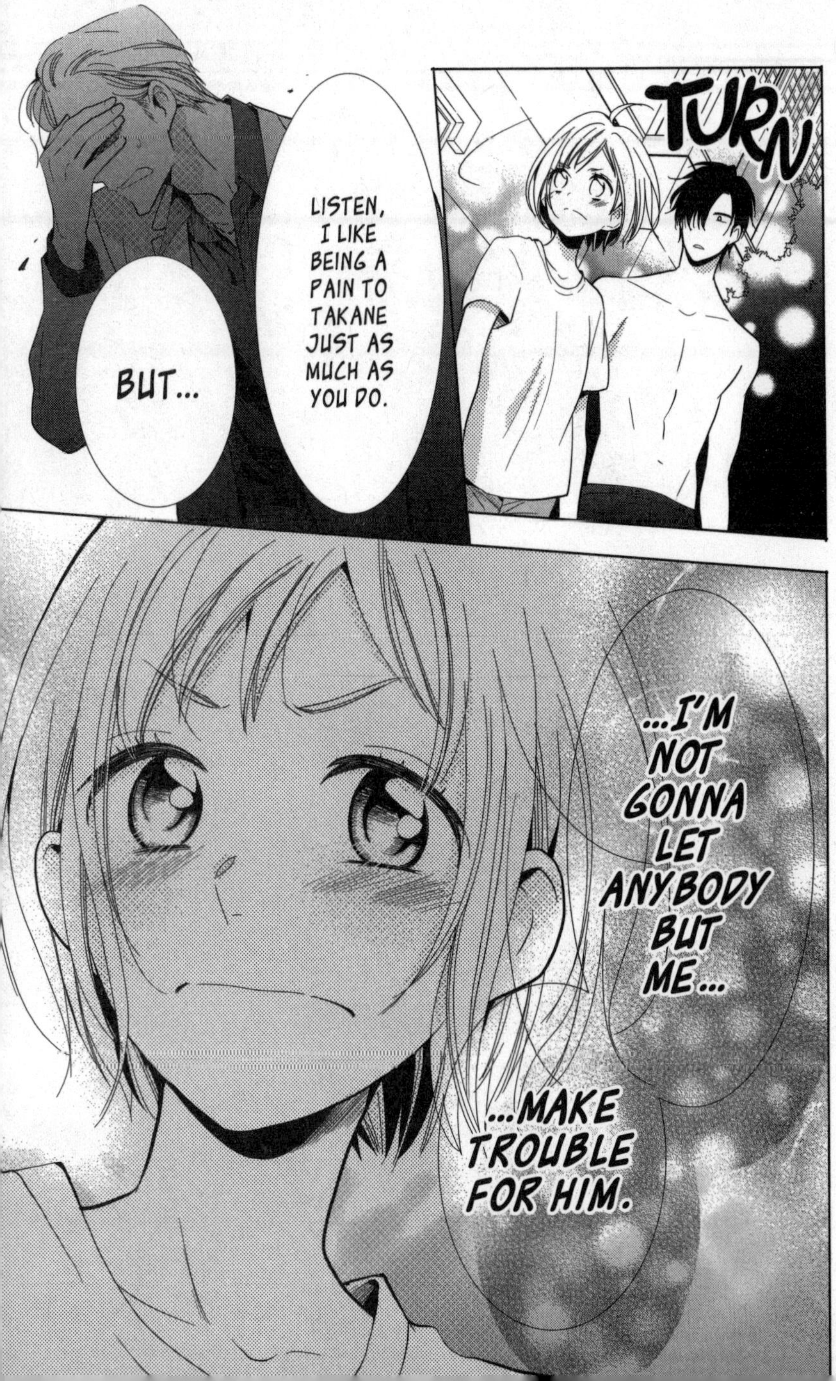
TURN
LISTEN, I LIKE BEING A PAIN TO TAKANE JUST AS MUCH AS YOU DO.
BUT...
...I'M NOT GONNA LET ANYBODY BUT ME...
...MAKE TROUBLE FOR HIM.

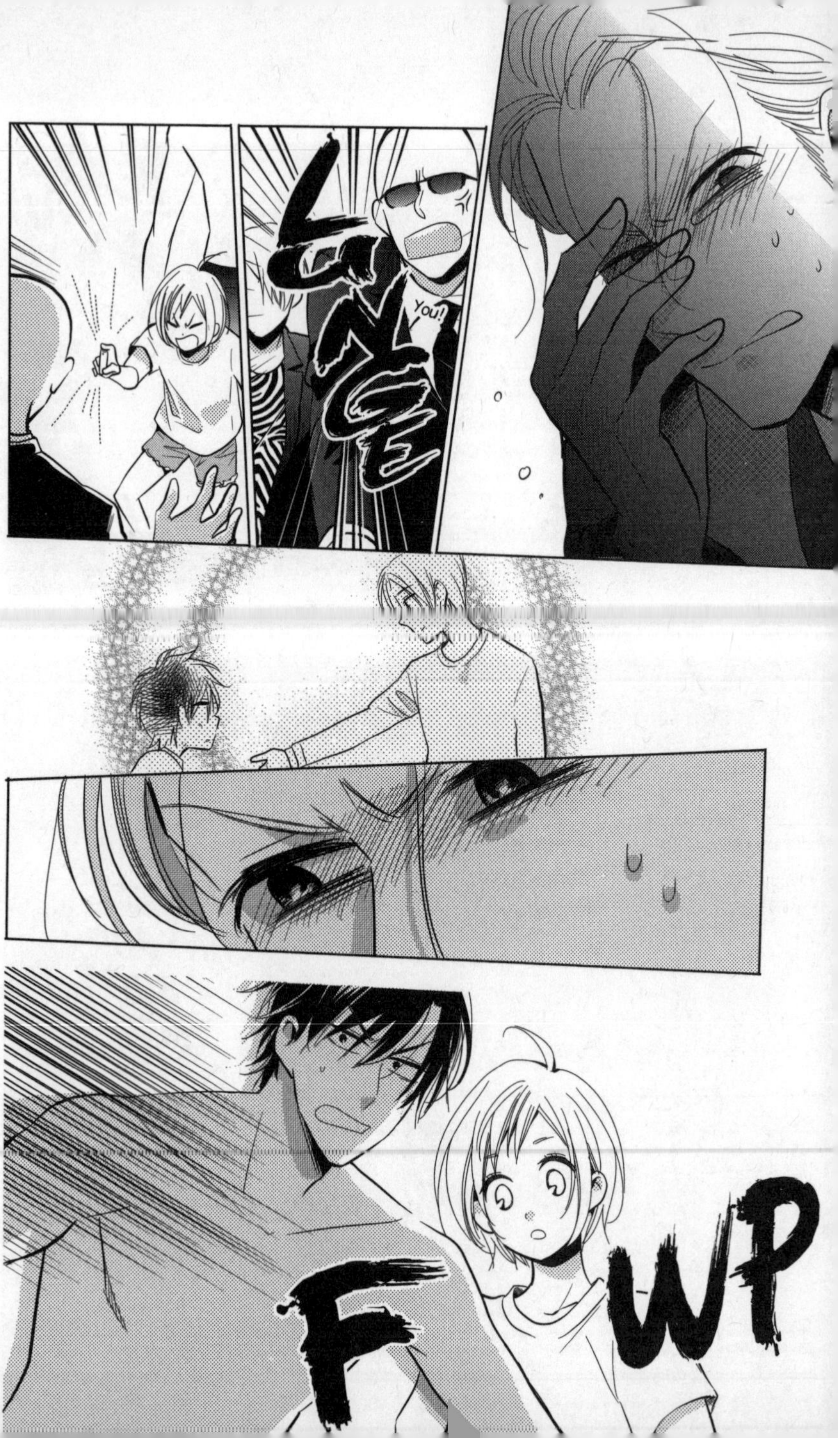
You!
FWP

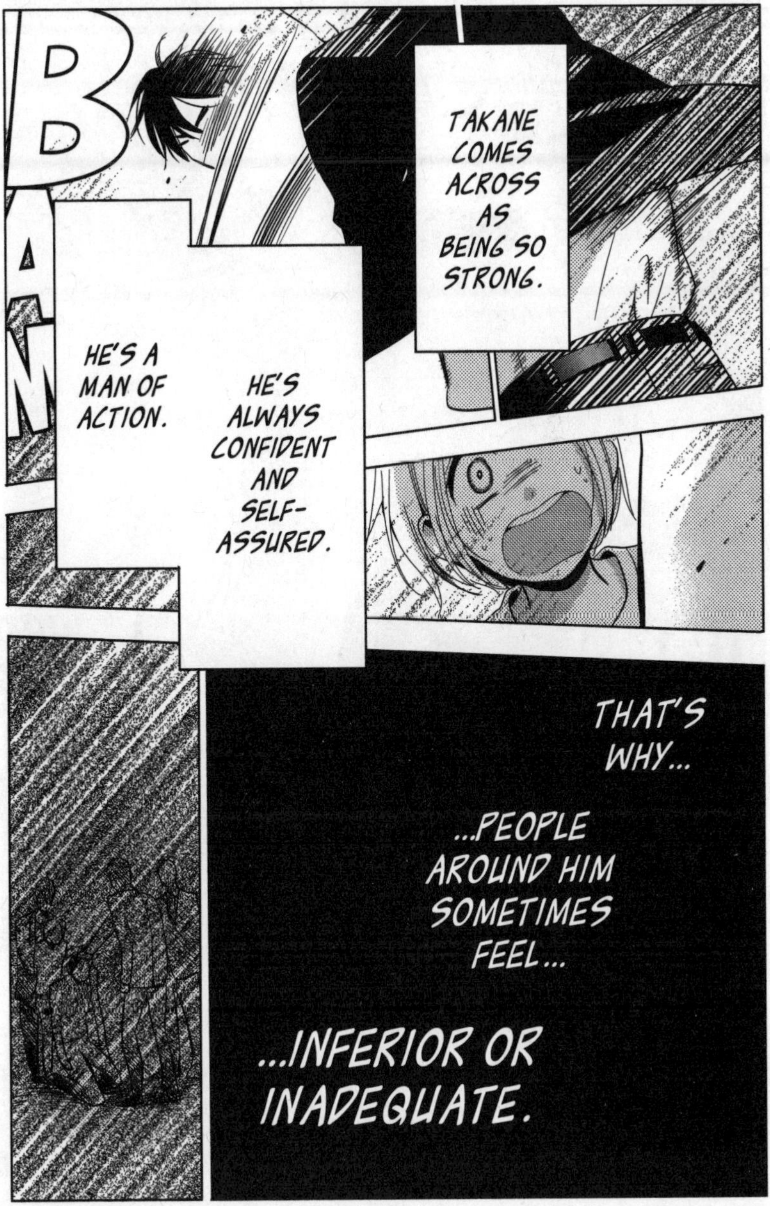
TAKANE COMES ACROSS AS BEING SO STRONG.
BAM
HE'S ALWAYS CONFIDENT AND SELF-ASSURED.
HE'S A MAN OF ACTION.
THAT'S WHY...
...PEOPLE AROUND HIM SOMETIMES FEEL...
...INFERIOR OR INADEQUATE.

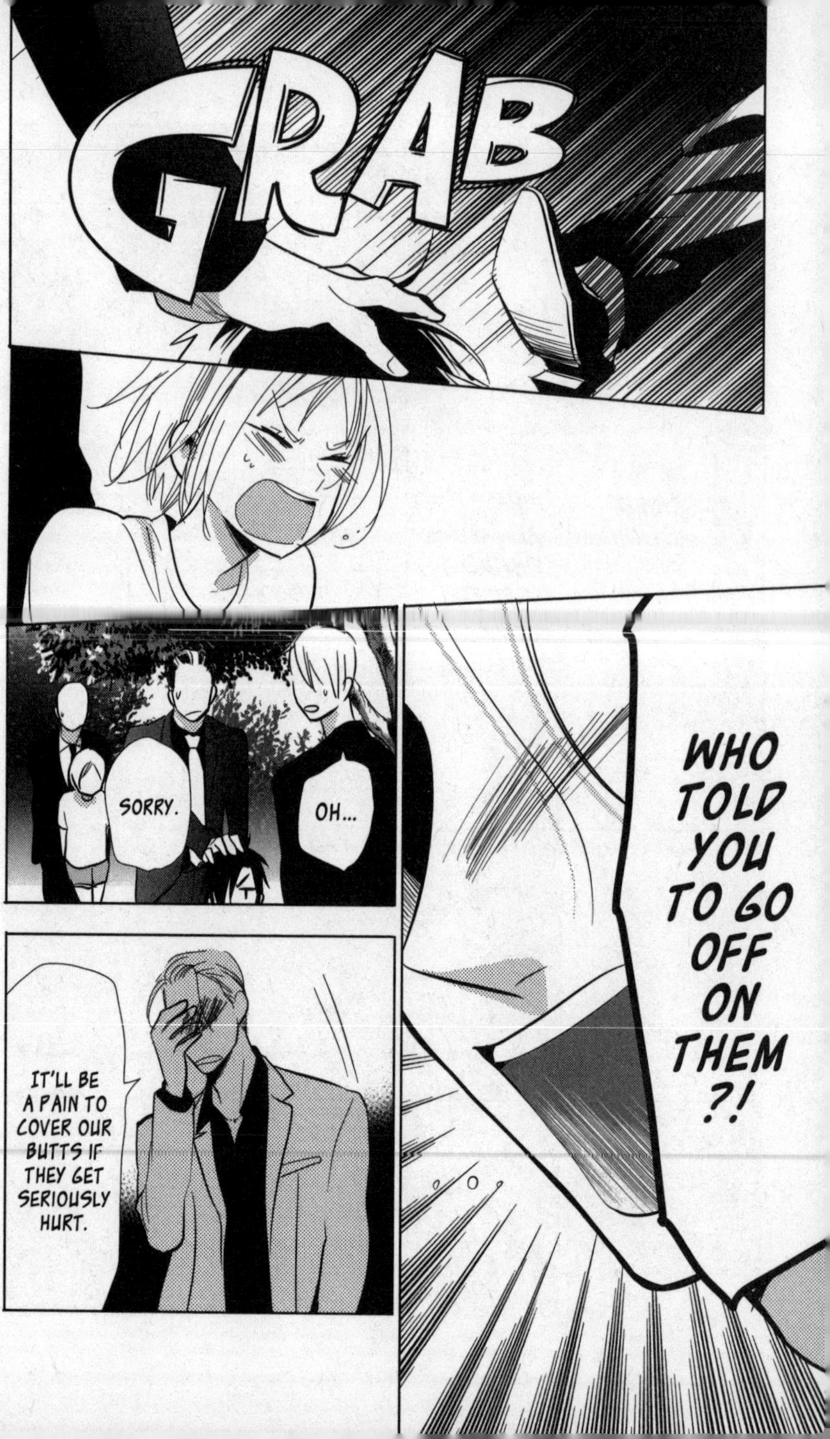
GRAB
WHO TOLD YOU TO GO OFF ON THEM?!
OH...
SORRY.
IT'LL BE A PAIN TO COVER OUR BUTTS IF THEY GET SERIOUSLY HURT.

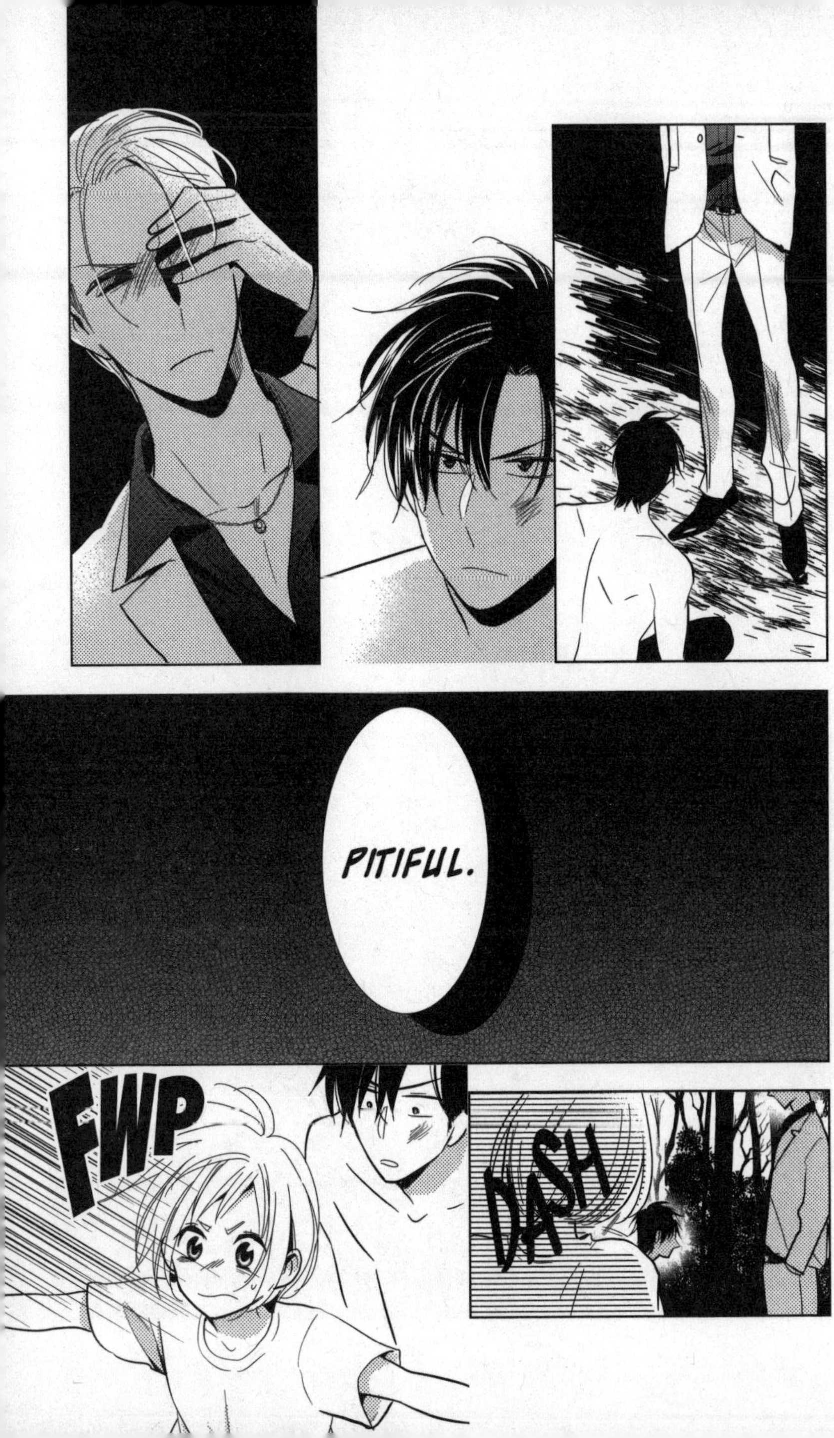
PITIFUL.
DASH
FWP

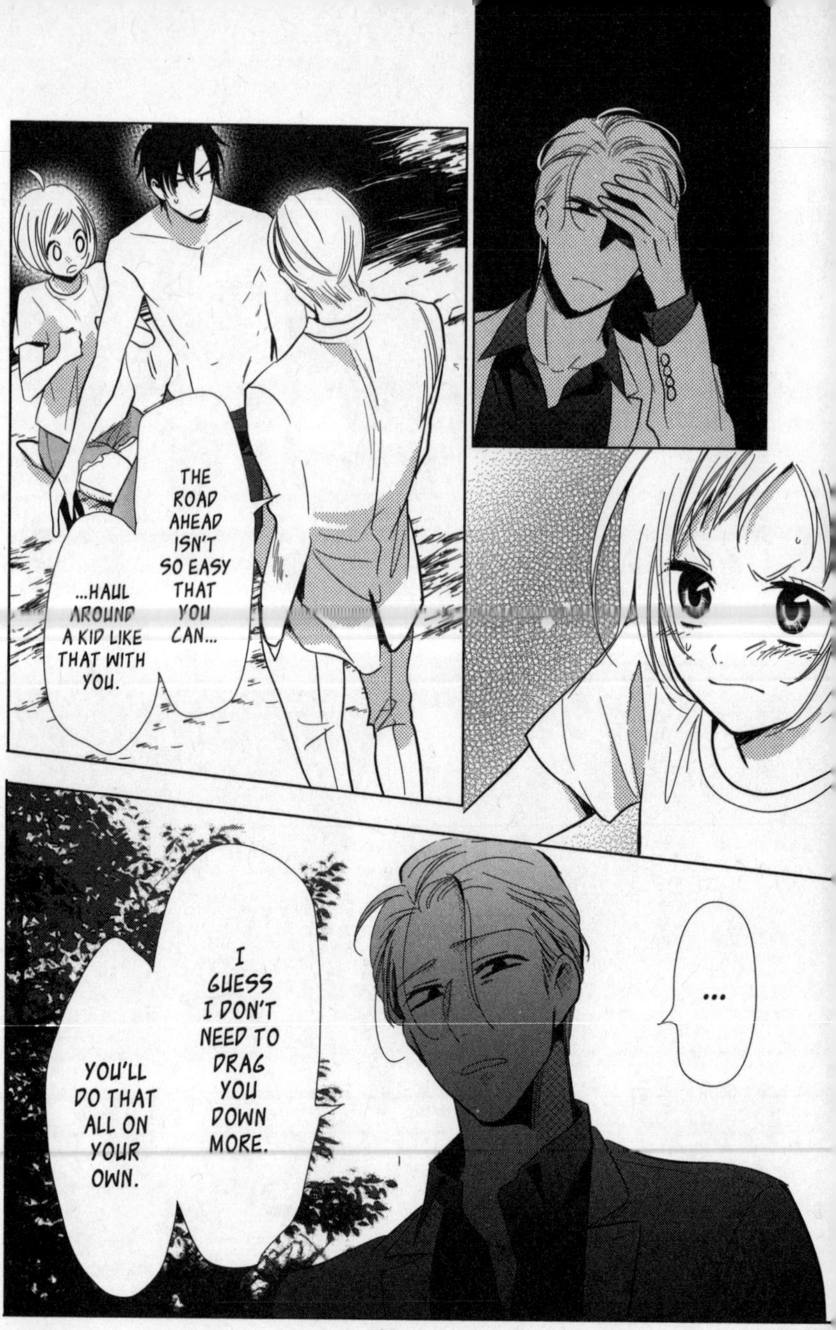
THE ROAD AHEAD ISN'T SO EASY THAT YOU CAN...
...HAUL AROUND A KID LIKE THAT WITH YOU.
...
I GUESS I DON'T NEED TO DRAG YOU DOWN MORE.
YOU'LL DO THAT ALL ON YOUR OWN.

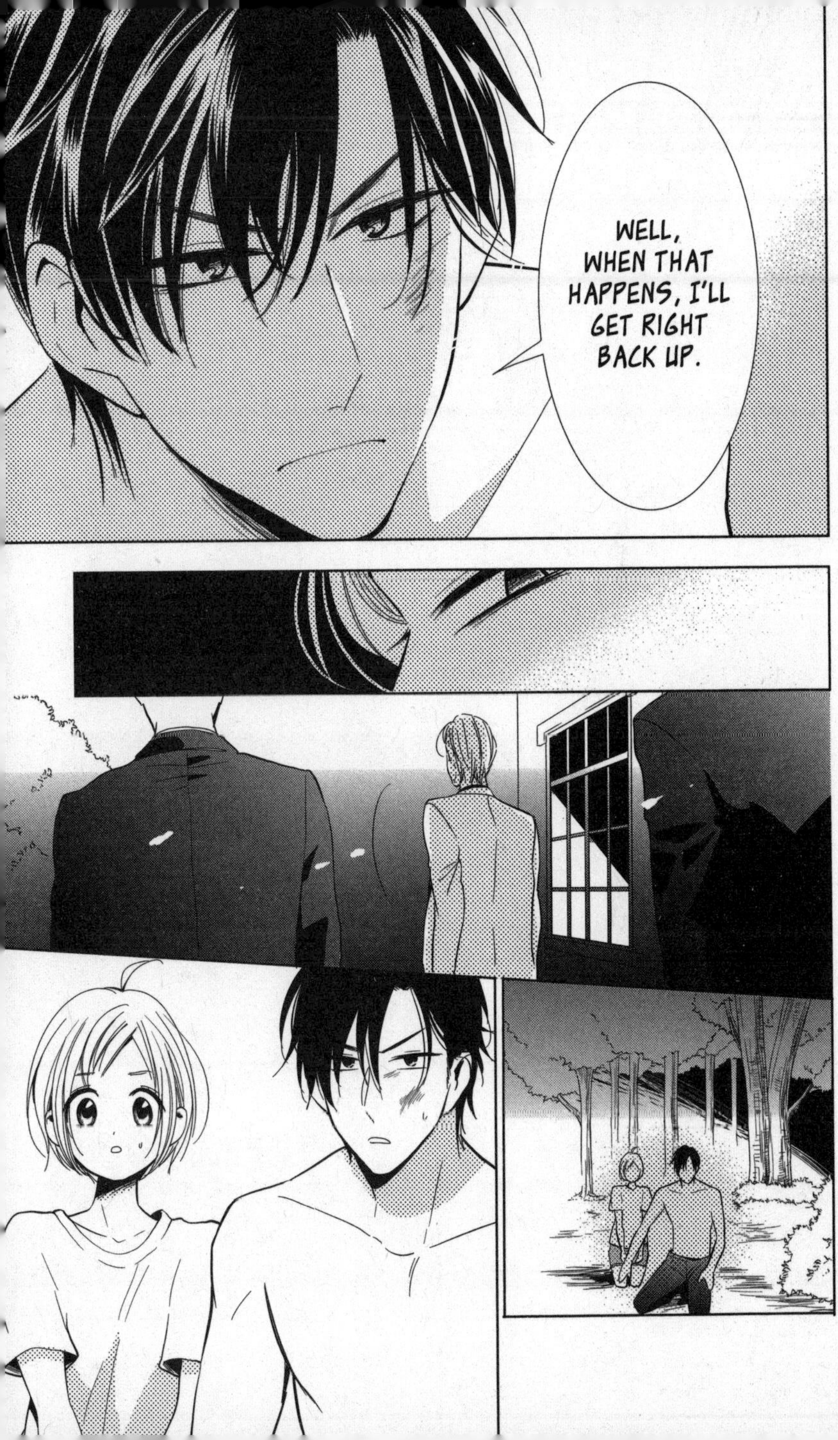
WELL, WHEN THAT HAPPENS, I'LL GET RIGHT BACK UP.

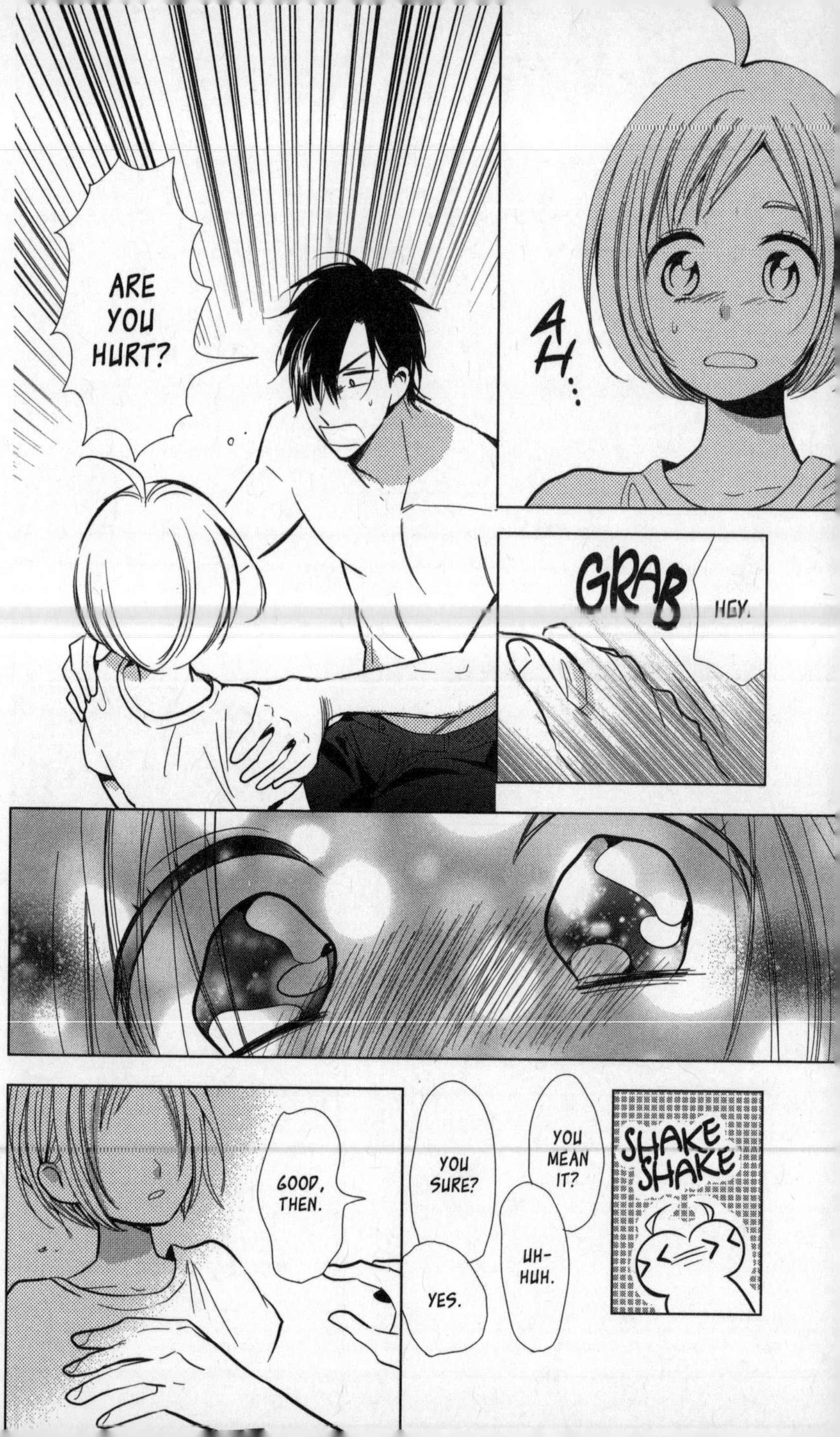
AH...
GRAB
HGY.
ARE YOU HURT?
SHAKE SHAKE
YOU MEAN IT?
UH-HUH.
YOU SURE?
YES.
GOOD, THEN.

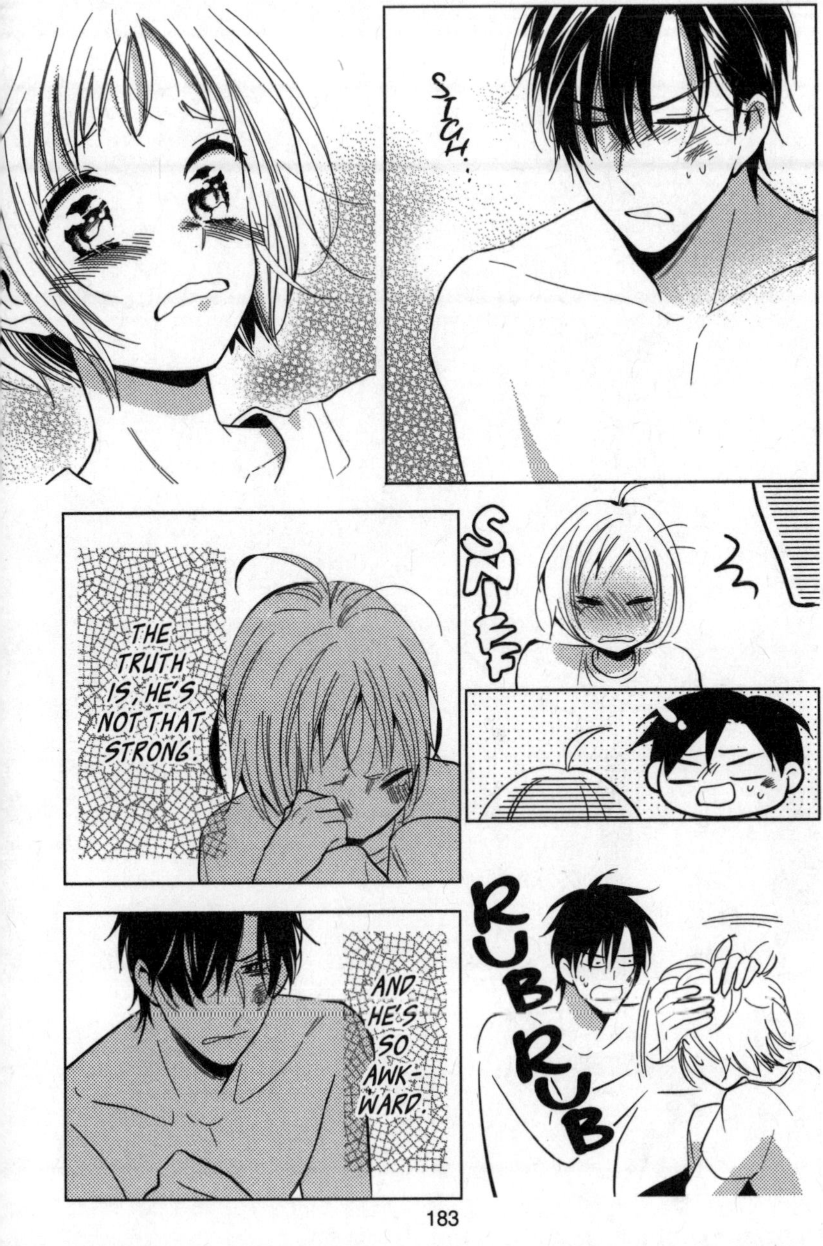
SIGH...
SNIFF
THE TRUTH IS, HE'S NOT THAT STRONG.
RUB RUB
AND HE'S SO AWKWARD.

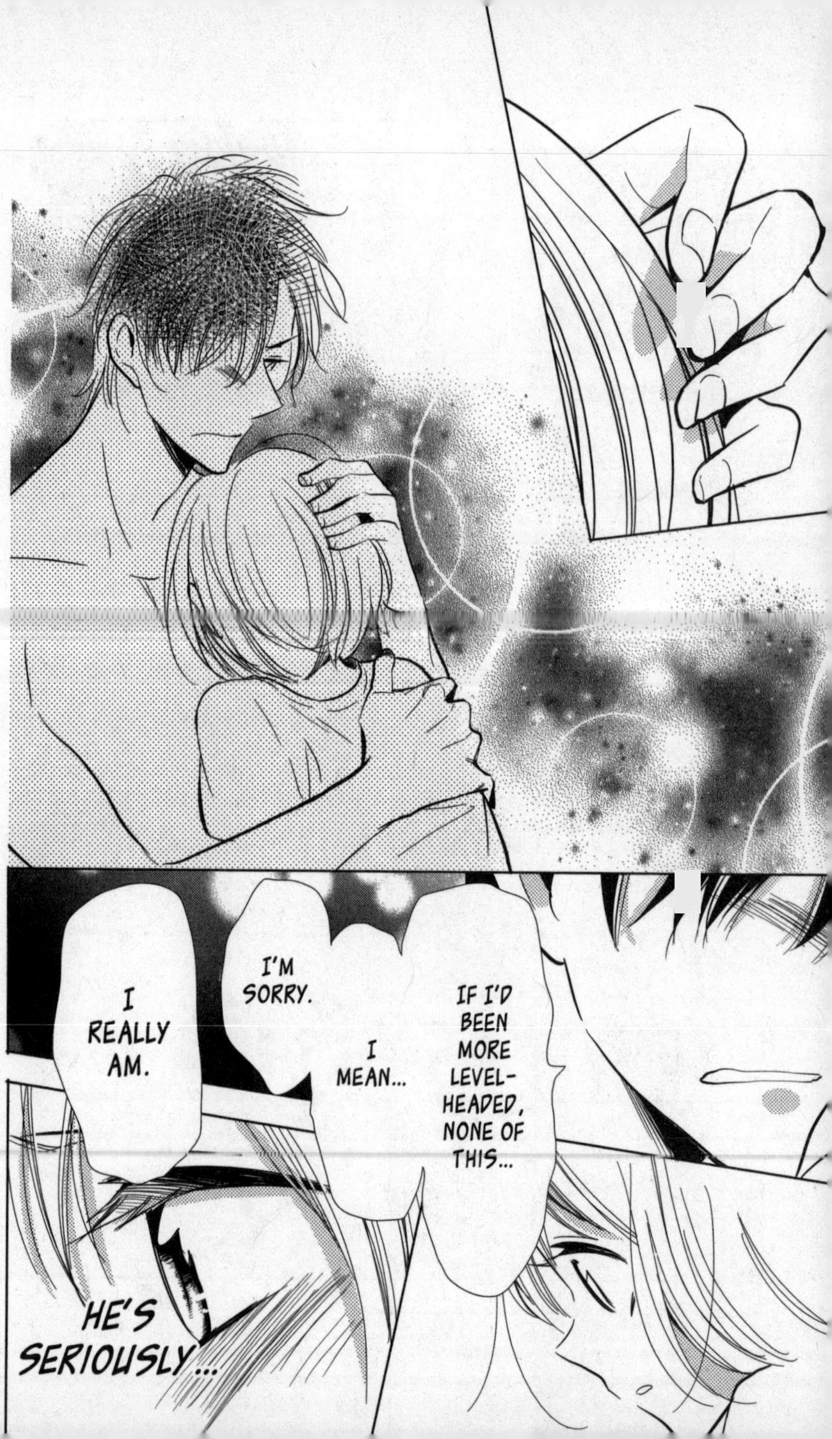
IF I'D BEEN MORE LEVEL-HEADED, NONE OF THIS...
I MEAN...
I'M SORRY.
I REALLY AM.
HE'S SERIOUSLY...

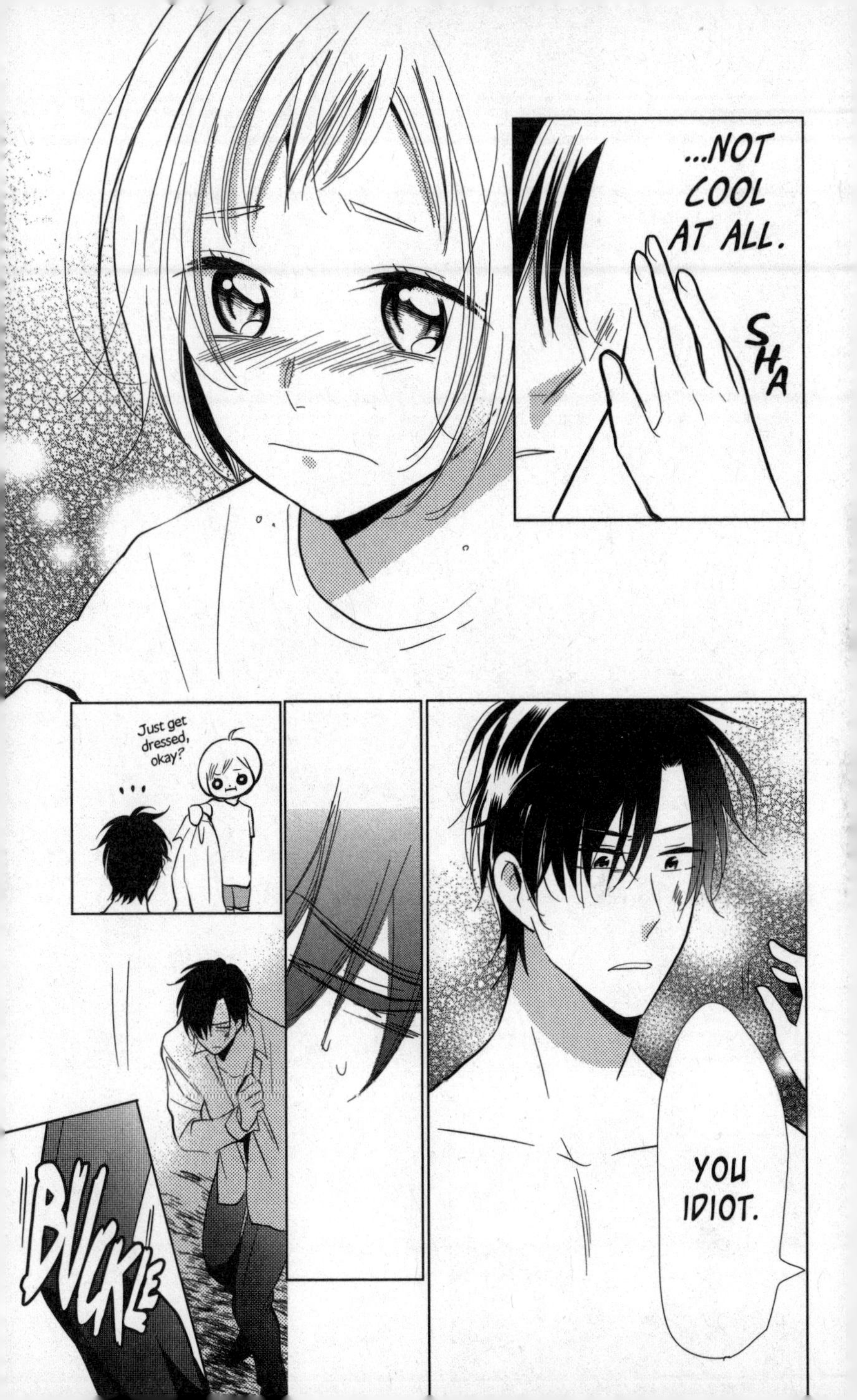
...NOT COOL AT ALL.
SHA
YOU IDIOT.
Just get dressed, okay?
...
BUCKLE

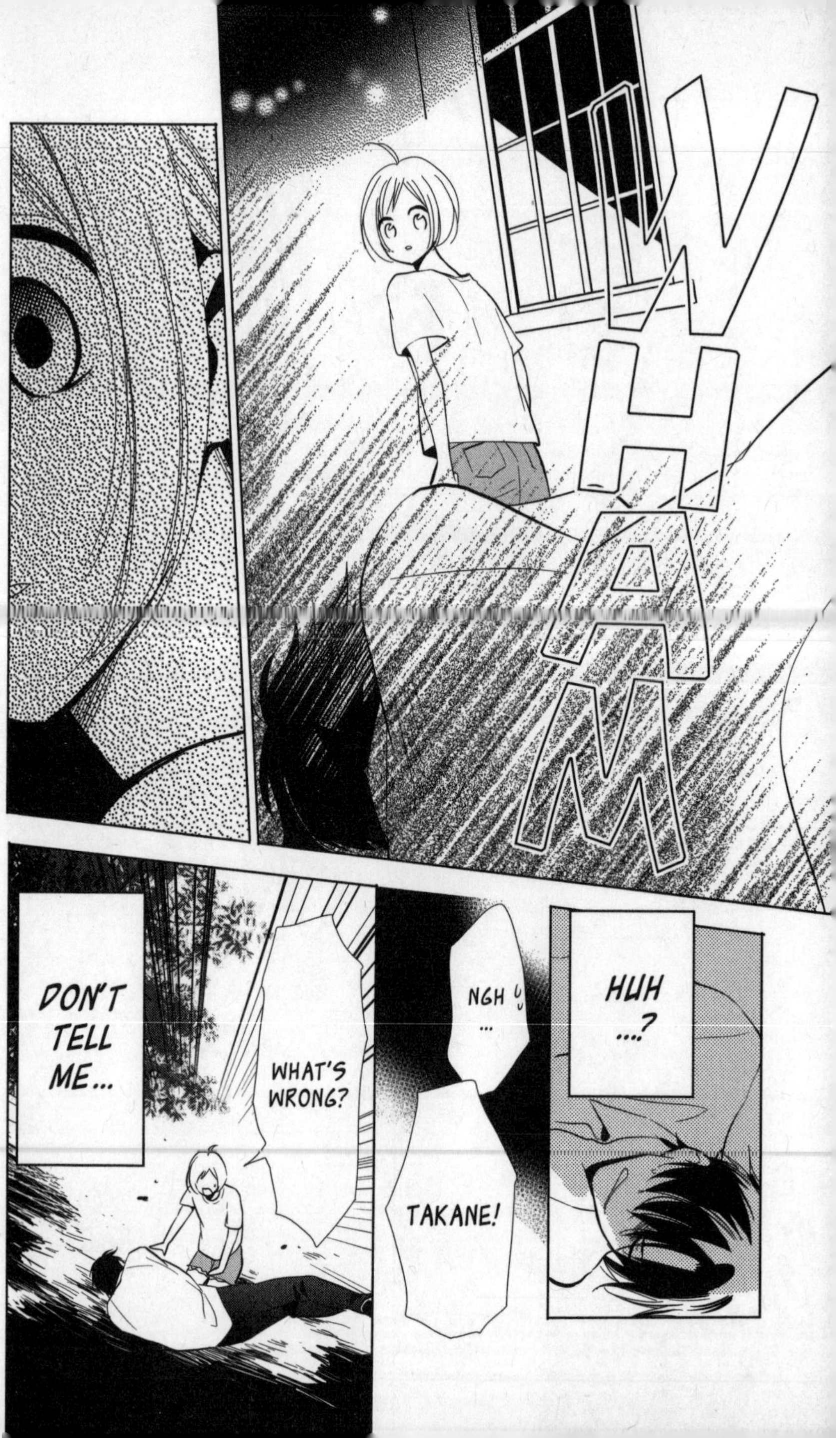
WHAM
HUH ...?
NGH ...
TAKANE!
WHAT'S WRONG?
DON'T TELL ME...

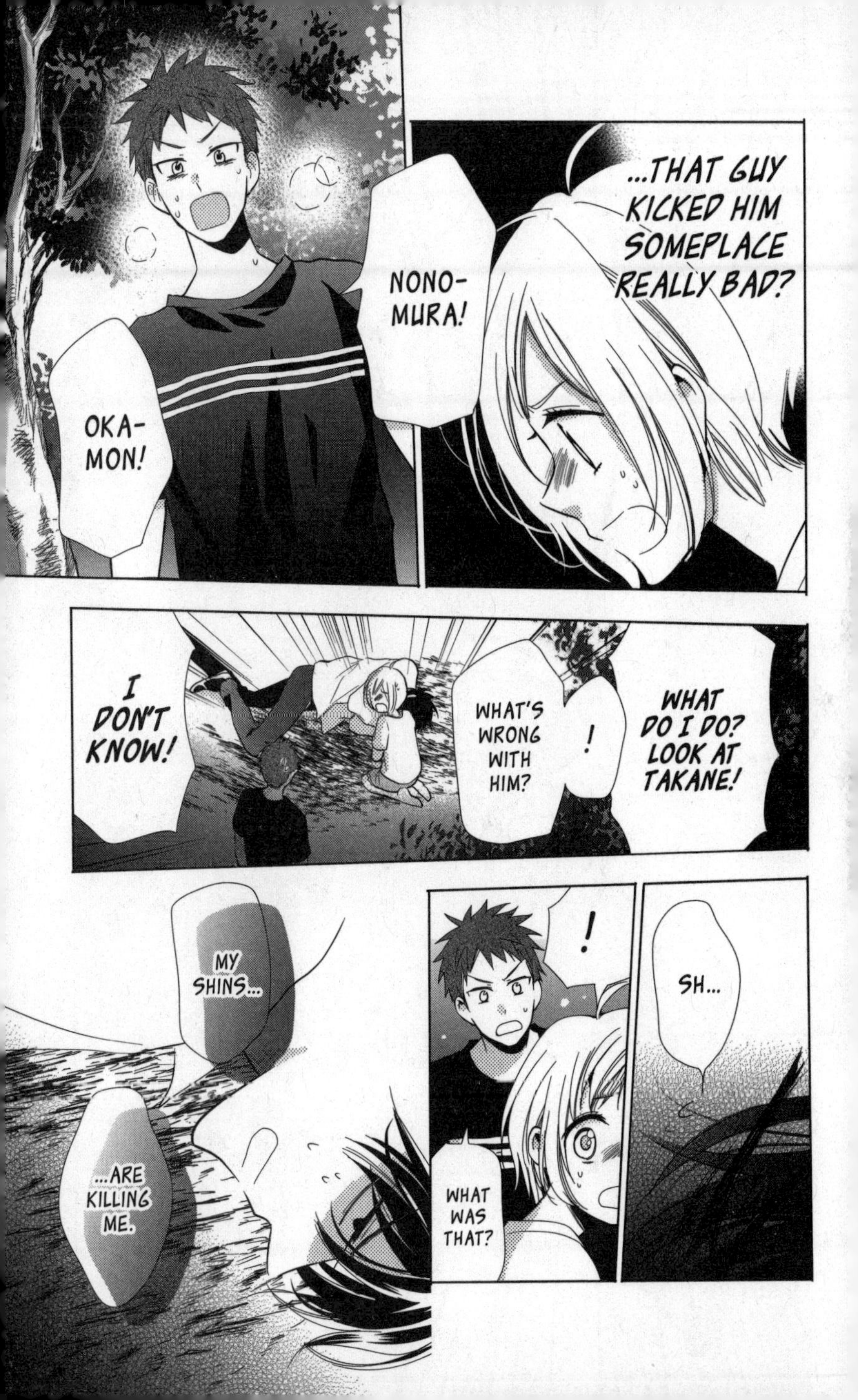
...THAT GUY KICKED HIM SOMEPLACE REALLY BAD?
NONO-MURA!
OKA-MON!
WHAT DO I DO? LOOK AT TAKANE!
!
WHAT'S WRONG WITH HIM?
I DON'T KNOW!
SH...
!
WHAT WAS THAT?
MY SHINS...
...ARE KILLING ME.

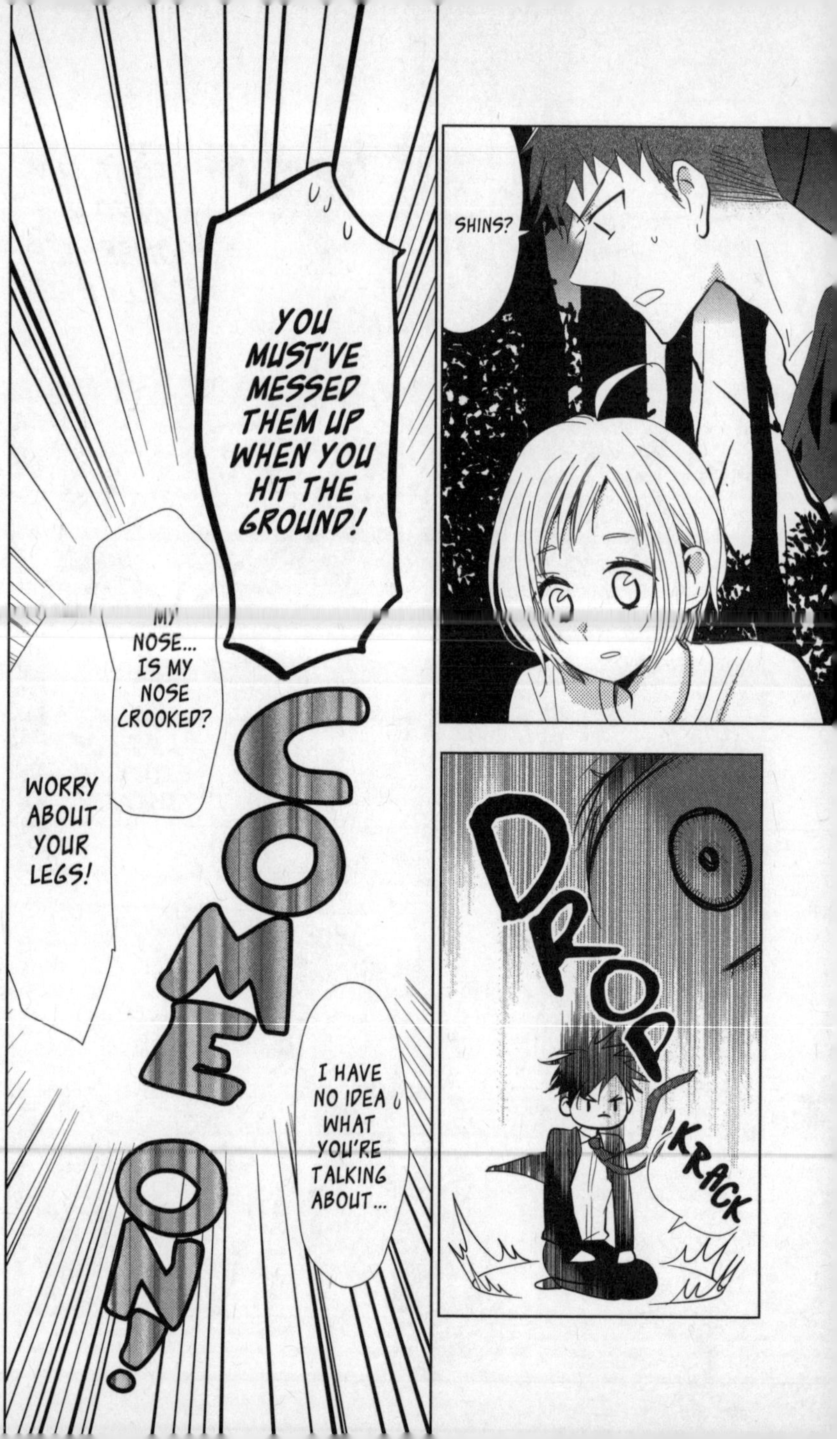
SHINS?
DROP
KRACK
YOU MUST'VE MESSED THEM UP WHEN YOU HIT THE GROUND!
MY NOSE... IS MY NOSE CROOKED?
WORRY ABOUT YOUR LEGS!
COME ON!
I HAVE NO IDEA WHAT YOU'RE TALKING ABOUT...

Chapter 47
• (in volume 9) •

You can tell a lot about a person by looking at their bookcase.

The illustration shows Hana checking out the magazines scattered all over Takane's room.

The sales copy I've chosen to talk about all seem to be skewed toward commentary (since they're coming from the author's perspective).

Chapter 53
• (in volume 10) •

Let me extend a summer greeting to you instead of letting Takane do it. That smug face will just make you sweatier.

The illustration shows Hana like a pinup girl (?) in a bathing suit.

I love the ones where Takane gets dissed since I feel like it makes his character stand out more. (*Ha ha.*)

And there it is! I picked one from every volume. There were more I wanted to include, but I ran out of space. To my head editor, thank you so much for all the wonderful sales copy!

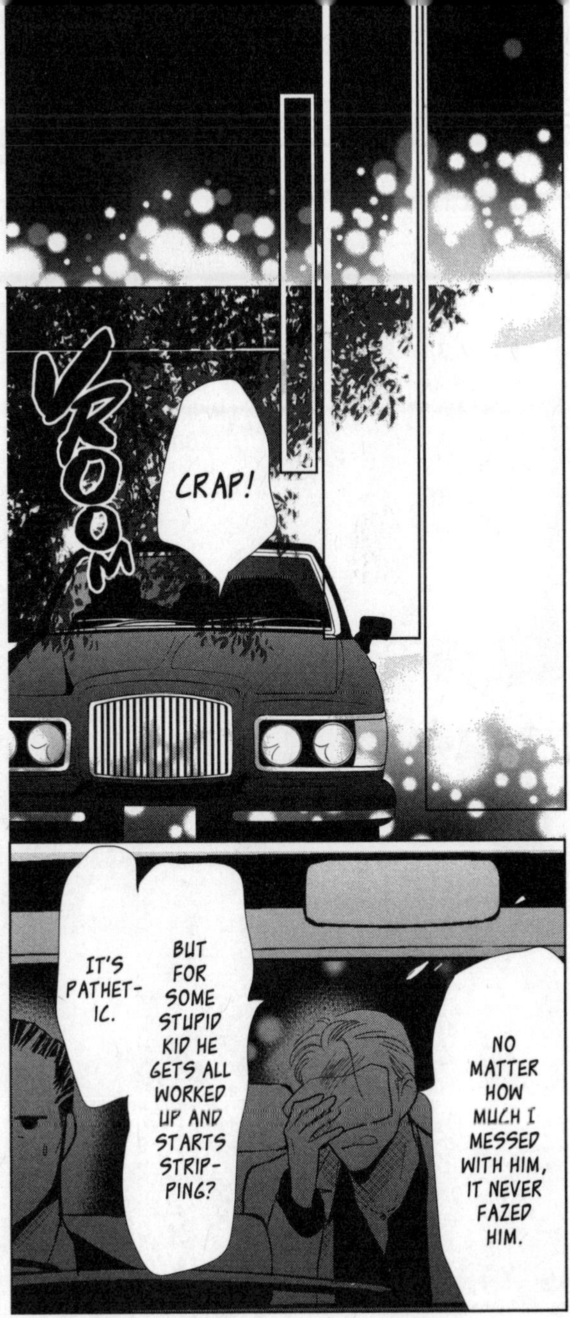
VROOM
CRAP!
NO MATTER HOW MUCH I MESSED WITH HIM, IT NEVER FAZED HIM.
BUT FOR SOME STUPID KID HE GETS ALL WORKED UP AND STARTS STRIP-PING?
IT'S PATHET-IC.

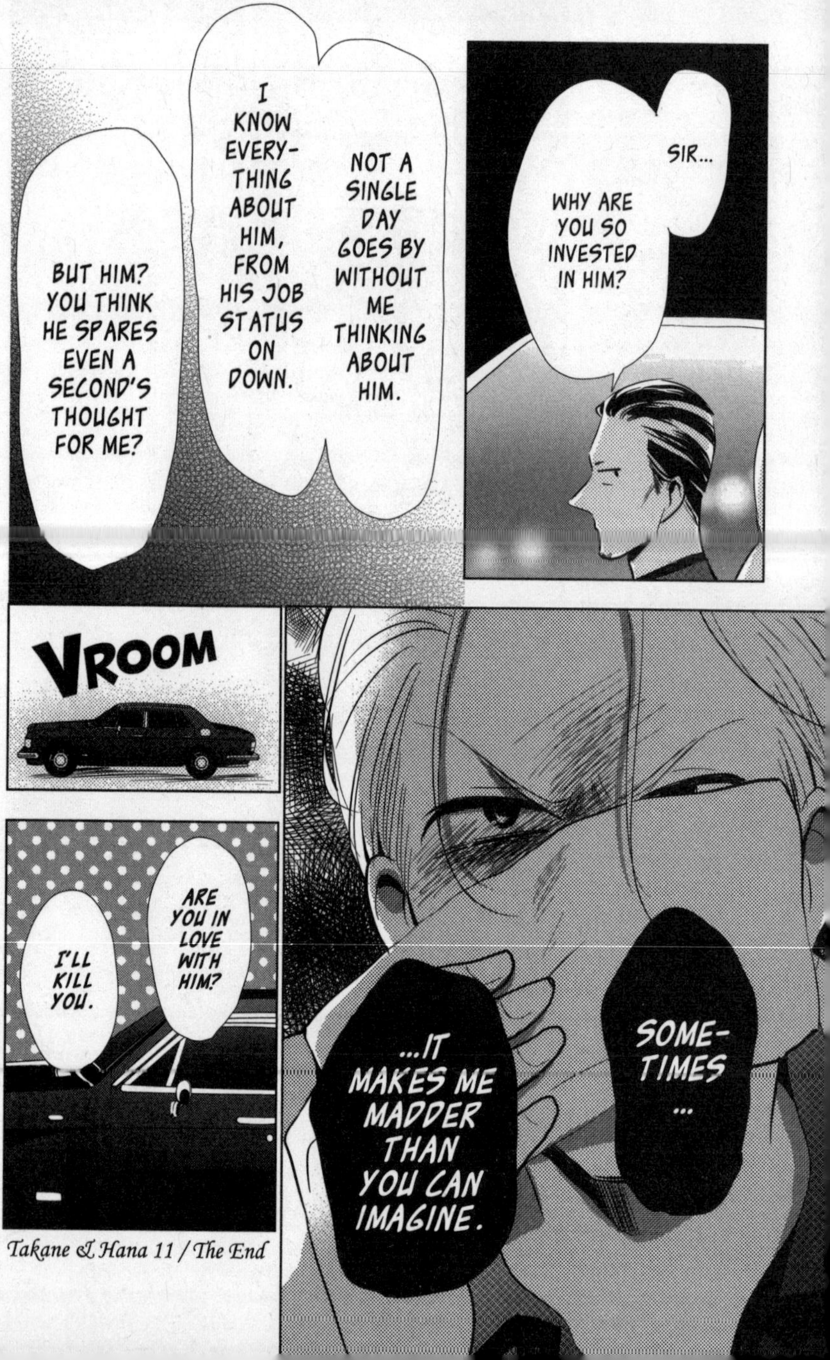
SIR...
WHY ARE YOU SO INVESTED IN HIM?
NOT A SINGLE DAY GOES BY WITHOUT ME THINKING ABOUT HIM.
I KNOW EVERYTHING ABOUT HIM, FROM HIS JOB STATUS ON DOWN.
BUT HIM? YOU THINK HE SPARES EVEN A SECOND'S THOUGHT FOR ME?
SOMETIMES...
...IT MAKES ME MADDER THAN YOU CAN IMAGINE.
VROOM
ARE YOU IN LOVE WITH HIM?
I'LL KILL YOU.

Takane & Hana 11 / The End

This "things falling from the sky"
series is alive and well.

—YUKI SHIWASU

Born on March 7 in Fukuoka Prefecture, Japan,
Yuki Shiwasu began her career as a manga artist
after winning the top prize in the Hakusensha Athena
Newcomers' Awards from *Hana to Yume* magazine. She
is also the author of *Furou Kyoudai* (Immortal Siblings),
which was published by Hakusensha in Japan.

Takane & Hana

VOLUME 11
SHOJO BEAT EDITION

STORY & ART BY **YUKI SHIWASU**

ENGLISH ADAPTATION **Ysabet Reinhardt MacFarlane**
TRANSLATION **JN Productions**
TOUCH-UP ART & LETTERING **Annaliese Christman**
DESIGN **Shawn Carrico**
EDITOR **Amy Yu**

First published in Japan in 2018 by HAKUSENSHA, Inc., Tokyo.
English language translation rights arranged with HAKUSENSHA, Inc., Tokyo.

Printed in the U.S.A.

Published by VIZ Media, LLC
P.O. Box 77010
San Francisco, CA 94107

10 9 8 7 6 5 4 3 2 1
First printing, October 2019

ratings.viz.com RATED T TEEN

PARENTAL ADVISORY
TAKANE & HANA is rated T for Teen and is recommended for ages 13 and up. This volume contains suggestive themes.

VIZ MEDIA
viz.com

Shojo Beat
shojobeat.com

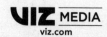

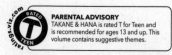